PICTURING ASIA: DOUBLE TAKE

THE PHOTOGRAPHY OF BRIAN BRAKE AND STEVE MCCURRY

Published on the occasion of the exhibition

Picturing Asia: Double Take organized
by Asia Society Hong Kong Center
Chantal Miller Gallery
Hong Kong
September 10, 2016—January 7, 2017

First published in Hong Kong, September 2016, by Asia Society Hong Kong Center

9 Justice Drive, Admiralty, Hong Kong

Project Manager : Dominique Chan

Guest Curator : Ian Wedde

Assistant Curators : Kristy Soo, Ashley Nga-sai Wu

Curatorial Support : Cara Tsui, Joyce Hei-ting Wong

Editor : Ian Wedde

Assistant Editors : Kristy Soo, Ashley Nga-sai Wu

Contributors : Anthony Bannon, Evans Chan, Jonathan Flaws, Athol McCredie, Kristy Soo, Ian Wedde, Ashley Nga-sai Wu

Art Direction and Design : Zero

Printing : Colham Printing Co. Limited

ISBN : 978-988-12272-7-0

www.asiasociety.org.hk

ORGANIZER

Asia Society
Hong Kong Center

EXHIBITION PARTNER

TE PAPA
OUR PLACE

Supported by the Museum of New Zealand Te Papa Tongarewa. Te Papa gratefully acknolwedges the gift of the Brian Brake Collection by Wai-man Lau.

LEAD SPONSOR

MetLife Foundation
Ensuring Access. Empowering Communities.

TABLE OF CONTENTS

EXECUTIVE DIRECTOR'S FOREWORD

S. Alice Mong
Executive Director, Asia Society Hong Kong Center

The 21st century has been dubbed the "Asian Century". While the world enthusiastically listens to Asian leaders, artists and entrepreneurs for insights to create a global future, we Asians find it equally intriguing to turn our heads and see how we were, and are perceived by those we call "westerners".

There is no better time than now as Asia Society celebrates our sixtieth anniversary, for the Hong Kong Center to present *Picturing Asia: Double Take*, the first exhibition in Hong Kong to feature the works of two great contemporary photojournalists, Brian Brake and Steve McCurry. Despite their different styles, both photographers embrace a long-standing passion in picturing Asia for a global audience. Their documentation of Asia has immense historical value. But beyond the importance as ethnographic records, both Brake and McCurry's works radiate an interest in, and a longing to understand their human subjects. Many know Brake simply as the only independent western photojournalist allowed to shoot the People's Republic of China's tenth anniversary, and McCurry as the master behind the haunting green eyes of the "Afghan Girl", but their empathy for Asians is what gives their work enduring impact, resonating in all parts of the world by stressing the possibility to understand one another regardless of geographical boundaries and cultural differences.

First and foremost, I am indebted to Jonathan Flaws for initiating *Picturing Asia: Double Take*. I most gratefully acknowledge the endless inspiration Steve McCurry brings us with his work. I must also extend my warmest gratitude to our Exhibition Partner, Museum of New

Zealand Te Papa Tongarewa and Wai-man Lau for sharing works from the Brian Brake Collection with a worldwide audience. I am especially grateful to Ian Wedde, our Guest Curator for his exceptional knowledge and dedication which bring this exhibition to life. My deepest gratitude goes to MetLife Foundation, the Lead Sponsor of this exhibition and long-time supporter of our endeavors, for their generosity which makes this ambitious project possible. I must also thank the Education Development Foundation Association for supporting our education programs, as well as Epson and Phase One for being our Supporting Partners. My gratitude also goes to Hang Lung Properties for being our Outreach Partner once again. I must acknowledge my colleague Dominique Chan, Head of Gallery and Exhibition and his team, in particular Assistant Curators Ashley Wu and Kristy Soo, for their hard work and commitment to this project. Last but not least, my wholehearted gratitude is due to all staff and volunteers of Asia Society Hong Kong Center for bringing this challenging venture to fruition.

Sixty years ago, Asia Society was founded with a mission to be a bridge between "the east" and "the west". Brake and McCurry's continuous effort to look outwards, to understand and appreciate a world that is not their own is a true inspiration. Presenting the diverse Asian heritage and culture through the lens of two "westerners" in Hong Kong, a global city that fascinates both men, makes this exhibition all the more exciting.

GLOBAL PRESIDENT'S FOREWORD

Josette Sheeran
President and CEO, Asia Society

There is reality, and then there is the lens through which we view reality. Photographers occupy a unique space between reality and what we see. This exhibition covers works by Brian Brake and Steve McCurry spanning over sixty years in countless cities and hamlets across Asia's vast plains and valleys.

There are other kinds of visionaries—those who have the ability to look far, and with wisdom, into the future.

For the last six decades, Asia Society has been on a mission led by one such visionary—John D. Rockefeller 3rd—who founded Asia Society in his pursuit for "broader and deeper understanding between the peoples of the United States and Asia."

In 1956, while others saw only the wreckage of war in Asia, Rockefeller saw—through his own lens—an Asia of "shared hopes, fears and aspirations" with the United States. This was an unusual view at the time, and a reflection of the Rockefeller family's long and profound engagement with Asia. That engagement had begun in 1863, when Asia was for most Americans an unfathomable and inaccessible concept. In that year the 24-year-old John D. Rockefeller Sr. recorded his first interest in the continent—a $10 donation to a missionary organization in China.

Our founder projected a clear vision of "understanding" for us—as "the most subtle and delicate, difficult and elusive bond that can link continents and nations and even men" and that "it strikes deeper than mere tolerance; it reaches further than mere acquaintance or formal association;

it is that quality of mind and spirit whose existence is essential to true peace."

To this day, this is the vision and identity of Asia Society, against which we measure our efforts worldwide.

More than ever before, Asians and Americans, and indeed the world at large, share a common destiny—one that rests upon "broader and deeper understanding" as Asia faces unprecedented challenges and finds itself home to a host of new flashpoints.

Fortunately for Asia Society, we have a decades-long foundation on which to build. And today we are deploying cutting-edge tools, in multiple disciplines, through an unparalleled global network, in pursuit of the original Rockefeller vision.

Arts and culture, as an equal pillar alongside policy and education, is central to Asia Society's mission. Today, our critically-acclaimed work in the arts celebrates the vibrancy of Asia's creative spirit through seminal exhibitions and performances at Asia Society Museum in New York as well as at our cultural spaces in Hong Kong and Houston. *Transfuze: The Asia Arts and Museum Network* seeks to foster collaboration in the cultural sector through programs, projects, and digital resources. In 2015, Boon Hui Tan, the former head of the Singapore Arts Museum, joined Asia Society as Vice President for global arts and cultural programs and museum director to lead these efforts and build on our rich history of arts and culture programming.

Today, amid the non-stop deluge of information, it is easy to mistake seeing for vision, knowledge for understanding. We endeavor every day to provide some needed vision and understanding, and in their own ways, Brian Brake and Steve McCurry have provided the world with profound examples of both. I hope you enjoy this exhibition and collection as a journey of discovery and understanding, through the lens two perceptive, careful and thoughtful artists.

SPONSOR'S STATEMENT

On behalf of MetLife Foundation, I warmly welcome you to the exhibition *Picturing Asia: Double Take—The Photography of Brian Brake and Steve McCurry.*

MetLife Foundation has a longstanding tradition of corporate contributions and community involvement. Visual art, we believe, is vital to our communities in a way that it bridges understanding among diverse cultures, and promotes learning in the world.

I am pleased to continue this tradition by partnering with Asia Society Hong Kong Center, to bring an exhibition of Brian Brake and Steve McCurry's works to Hong Kong for the first time. The photographs of these two masters sketched an impression of Asia for the world before the age of internet, and now, in this part of the world, we can look back and reflect on how the east was once perceived, and through this, understand the many intrigues of the east-west encounters.

MetLife also actively supports cultural and educational works. We are especially proud of the educational effort that will be produced by the learning and school visit programs that are associated with *Picturing Asia: Double Take.*

As a company serving approximately 100 million customers around the world in nearly fifty countries and over sixty years of experience in Asia, MetLife is focused on continuous improvement for ourselves and our business to help our customers, partners and communities pursue more from life. The arts make communities better places to live by bringing people together to learn and share. MetLife is committed to providing access to the arts via

Chris Townsend
President, MetLife Asia

community-level programming that engages individuals of all ages, backgrounds and cultures.

We hope the exhibition inspires you as much as it does us, and that you have the opportunity to share this experience with your family and friends.

ACKNOWLEDGEMENTS

The exhibition and catalog project *Picturing Asia: Double Take—the Photography of Brian Brake and Steve McCurry* originated in a concept proposed by the New Zealand collector Jonathan Flaws and the art dealer John McCormack. I am grateful for their vision and ongoing support. They established the possibility of a fascinating conversation between these two master photographers, which it has been my privilege to develop as curator; my thanks to Asia Society Hong Kong for offering me that opportunity.

The project would not have been possible without the support of the late Brian Brake's Trustee, Wai-man Lau, and of the Museum of New Zealand Te Papa Tongarewa, where the Brian Brake Collection resides as a gift to the nation. The *Picturing Asia* project team is grateful to New Zealand's national museum for its substantial partnership support for the project. We are particularly grateful to the museum's Curator Photography, Athol McCredie, for sharing his expertise and knowledge; and to Jeremy Glyde for impeccable digital imaging.

Steve McCurry and his team in New York have been generous supporters of the project; we are especially grateful to McCurry himself, and to Dalia Amara, his studio manager at Steve McCurry Studios LLC.

McCurry's exhibition prints were made by Steve McCurry Studios in New York, and Brake's by Kevin Church at Opticmix Ltd., Auckland, New Zealand. The high quality of the exhibition experience owes much to their combined finesse and craft.

Ian Wedde
Guest Curator

I acknowledge the expertise and scholarship of the catalog writers: Athol McCredie on Brake, Anthony Bannon on McCurry, Evans Chan for his contemporary insider perspective on the picturing of Asians, Kristy Soo and Ashley Wu for extending the conversation into the experiences of young Hong Kongers in the age of selfies; and, at the originating historical moment of the exhibition, Jonathan Flaws for his memories of encountering Asia in the magazine photo essays of the 1950s and 60s.

We are indebted to Jonathan Flaws and to Steve McCurry for lending material for case displays in the exhibition. Many agencies and individuals have facilitated and granted permission to publish the images that accompany catalogue essays; my thanks especially to Kristy Soo at Asia Society Hong Kong, and to Yiyang Hou in New York, for their work enriching this aspect of the catalog's "Picturing Asia" story.

I am especially grateful to the team I have worked with at Asia Society Hong Kong: Dominique Chan, Ashley Wu and Kristy Soo. Their care, skill and commitment have always been matched by generosity and openness to discussion.

PICTURING ASIA: THE NARRATIVE PHOTOGRAPHY OF BRIAN BRAKE AND STEVE MCCURRY

Ian Wedde
Guest Curator

THE ASIAN CONTEXT

The exhibition concept "Double Take" originates in a proposal by the New Zealand collector Jonathan Flaws and a New Zealand art dealer, John McCormack, who share a long-term interest in the art and photography of Asia. Their concept involves two distinct "takes" on Asia by two photographers: that of the New Zealander, Brian Brake (1927–1988) and the American, Steve McCurry (born 1950). The proposal anticipates the sixtieth anniversary in 2016 of Asia Society and the Society's mission to promote greater understanding of globally.

This mission articulates the liberal political altruism of the Society's founder, John D. Rockefeller 3rd who, after visiting Japan in 1950 as part of an official American delegation, saw the need to improve knowledge in the United States about Asian societies, cultures and histories. His report stressed "the importance of the exchange of ideas and information on a 'two-way' street".[1] His impulse for dialogue had its particular history in the family's engagement with Asian culture—his mother, Abigail Greene "Abby" Aldrich Rockefeller (1874–1948) was a connoisseur of Asian arts; her son John D. and his wife Blanchette Ferry Hooker went on to assemble the Mr. and Mrs. John D. Rockefeller 3rd Collection of Asian Art, gifted to Asia Society in 1978 when John died.[2]

But Rockefeller's impulse should be read in a more urgent historical context that included four major events. Firstly, the World War II Japanese surrender in 1945 produced conflicted themes of punishment, détente and reparation in Japan as well as in the United States. Shomei Tomatsu's *Chewing Gum and Chocolate* photographs of American military bases in Japan and Okinawa in the

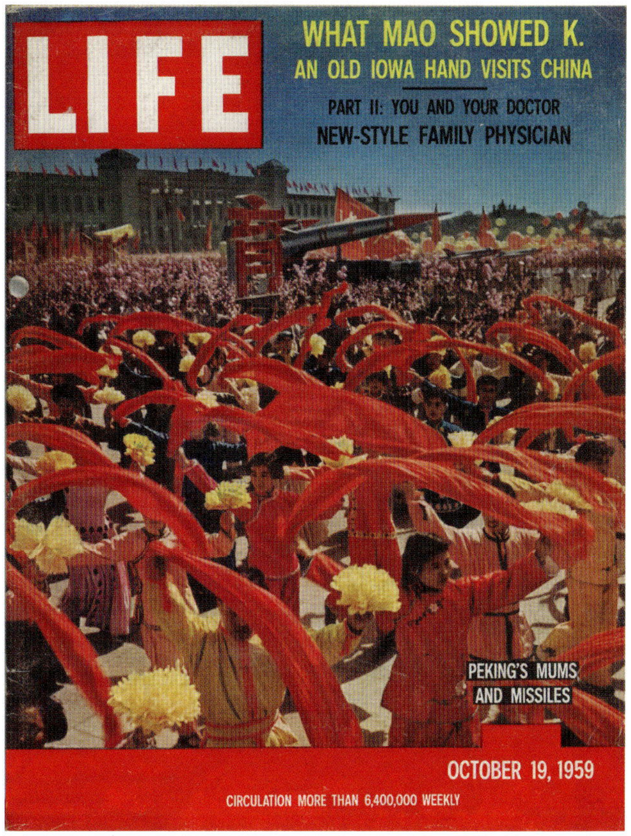

Brian Brake. "Peking's Mums and Missiles". Cover, *Life,* vol. 47, no. 16, 19 October 1959. LIFE logo and cover design © Time Inc. LIFE and the LIFE logo are registered trademarks of Time Inc. used under license.

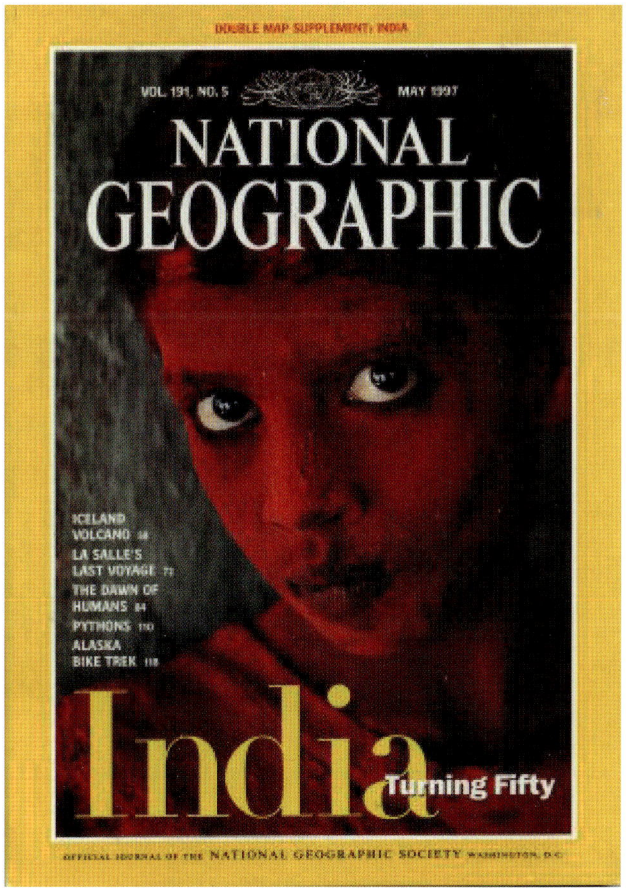

Steve McCurry. "India Turning Fifty". Cover, *National Geographic*, vol. 191, no. 5, May 1997. © NATIONAL GEOGRAPHIC CREATIVE.

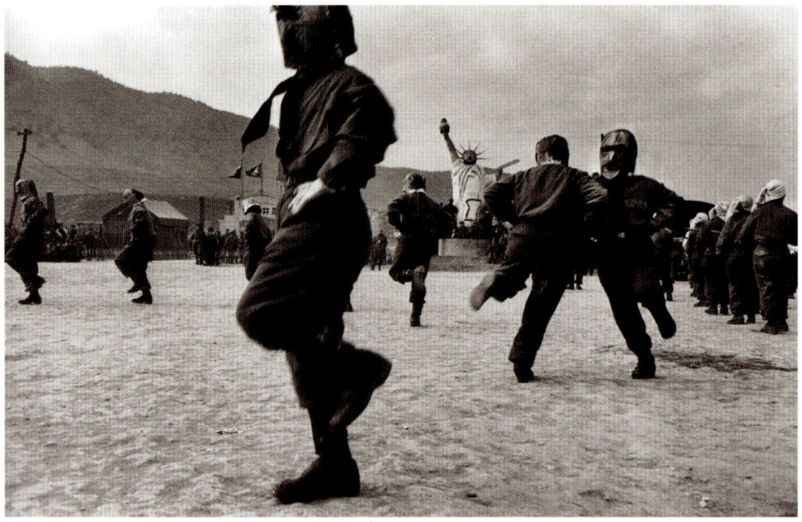

Werner Bischof (1916–1954). *South Korea, Island of Koje Do,* 1952. © Werner Bischof/Magnum Photos/Imaginechina.

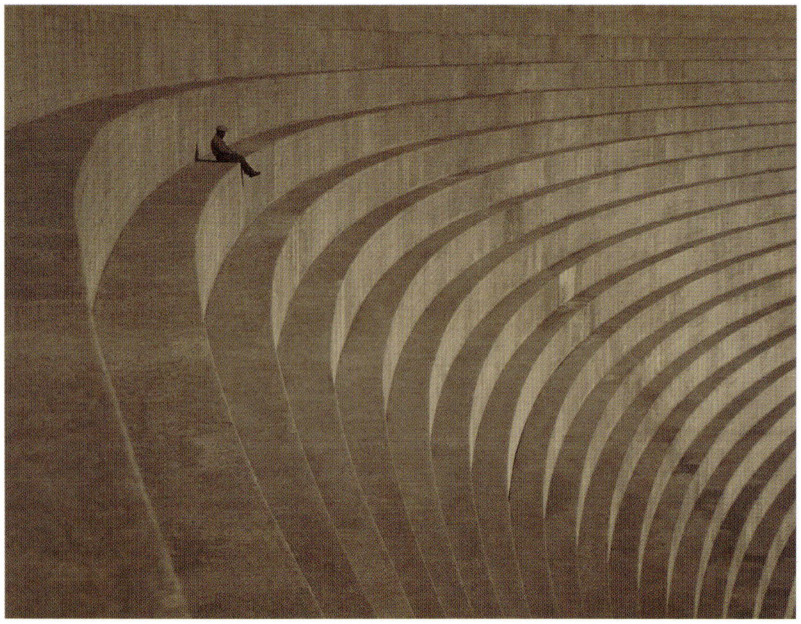

Hiromu Kira (1898–1998). *Man on Steps, Bowl (The Thinker),* c. 1930. © Digital Image 2016 Museum Associate/LACMA, Licensed by Art Resource, NY/Sadamura Family Trust.

1960s and 1970s (see illustration on p. 161) may seem hostile to the American presence but Tomatsu himself has written that, "They say the separation between love and hate is paper-thin. Truly, for me, 'occupation' is a unity of contradictions."[3] Secondly, the founding of the Peoples' Republic of China in 1949 generated xenophobic panic about "the Reds" in the Time Inc. publications *Time* and *Life*; Henri-Cartier-Bresson's photo essays of 1949 and 1959 for *Life* magazine were accompanied by alarmist texts and captions, discussed later in this essay. Thirdly, the Korean War truce in 1953 increased American fear of Chinese communist expansion in Asia. Werner Bischof's 1952 Korean War photographs of "reeducation camps" convey deep unease and war-weariness, as in his image of masked North Korean prisoners of war performing a "square dance" in front of a crude facsimile Statue of Liberty. Finally, the Vietnam War 1955–75, known in Vietnam as the Resistance War Against America (*Kháng chiến chống Mỹ*), resulted in widespread international sympathy for the victims of American and allied military interventions in Vietnam, Laos and Cambodia. The anti-war demonstrations that gathered momentum in the United States and elsewhere from a surge in 1965 contributed to a shift in Western attitudes to Asia. In America, anti-war protests increased the profiles of artists and writers who had championed Chinese and Japanese cultures; they included the poet Kenneth Rexroth who had helped Japanese-Americans to escape West Coast internment camps, and the American Buddhist monk and poet Philip Whalen. And as Leo Rubinfien notes in *Chewing Gum and Chocolate*, "… while it is well known that many elements of American culture have penetrated Japan, Japanese culture has penetrated America too, becoming an ubiquitous feature in its imagination."[4] These lines of dialogue reach back to the pre-World War II origins of Modernism, for example to the Japanese-American photographer Hiromu Kira (1898–1998); they are evidence of progressive intercultural influences that Rockefeller hoped to give mainstream legitimacy.

In addition to Asia Society, Rockefeller also supported the Institute of Pacific Relations (IPR) through the philanthropic Rockefeller Foundation—the IPR folded in 1960 under pressure from McCarthyite anti-communist lobbies and Cold War paranoia; and the Japan Society that, after shutting down from 1941 to 1952, continues to flourish in 2016.

As well as such immediate contexts we need to consider a longer historical view-shaft. The homogeneous term "Asia"—like the reductionist conflation "The Third World"—may often be colonialist in its effects: it shapes and simplifies a geocultural space by occupying it conceptually. Edward W. Said's influential text in post-colonial studies, *Orientalism*,[5] invigorated a discussion that continues to this day. A decade after this book's publication in 1978, Said revisited its key themes: "the representation of other cultures, societies, histories; the relationship between power and knowledge".[6]

How Asia is represented to and by the "West", and how the relationship between power and knowledge shapes that representation, are the core issues of *Picturing Asia: Double Take.* Representation shaped by knowledge that has itself been determined by power may involve "the exchange of ideas and information on a 'two-way' street"; or the tyrannies of prejudice and appropriation: representation shaped by ignorance determined by power. Historically, one of the effects of ill-informed, tendentious representation has been to normalize an us-them binary; to mark Asian difference as extrinsic, a "foreign body".

A consequent effect of distancing, whether by state policies, citizen groups or individuals, has been to isolate immigrant Asian communities that have extended the geocultural borders of "Asia" into Europe, the United States and the Pacific. Discriminatory anti-Chinese poll taxes were enforced in New Zealand during the nineteenth and early twentieth centuries, following the examples of California and certain Australian states. The racist representation "Yellow Peril", coined by the German Emperor Wilhelm II in 1895, became pervasive in New Zealand, Australia and the United States, in reaction against the influx of "coolie" labor from East and Southeast Asia. The term's racist xenophobia was symptomatic of a rejection of "foreign bodies" by the citizens of states whose colonialist and economic interventions in Asia had their own counterbalancing consequences such as the 1900 anti-colonial Boxer Rebellion in China; this, in turn, generated the paranoid neologism "Boxerism" in the West.

THE REPRESENTATION CHALLENGE

This history of reactionary resistance to foreign bodies generates the challenge encountered by Western photographers wanting to represent the diverse differences of Asian cultures, particularly at times of xenophobic anxiety.

By complicating the homogeneous stereotyping of diverse peoples, Western photographers may facilitate the acceptance of difference hoped for by cultural optimists like John D. Rockefeller 3rd and implicitly endorsed by cultural anthropologists since Franz Boas. Almost inevitably, such progressive attitudes may also seek out the exotic and the exotic's managed encounter zones exploited by tourism, including the virtual tourism of travelogs and coffee-table picture books. Photography may make foreign bodies safe by distancing them either to representation or to "destinations".

Often, this distancing will include a suppression of the modern in favor of the exotic "traditional", even when economies and cultures such as Japan's have become leaders of capitalist modernity. One of Said's ironic epigraphs to *Orientalism* is from Karl Marx: "They [Orientals] cannot represent themselves; they must be represented."[7] The second of Said's epigraphs is from Benjamin Disraeli: "The East is a career."[8] The patronizing implication of Said's shrewd pairing of epigraphs is that representing backward or inarticulate "Orientals" may be a "career" opportunity for Western agents in both political and artistic discourses.

The reactionary effect of the representation challenge is that highlighting difference may increase not diminish xenophobia, marking the exotic as "primitive" and therefore backward, "colorful" and therefore unsophisticated, "traditional" and therefore pre-modern, and so forth—as well, often enough, as dangerous. The disparaging inference of inferiority is often present on this reactionary side of the challenge.

To suggest that "Asia" is exclusively a Western construct ignores a long history of regional configurations.[9] In the wider Southeast Asia region between the second century BC and the sixth century AD, supple systems of concentric *mandala* polities grew along major water-borne conduits for trade.[10] The best known is the Sumatran Śrīvijaya which endured from the seventh to the thirteenth century, maintaining a pragmatic approach to cultural and social difference.[11] The cultural effects and assets of such *mandala* polities often survived the impacts of aggressive Western power, becoming the artifactual and ceremonial residues of *mandala* societies, sought after by Western orientalist connoisseurs—and tourists.

The American businessman Jim Thompson, whose "House on the Klong" in Bangkok became a national museum following his mysterious disappearance in March 1967, sought artifacts associated with *mandala* societies. The house and its contents were themselves represented by Brian Brake and the writer William Warren in a book: *The House on the Klong: The Bangkok Home and Asian Art Collection of James Thompson* (1968).[12] The post-colonial successors of *mandala* trade-based polities may be found in organizations such as ASEAN (Association of Southeast Asian Nations) established in 1967. ASEAN's Southeast Asia tourism site invites us to "Feel the warmth"; its destination categories include

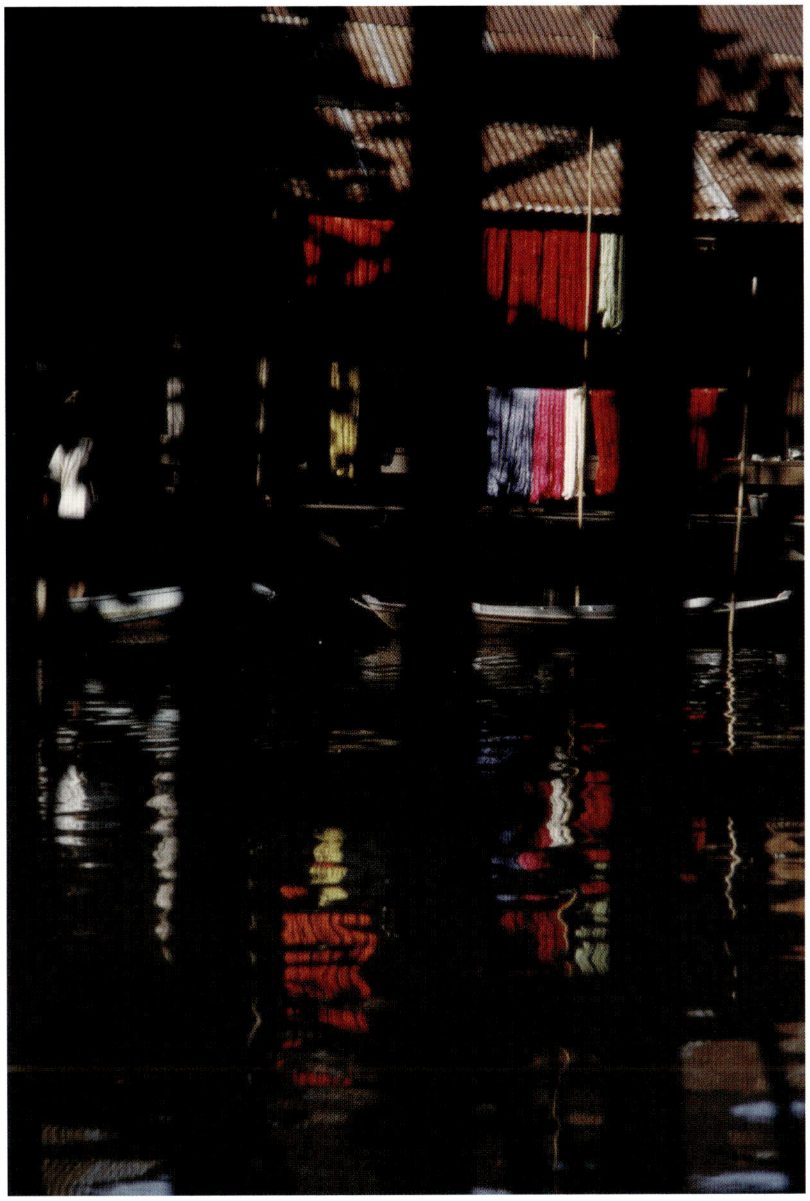

Brian Brake. From the series: The House on the Klong, Thailand, circa 1968. 35mm color transparency. Collection Museum of Te Papa Tongarewa. Gift of Wai-man Lau, 2001.

Pilgrimage Tourism ("Simplicity, Sincerity, Serenity and Sacred Sites").[13] Such inducements seem haunted by *mandala* cultures; the sacred sites and artifacts on offer are their commercially positive traces. Among the warmly welcomed traders of the twenty-first century's post-*mandala* polities are the Western tourists photographed by Brian Brake at Borobudur, Central Java, in 1971 (plate 71 p 106). Brake's Hong Kong-based production company Zodiac Films made several cultural documentaries, among them *Borobudur: The Cosmic Mountain* (1972). Such representations have to negotiate the challenging interface between exotic tourism and scholarly documentation; to loosen up and work with the false dichotomy between immediacy and depth; to combine general appeal with accurate records. They have to enable their viewers to look through their exotic surfaces into the historical depth of the representation.

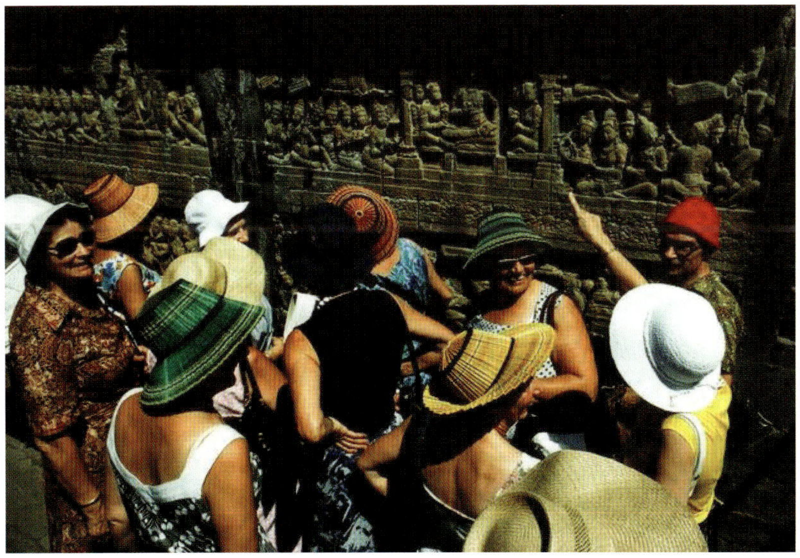

Brian Brake. *Tourists at the temples of Borobudur, Indonesia,* 1971. "The Cosmic Mountain: Borobudur". *India Magazine*, vol. 3, no. 1, December 1982. 35mm color transparency. Collection Museum of New Zealand Te Papa Tongarewa. Gift of Wai-man Lau, 2001.

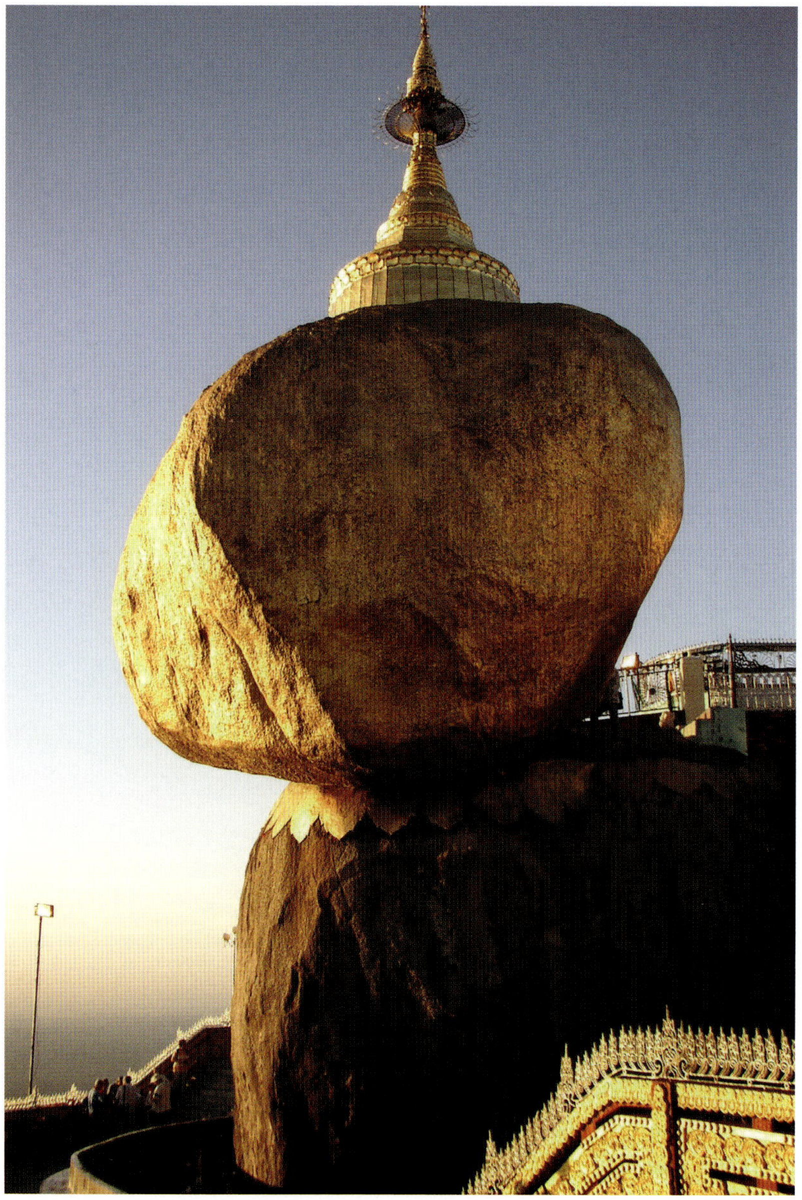

Ralf-André Lettau. *Golden Rock,* 30 November 2005. Courtesy of Andre Lettau/gallery/Myanmar, Wikimedia Commons.

NEGOTIATING THE REPRESENTATION CHALLENGE

Among the most spectacular post-*mandala* artifacts is the popular tourist destination Kyaiktiyo Pagoda or "Golden Rock" in Mon State, Myanmar. This was photographed by Steve McCurry in 1994 (plate 54 p 068) and by the Japanese photographer Hiroji Kubota in 1978 as *The Golden Rock at Shwe Pyi Daw*. Both photographers have cropped their shots to the rock itself, omitting the pagoda on top. The site is one of the most photographed along the South East Asia tourist itinerary; images incorporating the pagoda, such as Ralf-André Lettau's, are the commonplace norm. Kubota's and McCurry's pagoda-less framing raises the issue: to what extent can reality be edited?

The simple answer is that all photographs edit "reality". McCurry's astonishing photographs of cultural practices such as *Men playing chess*, *Jodhpur, Rajasthan, India*, 1996,[14] (plate 78 p 113), *Shaolin monks training, Zhengzhou, China*, 2004 (plate 81 p 118) *Stilt Fishermen, Weligama, Sri Lanka*, 1995 (plate 80 pp 116-117), or *Boy at Ganesh Chaturthi festival*, *Mumbai, India*, 1996 (plate 84 pp 120-121) use the full range of resources available to the modern digital camera—vibrant saturated color, High-Resolution, fast shutter speeds, and sophisticated editing resources. Yet these photographs' compelling surfaces are stretched across the depth of cultural practices that may be at once everyday and at-risk or anachronistic. The photograph is both an exotic experience and a precisely situated ethnographic record, immediate in terms of impact and slow in terms of content. The photographer is simultaneously gratifying his audience's desire for sensation and acting as an ethnographic historian. Negotiating a balance between surface and depth is one of many sub-themes of the representation challenge.

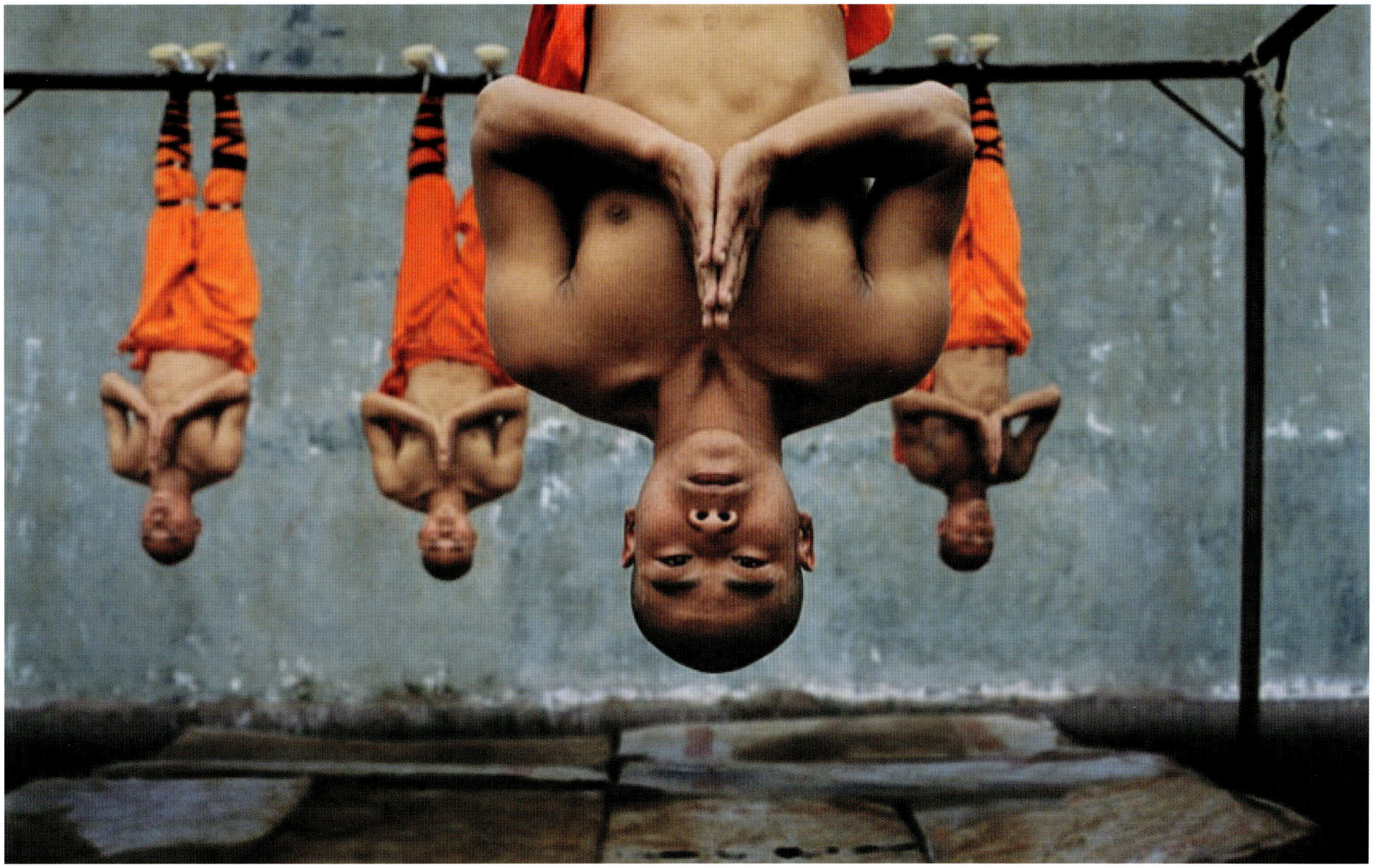

Steve McCurry. *Shaolin monks training, Zhengzhou, China,* 2004. *The Iconic Photographs* (London & New York: Phaidon Press, 2010).
© Steve McCurry.

TRUTH AND CONTEXT

Discussion of photographic representation circulates around regimes of truth. How does the viewer know what power has edited the knowledge that determines the truth of the representation? These terms of reference have become more complex since the proliferation of image-rich photographic media and technologies, beginning with mass-circulation picture magazines in the 1930s, and accelerating through standardized computer desktop editing softwares such as Adobe Photoshop in 1990, Apple's iPhoto in 2002, and distribution and storage facilities such as Instagram in 2010—and Instagram's own "adjust" and "filter" tools. The term "photoshopped"—or just "shopped"—has been in common usage for two decades and now speaks to an expectation that most publicly circulated photographs will have been "tweaked", whether for professional online or print publication, or for sharing on social media. Only rarely is this controversial. The polarizing international controversy that followed disclosure of Brake's having art-directed a young actress, Aparna Das Gupta (now Sen), to make his iconic photograph *"Monsoon girl"* (1960) (plate 01 p 032) is now less likely as photo-editing technologies become ubiquitous across amateur and professional applications. The distinction between pre-production staging of a photograph (on a scale from shot-selection and framing, to studio-based art-direction) and post-production editing of the image (on a scale from amateur desktop cropping and filtering to professional remodeling and cloning) has become less clearly marked as digital post-production capacities have become increasingly sophisticated and available.

In a 1984 interview, Jean Baudrillard suggested that: "… the sign is, if you like, without recourse … On the contrary, *reality is the effect of the sign.*"[15] In 1953, in the pre-digital era, Roland Barthes suggested that, "Depth is born only at the moment the spectacle itself slowly turns its shadow toward man and begins to look at him."[16] Writing about the "press photograph" in 1961, Barthes concluded that the photograph develops its social function, "in the form of a paradox—that which makes of an inert object a language and which transforms the uncultured of a 'mechanical' art into the most social of institutions."[17]

The issues of autonomy, depth, and social agency discussed by these writers in the early stages of the mass distribution and consumption of photographs have now entered contemporary popular discussion. This occurs not just in truth-evaluating terms such as "photoshopping" but in relation to how the photograph has become what Barthes—half a century before selfies—called "the most social of institutions", from family snaps to Snapchat, Pinterest and "Insta-celebrities" known as "influencers"; and also with significant sociopolitical agency, as in cellphone camera documentations of Taksim Square demonstrations in Istanbul 2013–14 or the Umbrella Occupation in Hong Kong 2014–15. Such nonprofessional photographs now overlap with and in some cases supplant the "press photograph" whose regime of truth was once epitomized by heroic frontline photographers in the mold of Robert Capa—despite controversy surrounding the possible staging of his most famous photograph, *Loyalist Militiaman at the Moment of Death, Cerro Muriano, September 5, 1936.*[18]

For Baudrillard, the photograph's uncanniness is the consequence of its being "without recourse"—making reality, not signifying it. However, in the wider context of mass consumption photography as documentary reportage or what Barthes characterized in 1961 as "the press photograph", issues of truth remain contingent on the historicity and situatedness of the photograph's moment.

In 1961, when Barthes noted the paradoxical transformation of "'mechanical' art into the most social of institutions", the truth of a photograph was still routinely sought at the "candid" convergence of a mechanical capacity (the speed and portability of the Leica camera); the mantra of the *instantané* or "decisive moment" associated with Henri Cartier-Bresson and, to some extent, with Magnum, the photo agency he co-founded; and the credo of the photographer's self-denial.[19] Truth depended on non-conformity, improvisation and chance; perceptual triggers related to surrealism. It was the world and the world's time that took the photograph; the photographer was reality's instrument, albeit a finely tuned, hyper-conscious and refined one.

What, within the terms of the *instantané*, do we make of Steve McCurry's *Flower seller at Dal Lake, Srinagar, Kashmir* (1996)? (plate 77 p 112) This enchanting image contains an element that seems to conform brilliantly to the "decisive moment" test of truth and reality. Moving forward into a beautiful *repoussoir* perspective, the boat's prow, the flower seller, and in particular the man's hand holding the shaft of his paddle are silhouetted within the reflected V of light entering the picture from a luminous gap in the trees ahead. But this apparently momentary effect was the culmination of two weeks spent travelling with the flower sellers and is the result of a slow process in which the photographer's presence over time, rather than instantaneous, heightened consciousness, is the arbiter of truth.[20]

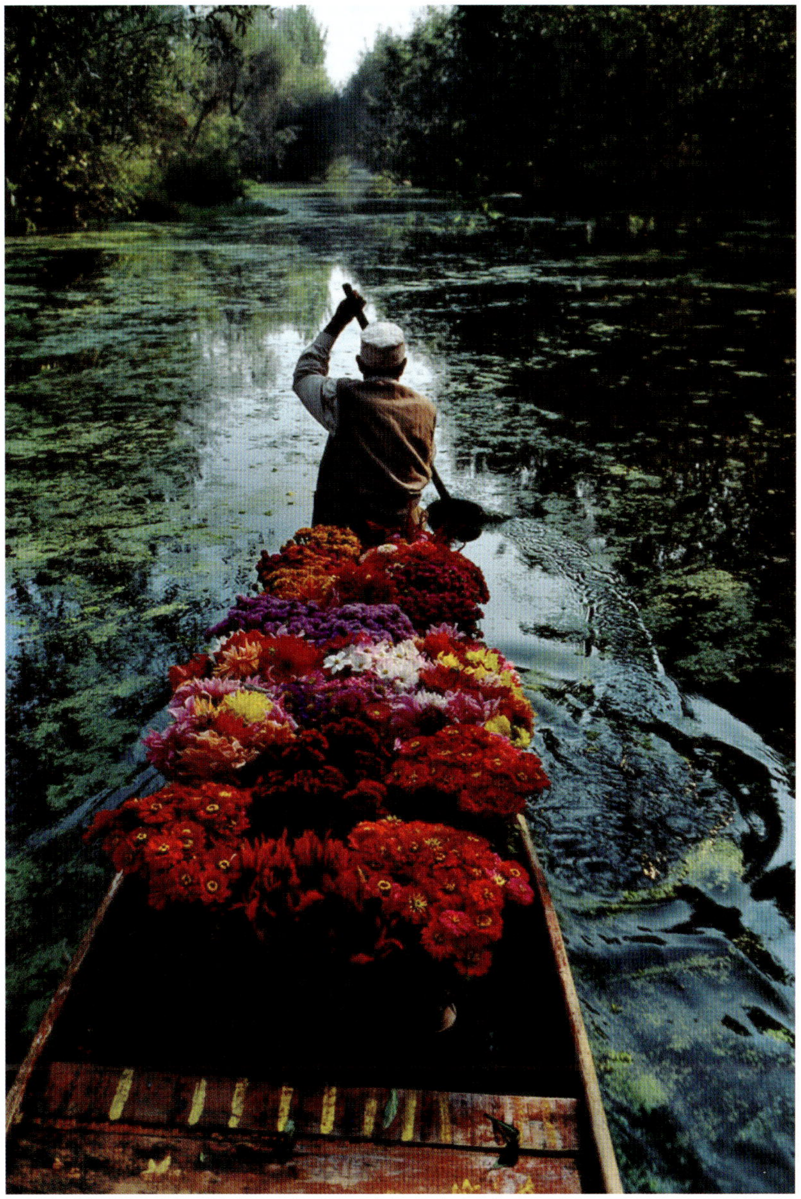

Steve McCurry. *Flower Seller at Dal Lake, Srinagar, Kashmir*, 1996. "Kashmir: Trapped in Conflict". *National Geographic,* vol. 196, no. 3, September 1999. © Steve McCurry.

Recently, the German photographer Barbara Probst (born 1964) has made deliberately anti-decisive moment serial works by triggering multiple simultaneous exposures of the same moment from different viewpoints.[21] In addition, through the 1950s photography became progressively consolidated within the art mainstream. Andy Warhol took thousands of Polaroid photographs of himself and his friends, 700 of which were recently published by the leading fine-art house Taschen in *Andy Warhol: Polaroids 1958–1987*. Artists including Cindy Sherman turned photography's gaze against itself to expose its ability to frame and manipulate its objects, especially women—exposing the anachronistic, even narrowly ideological, principles of *instantané* truth. Sherman's self-staged portraits ask to be read as allegories, not instances of unmediated reality.

McCurry's flower-seller image can also be read allegorically: the boatman steering his beautiful cargo towards a bright future. But the photograph's historicity and situatedness are annotated otherwise in the title of the photo essay where the image first appeared in *National Geographic* magazine: "Kashmir: Trapped in Conflict".[22] In 1996 the armed conflict in Kashmir entered its seventh year, with Indian security forces and Kashmiri militant separatists engaged in a bitter struggle characterized by torture and violations of human rights. The exotic surface of the photograph "slowly turns its shadow", as Barthes wrote; what then confronts us is the possibility that these flowers are funerary offerings. The "exotic" in this allegorical mode operates across the grain of the historical moment and, though the photograph has appeared in books and exhibitions detached from the magazine text that first provided its context, that context constitutes what Barthes called the photograph's "depth".

Issues of truth and context may spill out into wider fields of representation. The 22 December 1941 issue of *Life* displayed a full page image of the American flag on its cover. Pearl Harbour had been attacked on 7 December and America was at war with Japan. Inside was a two page feature on "How to Tell Japs From the Chinese".[23] The article could charitably be seen as well-intentioned: "angry citizens" had failed to distinguish between Japanese and Chinese U.S. citizens and *Life* provided a photographic "rule-of-thumb from the anthropometric conformations that distinguish friendly Chinese from enemy alien Japs". The Japanese-American photographer Susumo Ito's documentary photographs of the all-Japanese American 442nd Regimental Combat Team in Europe move a counter-narrative into the anxious field marked out by *Life*'s feature.[24] The families of many Japanese 442nders were in internment camps in the United States: Ito's own parents were in the Rohwer internment camp in Arkansas. His all-Japanese unit became the most decorated unit in U.S. history. This narrative spills further into *Bad Day at Black Rock* (1955), the John Sturges movie starring Spencer Tracy as the war-wounded John J. Macreedy who comes to a small country town, Black Rock, to give a medal to a Japanese farmer, Komoko, father of a deceased 442nd Regimental Combat Team army officer, Joe, who had saved Macreedy's life. Komoko, however, has been killed by townspeople in a racially motivated attack on a "Jap".[25]

The consumers of photo essay magazines together with movies and newsreels (especially Henry Luce's Time Inc. "March of Time" series) and an emergent television industry in the post-WWII years would routinely have been immersed in such complex, contradictory visual environments—complicated by advertising targeting prosperous middle-class consumers, and the admission of photography to the high temples of art. Both Brake and McCurry reflect the influence of Edward Steichen's *The Family of Man* in 1955—the internationally successful Museum of Modern Art (MoMA) photographic exhibition and book project that promoted a universalizing, humanist post World War II ethos. Despite successfully touring the world for eight years, it was criticized for generalizing difference. Critics also noted the significance of Steichen's debt to photo essay magazine formats. MoMA pursued this theme with John Szarkowski's 1965 *The Photo Essay* exhibition, which included several of Brake's *Monsoon* photographs. The tension between generalized humanism—or transculturalism—and cultural difference remains critical. In 1994 Homi Bhabha noted that, "… we find ourselves in the moment of transit where space and time cross to produce complex figures of difference and identity, past and present, inside and outside, inclusion and exclusion."[26]

This environment of "complex figures of difference and identity", together with ongoing developments in media technologies, is where the photographs of Brake and McCurry must be read first—Brake from his China portfolios of 1957 and 1959 in *New York Times Magazine, Paris Match,* and *Life*, through diverse publications until his death in 1988; and McCurry twenty years on from Brake's China photographs, beginning with his coverage of the war in Afghanistan for the *New York Times* in 1979 and *Time* magazine in 1980 and continuing through numerous assignments, especially for *National Geographic*, to the present day. The exhibitions and coffee-table books where the photographs have appeared are important too, especially in McCurry's case, as are Brake's films and artifact-based ethnographic catalogues. But the significance of their work in general sheets back to the complex, contested environment of the mass distribution picture embedded in a photo essay with more or less text and a significant story to tell. This is where their engagements are most critically tested: to quote Said again, in the challenges of "the representation of other cultures, societies, histories; the relationship between power and knowledge."

Contemporary on-line distribution systems including Instagram have expanded the reach of professional photography far beyond the capacities of mass distribution magazines. Equally accessible now are the elaborately staged "realist" photo-shoots of Gregory Crewdson, whose photographs reverse-mime the exaggerated naturalism of photo-realist art;[27] the anti-exotic series on the vernacular culture and architecture of Asian mega-cities by Hong Kong-based Michael Wolf;[28] the true-to-genre documentarism of Warren Richardson's 2016 Photo of the Year in the World Press Photo Contest;[29] and, at another extreme, the ironic subterfuge of the Argentinian artist Amalia Ulman's Instagram project *Excellences and Perfections* (2014).[30] In September 2015, the Instagram blog announced its 400 millionth user—an indicator of how the photograph has extended its global reach since the decline of major weekly photo-magazines in the 1970s.[31]

A concise rendition of the rich historical ironies in this expanded field of photographic practice is provided by the title of the 2016 Auckland Festival of Photography, *Otheries are the New Selfies*; its tag-lines are "We're glad to share the joy of true photography," and "Some things should be kept sacred." That Sacred Hill Vineyards is a Festival sponsor tweaks the by-now familiar word-string: "Other[ie]s", "true" and "sacred". Said's challenge in respect of "the representation of other cultures, societies, histories" pertains in this expanded environment—but in more complexly articulated ways.

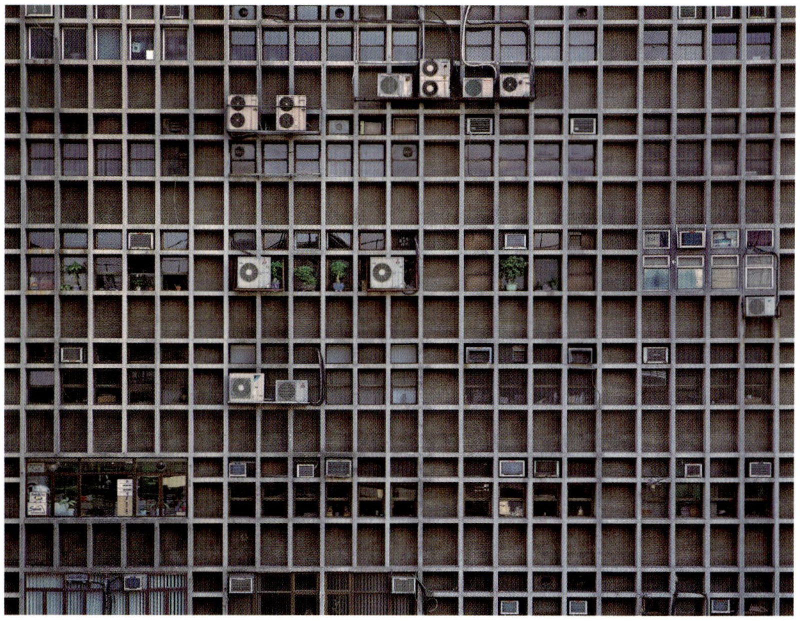

Michael Wolf (b. 1954). *industrial 24,* Hong Kong, 2014. @michael wolf.

THE MAGAZINE PHOTO ESSAY

As noted by Jonathan Flaws in his essay "Opening the Door" in this catalog, the magazine photo essay gave many their first glimpse of different cultures and places. During its heyday from the 1940s through 70s, the photo essay reached large audiences for magazines such as *Life* and *Paris Match*. By 1942, four years after being launched as a weekly, *Life* already had an American circulation of four million.[32] What this expansive audience encountered in the work of documentary photographers such as Brake and, twenty years later, McCurry, was not just the *picturing* accomplished by mechanical reproduction, but invitations to "picture this", to use the photograph as a means to expand the reach of visual thought.

Viewers' thinking also encountered *Life*'s page-sharing collages of photo essays on, for example, communist China, and advertising spreads featuring cheerfully prosperous portraits of middle-class American life (cigarettes, cars, liquor, TV sets)—as well as the hidden influences of photo-editors and blatantly tendentious messaging by caption writers. *Life*, under the direction of its founder Time Inc.'s Henry R. Luce, was politically conservative and anti-communist—in *Time* (9 June 1930) Stalin was described as having a "mask of Oriental ruthlessness". However, Luce was born in China to Presbyterian missionary parents and received some of his education there; and though his internationalist brand of American "manifest destiny" led him to predict that the twentieth century would be "the American century" —"The drama of Western Culture culminates in the creation of the United States of America"[33]— his interest in Asia and especially China was reflected in *Life*'s feature programming. In its first issue (23 November 1936), the magazine visited a Catholic parochial school for Chinese children in San Francisco. The feature's text concludes, "... when the 3 o'clock bell clangs at the end of school, home they skip to Chinatown to lapse again into the speech of their ancestors."[34] The intention of the text is benign, its tone patronizing, but the key message identifies a ghettoized "foreign body" that will "lapse" into its customary language. This would be *Life*'s characteristic tone.[35]

In addition, Luce's vision—prompted by his second wife, Clare Boothe Luce—was to tell stories in pictures rather than text.[36] *Life*'s photographers included Margaret Bourke-White, who provided the magazine's first cover image and set up its first photo-lab; and Dorothea Lange, who covered the internment of Japanese Americans after the Japanese attack on Pearl Harbour. The availability of 35mm color film and small, portable cameras such as the Leica M series in the mid-1950s also contributed to the ability of many photo essay magazines including *Life* to undertake international assignments—though *Life* was initially resistant to 35mm film. A cadre of distinguished photographers including Henri Cartier-Bresson (1908–2004) and his younger French compatriot Marc Riboud (born 1923) photographed widely in Asia. In January 1949 Cartier-Bresson contributed "A Last Look at Peiping" ten months before the establishment of the People's Republic of China. Embedded in the accompanying text is Luce's militaristic partisanship towards the Kuomintang of his hero, Chiang Kai-shek: "... everywhere the desire for peace, no matter what the price, was doing almost as much as the Communists to destroy Chiang Kai-shek's China."[37] In 1958, Cartier-Bresson returned to China to photograph impacts of the Great Leap Forward. The text ("Red China Bid for a Future") is replete with phrases such as "back-breaking toil", "iron grip" and "bloody record".[38] Cartier-Bresson's photographs are "real", but less judgmental.

Riboud and Brake worked together in China in 1957. It is clear that Brake liked and respected the Chinese. His photographs published in *New York Times Magazine* in May 1957 under the title "Reception in Peiping" show Chairman Mao Zedong meeting with Marshall Kliment Y. Voroshilov, the Soviet chief of state.[39] These photographs do not represent the sympathetic range and variety of work Brake made in China, most of which was not published until 1995:[40] scenes of ordinary life and work and, with Riboud, documentation of traditional Chinese medicine subsequently published in the medical journal *MD* and the French magazine *Science et Avenir.*[41]

In 1959, Brake was the only independent Western, non-communist journalist permitted entry to China to photograph the tenth anniversary of the Peoples' Republic and the visit of the Soviet premier Nikita Khrushchev. His access was probably assisted by the presence in China of another New Zealander, Rewi Alley, a member of the Chinese Communist Party respected for his work with the "Gung Ho" Chinese Industrial Cooperatives.[42] Such an association, while useful to *Life*, was not going to inflect its negative attitude toward "Red China".

In this often conflicted context, Brake's monsoon essay in the 8 September 1961 issue of *Life* was unusual. He spent nine months photographing the stages of the monsoon in India in 1960, taking over 1,000 35mm Kodachrome transparencies which he eventually whittled down to a presentation set of about 110.[43] According to his partner Wai-man Lau, Brake was persuaded by his Indian colleagues and especially perhaps by his assistant in 1960, Asoke Roy Chowdhury, to reshoot much of his first work because it was too light.[44] The resulting images and texts, distributed over nineteen pages, break with many of the ingrained conventions of the magazine photo essay. Though there are bright, colorful photographs of festivals and flowering trees, a number of others are very dark and might usually have been rejected by photo-editors; however, Brake's "Monsoon", despite initial hesitation on the part of *Life*'s art director Bernard Quint, resulted in competition between *Paris Match* and *Life*, and subsequent versions in a variety of magazines.[45]

RISK AND DIALOGUE

How to engage with Brake's dark monsoon photographs, for example *Villagers shelter from torrential rain, Nimitia, West Bengal, India*, 1960 (plate 07 p 038)? The image is neither conventionally exotic, nor dramatically catastrophic. Its darkness is at once truthful and hard to see into. Looking for dialogue, we encounter texts by the Indian poets Rabindranath Tagore, Kalidasa, Jasim Uddin and Nuripama Debi. They challenge us to engage with the picture, to look past its surface into the situated cultural

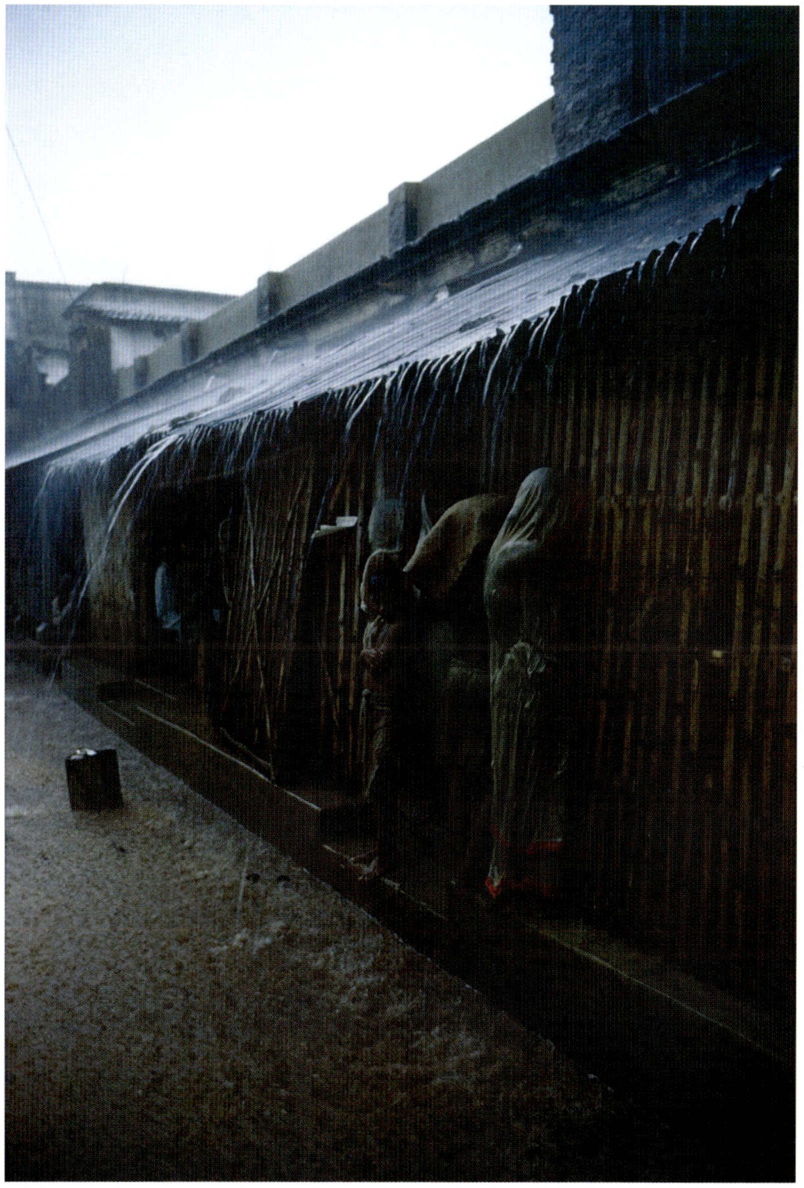

Brian Brake. *Villagers shelter from torrential rain, Nimitia, West Bengal, India.* From the series: Monsoon, 1960. "Monsoon". *Life,* vol. 51, no. 10, 8 September 1961. 35mm transparency. Collection Museum of New Zealand Te Papa Tongarewa. Gift of Wai-man Lau, 2001.

conditions and narratives to which it offers a portal. The photograph also blurs distinctions between the pictorialist "art photograph", and documentary reportage.

Making photographs that could take such risks—and that could be unappealing at first sight—became more challenging with the passing of the American Airline Deregulation Act of 1978, which facilitated the growth of cheaper international air travel. When *National Geographic Traveler* was launched in 1984, global tourism was a growth industry. Magazine editors relied on key words like "exotic" to convey the allure of foreign destinations—especially in Asia. The title "Exotic, Enticing Hong Kong" was a familiar sub-editor's contribution to McCurry's essay in *National Geographic Traveler* (Winter 1986–87). But by comparison with the Luce policy at *Life* of privileging image over text, *National Geographic* routinely included substantial writing; distinguished journalists McCurry has collaborated with include the historian Geoffrey Ward,[46] the Pulitzer Prize-winning correspondent Lewis Simons,[47] and the travel writer Paul Theroux.[48]

A majority of McCurry's many celebrated portraits engage directly and frankly with their subjects—framing them as equal participants and challenging the glib exoticism of voyeuristic representation.[49] But a portrait that may best show McCurry's ability to meet the complexities of the representation challenge is of a mental patient, a former army officer, possibly war-damaged, in an asylum in Kabul in 1992 (plate 40 p 076). In this picture, the asylum patient is seen in the middle distance in an empty corridor with strong shafts of sunlight piercing its gloom from large windows that cast the shadows of their frames on the floor. These barred shapes both contain, and separate us from, the man whose awareness of the photographer seems at once focused and quizzical. Strongly side-lit, one half of his face is in shadow as if to conceal his intention; yet a perplexed furrowing of his brow is visible. With his head tilted to one side, his back to a wall, and with the function of the door to his left unclear, his status in the space is ambiguous: has he been encountered there in the corridor, has he agreed to stand there and be photographed, is this where he might usually be met with, has he been in some way coerced? What emerges from Anthony Bannon's commentary on this photograph suggests another slow take: "Day after day, McCurry saw him return to this spot and stand there, motionless, without a word, pondering the designs of light on the floor."[50]

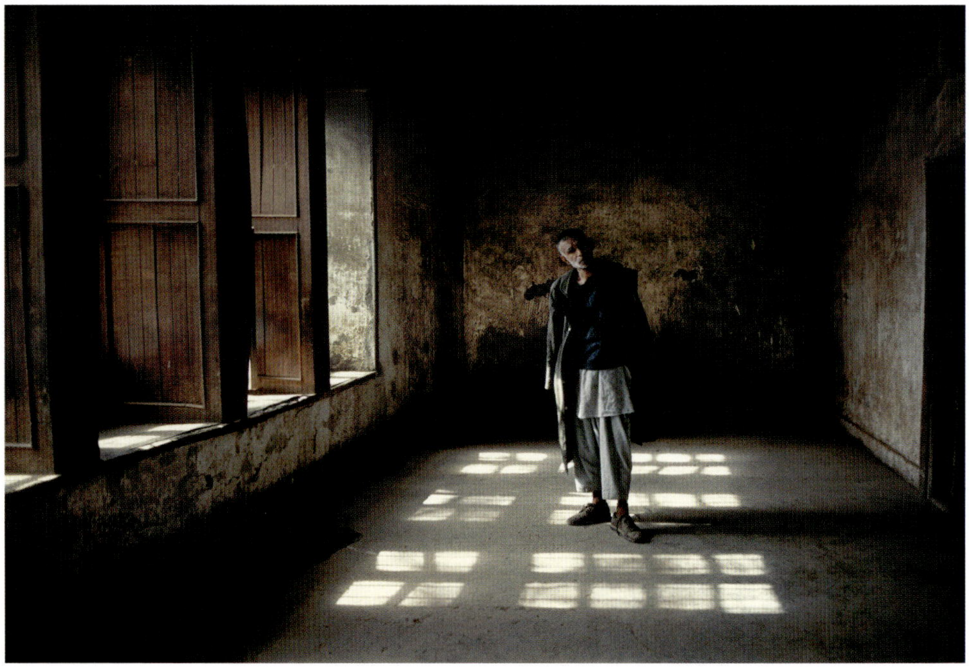

Steve McCurry. *Asylum, Kabul, Afghanistan,* 1992. "Afghanistan's Uneasy Peace". *National Geographic,* vol. 184, no. 4, October 1993. © Steve McCurry.

The portrait as news is a stock-in-trade of intercultural photography: McCurry's famous *Afghan Girl* (plate 20 p 062) became "the face" of the Afghan conflict 1979–89; Annie Leibowitz's photograph of the Indian Nobel Peace prize-winner Malala Yousafzai brought her story into the exhibition *Women: New Portraits* touring to ten major cities worldwide in 2016.[51] The high visibility and fame of these portraits edge them into another ubiquitous contemporary category, the celebrity photograph. But a great many of McCurry's subjects are not and will not become celebrities: his Afghan miner (plate 83 p 119), the woman pilgrim at a stupa in Tibet (plate 82 p 119), the wonderful portrait photographer in Kabul (plate 63 p 100).

The portrait of the asylum patient in Kabul will not elide smoothly with "news", nor with celebrity, nor with the stock confrontations of war photography—what David Shields, author of *Reality Hunger—a Manifesto* (2010) has recently critiqued in *War Is Beautiful: The New York Times Pictorial Guide to the Glamour of Armed Conflict**. [52] Nor can it be coopted by the exotic. McCurry allows the man to keep his distance and the distance of his story. His engagement with the moment of the photograph is ambiguous, and so, therefore, is ours. The hints of allegory, such as the barred shadows on the floor and the darkness that masks part of the man's face, are unobtrusive. Though the historical and narrative depth of the man's condition may be guessed at through the photograph, it does not weigh the image down with demands for significance. The question of how "the relationship between power and knowledge" shapes this representation of a particular man in a particular place at a particular time in a particular region of Asia, initiates a complex and productive narrative. The picturing it enables will not be exhausted easily.

Biographical note

Ian Wedde ONZM is an independent writer and curator based in Auckland, New Zealand. From 1994–2004 he was head of art and visual culture at the Museum of New Zealand Te Papa Tongarewa. Between 2011–13 he established and taught a postgraduate course in curatorial practice and art writing at the University of Auckland. His recent books include a monograph on the artist Bill Culbert: *Bill Culbert: Making Light Work* (Auckland: Auckland University Press, 2010).

Notes

1: *A Passion for Asia: The Rockefeller Legacy*, ed. by Sally Fisher (New York and Manchester: Asia Society in association with Hudson Hills Press, 2006), p. 27.

2: Cynthia Bronson Altman, "A Family's Love of Asian Art", in *A Passion for Asia*, pp. 50-106.

3: Shomei Tomatsu, from *Taiyo no Empitsu* (The Pencil of the Sun), 1975; quoted in *Chewing Gum and Chocolate: Photographs and Texts by Shomei Tomatsu*, ed. by Leo Runbinfien and John Junkerman, with texts by Tomatsu and an afterword by Rubinfien (New York: Aperture, 2014), p. 65.

4: Rubinfien, Notes to "Echoes of War", in Tomatsu (2014), p. 191.

5: Edward Said, *Orientalism* (New York: Random House, 1978).

6: Edward Said, in "Orientalism Reconsidered", *Cultural Critique* No. 1 (Autumn, 1985), University of Minnesota Press, pp. 89-107.

7: Marx, Karl, *The Eighteenth Brumaire of Louis Bonaparte* (1852).

8: Benjamin Disraeli, *Tancred* (1847).

9: See Ashis Nandy, *Traditions, Tyranny and Utopias: Essays in the Politics of Awareness* (New York: Oxford University Press, 1988; reprinted 1993).

10: Rosita Dellios, "Mandala: From Sacred Origins to Sovereign Affairs in Traditional Southeast Asia". *The Centre for East-West Cultural and Economic Studies Research Paper No. 10,* 1 January 2003.

11: See for example: R.A. Donkin, *Between East and West: The Moluccas and the Traffic in Spices Up to the Arrival of Europeans* (Philadelphia: American Philosophical Society, 2003).

12: Brian Brake and William Warren, *The house on the Klong: The Bangkok home and Asian art collection of James Thompson* (New York: Weatherhill, 1968).

13: http://www.aseantourism.travel/explore/detail/pilgrimage-tourism. Accessed 15 March 2016.

14: Gordon Campbell, *The Grove Encyclopedia of Decorative Arts: Two-Volume Set* (New York: Oxford University Press 2006), p. 227.

15: Ted Colless, David Kelly and Alan Cholodenko, "An Interview with Jean Baudrillard", trans. by Philippe Tanguy, in Jean Baudrillard, *The Evil Demon of Images* (Sydney: The Power Institute of Fine Arts, 1987), p. 47.

16: Roland Barthes, "The World as Object", in *Barthes: Selected Writings*, ed. and with an introduction by Susan Sontag (Fontana Paperbacks 1982), p. 73.

17: Barthes, "The Photographic Message", in *Selected Writings* (1982), p. 210.

18: See, for example, Larry Gross, John Stuart Katz and Jay Ruby, eds., *Image Ethics: The Moral Rights of Subjects in Photographs, Film, and Television* (New York & Oxford: Oxford University Press, 1988); and Phillip Knightley, *The First Casualty: From the Crimea to Vietnam; The War Correspondent as Hero, Propagandist, and Myth Maker* (New York: Harcourt, Brace, 1975), pp. 209-12.

19: "To me, photography is the simultaneous recognition, in a fraction of a second, of the significance of an event as well as of a precise organization of forms which give that event its proper expression." Henri Cartier-Bresson, Preface to *The Decisive Moment. Texts and photographs by Cartier-Bresson* (New York: Simon & Schuster, 1952).

20: See Anthony Bannon's note on this photograph in Anthony Bannon, *Steve McCurry* (London: Phaidon Press Limited, 2005), p. 92.

21: http://barbaraprobst.net. Accessed 28 January 2016.

22: Steve McCurry, "Kashmir: Trapped in Conflict". *National Geographic*, vol. 196, no. 3, September 1999, pp. 2-28.

23: "How to tell Japs from the Chinese: Angry citizens victimize allies with emotional outburst at enemy". *Life*, vol. 11, no. 25, December 22, 1941, pp. 81-82.

24: One of the more unexpected appearances of the much discussed diagrammatic racial profile is in a prose poem by the American poet Sesshu Foster. See the diagram at: http://www.english.illinois.edu/maps/poets/a_f/foster/lifemag.htm. Accessed 10 December 2015.

25: *Before They Were Heroes: Sus Ito's World War II Images* exhibition at the Japanese American National Museum, 2015. http://www.janm.org/exhibits/sus-ito/sus/. Accessed 28 January 2016.

26: Homi K. Bhabha, "Border Lives: The Art of the Present", in *The Location of Culture* (London and New York: Routledge, 1994), p.1.

27: See for example http://www.gagosian.com/artists/gregory-crewdson, and http://theamericanreader.com/interview-with-photographer-gregory-crewdson/. Both accessed 28 January 2016.

28: Michael Wolf (born 1954, Germany), http://photomichaelwolf.com. Accessed 28 January 2016.

29: Warren Richardson (born 1968, Australia), *A man passes a baby through the fence at the Hungarian-Serbian border at Röszke, Hungary, 28 August* 2015. View at http://www.worldpressphoto.org/news/2016-02-18/world-press-photo-year-2015-goes-warren-richardson. Accessed 18 February 2016.

30: Find Amalia Ulman's *Excellences and Perfections* at http://webenact.rhizome.org/excellences-and-perfections/20141014150552/http://instagram.com/amaliaulman. Accessed 18 March 2016.

31: blog.instagram.com, 22 September 2015. Accessed 18 March 2016.

32: http://www.newworldencyclopedia.org/entry/Life_(magazine). Accessed 15 January 2016.

33: Alan Brinkley, *The Publisher: Henry Luce and His American Century.* (New York: Alfred A. Knopf, 2010; Kindle edition 7074).

34: "Chinatown School", *Life,* vol. 1, no. 1, 23 November 1936, p. 24.

35: "We believe that the long range happiness of the U.S. depends more upon the salutary relations between Asia and the 'white man' than upon any other factor." Henry R. Luce, *memo* 1943, quoted in Brinkley, *The Publisher* (Kindle 6672).

36: Brinkley, *The Publisher* (Kindle 4393).

37: "Last Look at Peiping", *Life*, vol. 26, no.1, 3 January 49, pp. 13-21.

38: "Red China Bid for a Future", *Life*, vol. 46, no. 1, 5 January 1959, pp. 44-61.

39: *New York Times Magazine*, 12 May 1957, pp. 10-11.

40: *Brian Brake: China, the 1950s.* (Wellington: Museum of New Zealand Te Papa Tongarewa, 1995). Exhibition Catalog.

41: "Chinese medicine yesterday and today". *MD*, April 1958, pp. 30-5; "Que faut-il penser de la médecine chinoise?" *Science et Avenir*, No. 149, July 1959, pp. 364-9.

42: Conversation with Wai-man Lau, Auckland, 13 November 2015.

43: Gael Newton, "The Color Photo Essay 1960-1980", in *Brian Brake: Lens on the World*, ed. by Athol McCredie (Wellington: Te Papa Press, 2010), p. 172.

44: Conversation with Wai-man Lau, Auckland, 13 November 2015.

45: Newton, *Lens on the World*, p. 172.

46: Geoffrey Ward and Steve McCurry, "India: Fifty Years of Independence". *National Geographic*, vol. 191, no. 5, May 1997, pp. 4-57.

47: Lewis Simons and Steve McCurry, "Kashmir: Trapped in Conflict". *National Geographic*, vol. 196, no. 3, September 1999, pp. 2-29.

48: Paul Theroux and Steve McCurry, "By Rail Across India". *National Geographic*, vol. 165, no. 6, June 1984, pp. 197-743.

49: See *Steve McCurry: Portraits* (London & New York: Phaidon Press, 2 editions, 2013).

50: Bannon, *Steve McCurry*, p. 54.

51: http://www.theguardian.com/artanddesign/2016/mar/23/annie-leibovitz-malala-yousafzai-photography-women-new-portraits. Accessed 23 March 2016.

52: David Shields, *War Is Beautiful: The New York Times Pictorial Guide to the Glamour of Armed Conflict** (New York: powerHouse Books, 2015).

MONSOON MEETING

The professional lives of New Zealand photographer Brian Brake (1927-1988, New Zealand) and the American Steve McCurry (1950-, U.S.A.) come together during the season of the Asian monsoon, which Brake photographed in 1960 and McCurry twenty years later.

Brian Brake began to plan his "Monsoon" project in 1958, one year after becoming an Asia specialist with the Magnum photographic agency. He envisaged the monsoon season as an epic life-cycle narrative poem, in which dark days are followed by rebirth and celebration. As an eleven-year-old, McCurry saw Brake's 1961 "Monsoon" photo essay in *Life* magazine, and published his own comprehensive book project in 1988. McCurry understood the monsoon as a cosmological and spiritual phenomenon, as well as a natural seasonal event.

Brake's Indian friends and colleagues told him that his first monsoon photographs were too bright, that they did not show the darkness and oppression of weeks of torrential rain. Following their advice, Brake reshot the "dark days". The resulting photographs are among his most unusual and memorable. Using low sensitivity 12 ASA (ISO) Kodachrome film with minimal exposure latitude—and a steady hand—he found the oppressive grey-brown palette of the deluge. Typical of such dark images is the picture of people sheltering under the overhang of a building in Nimitia, West Bengal.

McCurry also photographed the rains, but his sympathetic portrait of the monsoon is often characterized by incident and color. An Indonesian girl's pink blouse contrasts with the green, floating duckweed in her yard; a marooned black dog waits in a flooded street of red walls.

01

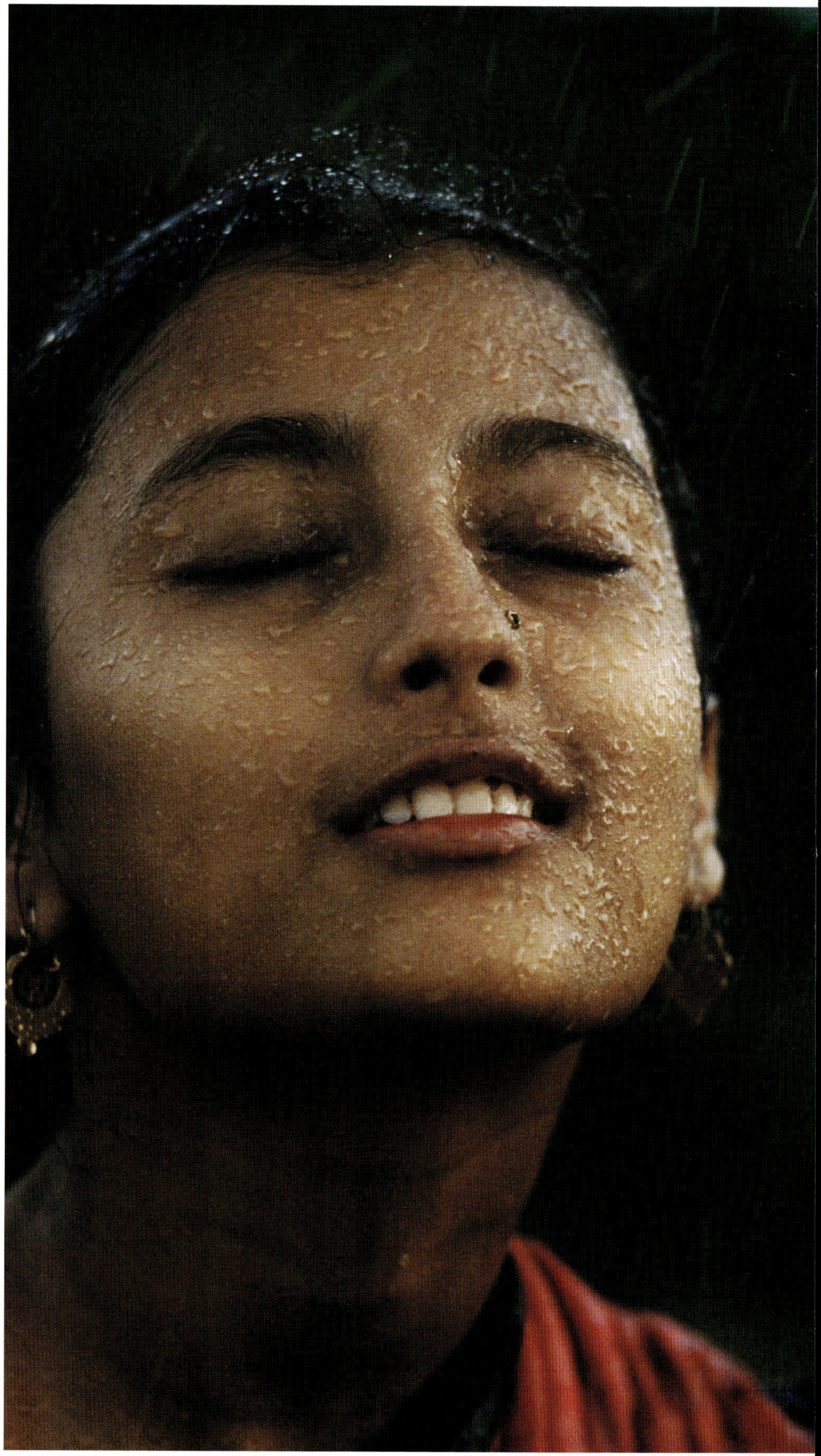

02

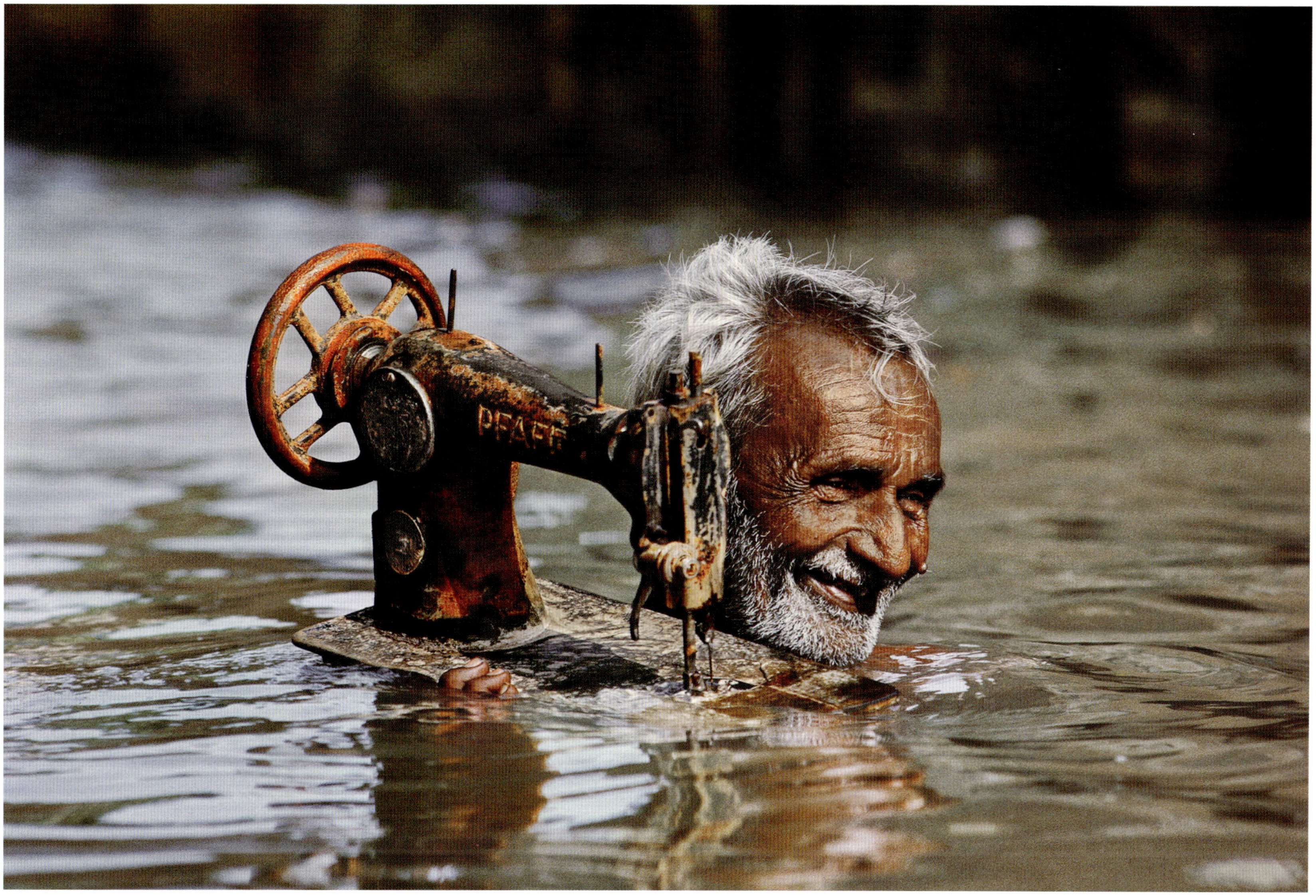

01 I Brian Brake. *"Monsoon girl" (Aparna Das Gupta), India*. From the series: Monsoon, 1960. "Monsoon". *Life*, vol. 51, no. 10, 8 September, 1961. 35mm transparency. Collection Museum of New Zealand Te Papa Tongarewa. Gift of Wai-man Lau, 2001.

02 I Steve McCurry. *Tailor in monsoon, Porbandar, India*, 1983. "Monsoons: Life Breath of Half the World". *National Geographic,* vol. 166, no. 6, December 1984. © Steve McCurry.

03

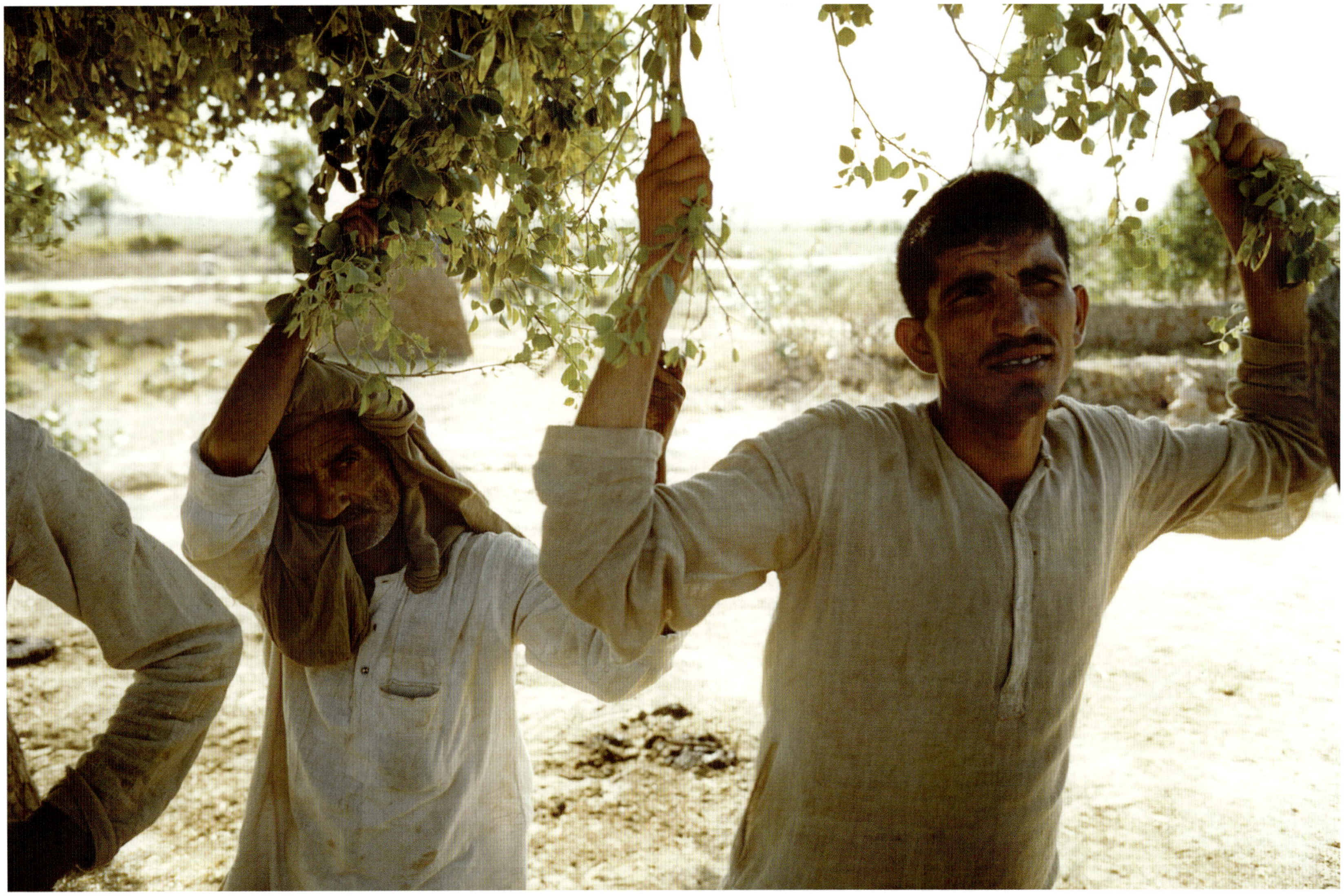

03 I Brian Brake. *Villagers in the shade of a tree during the afternoon heat, Punjab, India*. From the series: Monsoon, 1960. *Brian Brake – Monsoon*. Auckland: David Bateman, 2007. 35mm transparency. Collection Museum of New Zealand Te Papa Tongarewa. Gift of Wai-man Lau, 2001.

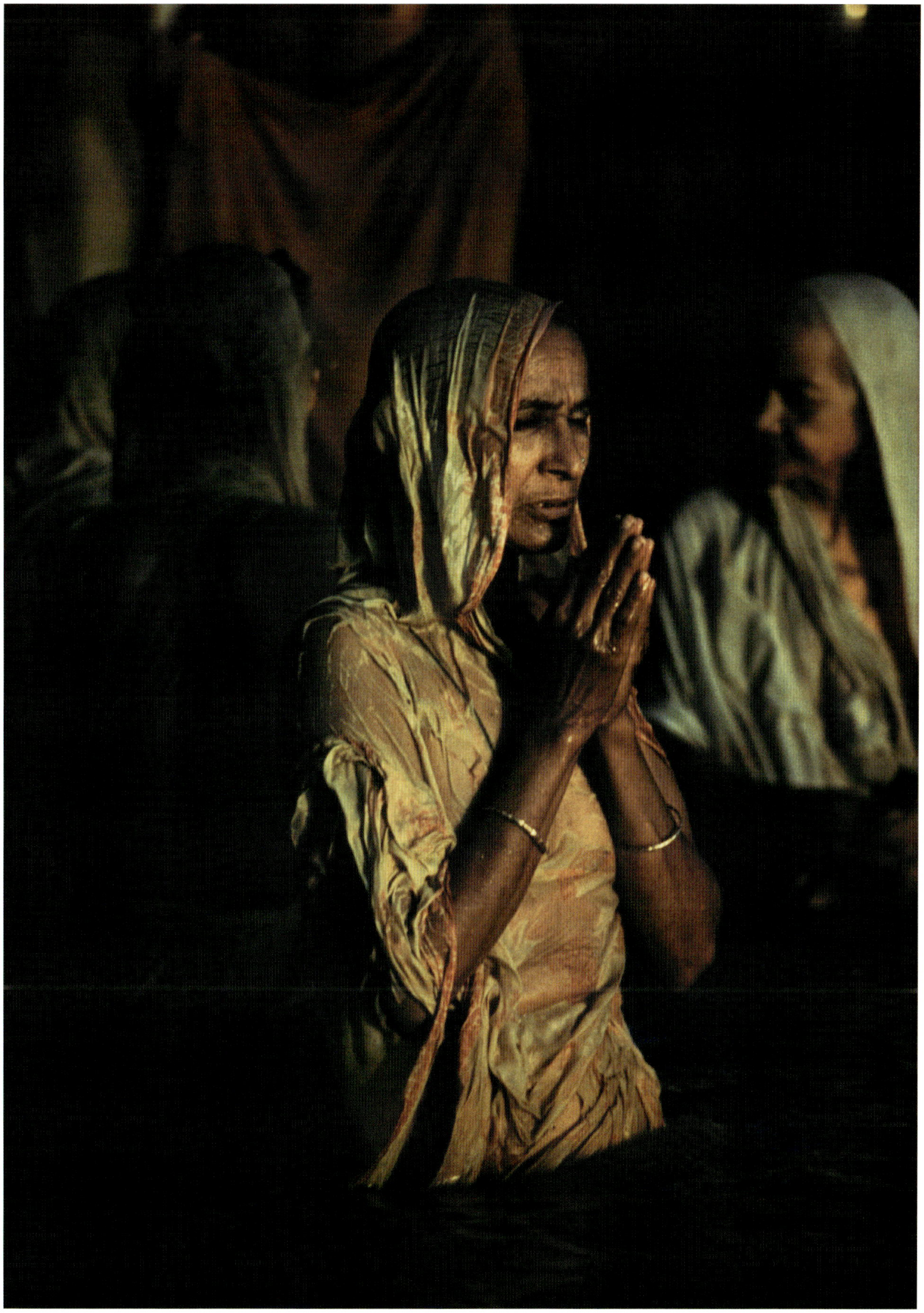

04 | Brian Brake. *Praying in the holy Ganges, Benares, India.* From the series: Monsoon, 1960. "Monsoon". *Life,* vol. 51, no. 10, 8 September, 1961. 35mm transparency. Collection Museum of New Zealand Te Papa Tongarewa. Gift of Wai-man Lau, 2001.

05

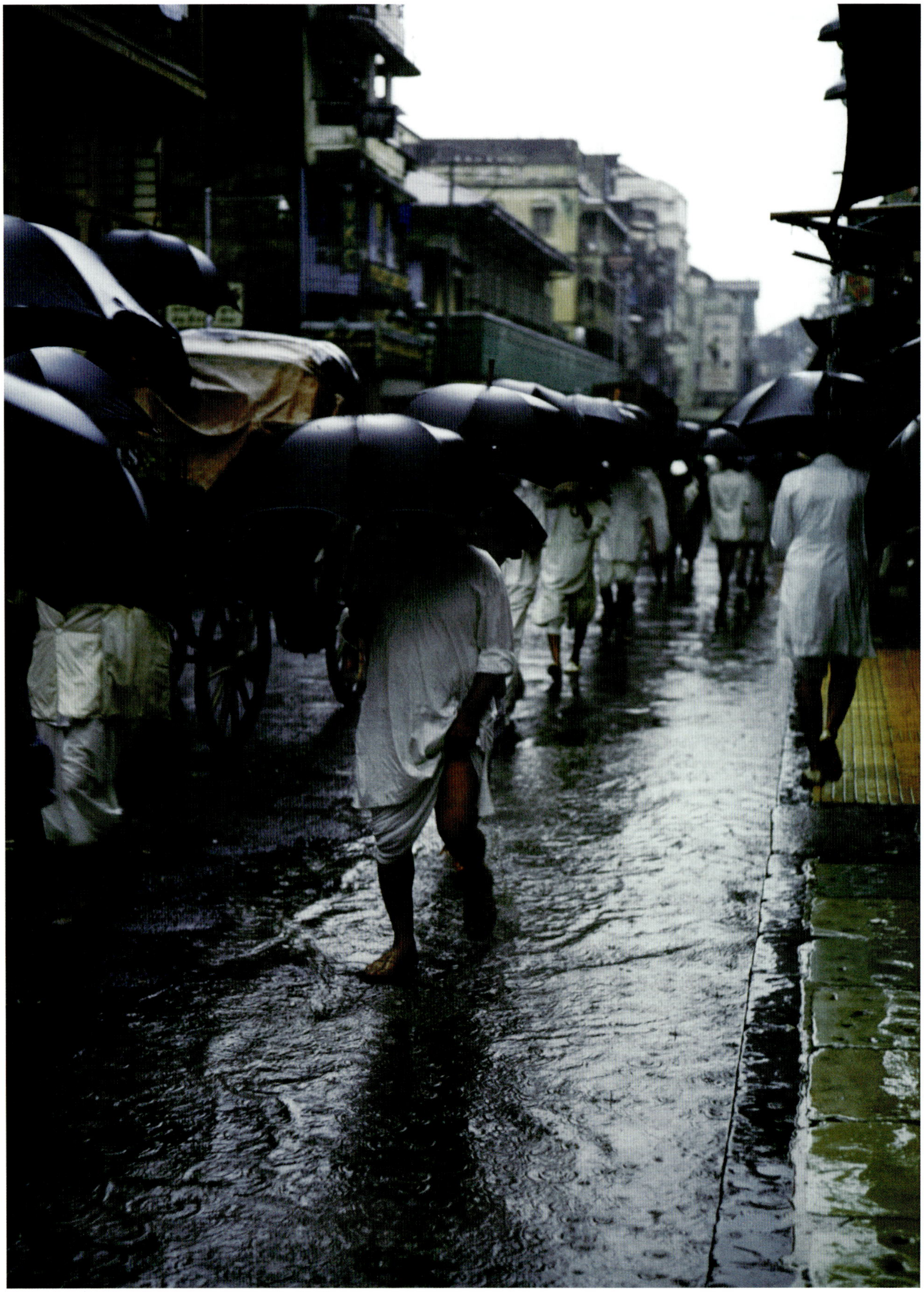

05 | Brian Brake. *"Every street runs like a river", Mumbai, India*. From the series: Monsoon, 1960. *Brian Brake – Monsoon*. Auckland: David Bateman, 2007. 35mm transparency. Collection Museum of New Zealand Te Papa Tongarewa. Gift of Wai-man Lau, 2001.

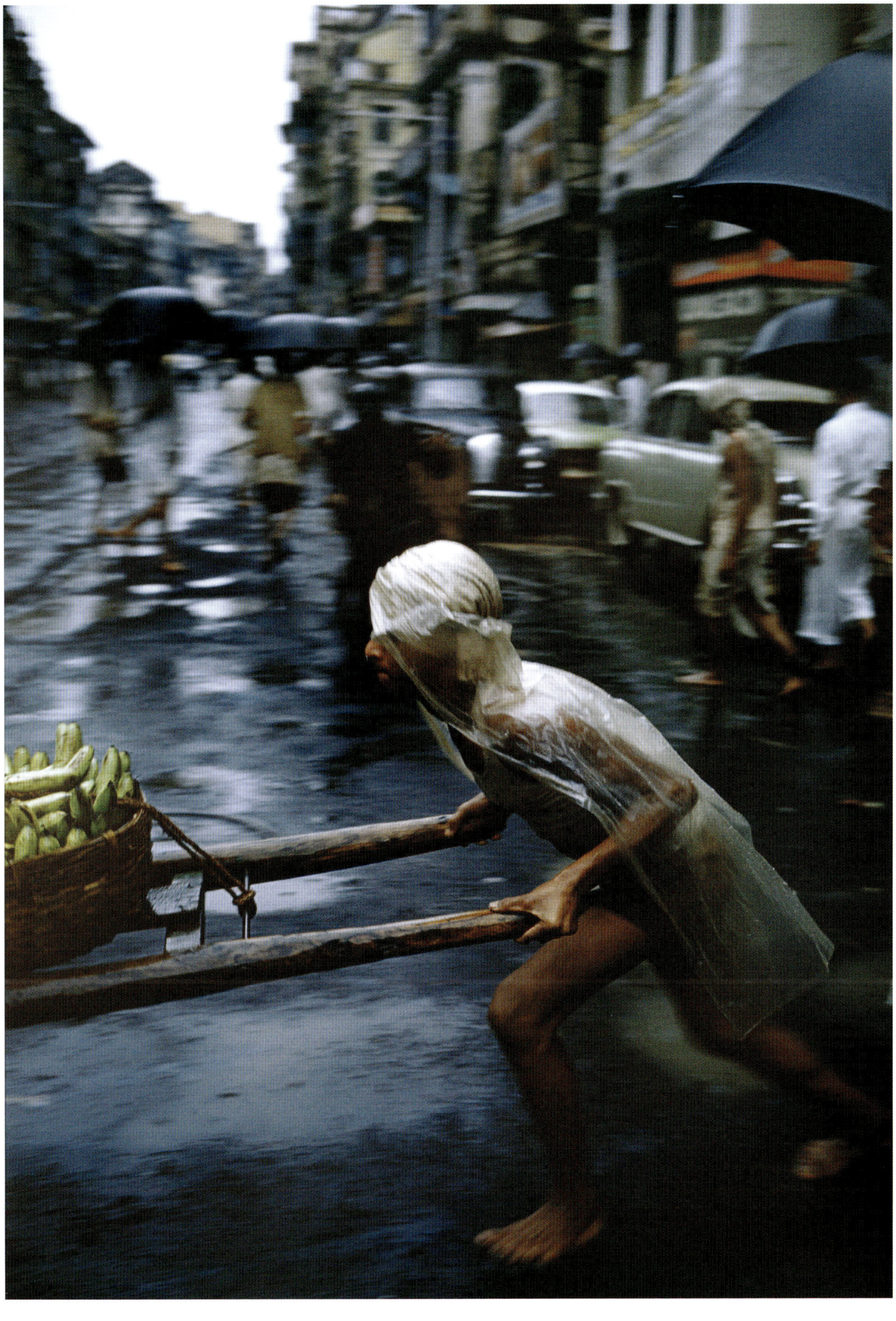

06 | Brian Brake. *Crawford Market, Mumbai, India*. From the series: Monsoon, 1960. “Monsoon”. *Life*, vol. 51, no. 10, September 8, 1961. 35mm transparency. Collection Museum of New Zealand Te Papa Tongarewa. Gift of Wai-man Lau, 2001.

07

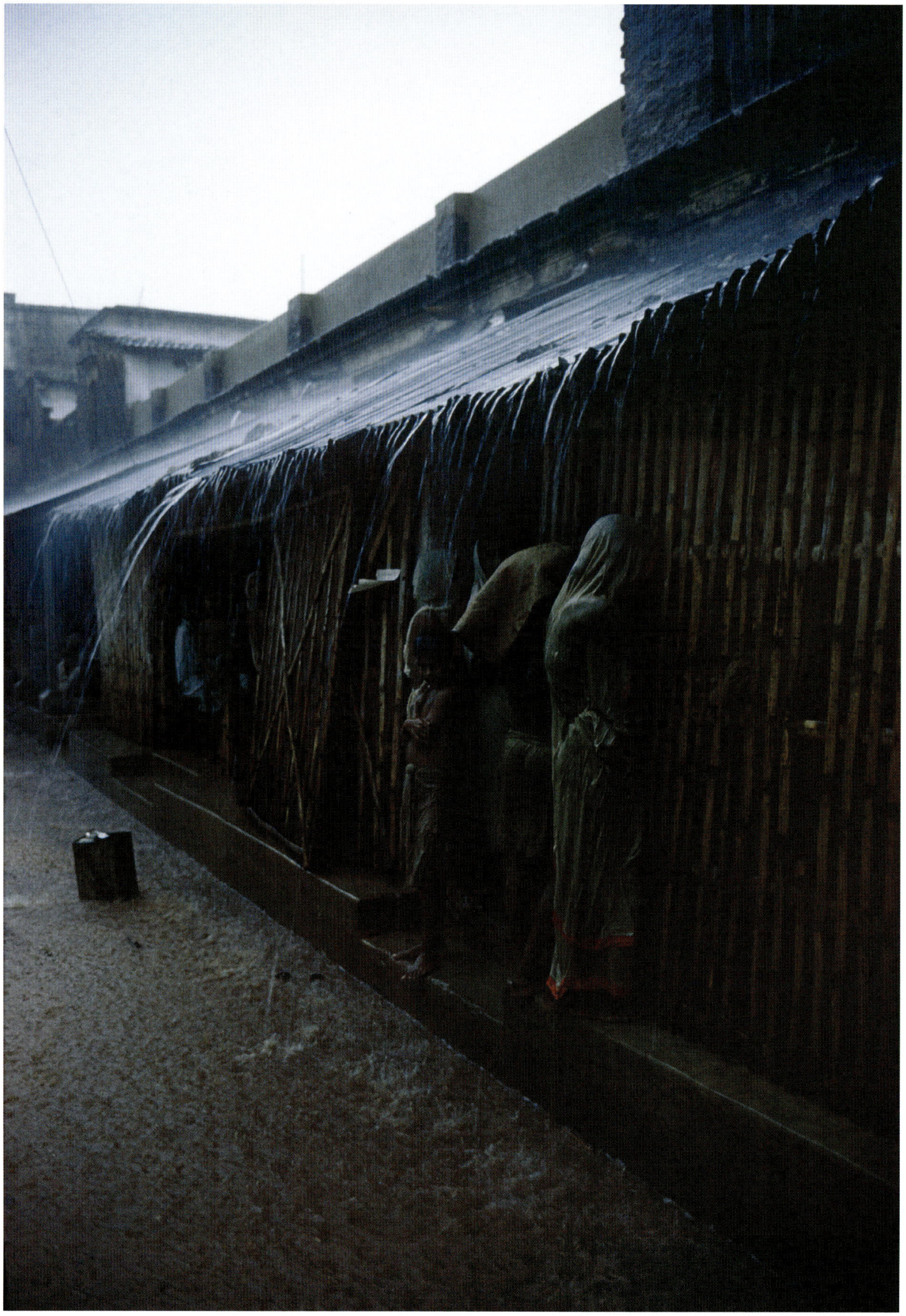

07 I Brian Brake. *Villagers shelter from torrential rain, Nimitia, West Bengal, India.* From the series: Monsoon, 1960. "Monsoon". *Life*, vol. 51, no. 10, 8 September, 1961. 35mm transparency. Collection Museum of New Zealand Te Papa Tongarewa. Gift of Wai-man Lau, 2001.

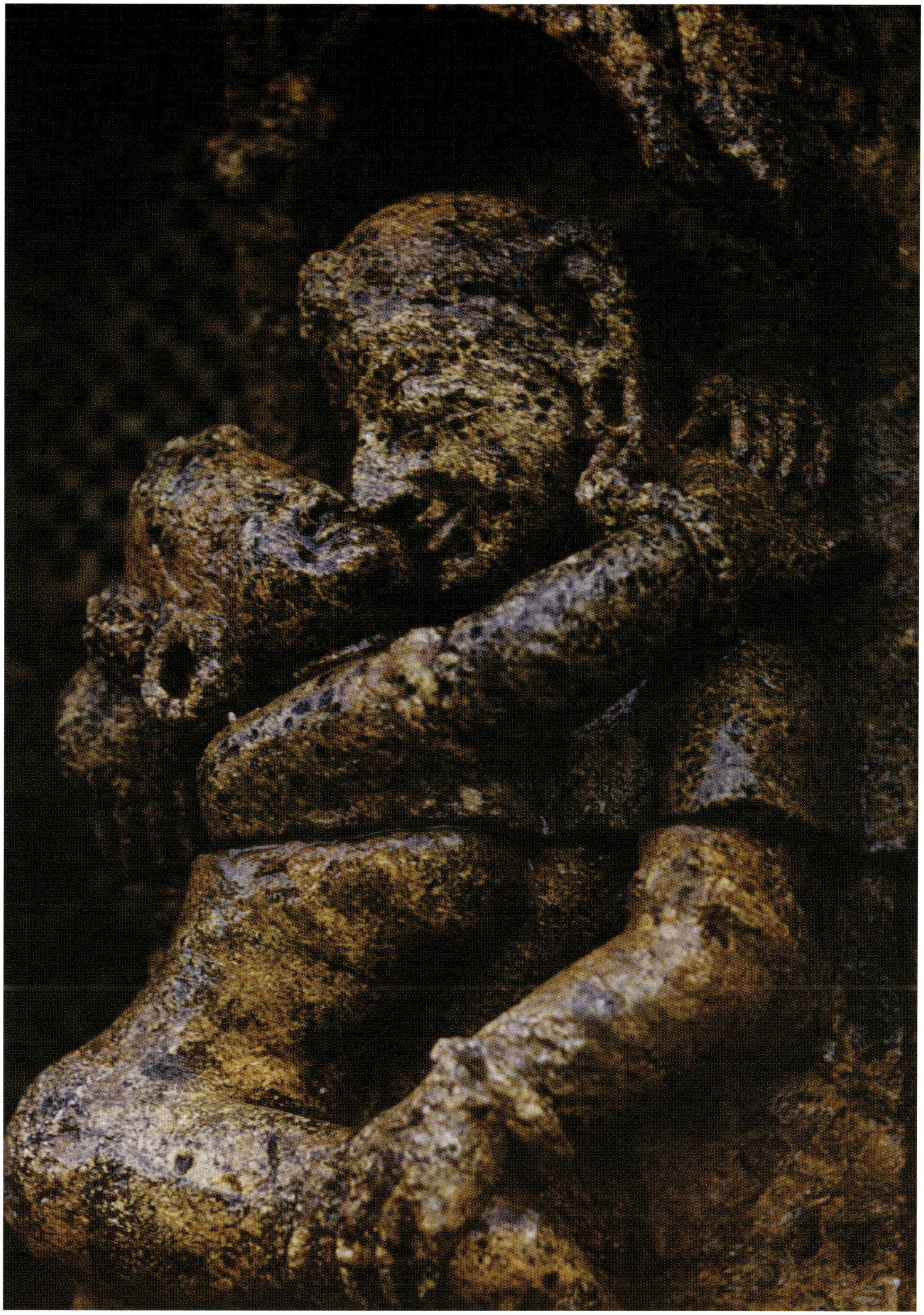

08 | Brian Brake. *Erotic sculpture in the Sun Temple, Konarak, India.* From the series: Monsoon, 1960. *Brian Brake—Monsoon*. Auckland: David Bateman, 2007. 35mm transparency. Collection Museum of New Zealand Te Papa Tongarewa. Gift of Wai-man Lau, 2001.

09

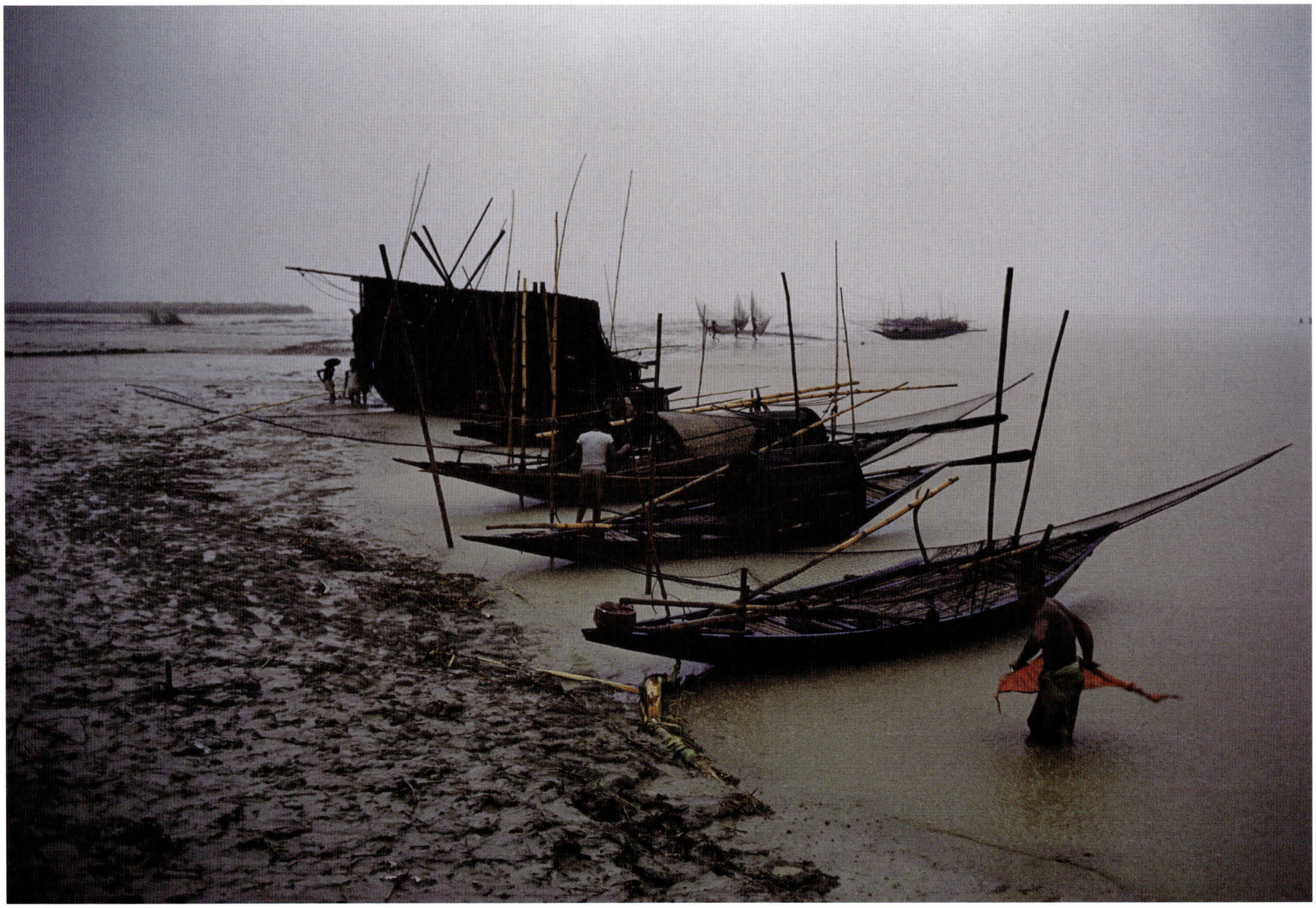

09 I Brian Brake. *Fishermen on the Padma River at Nimitia, West Bengal, India*. From the series: Monsoon, 1960. *Brian Brake – Monsoon.* Auckland: David Bateman, 2007. 35mm transparency. Museum of New Zealand Te Papa Tongarewa. Gift of Wai-man Lau, 2001.

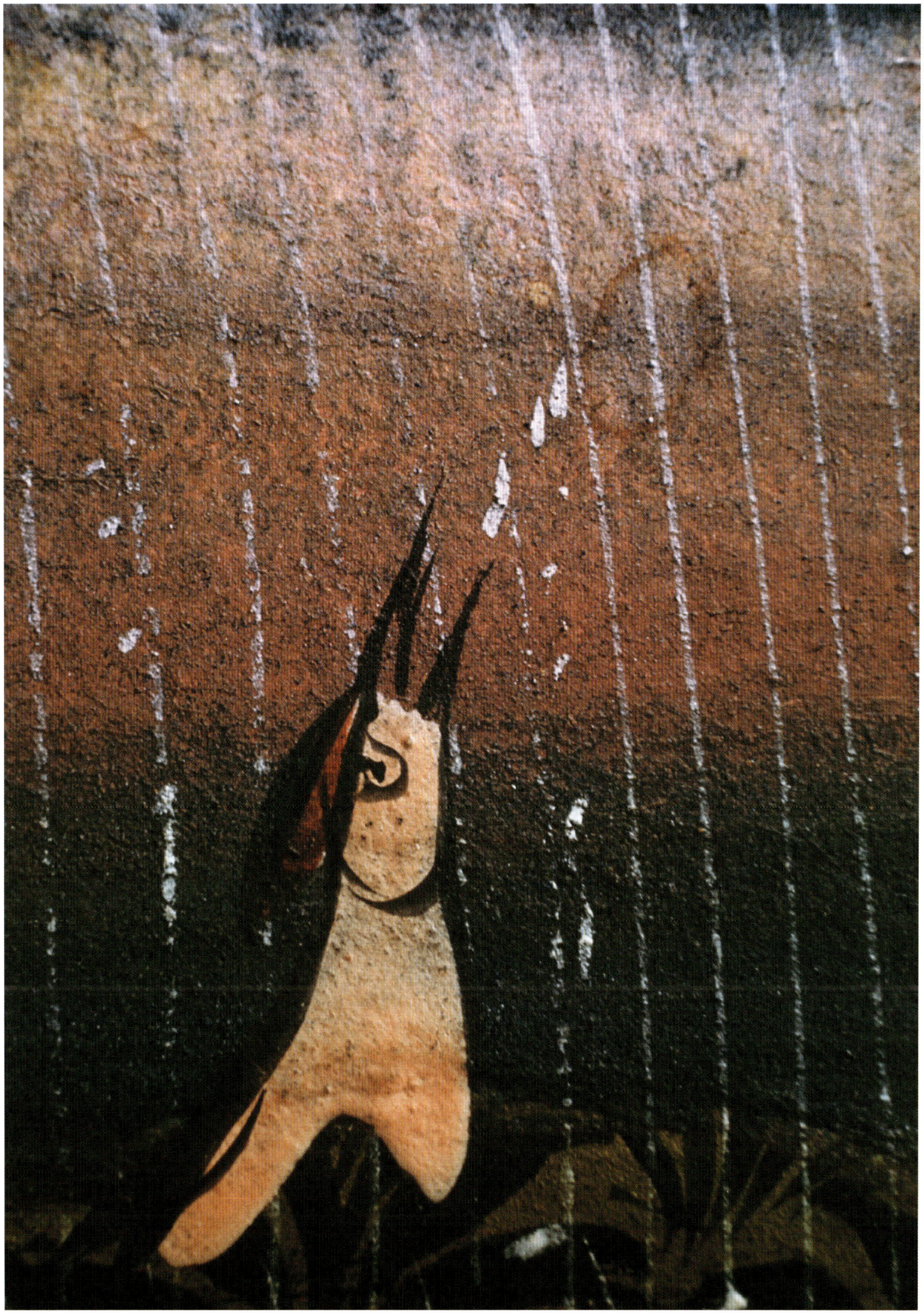

10 I Brian Brake. *The chatak bird* (detail from a miniature)*, India.* From the series: Monsoon, 1960. *Brian Brake – Monsoon.* Auckland: David Bateman, 2007. 35mm transparency. Collection Museum of New Zealand Te Papa Tongarewa. Gift of Wai-man Lau, 2001.

11

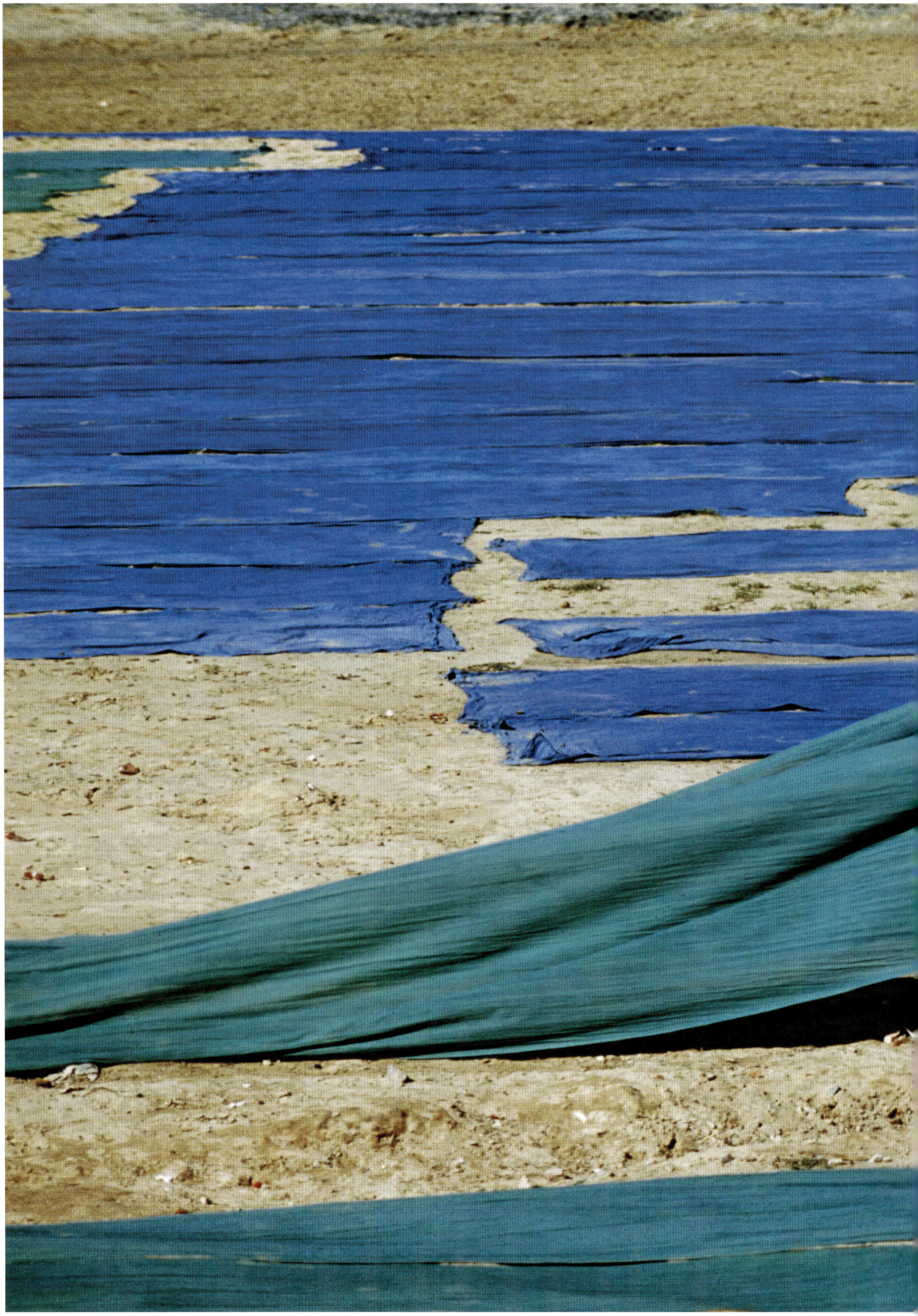

11 | Brian Brake. *Gathering dyed cloth on the banks of the Sabarmati River, Ahmedabad, India*, 1958. *Brian Brake: 40 Photographs.* Lower Hutt: Dowse Art Gallery, 1976. 35mm transparency. Collection Museum of New Zealand Te Papa Tongarewa. Gift of Wai-man Lau, 2001.

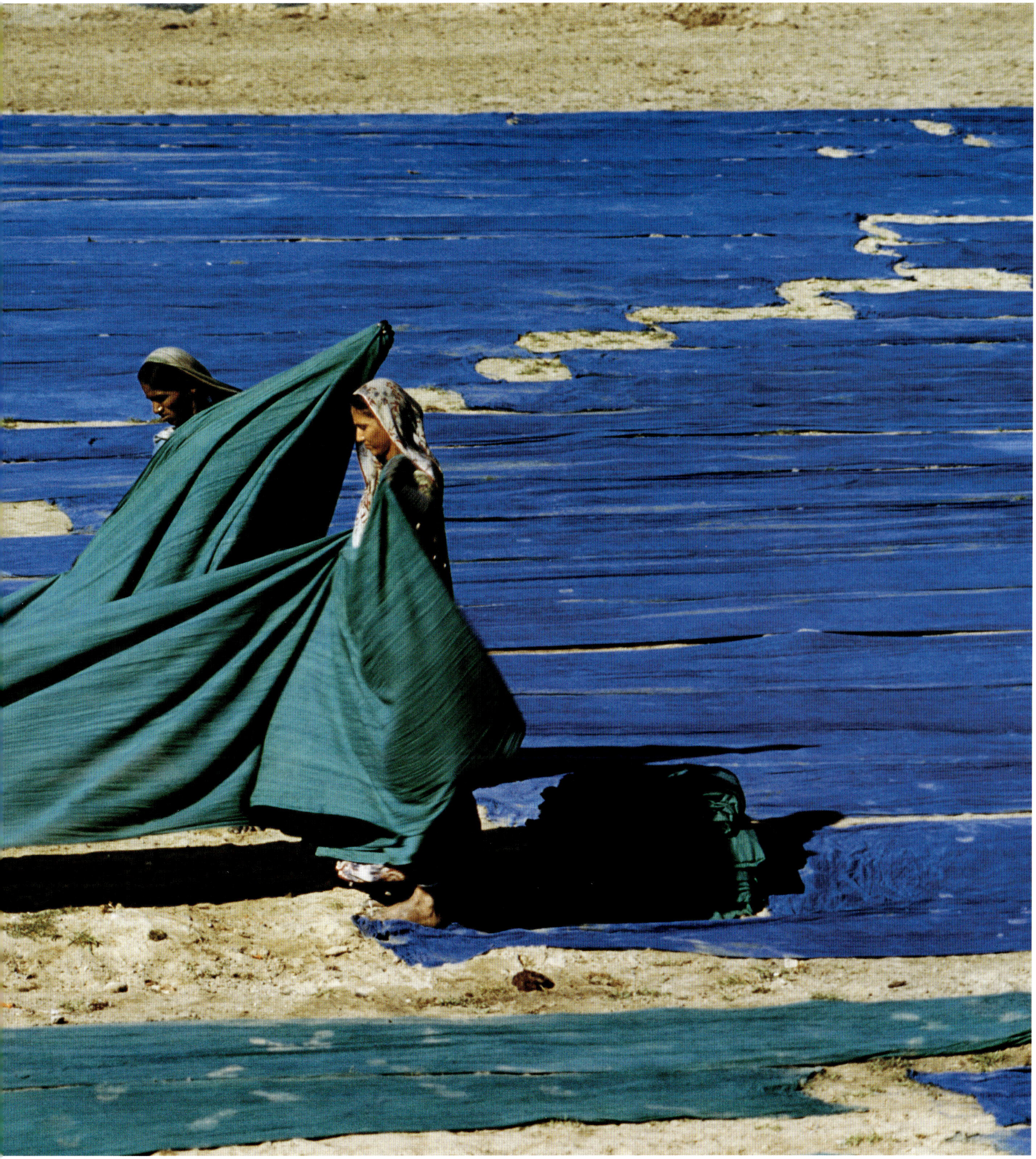

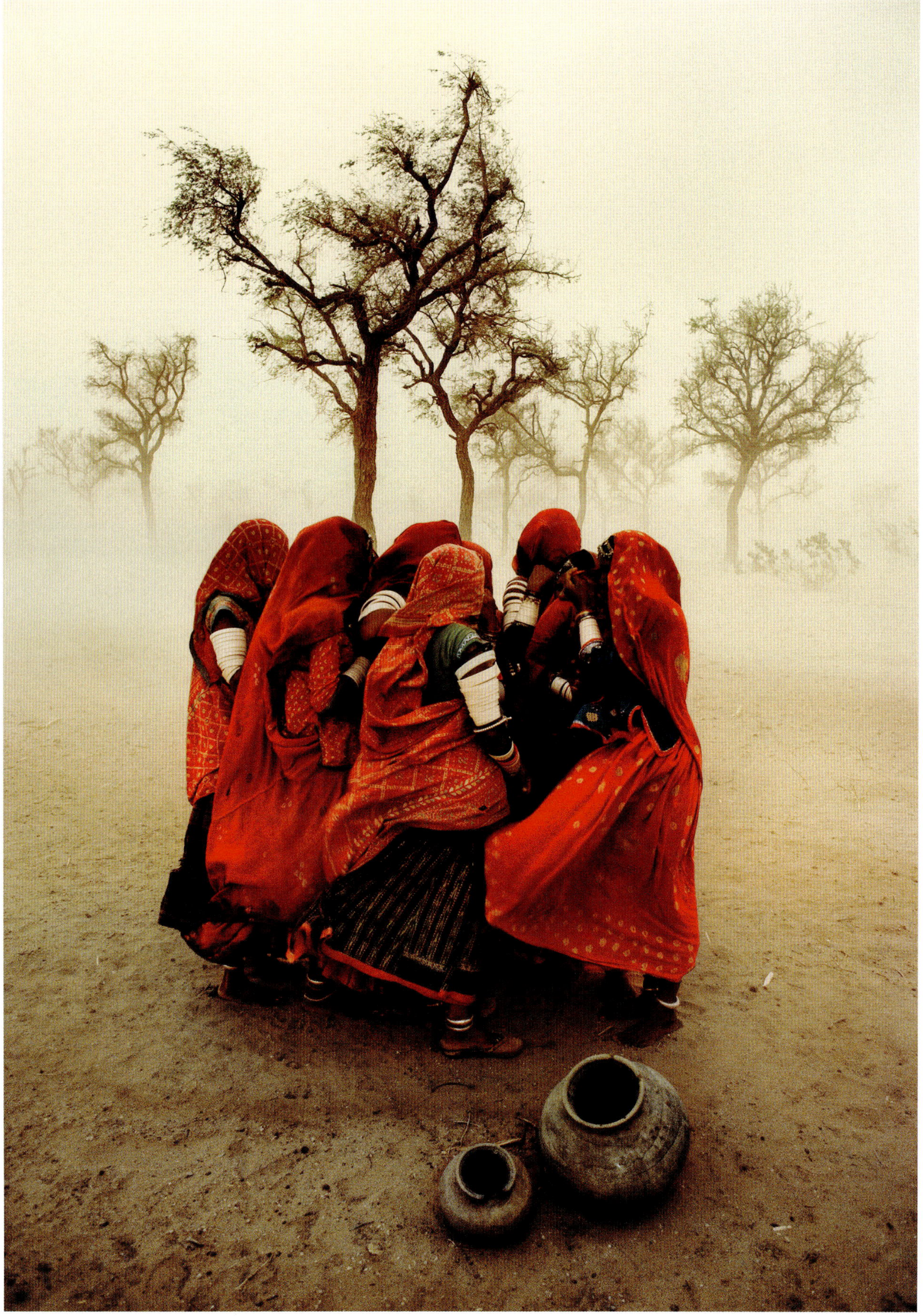

12 | Steve McCurry. *Dust storm, Rajasthan, India,* 1983. *Monsoon*. New York: Thames & Hudson Ltd., 1988. © Steve McCurry.

13

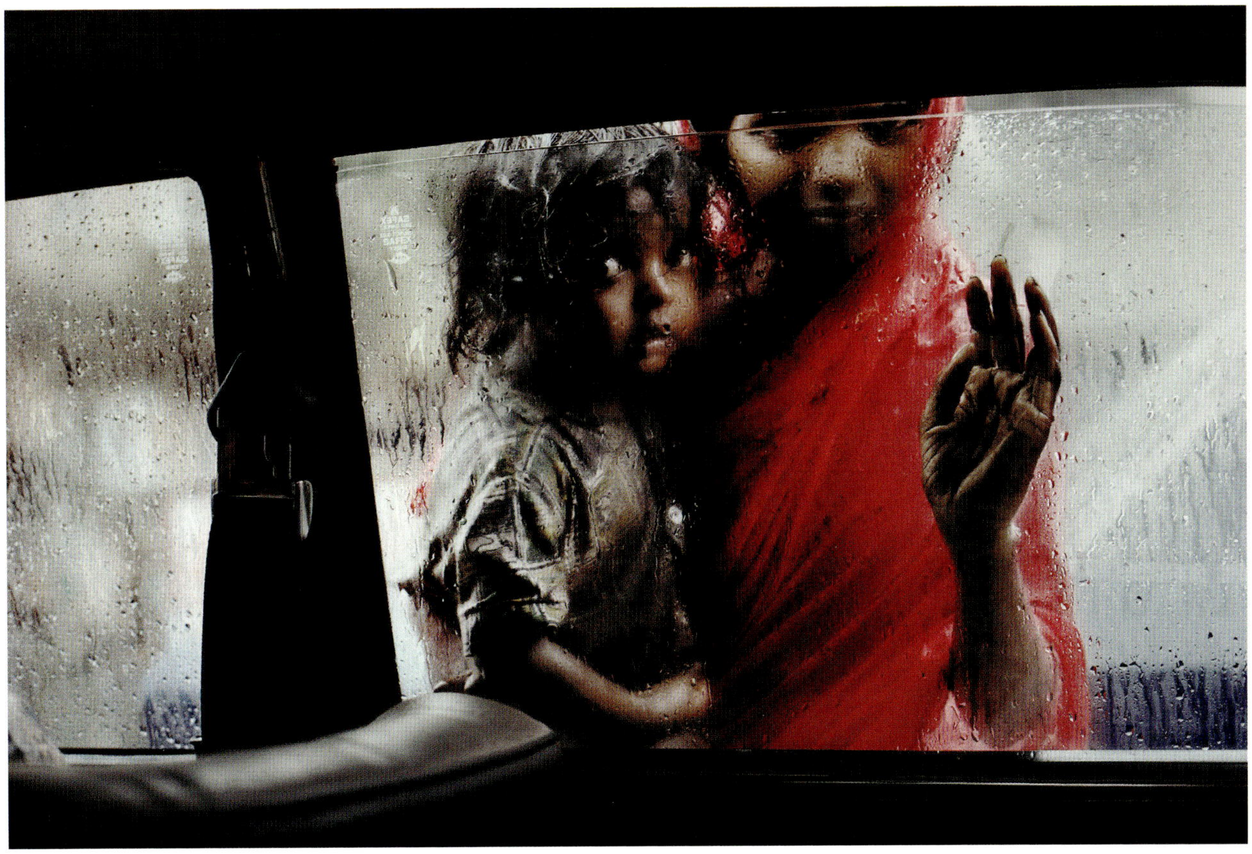

14

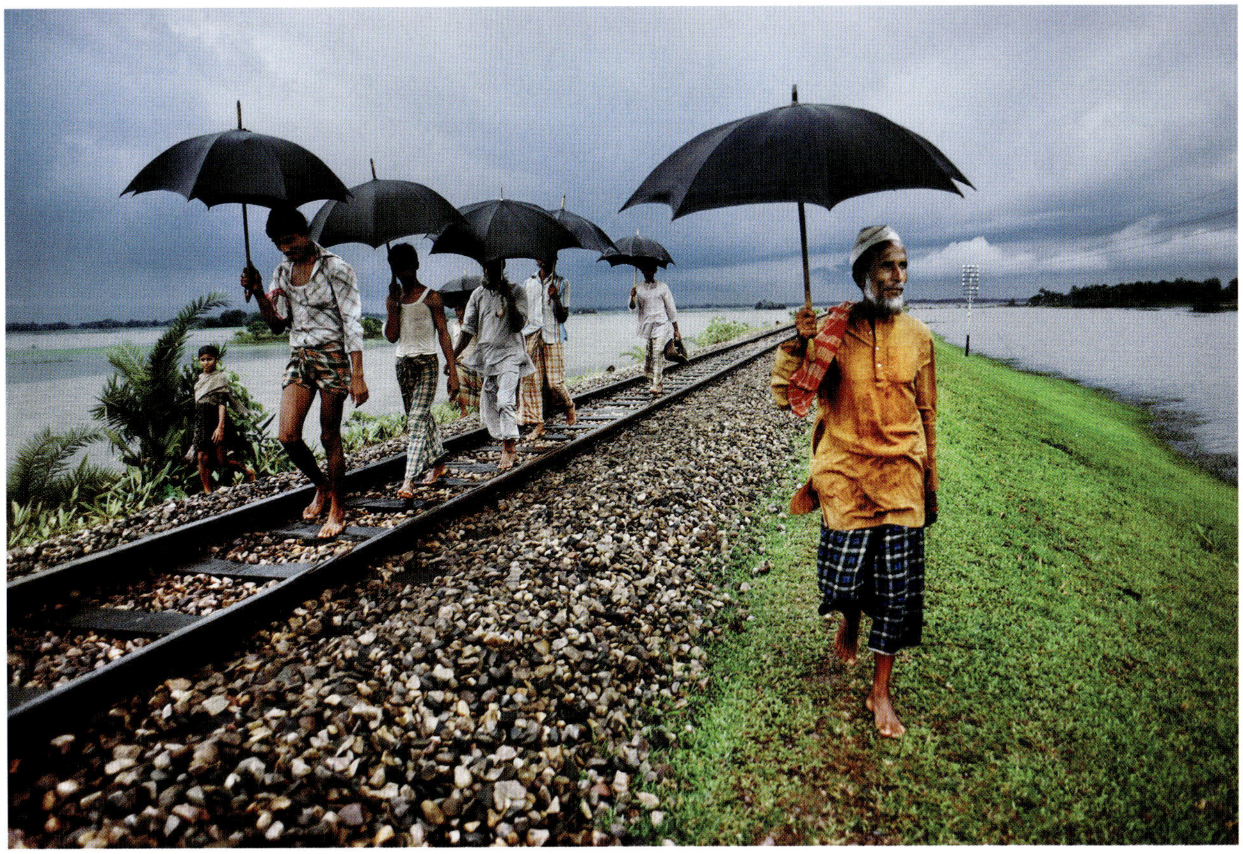

13 | Steve McCurry. *Mother and child at car window, Mumbai, India,* 1993. "Bombay: India's Capital of Hope". *National Geographic,* vol. 188, no. 3, March 1995. © Steve McCurry.

14 | Steve McCurry. *Railway track, Bangladesh,* 1983. McCurry, Steve and Paul Theroux. "The Imperial Way: By Rail Across the Indian Subcontinent". *National Geographic,* vol. 165, no. 6, June 1984. © Steve McCurry.

15

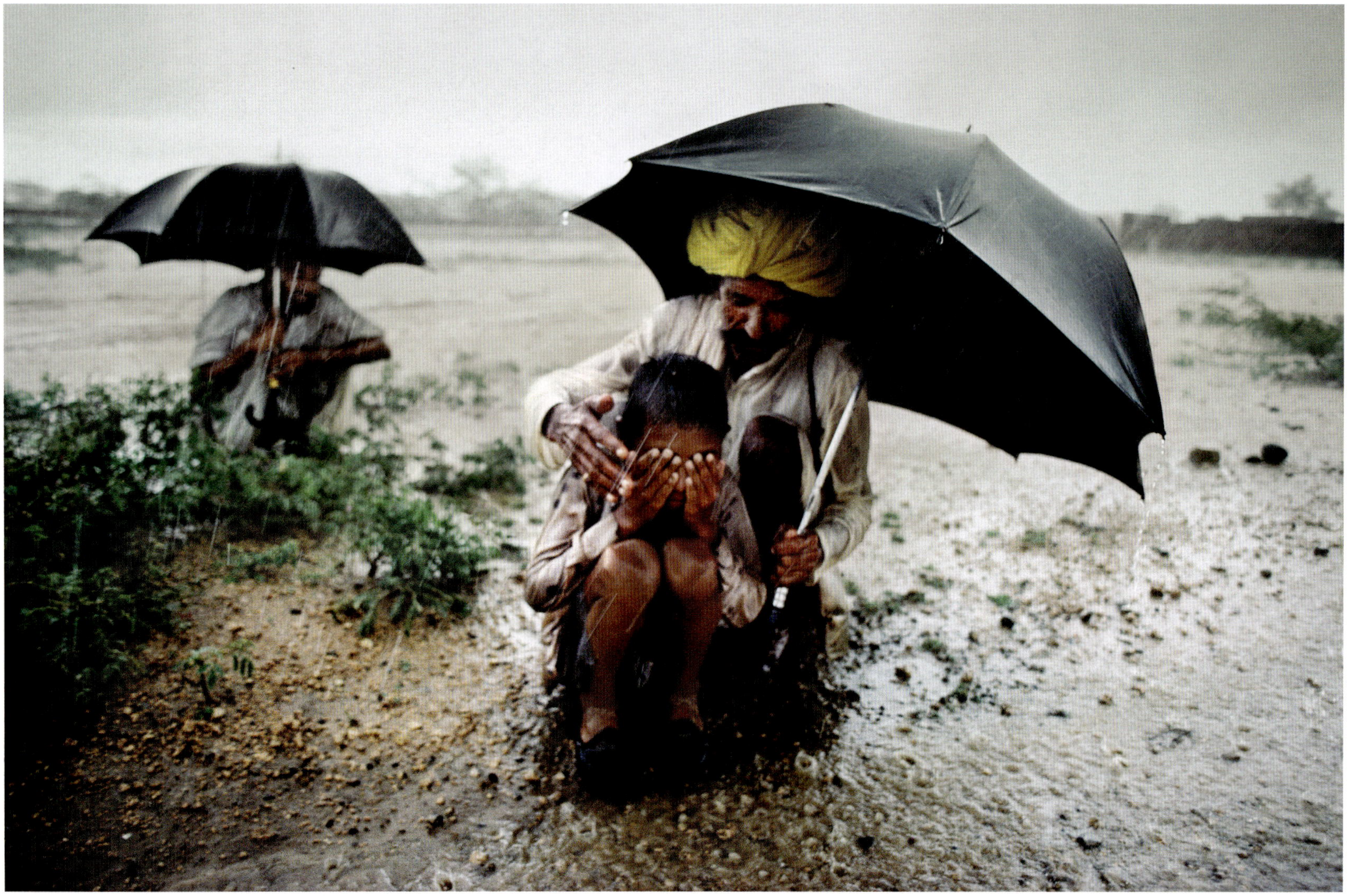

15 I Steve McCurry. *A father and son, Rajasthan, India,* 1984.
Monsoon. New York: Thames & Hudson Ltd., 1988.
© Steve McCurry.

16

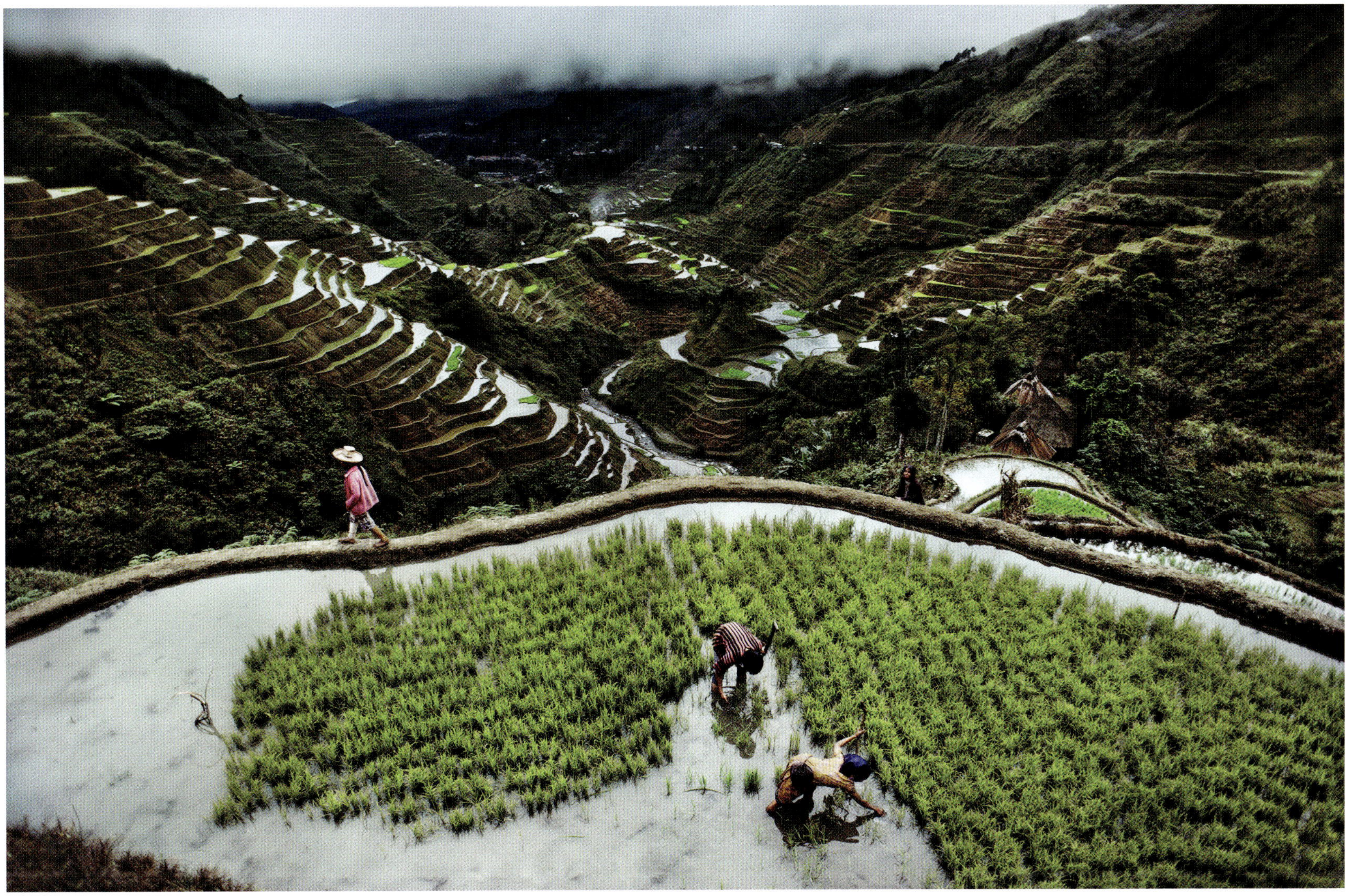

16 | Steve McCurry. *Rice paddy fields, Banaue, Philippines,* 1985. "The Philippines: A Time of Hope and Danger". *National Geographic,* vol. 170, no. 1, July 1986. © Steve McCurry.

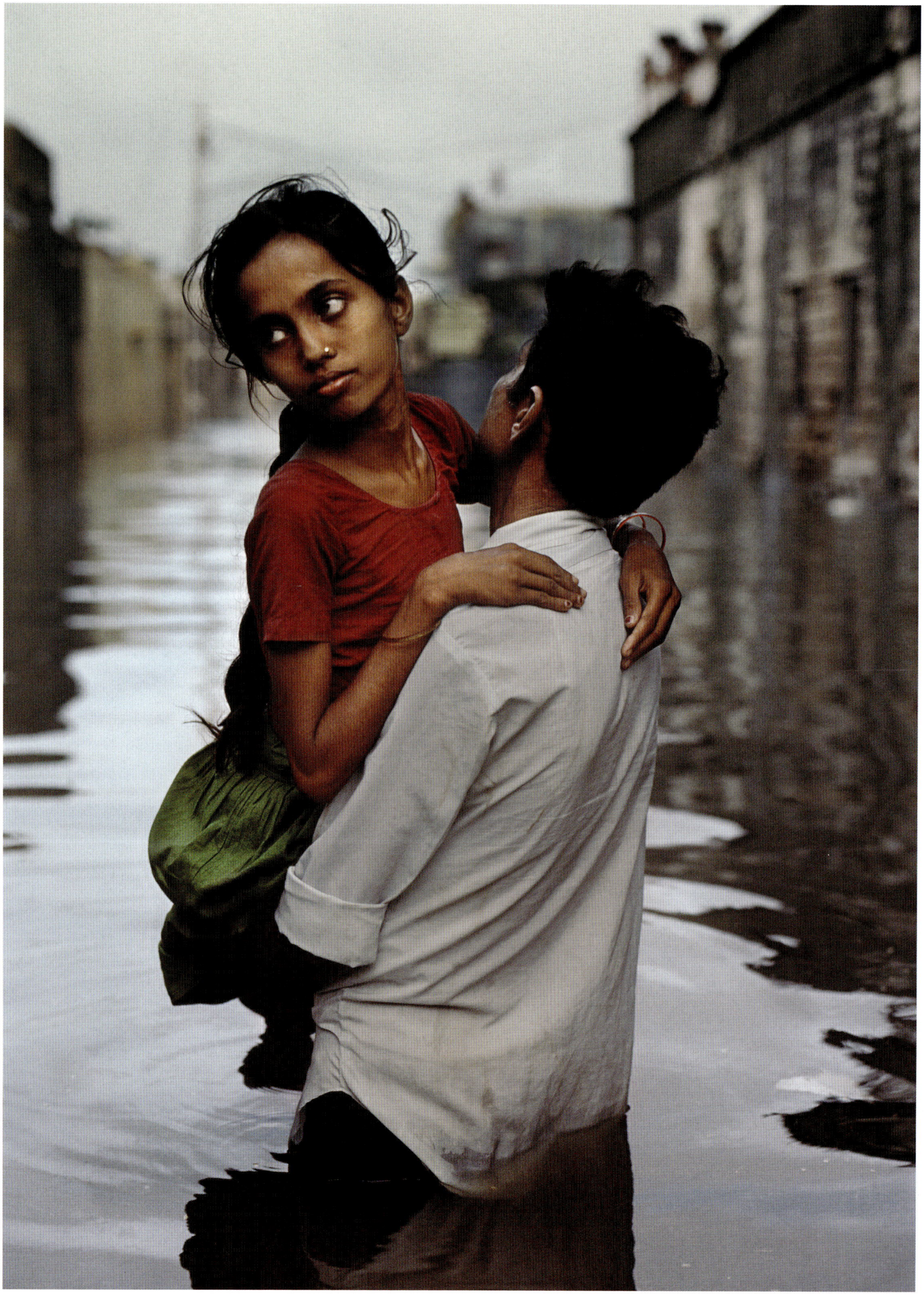

18

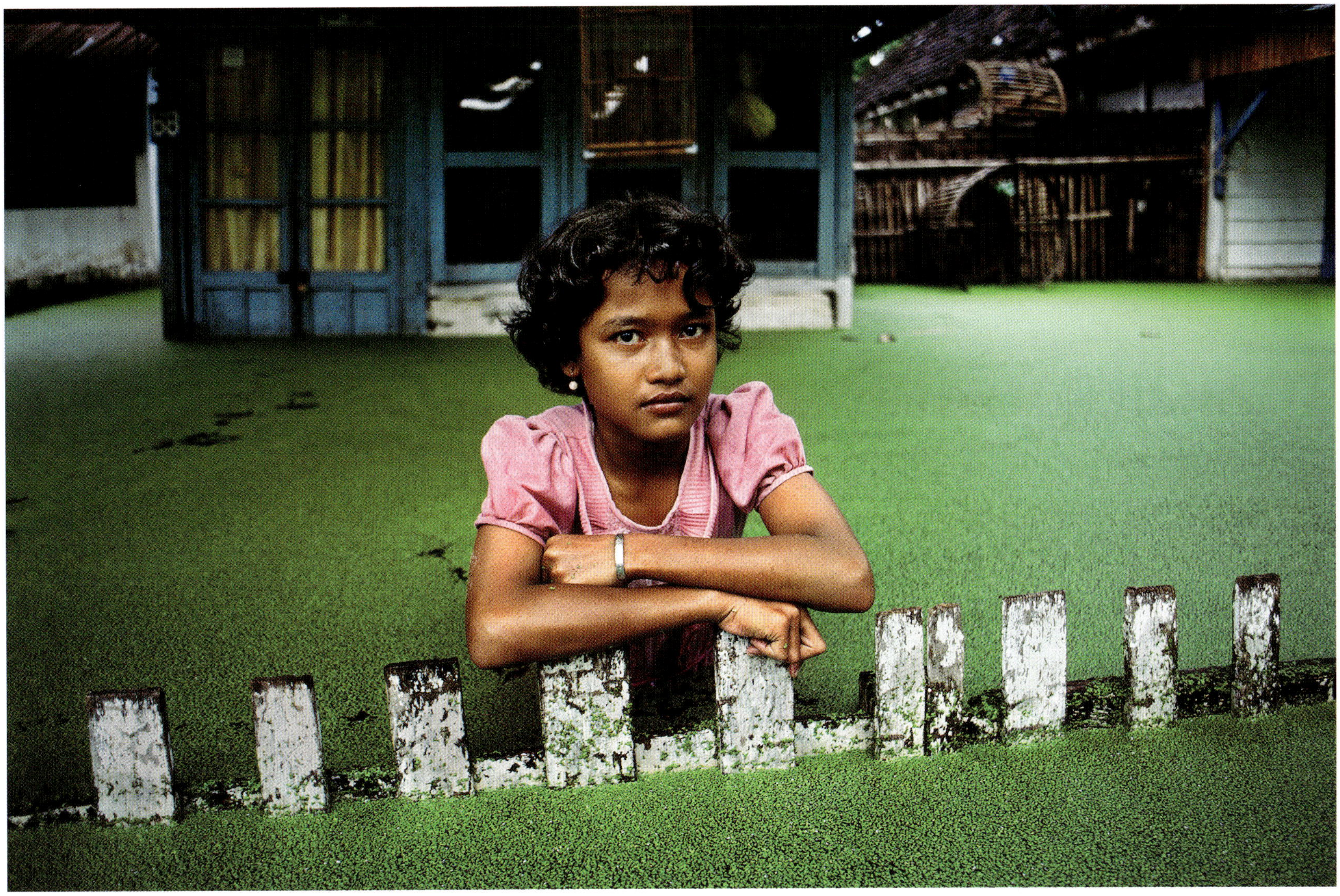

17 I Steve McCurry. *A flooded street, Porbandar, India,* 1983. *Monsoon.* New York: Thames & Hudson Ltd., 1988. © Steve McCurry.

18 I Steve McCurry. *Duckweed carpets the water in a girl's front yard at Bojonegoro, Java, Indonesia,* 1983. *Monsoon*. New York: Thames & Hudson Ltd, 1988. © Steve McCurry.

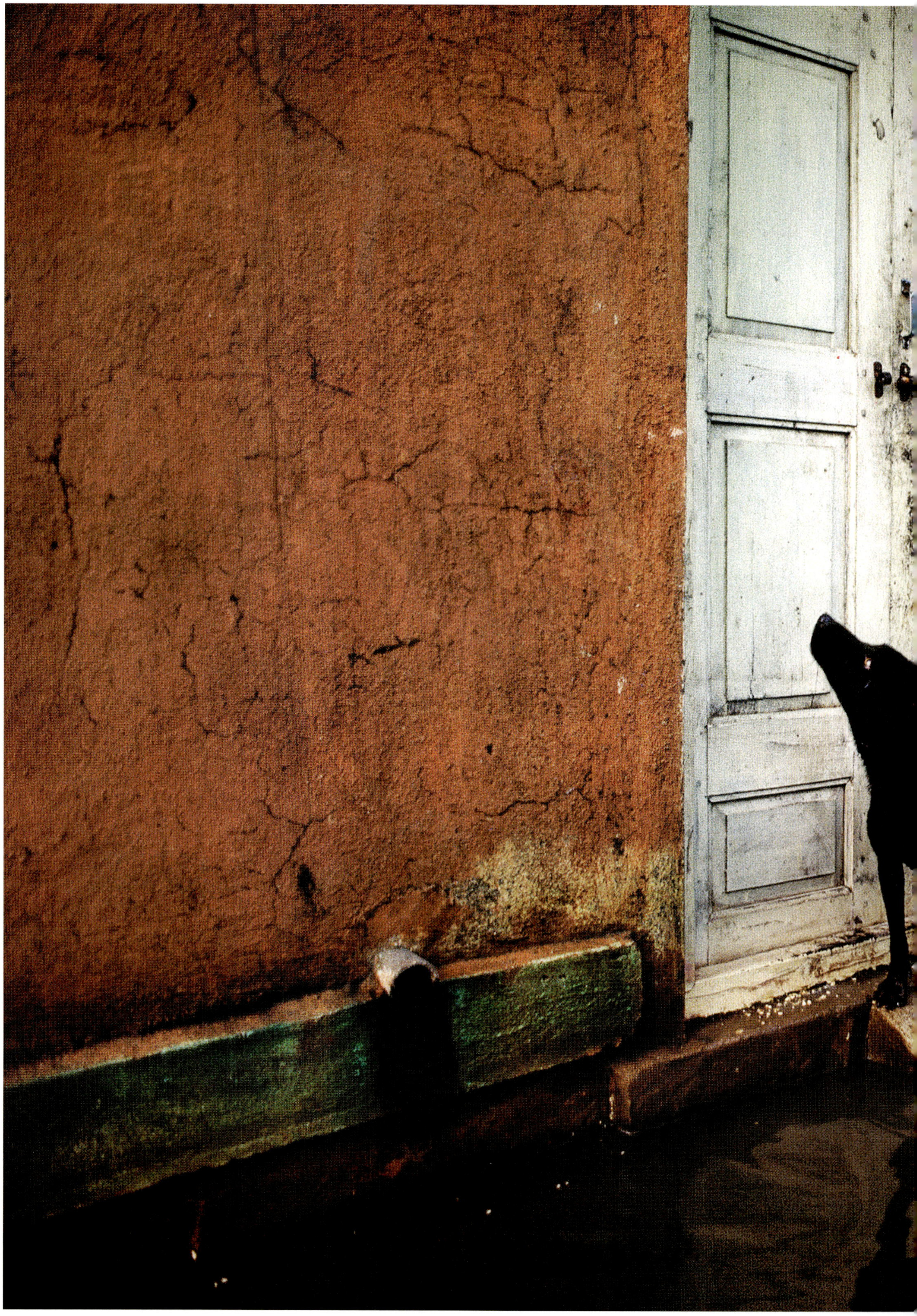

19 | Steve McCurry.
A dog caught in a monsoon, Porbandar, India, 1983.
Monsoon. New York: Thames & Hudson Ltd., 1988.
© Steve McCurry.

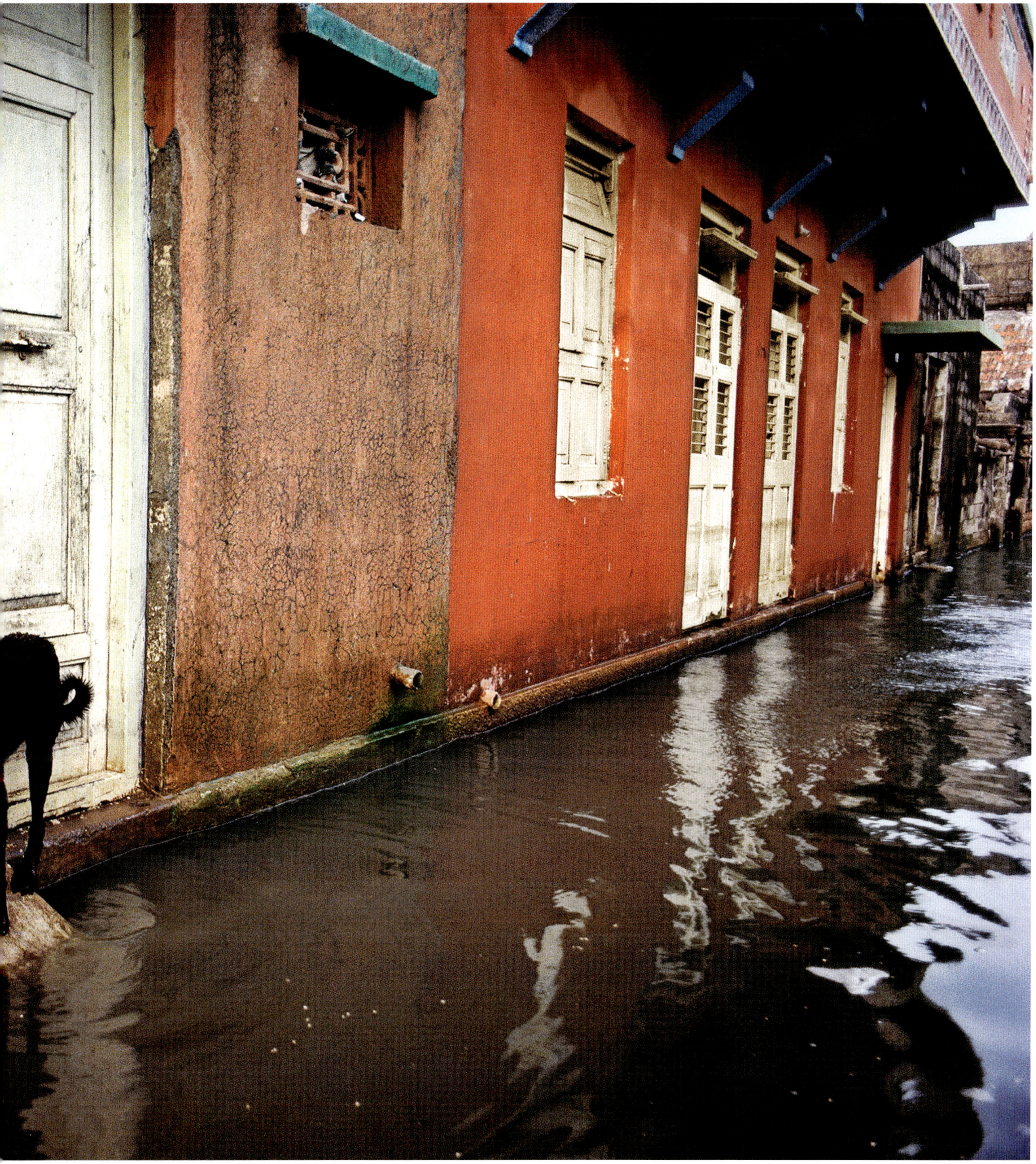

MAKING REPUTATIONS

Steve McCurry launched his career as a freelance photographer with an audacious expedition to Afghanistan in 1979. In April 1978 the communist People's Democratic Party of Afghanistan (PDPA) seized power, unleashing resistance by Mujahideen guerrillas, a group of Muslim Afghans who fought against the newly founded pro-Soviet government. In support of PDPA, the Russians invaded Afghanistan in December 1979 and only withdrew their troops in February 1989. Almost 10 million people had fled to Pakistan and Iran.

McCurry's black and white photograph of Mujahideen watching a military convoy was his first published image from this catastrophic war (*New York Times*, September 1979). More followed over the next twenty-five years, including the refugee "Afghan Girl" (1984). Many were collected in *In the Shadow of Mountains* (2007). But his first published Afghanistan photograph was when McCurry's international career as a photojournalist began.

Brian Brake's work with French photographer Marc Riboud in China in 1957 earned him significant international exposure. His photographs of Chairman Mao meeting the Soviet chief of state Marshal Voroshilov at May Day celebrations in Beijing were published in *New York Times* Magazine and twice in *Paris Match*. His photographs of traditional Chinese medicine in Beijing were published in *MD* and the French magazine *Science et Avenir*.

This engagement with the lives of ordinary people also characterized Brake's China portfolio of 1959, when he was the only independent Western photographer to cover the tenth anniversary celebrations of the People's Republic of China. His pictures were widely published, in *Paris Match, L'Europeo* (Italy), *Life, Life International, Quick and Bunte Illustrierte* (Germany).

20

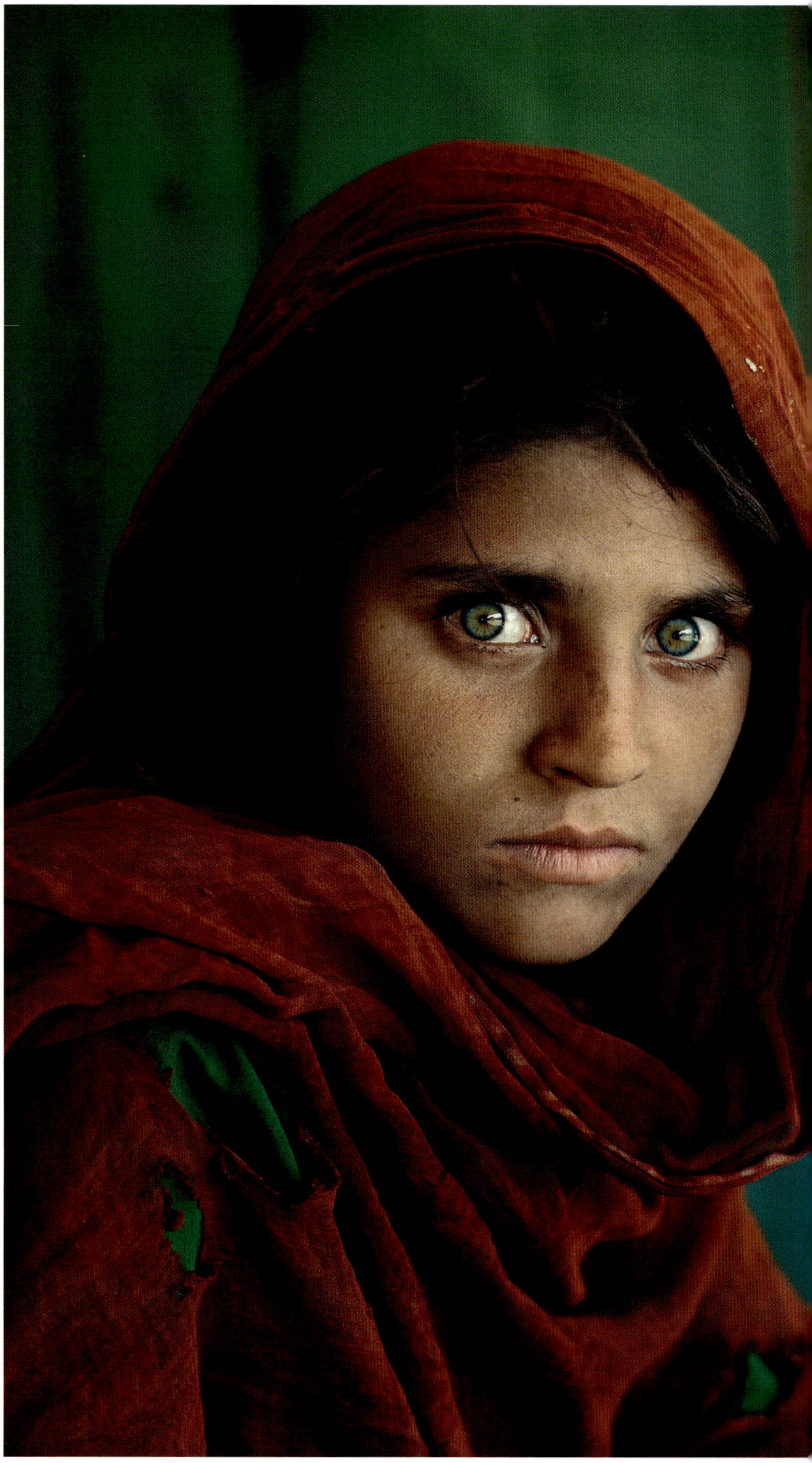

21

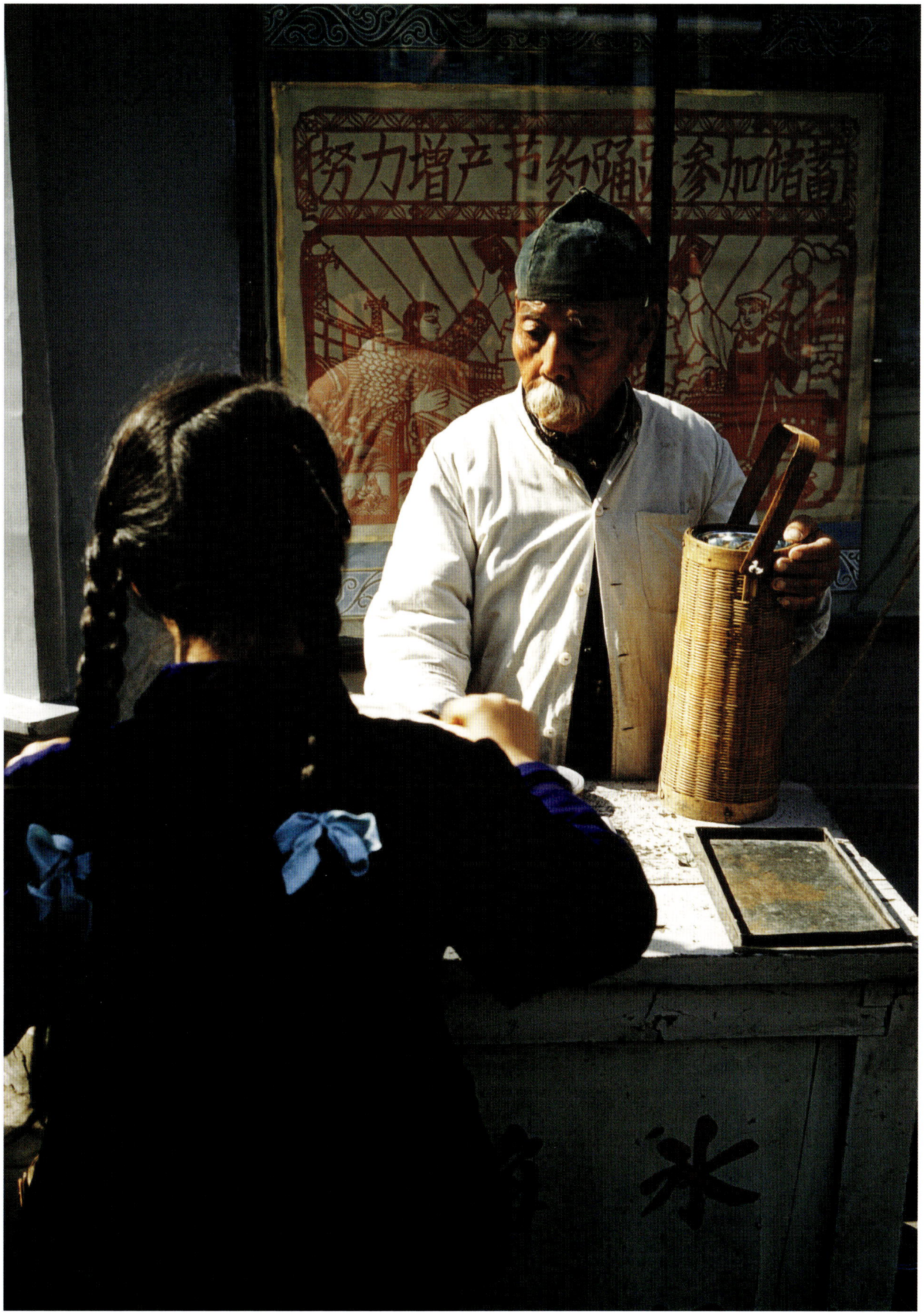

20 | Steve McCurry. *Sharbat Gula, "Afghan Girl", at Nasir Bagh refugee camp near Peshawar, Pakistan,* 1984. "Along Afghanistan's War-torn Frontier". *National Geographic,* vol. 167, no. 6, June 1985. © Steve McCurry.

21 | Brian Brake. *Old man selling popsicle to a girl, Beijing, China,* 1959. Variant in *Brian Brake: China, the 1950s.* Wellington: Museum of New Zealand Te Papa Tongarewa, 1995. 35mm transparency. Collection Museum of New Zealand Te Papa Tongarewa. Gift of Wai-man Lau, 2010.

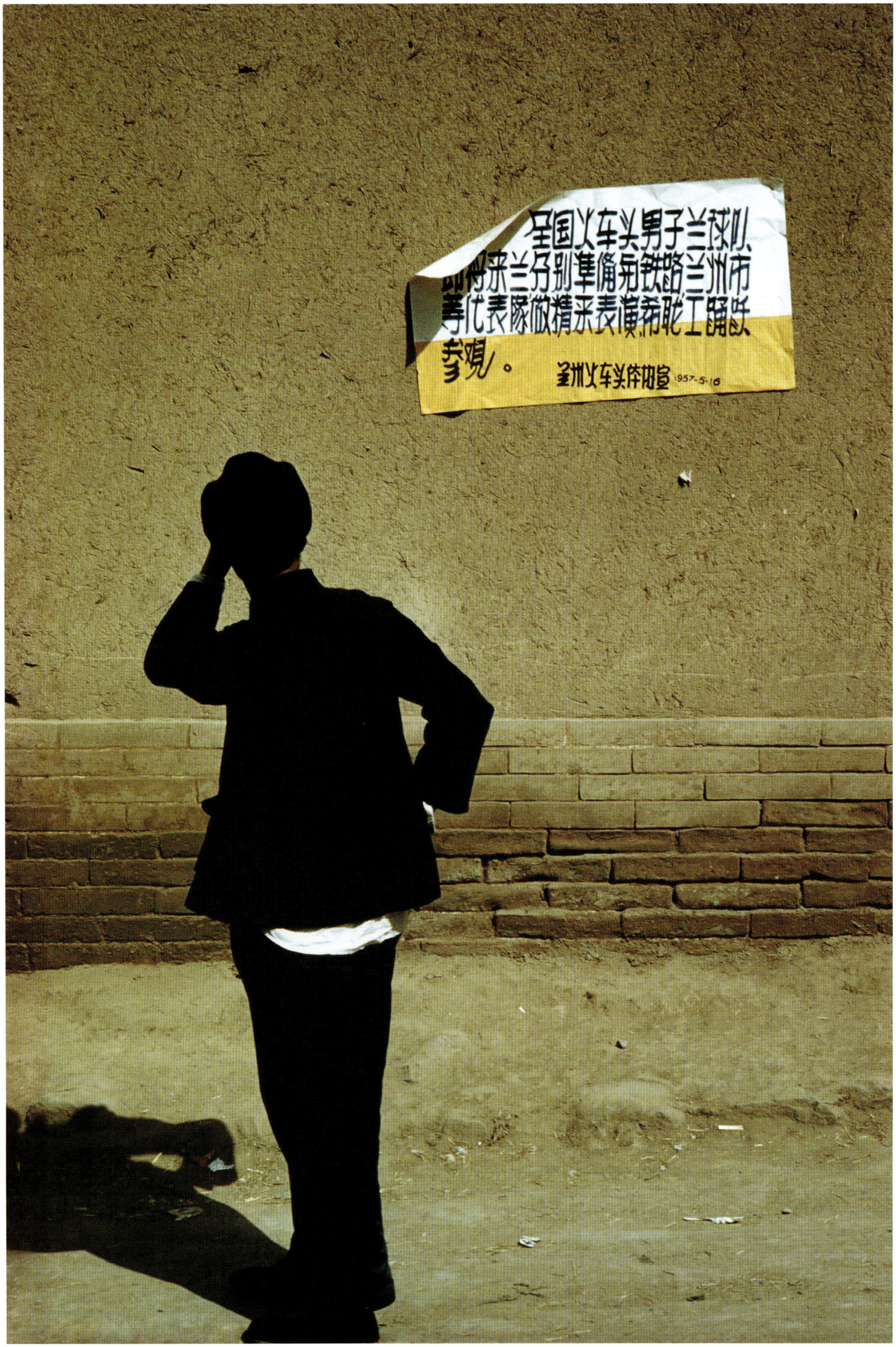
全国火车头男子兰球队、
参观。
兰州火车头体协宣 1957-5-16

23

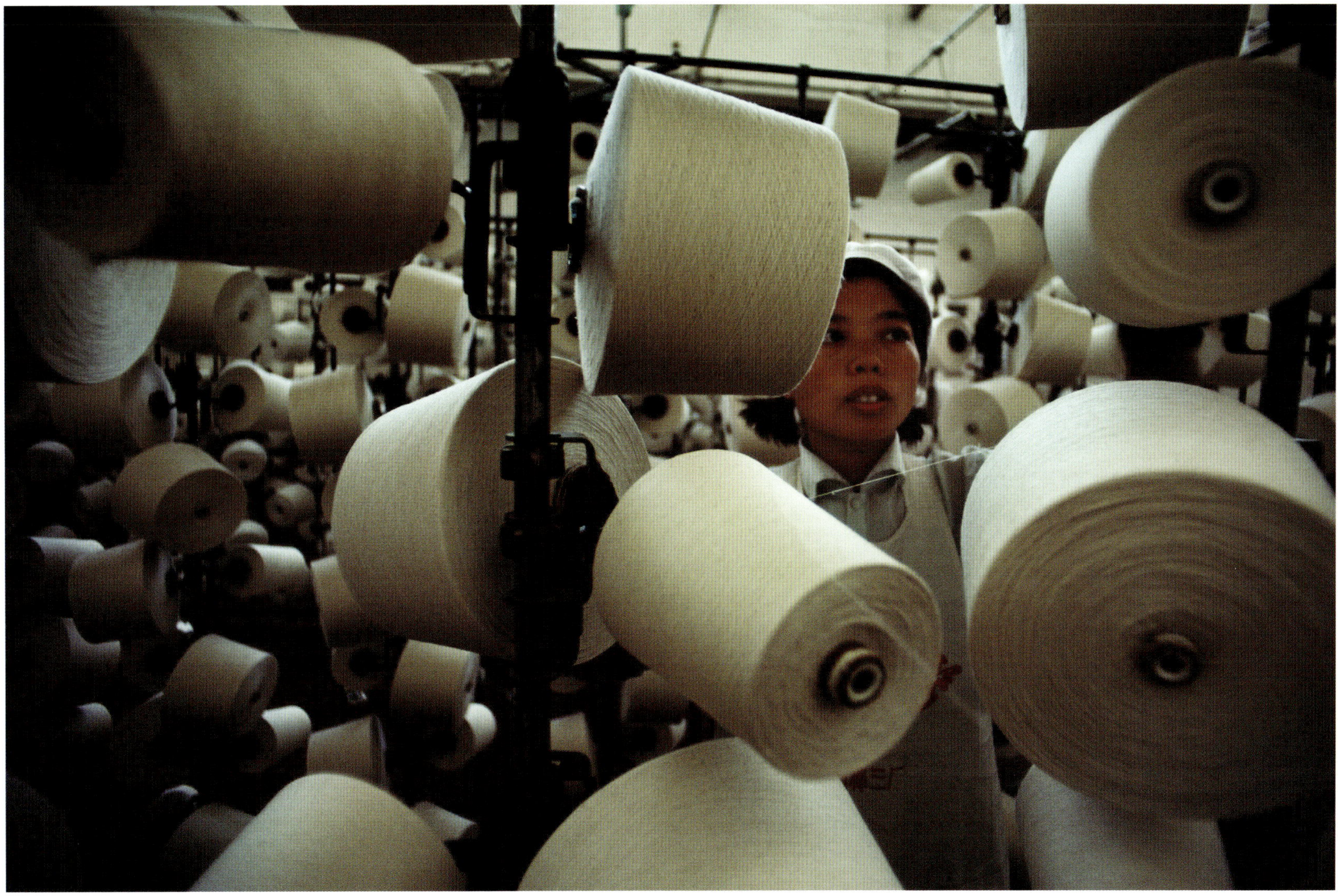

22 | Brian Brake. *Poster for a basketball match, Lanzhou, China,* 1957. *Brian Brake: 40 Photographs.* Lower Hutt: Dowse Art Gallery, 1976. 35mm transparency. Collection Museum of New Zealand Te Papa Tongarewa. Gift of Wai-man Lau, 2001.

23 | Brian Brake. *Woman tending bobbins in a synthetic-fiber factory, Beijing, China*, 1957. *Brian Brake: China, the 1950s.* Wellington: Museum of New Zealand Te Papa Tongarewa, 1995. 35mm transparency. Collection Museum of New Zealand Te Papa Tongarewa. Gift of Wai-man Lau, 2001.

24

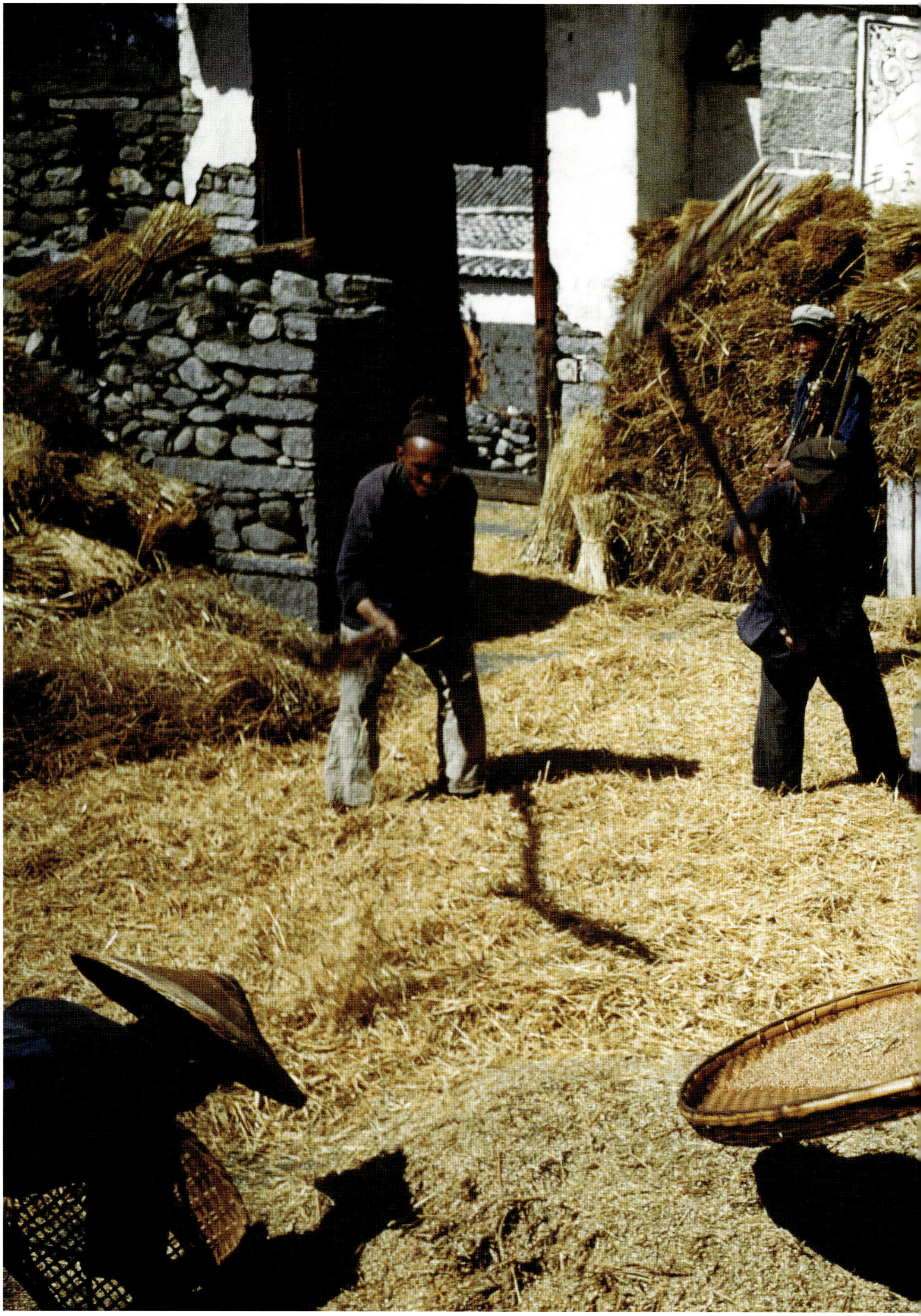

24 | Brian Brake. *Villagers threshing, Tali-Sakwan, Yunnan, China,* 1959. *Brian Brake: China, the 1950s*. Wellington: Museum of New Zealand Te Papa Tongarewa, 1995. 35mm transparency. Collection Museum of New Zealand Te Papa Tongarewa. Gift of Wai-man Lau, 2001.

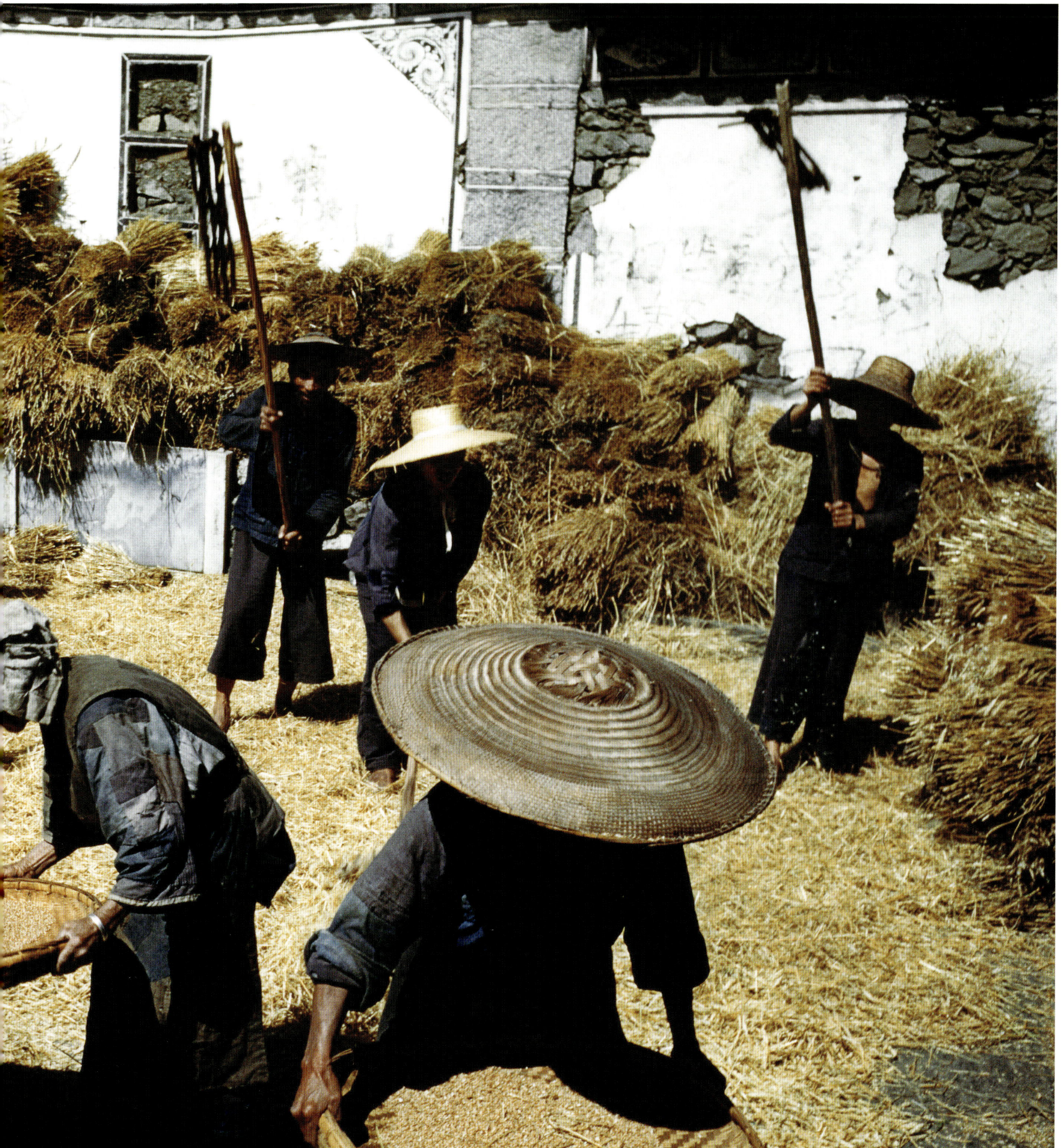

25

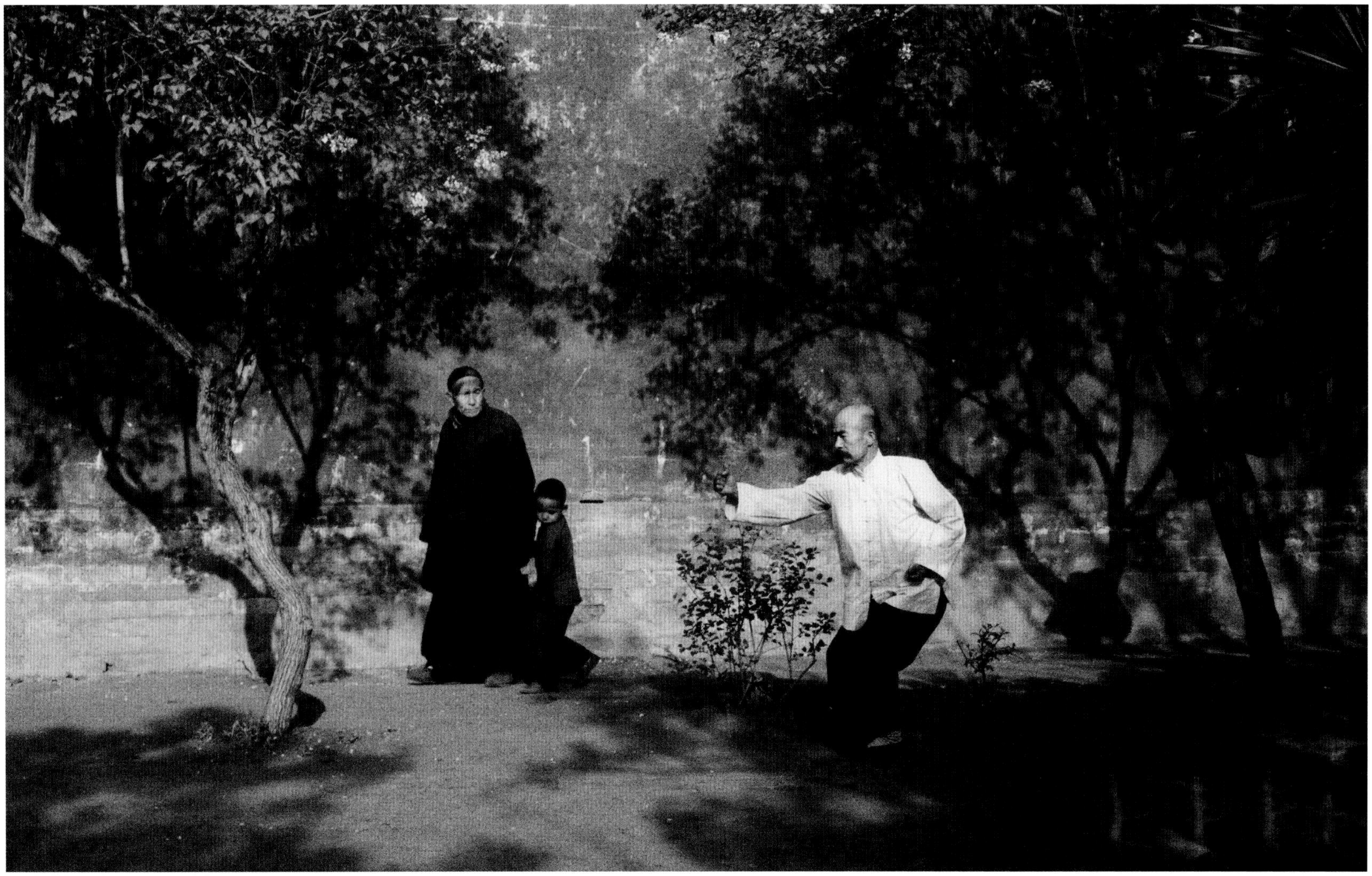

25 I Brian Brake. *Practising taijiquan by the palace wall, Beijing, China,* 1957. *Brian Brake: China, the 1950s*. Wellington: Museum of New Zealand Te Papa Tongarewa, 1995. Reproduced from a 35mm black and white negative. Collection Museum of New Zealand Te Papa Tongarewa. Gift of Wai-man Lau, 2001.

26

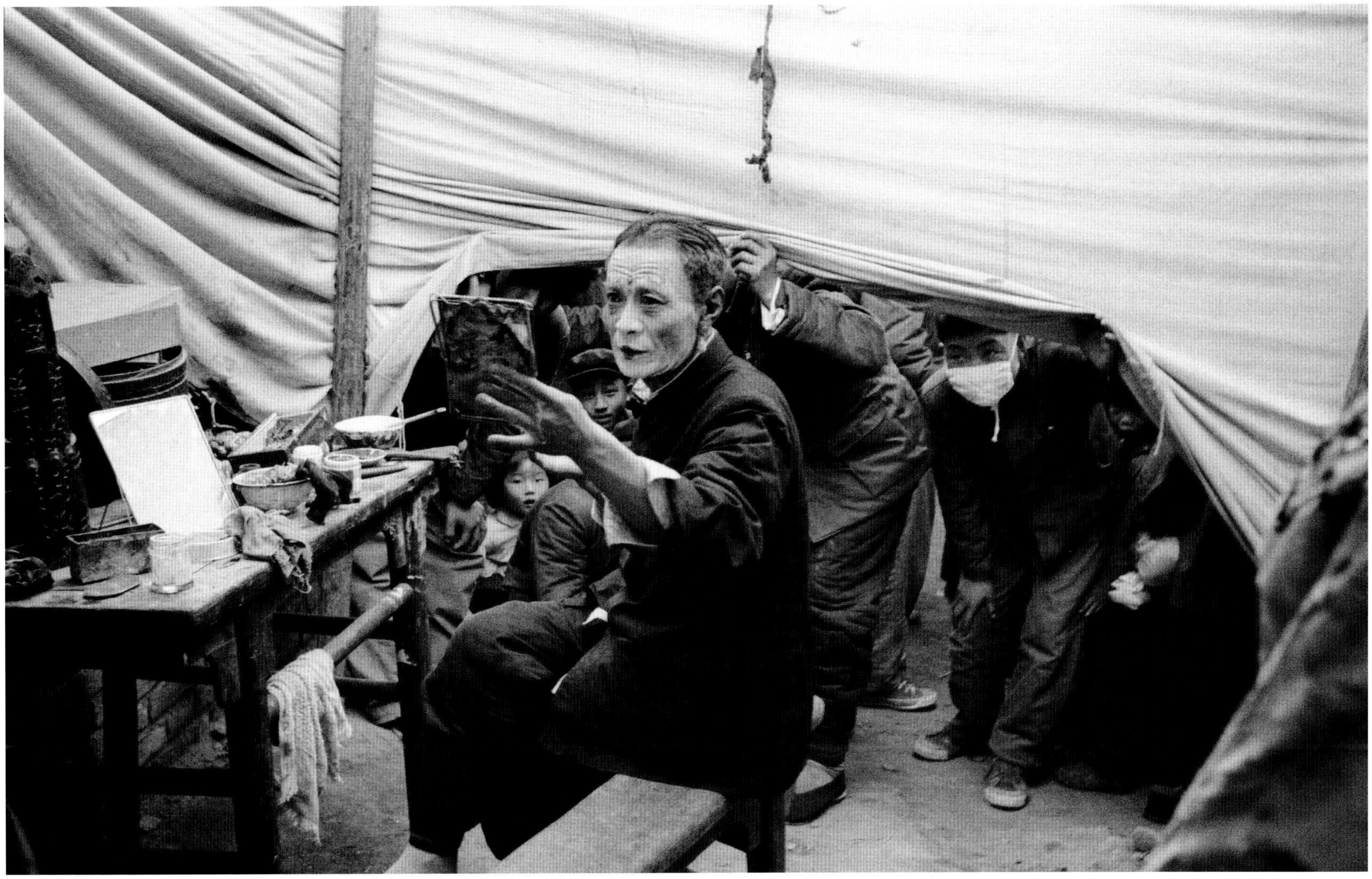

26 I Brian Brake. *Actor applying make-up, street opera troupe, Beijing, China,* 1957. *Brian Brake: China, the 1950s.* Wellington: Museum of New Zealand Te Papa Tongarewa, 1995. Reproduced from a 35mm black and white negative. Collection Museum of New Zealand Te Papa Tongarewa. Gift of Wai-man Lau, 2001.

27

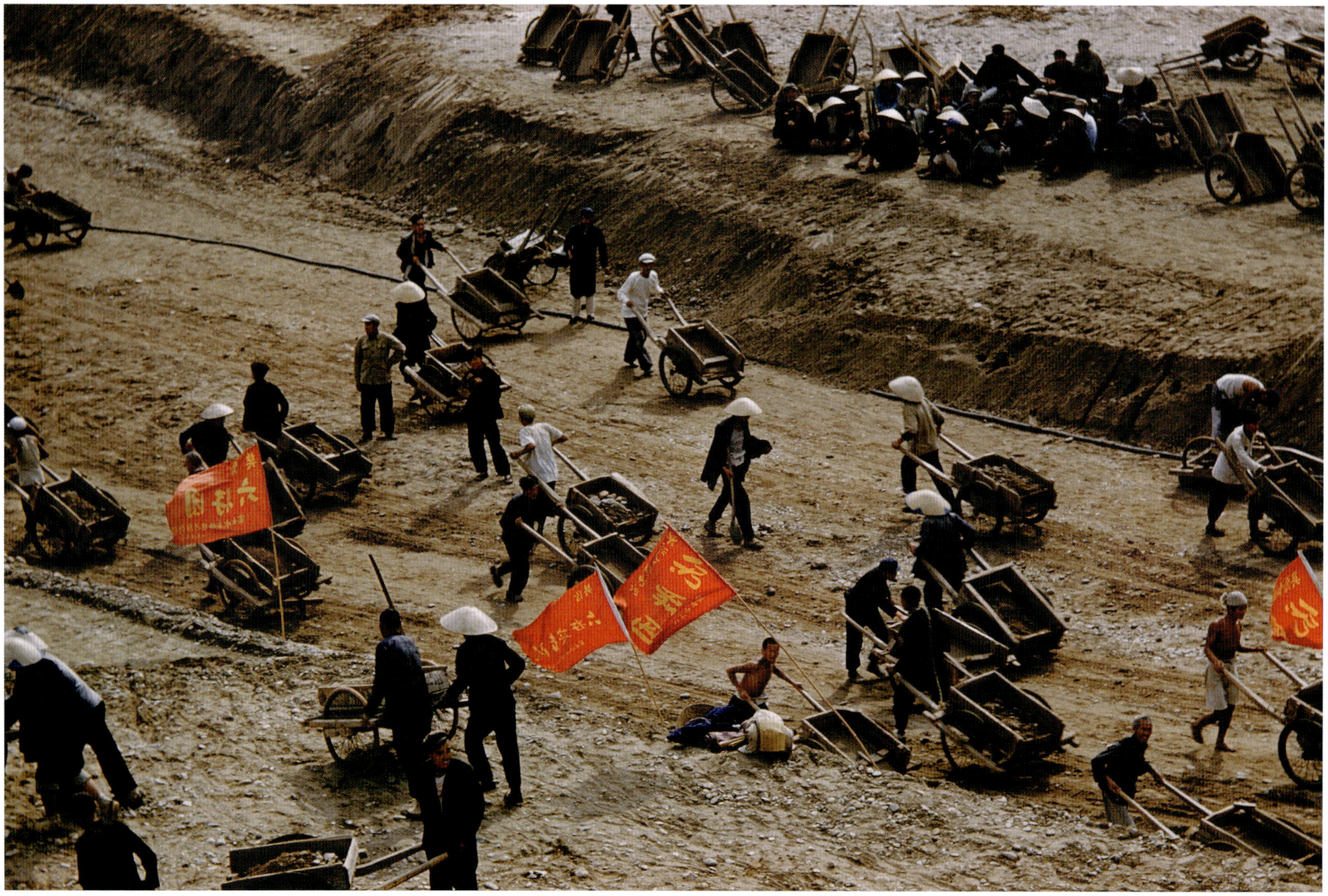

27 | Brian Brake. *Miyun reservoir construction, near Beijing, China,* 1959. Variant in *Brian Brake: China, the 1950s.* Wellington: Museum of New Zealand Te Papa Tongarewa, 1995. 35mm transparency. Collection Museum of New Zealand Te Papa Tongarewa. Gift of Wai-man Lau, 2010.

28

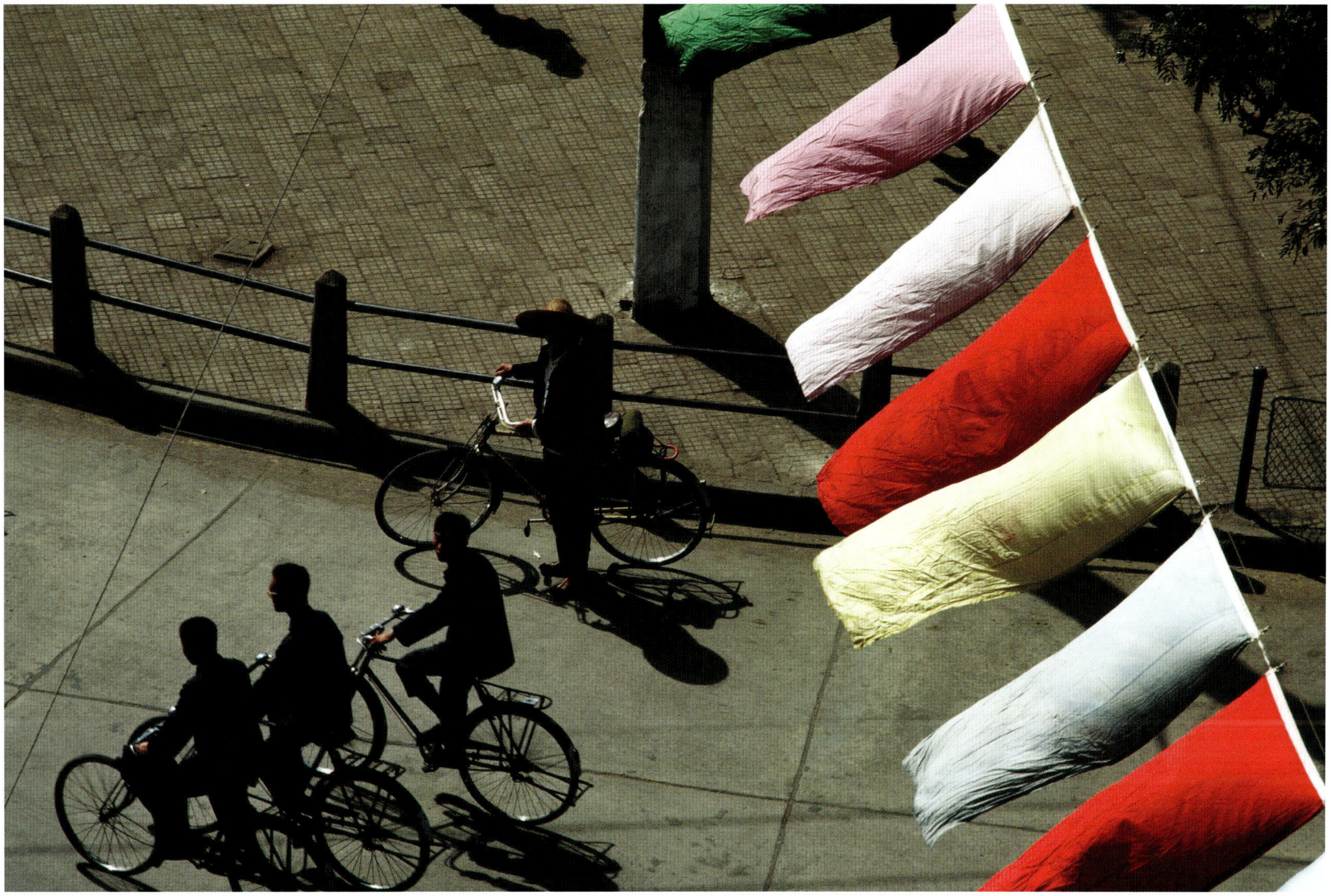

28 | Brian Brake. *Street flags, Beijing, China*. From the series: China, 1957-59. Unpublished. 35mm transparency. Collection Museum of New Zealand Te Papa Tongarewa. Gift of Wai-man Lau, 2001.

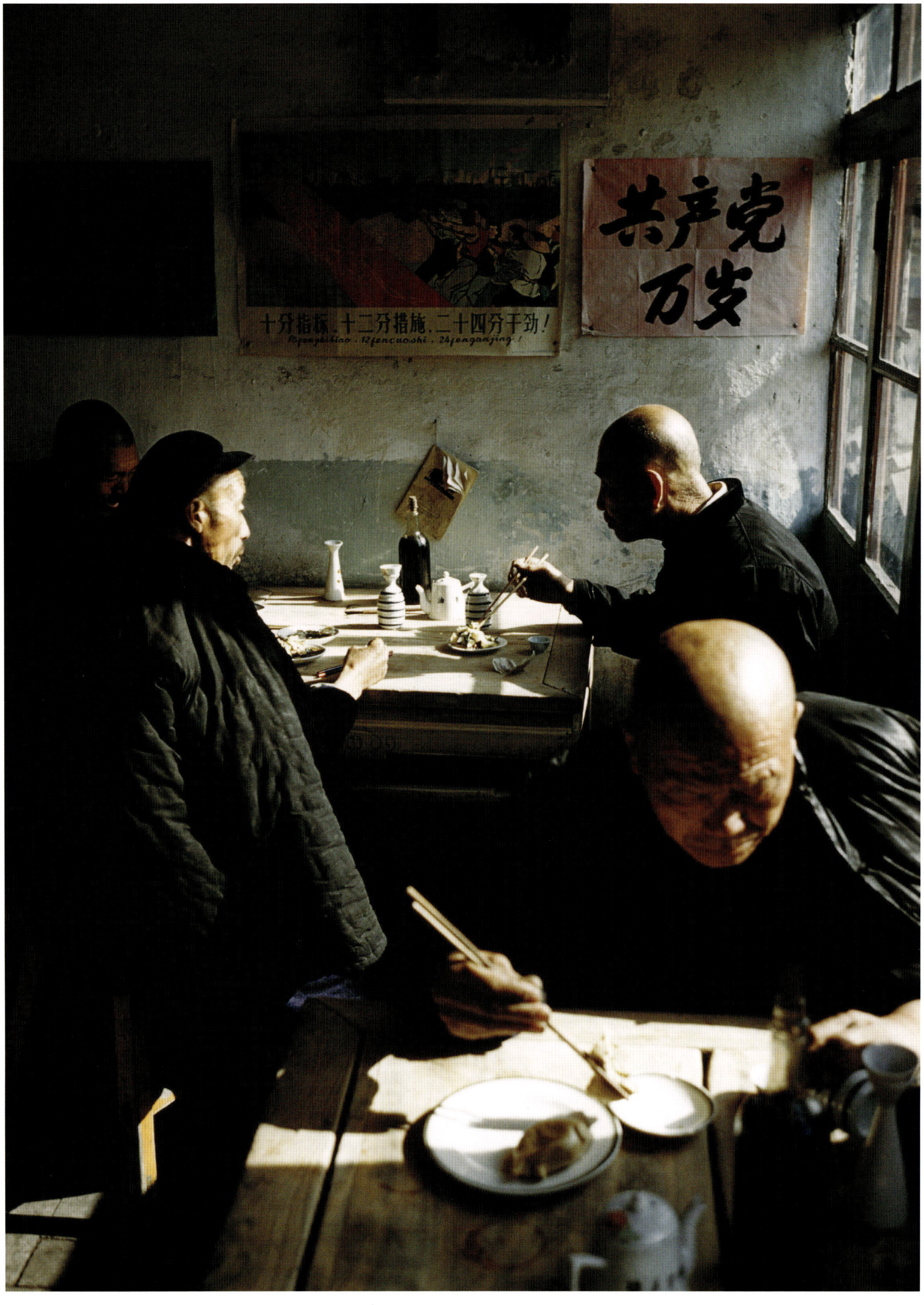
十分指标，十二分措施，二十四分干劲！
共产党
万岁

30

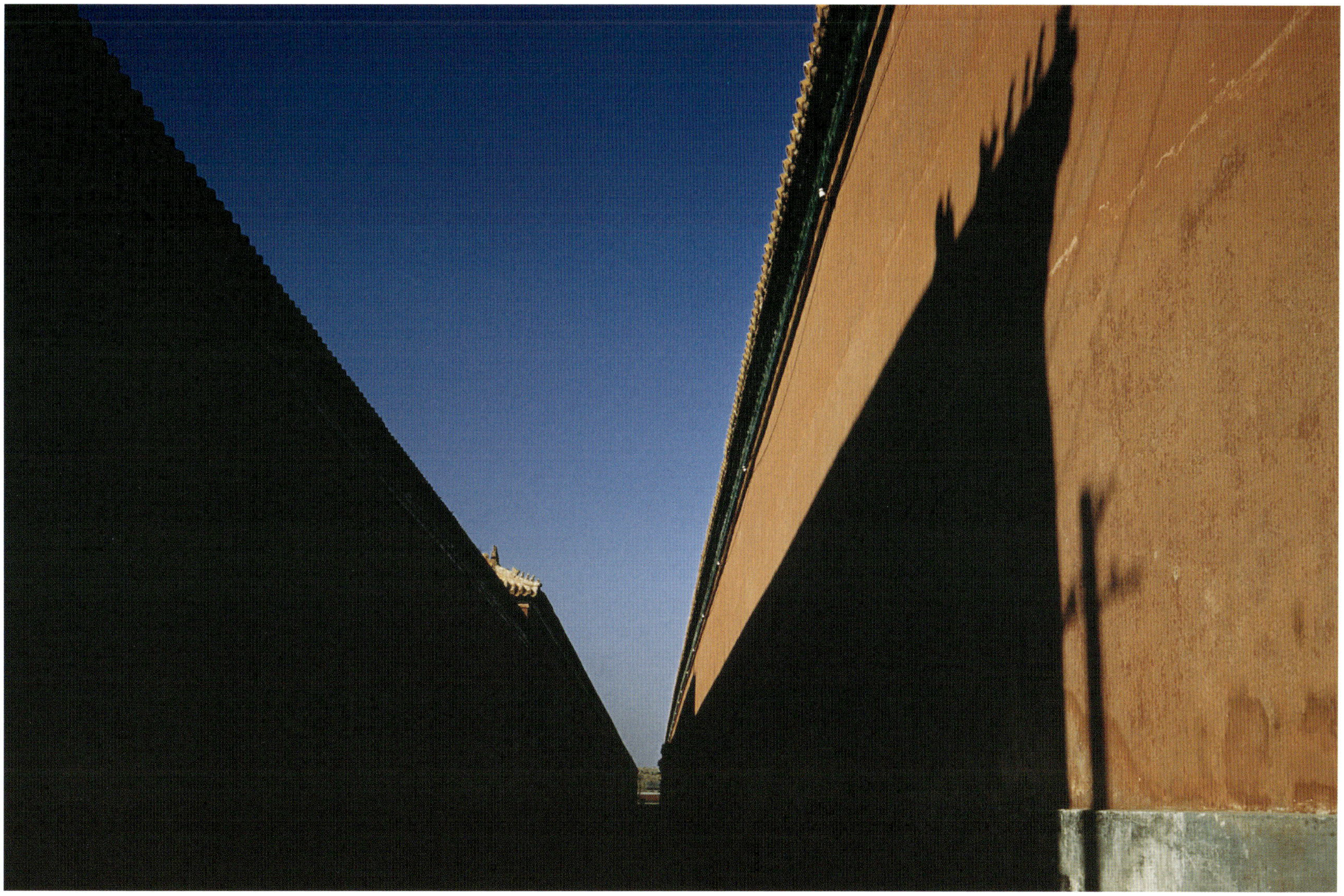

29 | Brian Brake. *Pedi-cab drivers in a restaurant in Liulichang Street, Beijing, China,* 1957. *Brian Brake: China, the 1950s.* Wellington: Museum of New Zealand Te Papa Tongarewa, 1995. 35mm transparency. Collection Museum of New Zealand Te Papa Tongarewa. Gift of Wai-man Lau, 2001.

30 | Brian Brake. *Walls of the Forbidden City, Beijing, China,* 1957. *Brian Brake: China, the 1950s*. Wellington: Museum of New Zealand Te Papa Tongarewa, 1995. 35mm transparency. Collection Museum of New Zealand Te Papa Tongarewa. Gift of Wai-man Lau, 2001.

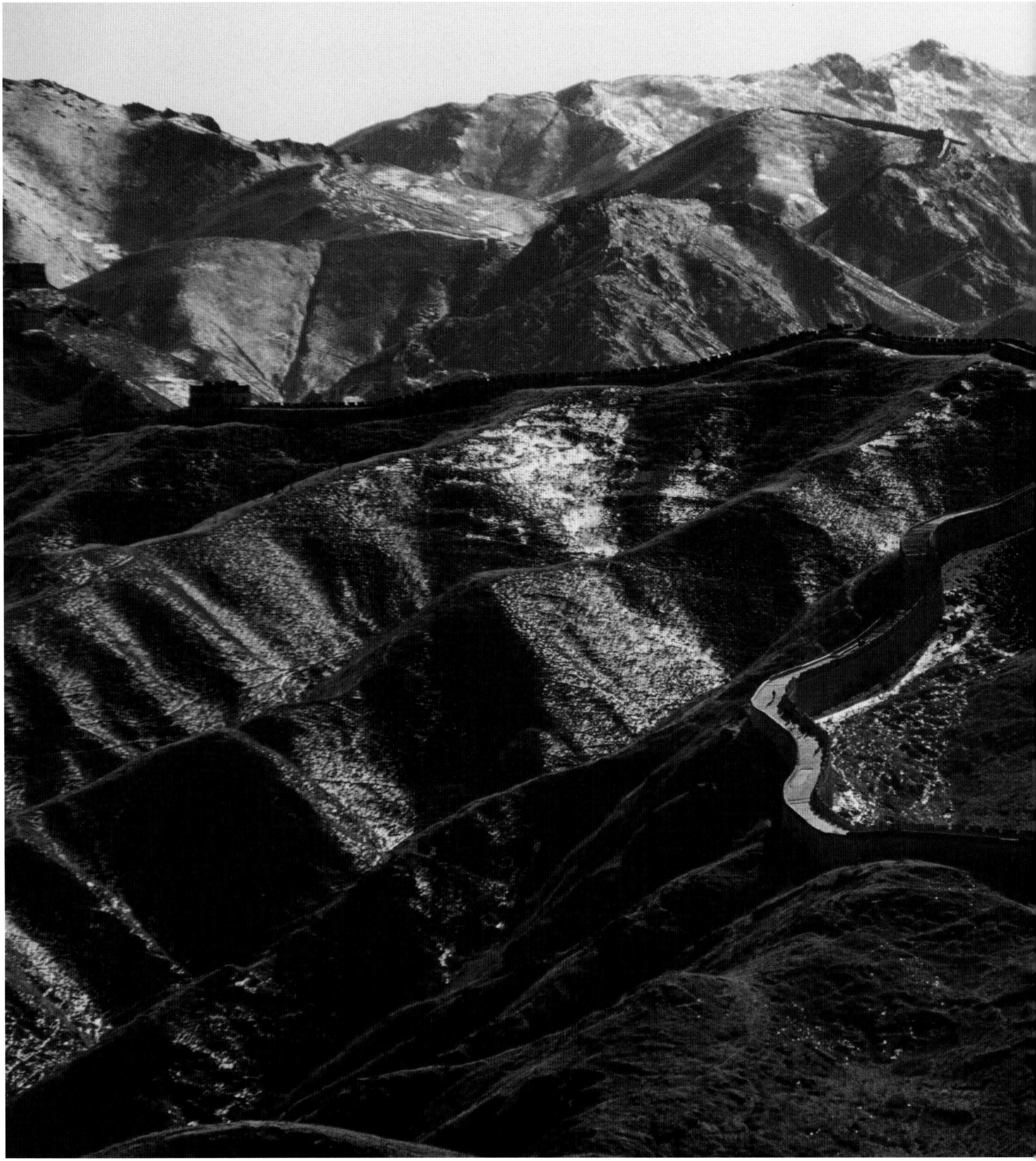

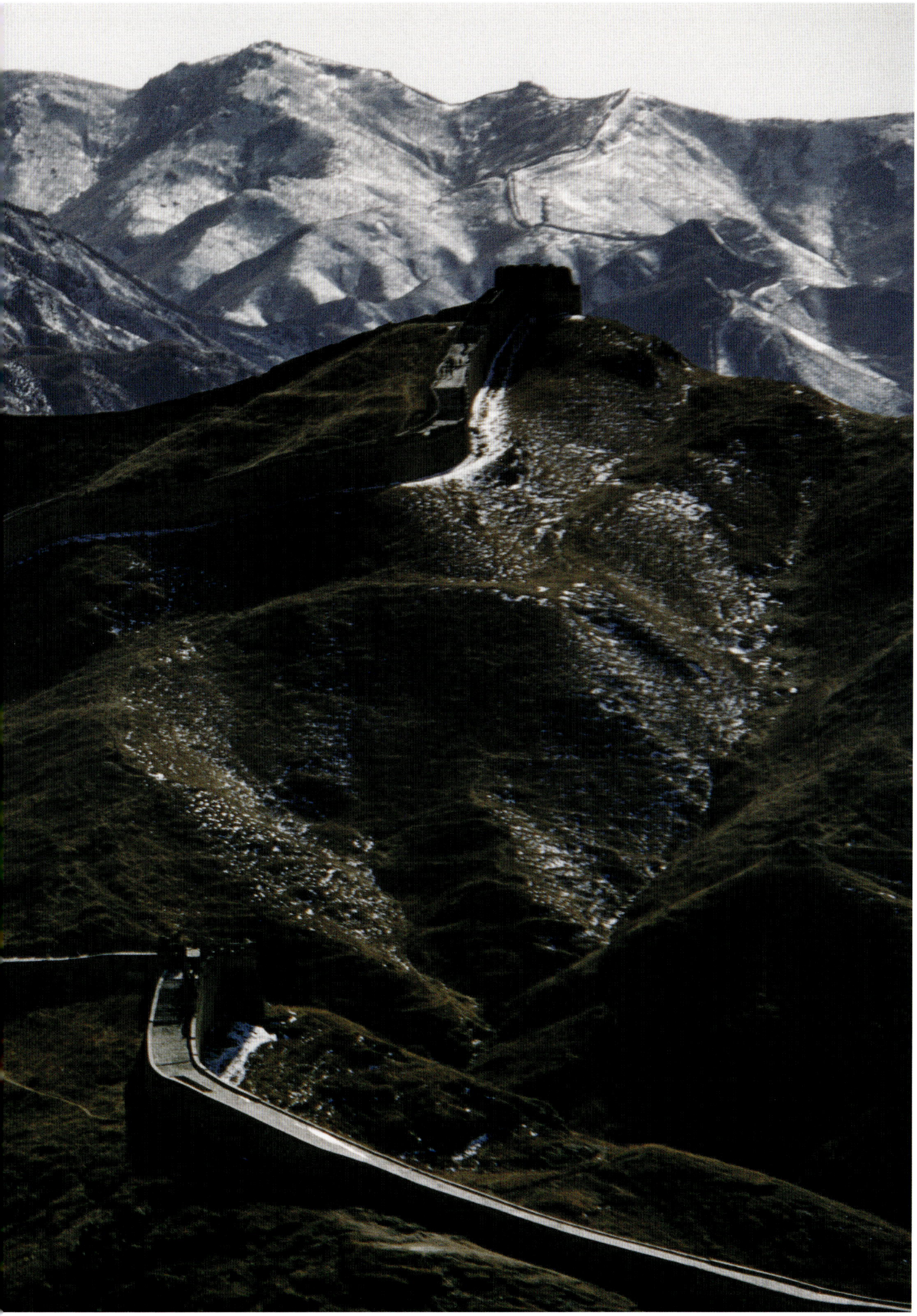

31 | Brian Brake. *The Great Wall, Chuyun Kuan, China,* 1957. *Brian Brake: China, the 1950s.* Wellington: Museum of New Zealand Te Papa Tongarewa, 1995. 35mm transparency. Collection Museum of New Zealand Te Papa Tongarewa. Gift of Wai-man Lau, 2001.

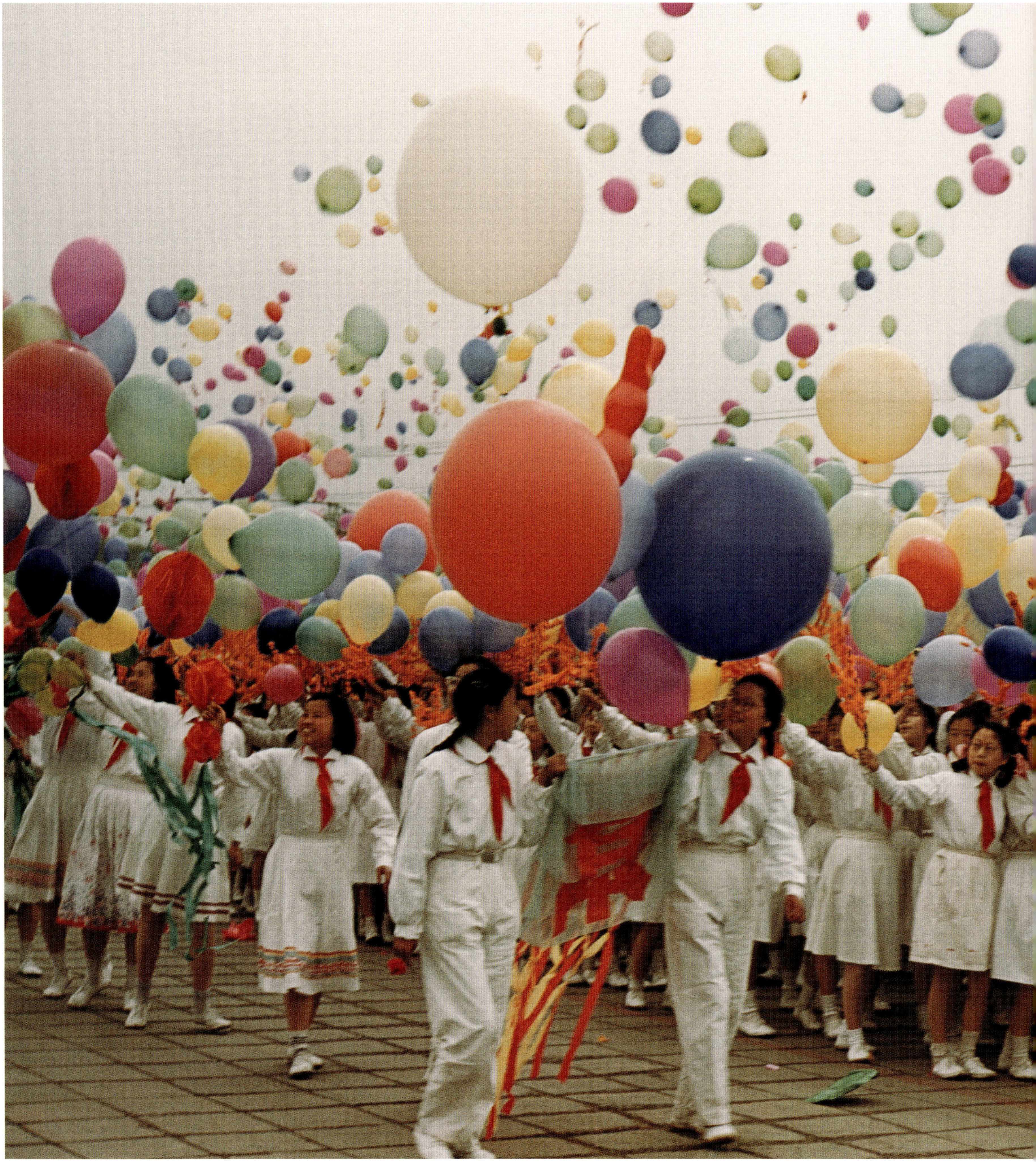

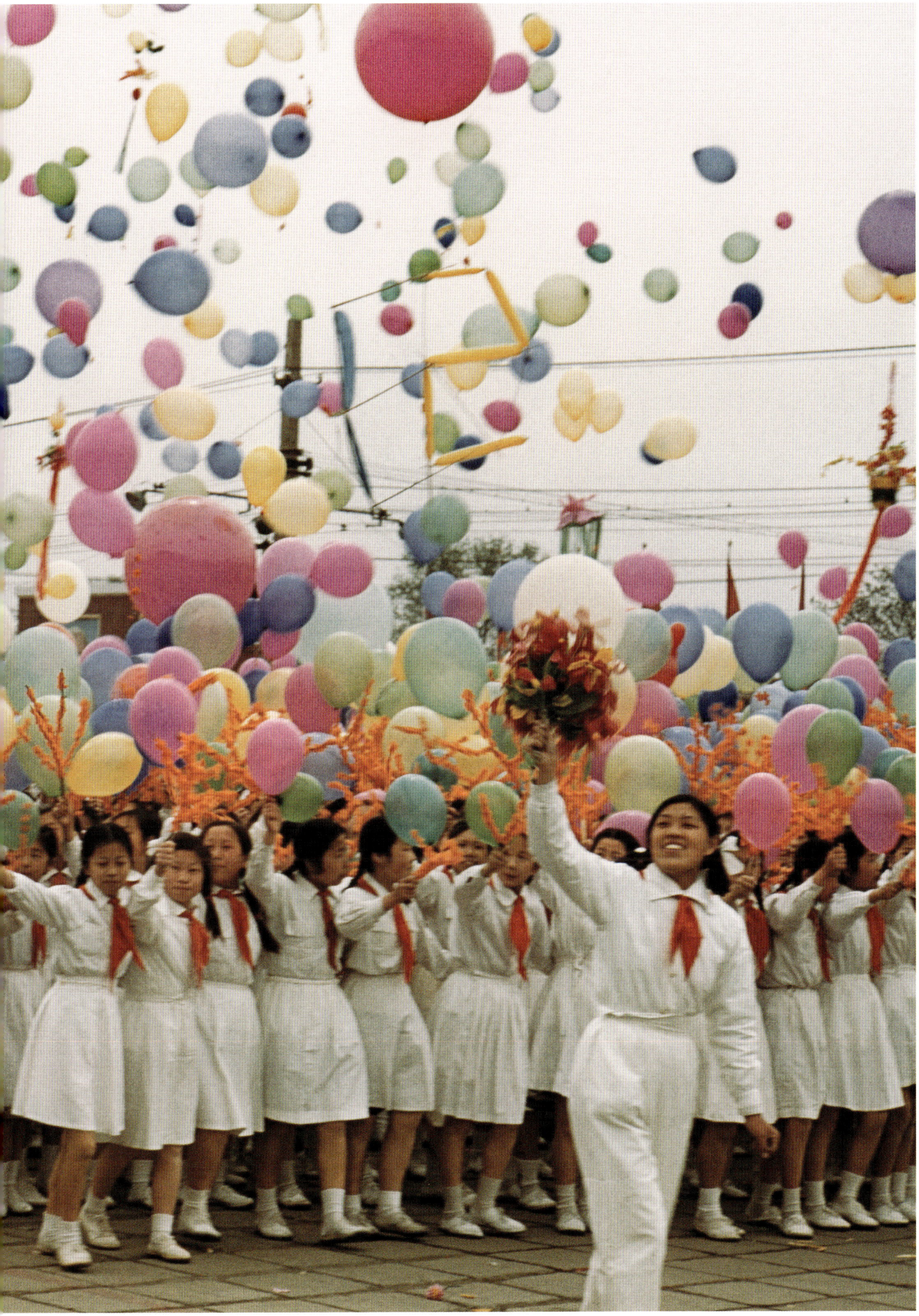

32 I Brian Brake. *May Day celebrations, Tiananmen Square, Beijing, China,* 1957. McCredie, Athol, ed. *Brian Brake: Lens on the World*. Wellington: Te Papa Press, 2010. 35mm transparency. Collection Museum of New Zealand Te Papa Tongarewa. Gift of Wai-man Lau, 2001.

33

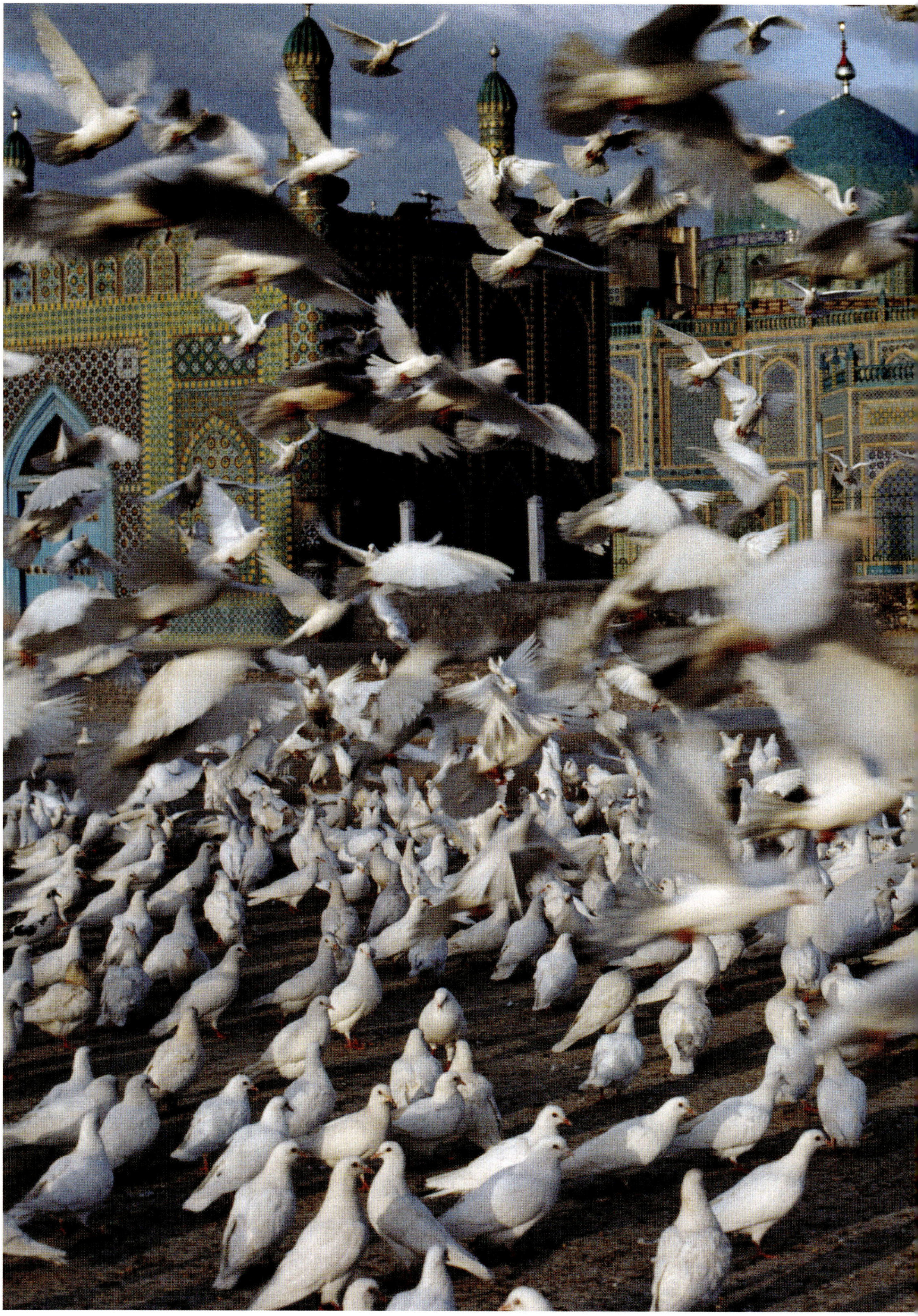

33 | Steve McCurry. *Blue Mosque, Mazar-i-Sharif, Afghanistan,* 1991. *South Southeast.* London & New York: Phaidon Press, 2000. © Steve McCurry.

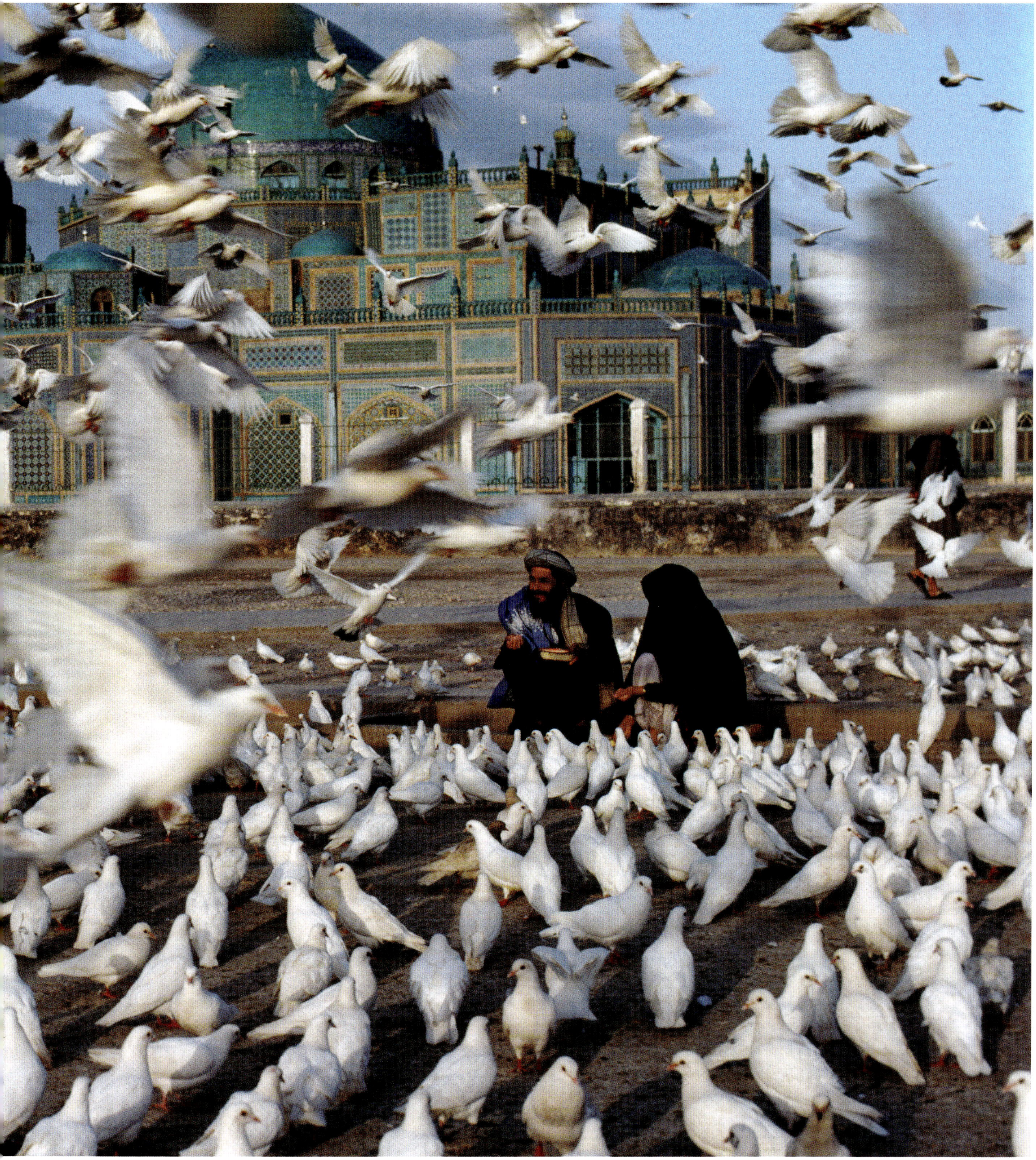

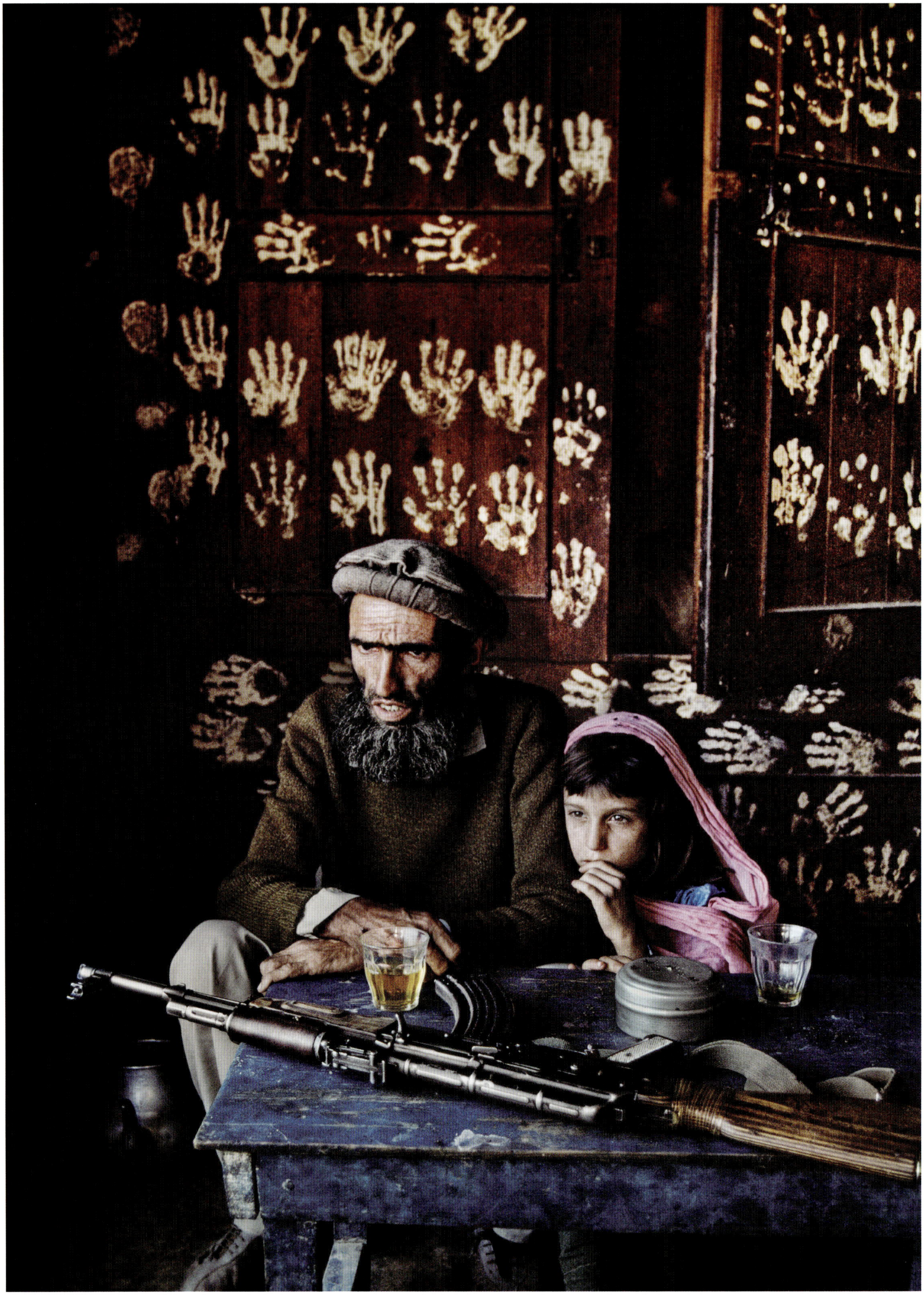

35

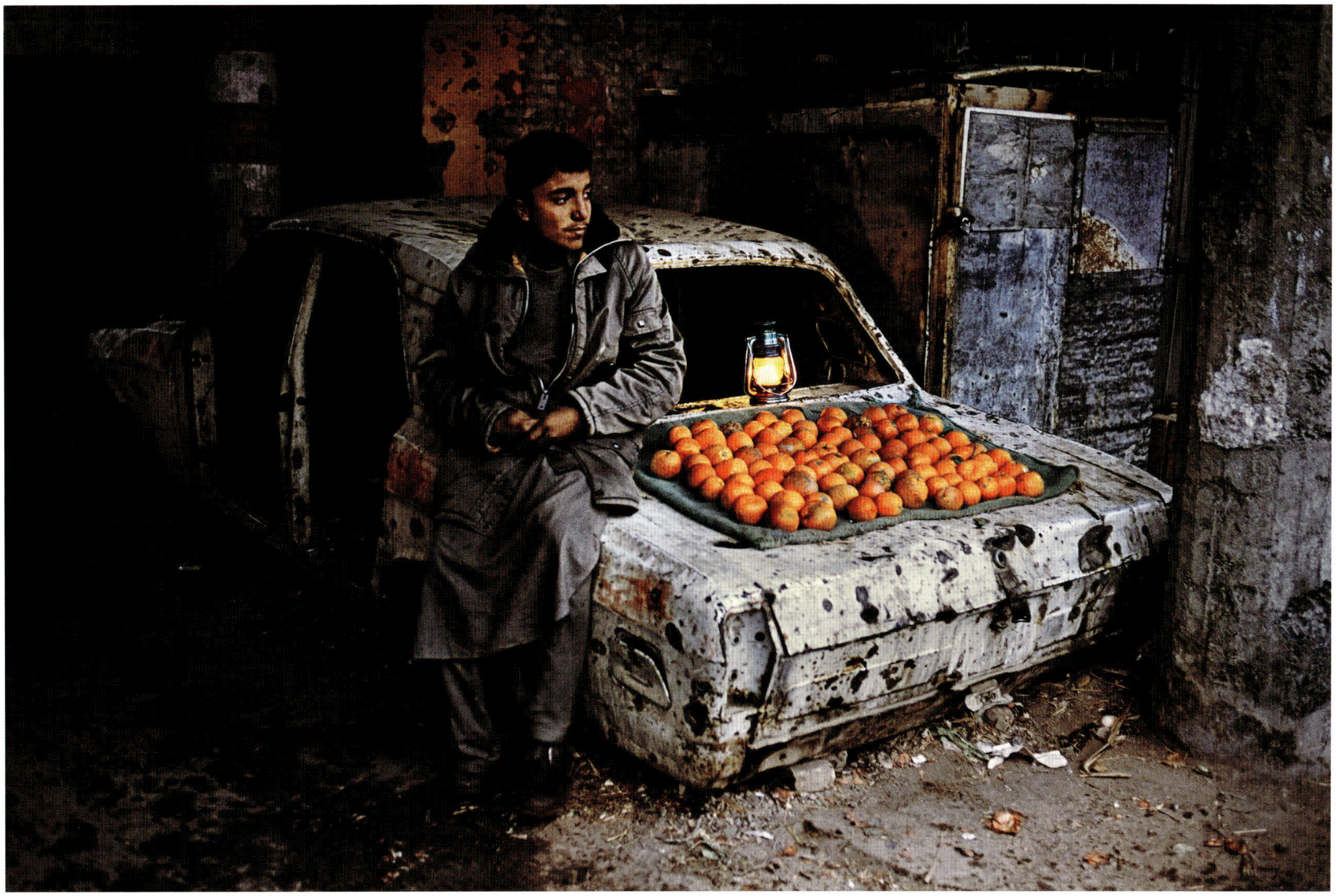

34 I Steve McCurry. *Father and daughter at home, Kamdesh, Afghanistan,* 1992. *In the Shadow of Mountains*. London & New York: Phaidon Press, 2007. © Steve McCurry

35 I Steve McCurry. *Orange seller, Kabul, Afghanistan,* 2003. *In the Shadow of Mountains.* London & New York: Phaidon Press, 2007. © Steve McCurry.

36

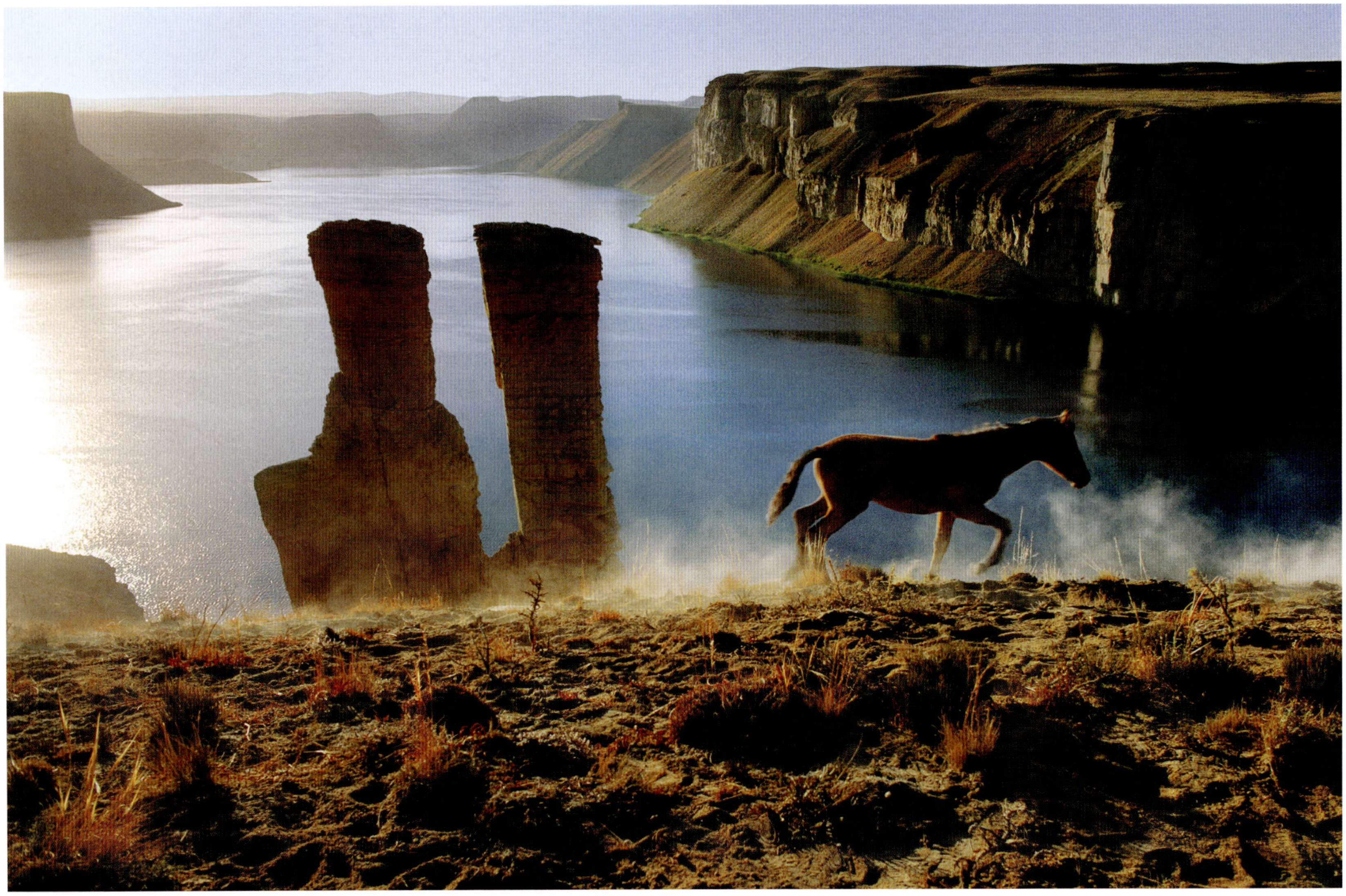

36 | Steve McCurry. *Band-i-Amir, Bamyan, Afghanistan,* 2002. "Afghanistan Between War and Peace". *National Geographic*, vol. 204, no. 5, November 2003. © Steve McCurry.

37

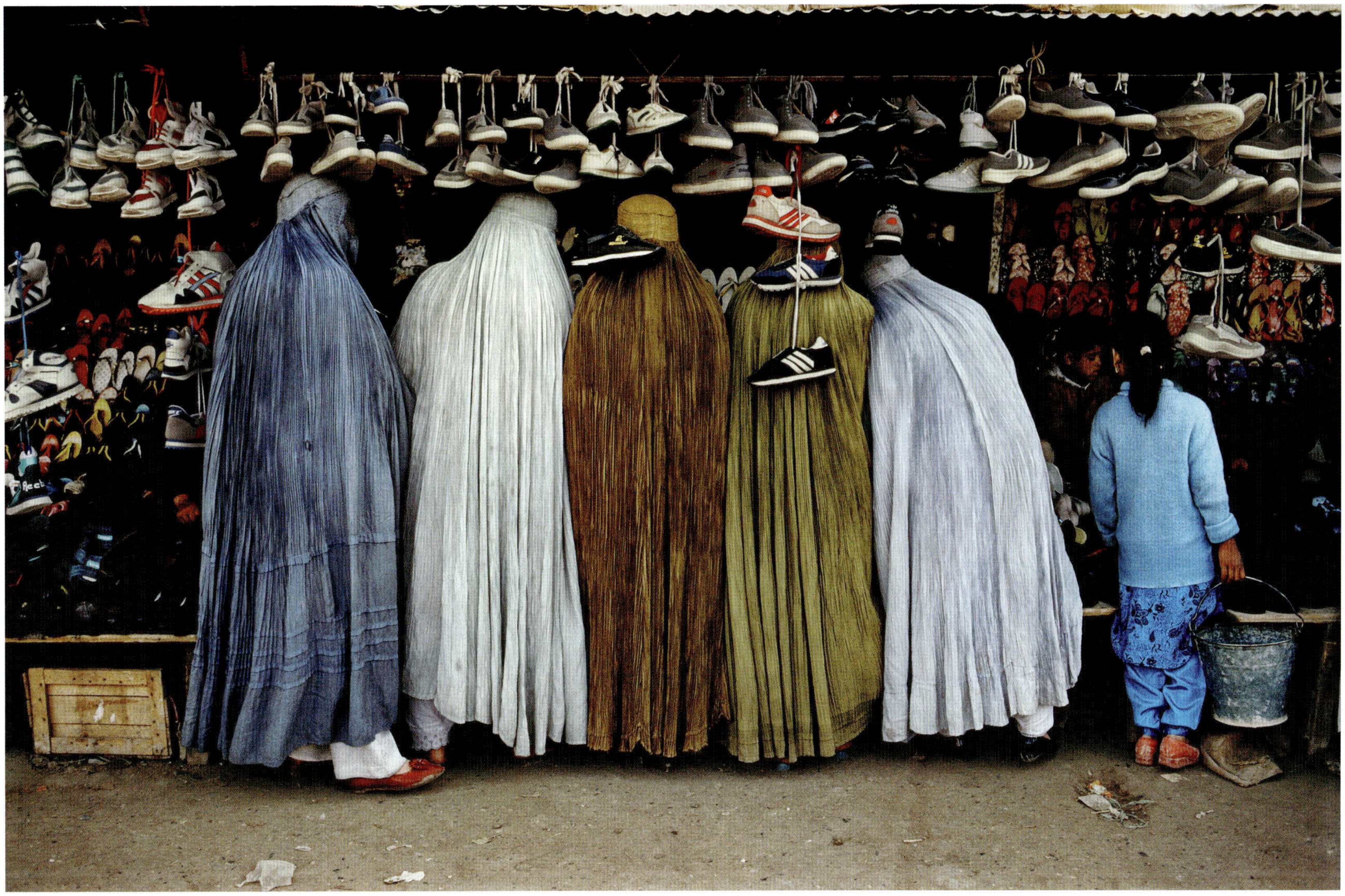

37 | Steve McCurry. *Kabul, Afghanistan,* 1992. “Afghanistan’s Uneasy Peace”. *National Geographic,* vol. 184, no.4, October 1993. © Steve McCurry.

38

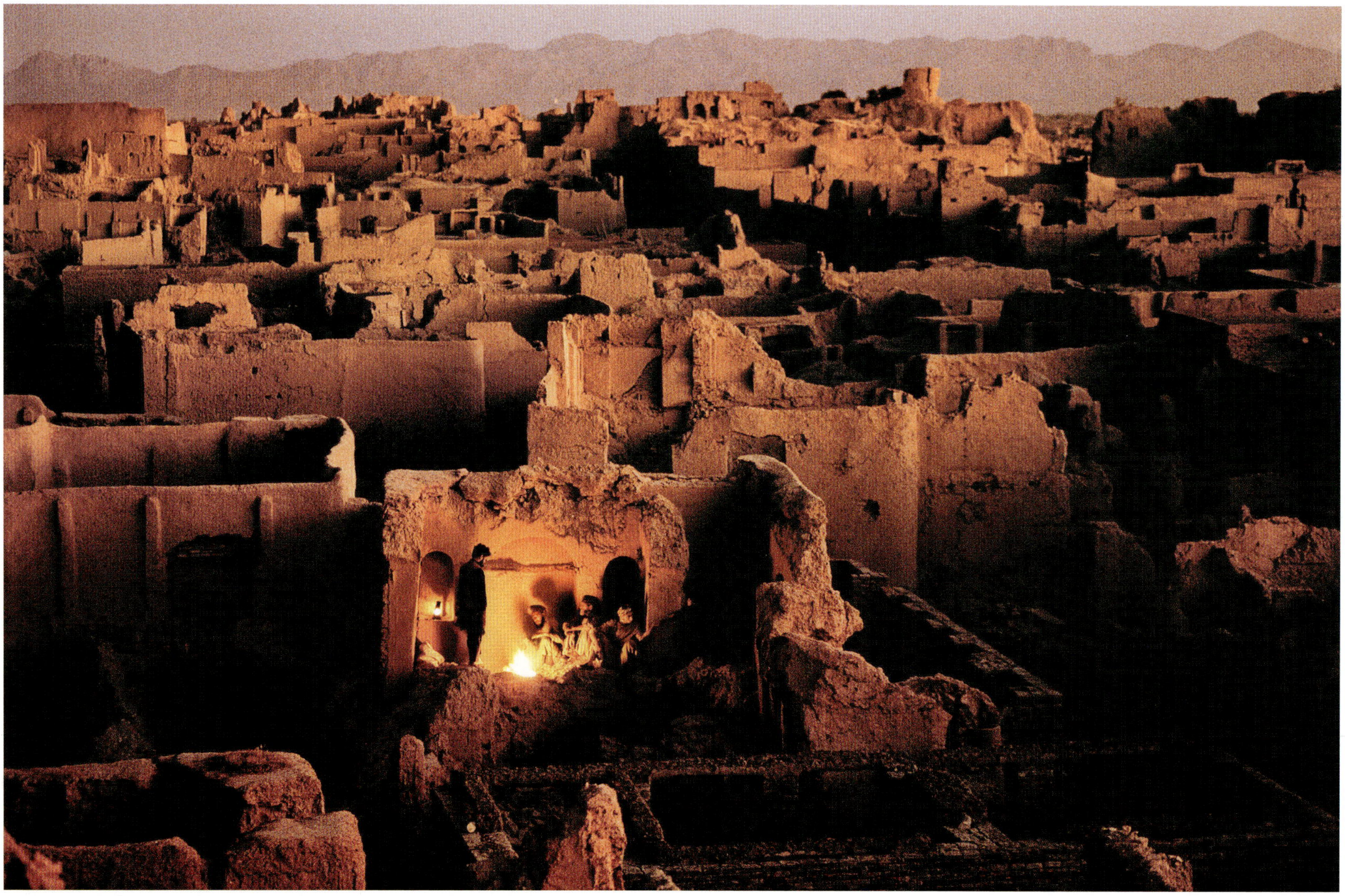

38 | Steve McCurry. *Bombed townscape, Herat, Afghanistan,* 1992. "Afghanistan's Uneasy Peace". *National Geographic*, vol. 184, no. 4, October 1993. © Steve McCurry.

39

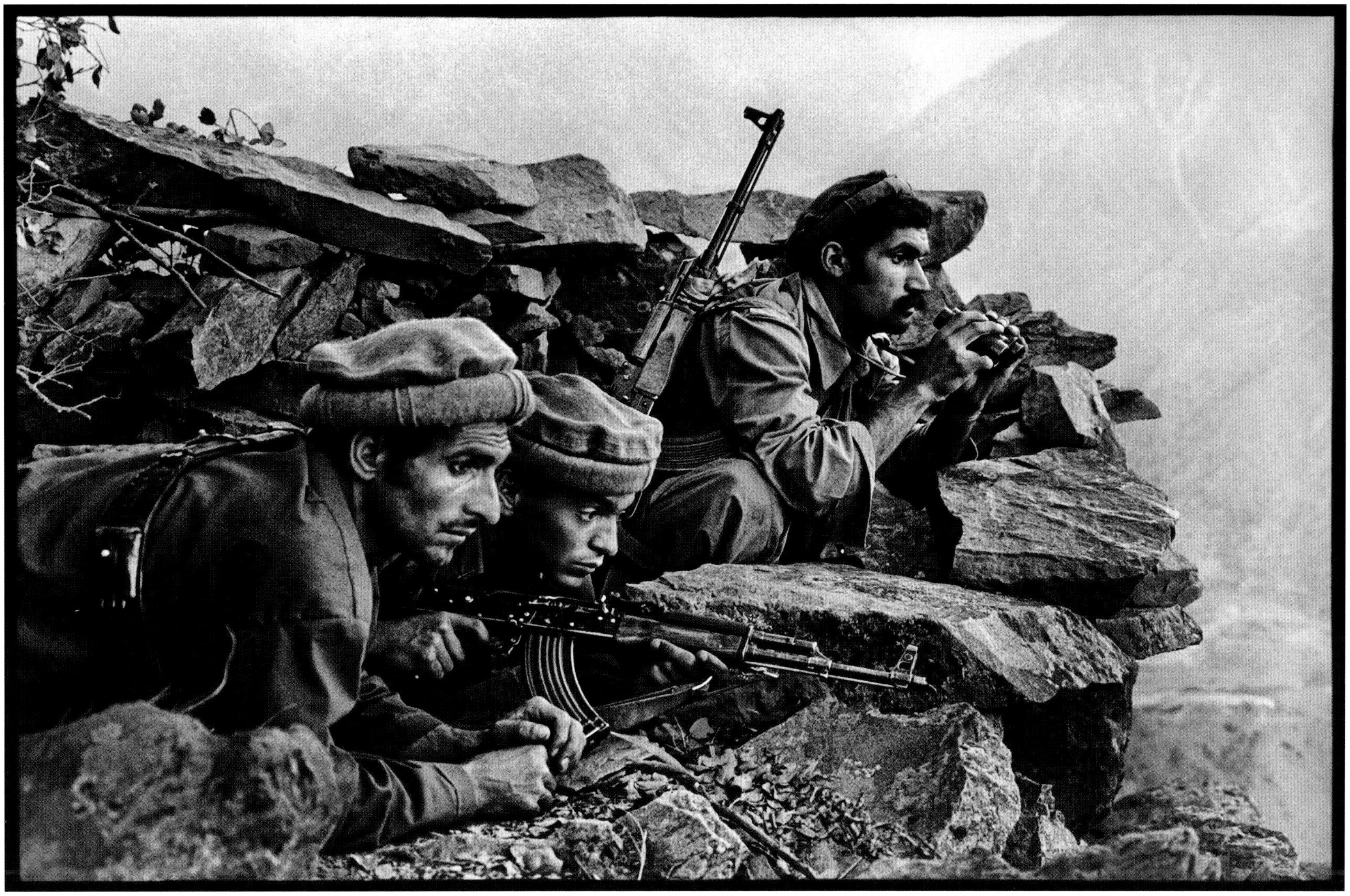

39 I Steve McCurry. *Mujahideen fighters watch convoy, Nuristan, Afghanistan,* 1979. Bannon, Anthony. *Steve McCurry.* London & New York: Phaidon Press, 2005. © Steve McCurry.

40

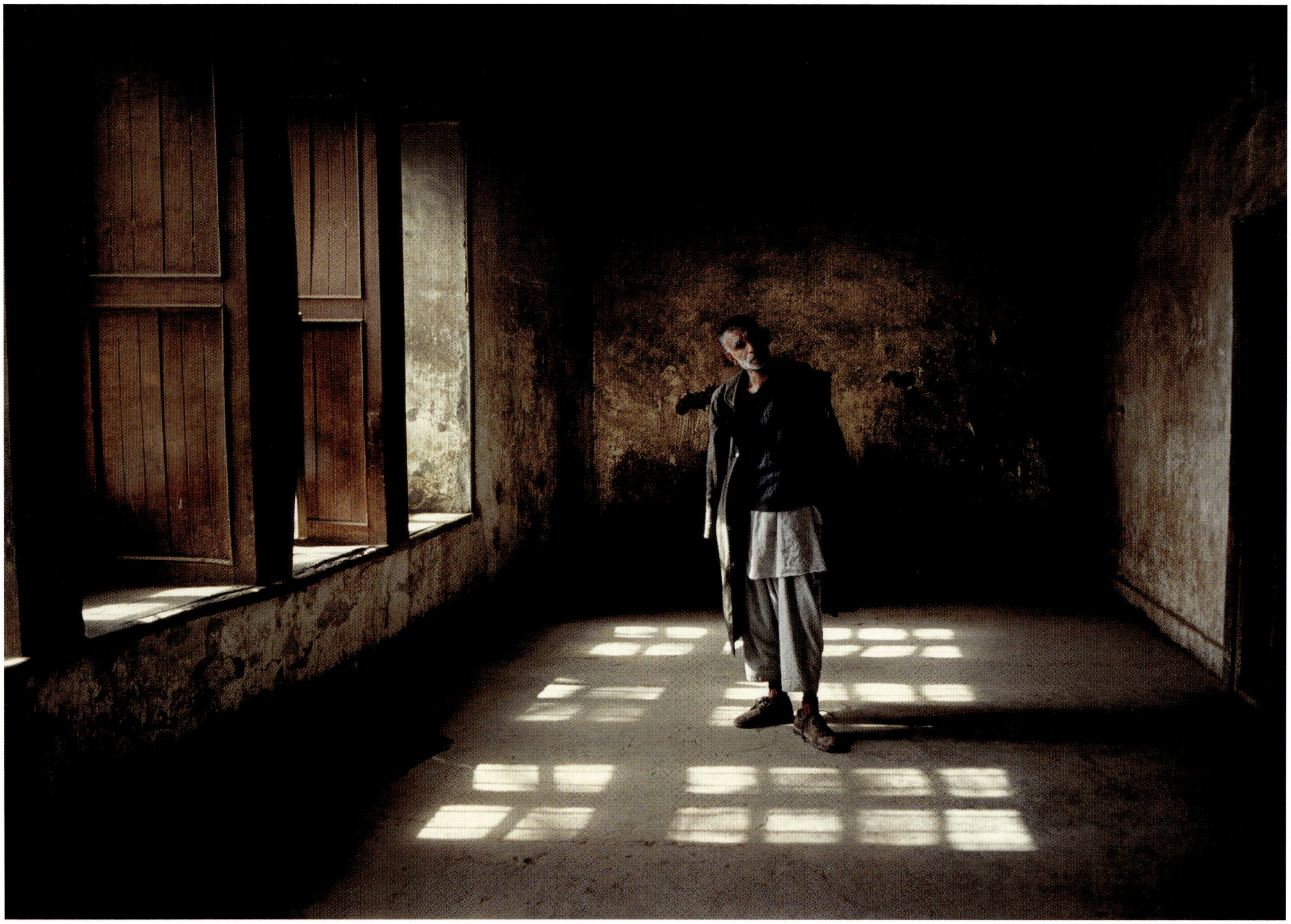

40 | Steve McCurry. *Asylum, Kabul, Afghanistan,* 1992. "Afghanistan's Uneasy Peace". *National Geographic,* vol. 184, no. 4, October 1993. © Steve McCurry.

41

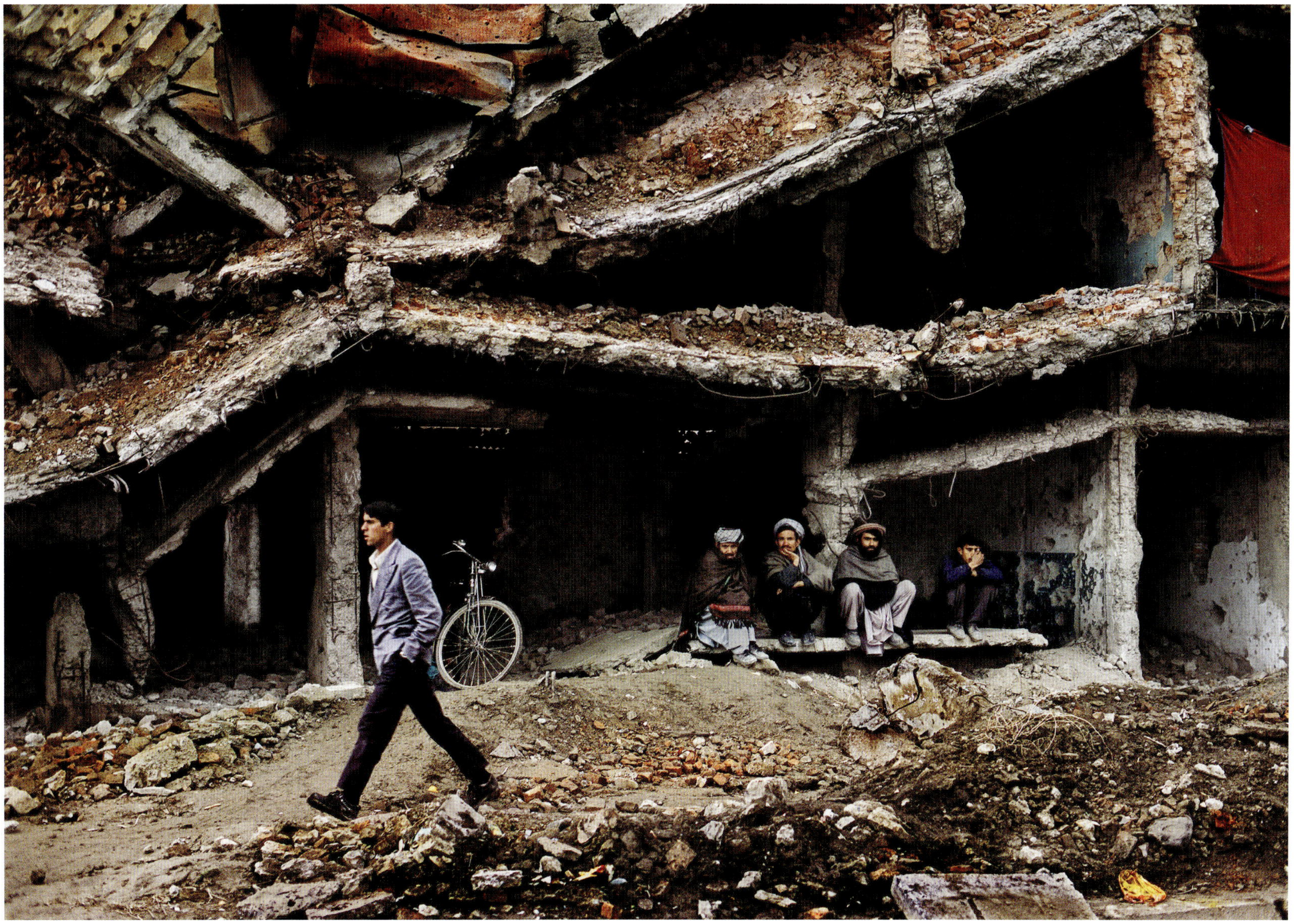

41 | Steve McCurry. *A ruined building, Kabul, Afghanistan,* 2002. "Afghanistan Between War and Peace". *National Geographic*. vol. 204, no. 5, November 2003. © Steve McCurry.

ANCIENT AND MODERN

In a 2009 interview with the Curator Photography of the Museum of New Zealand Te Papa Tongarewa, Athol McCredie, Brian Brake's London agent John Hillelson suggested that he had a "gentle" lens. The humanist ethos of the New York Museum of Modern Art's photography exhibition *The Family of Man* (1955) permeates Brake's photographs. He looked for shared human qualities rather than exotic differences.

The picture editors of his 1964 *Life* essay "Japan: The modern paradoxes" and of its *Paris Match* version, "Fabuleux Japon", favored images of traditional practices. But Brake's photographs emphasize historical continuities. The traditional ritual of a woman, Toshi Satow, offering a candle to the unknown dead, and the contemporary one of a baseball game cheerleader both involve living people—like those jammed into a Tokyo subway. And his 1963 *Life* essay on the Asian film industry folds ancient and modern together within the narrative frame of cinema.

Steve McCurry has a keen eye for what is distinctive and unexpected in the diverse cultures he has photographed. Often, the impact of his photographs involves rich, saturated color, eye-catching situations, and careful choices of time and location—such as Buddhist monks praying just after sunset at Golden Rock in Kyaiktiyo, Burma/Myanmar.

And yet scenes that at first glance appear exotic to Western readers of magazines like *National Geographic* often disclose sympathetic glimpses of ordinary life: a bicyclist in the distance beyond a huge reclining Buddha, or the women in a crowded garment factory in Rangoon whose pink uniforms match the traditional robes of Buddhist nuns, but whose cheap labor serves the desires of Western consumers.

42

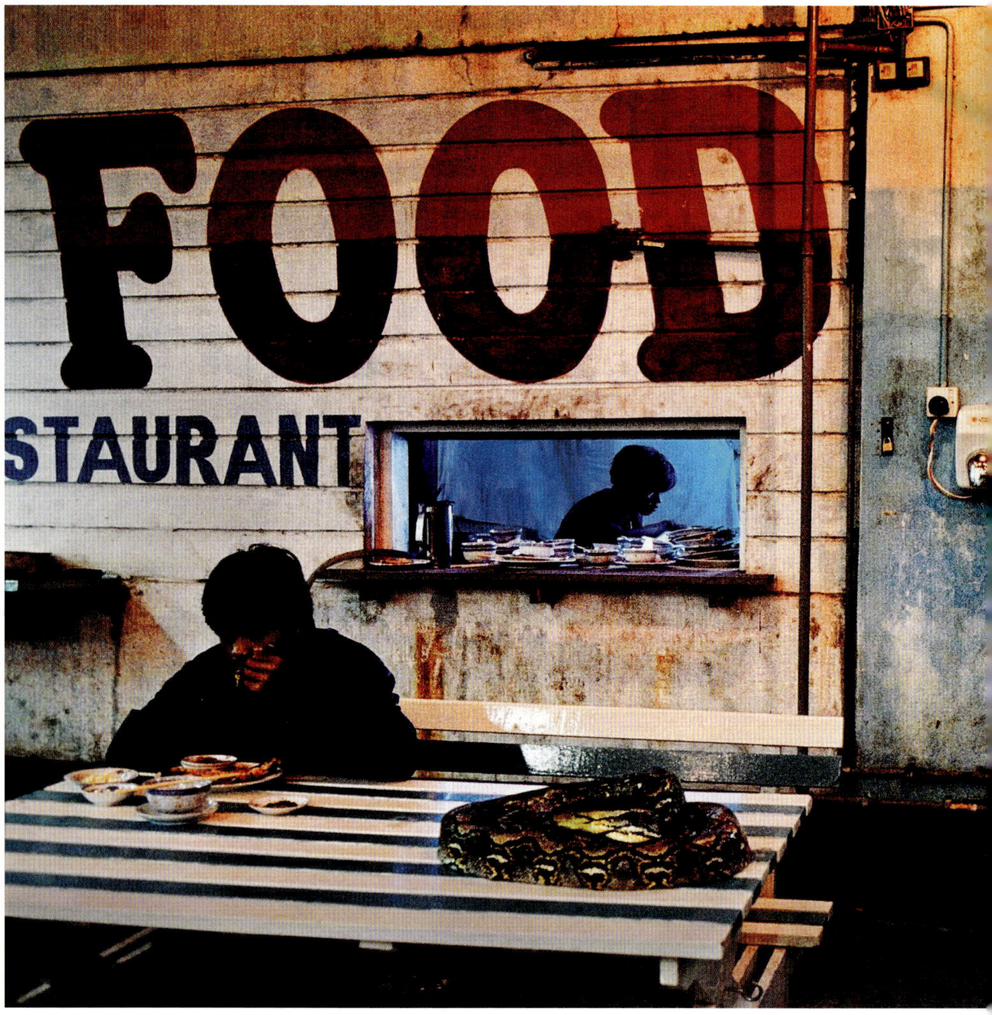

42 I Steve McCurry. *"Food", Rangoon, Burma/Myanmar,* 1994. *South Southeast.* London & New York: Phaidon Press, 2000. © Steve McCurry.

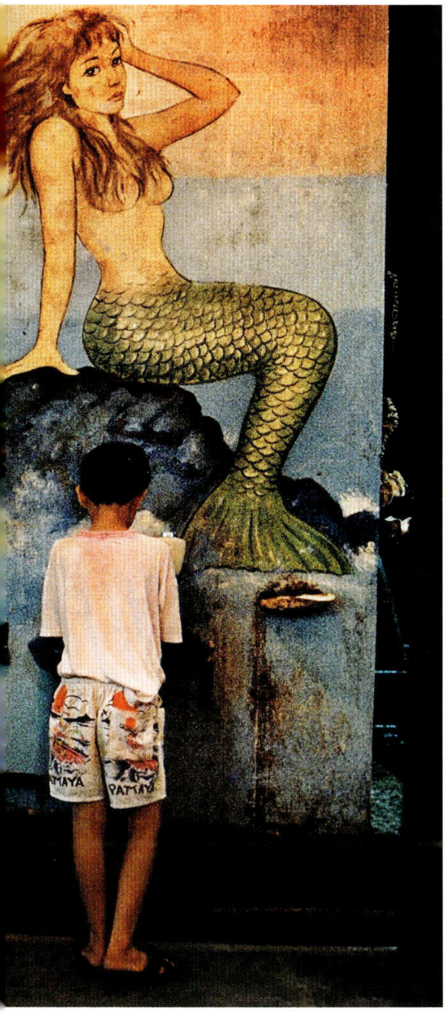

43

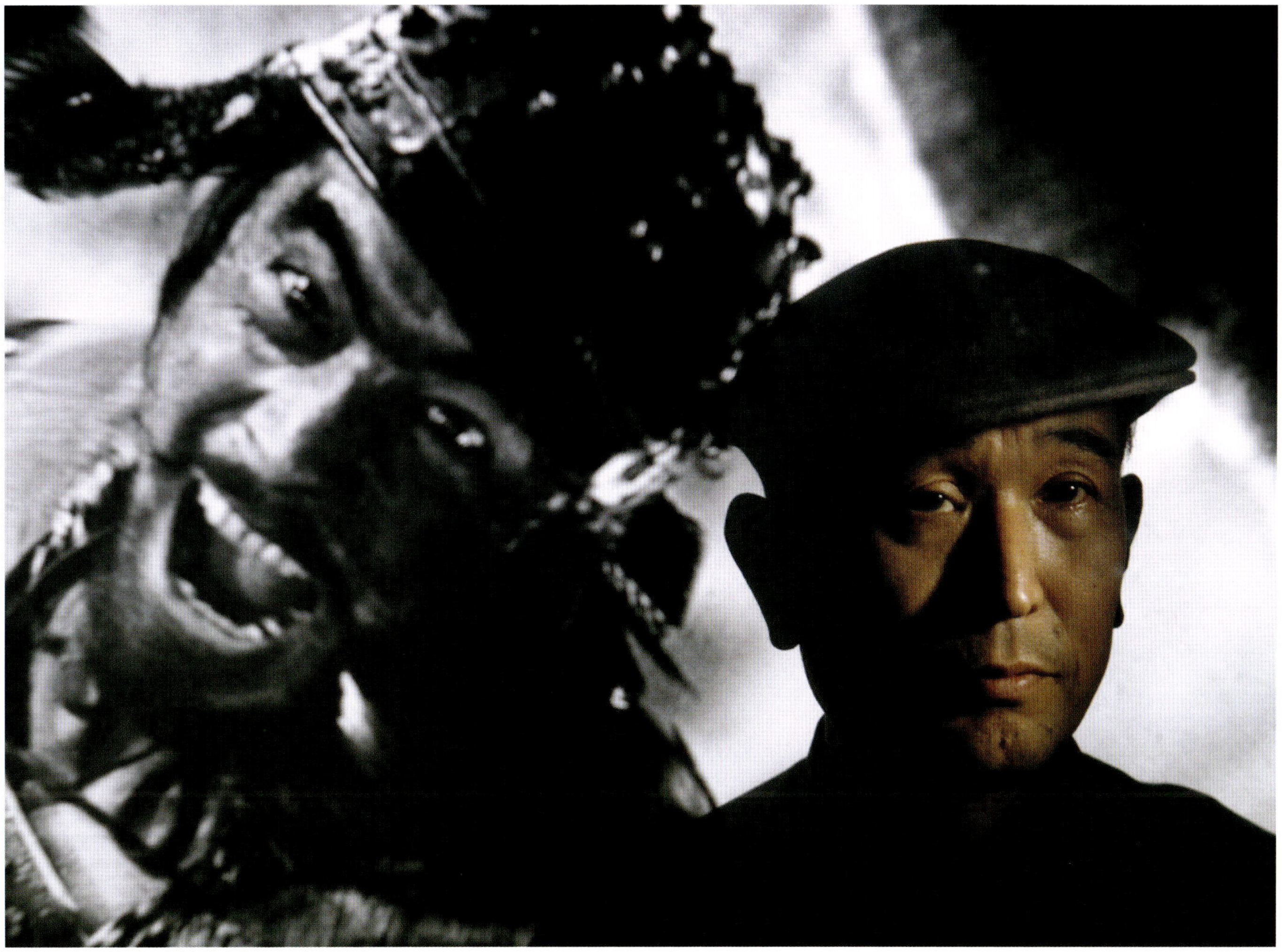

43 | Brian Brake. *Film director Akira Kurosawa standing before an image of his principal star, Toshiro Mifune, Tokyo, Japan,* 1963. "The Universal Magic of the Movies". *Life*, vol. 55, no. 25, December 1963. 35mm transparency. Collection Museum of New Zealand Te Papa Tongarewa. Gift of Wai-man Lau, 2001.

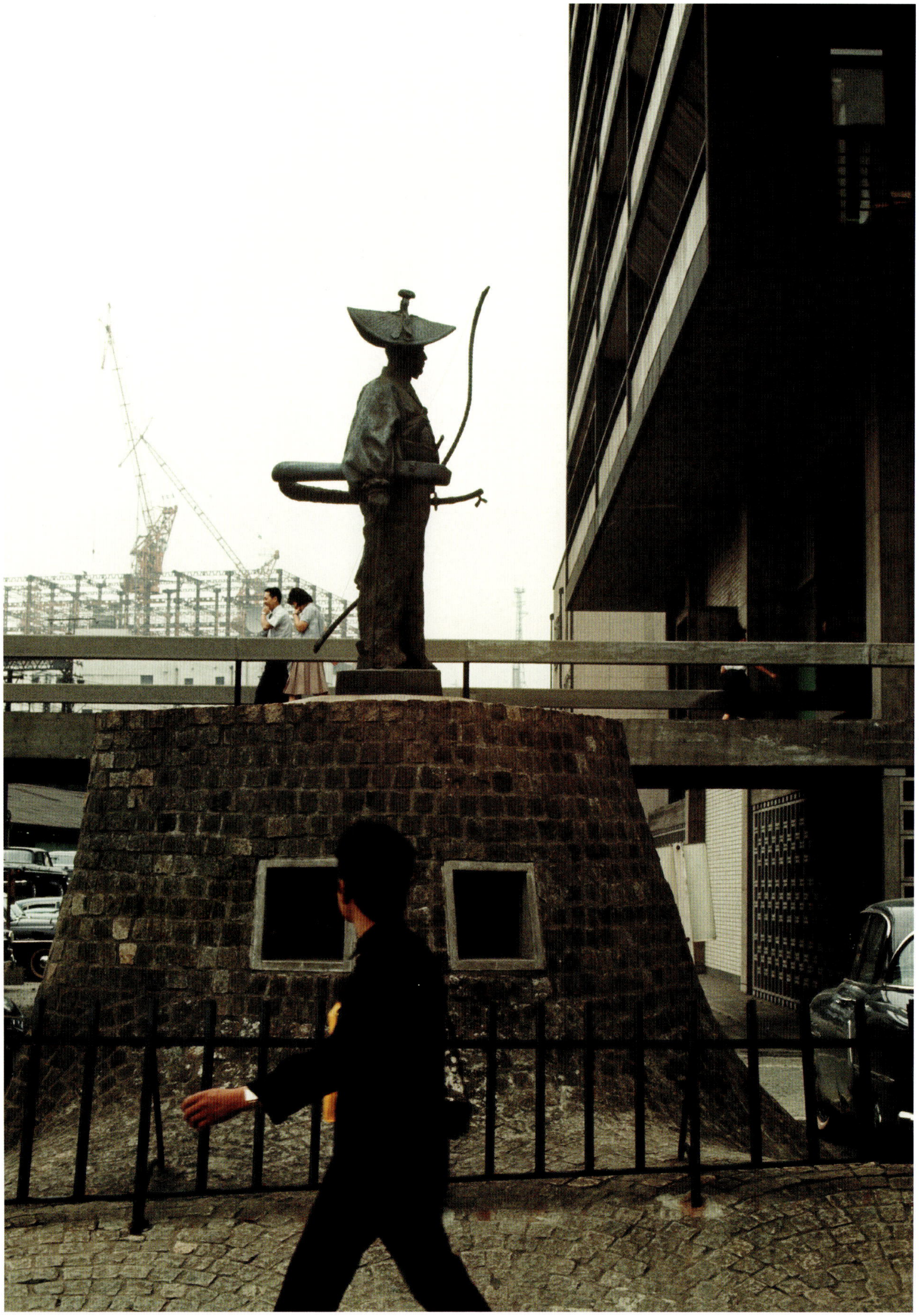

44 I Brian Brake. *Sculpture, Kanto, Japan*. From the series: Japan, 1960s-80s. Unpublished. 35mm transparency. Collection Museum of New Zealand Te Papa Tongarewa. Gift of Wai-man Lau, 2001.

45

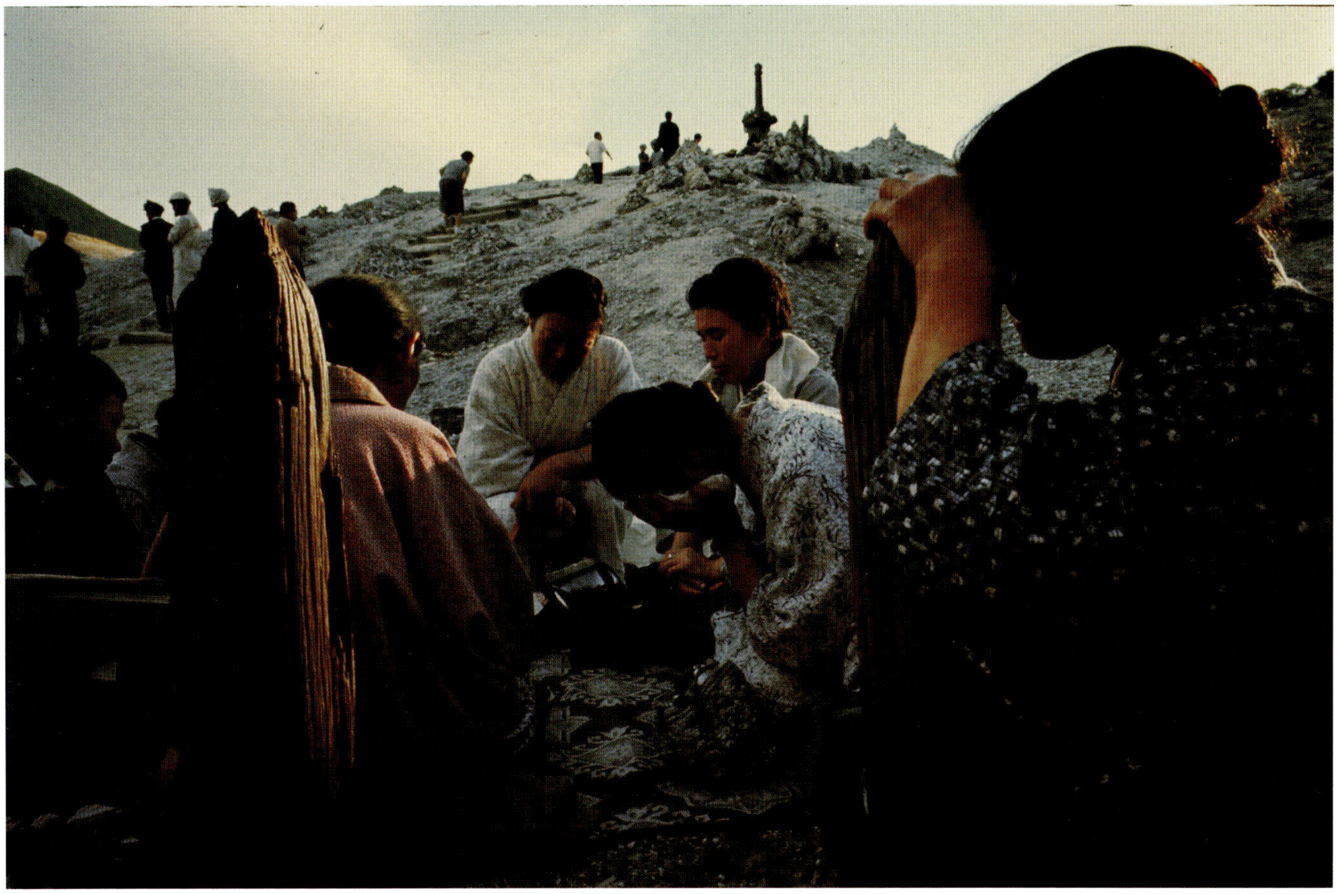

46

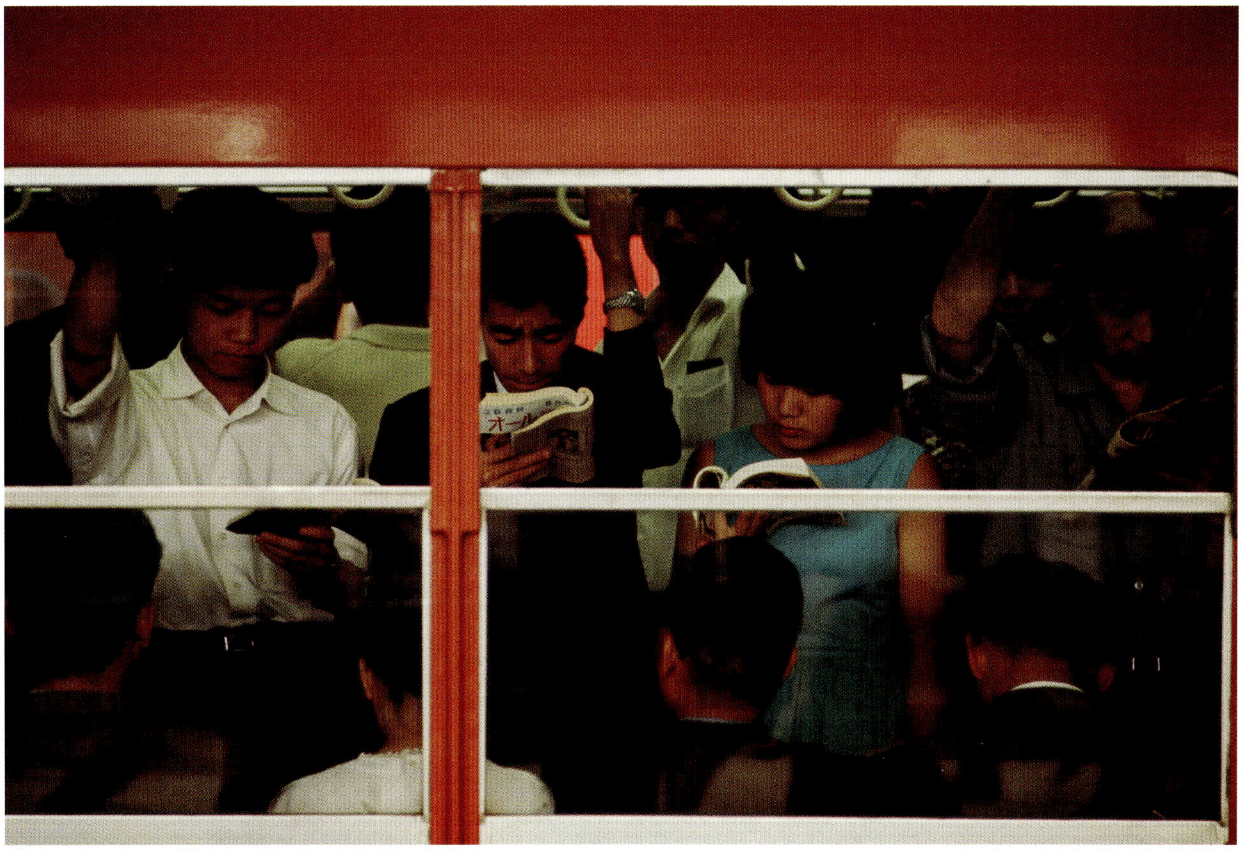

45 | Brian Brake. *Blind Japanese women claiming to be mediums gather once a year in Northern Honshu, Japan*. From the series: Japan, 1960s-80s. Unpublished. 4 x 5 inch color copy transparency. Collection Museum of New Zealand Te Papa Tongarewa. Gift of Wai-man Lau, 2010.

46 | Brian Brake. *Subway, Tokyo, Japan,* 1964. "Japan: The Modern Paradoxes". *Life*, vol. 57, no. 11, 11 September 1964. 35mm transparency. Collection Museum of New Zealand Te Papa Tongarewa. Gift of Wai-man Lau, 2001.

47

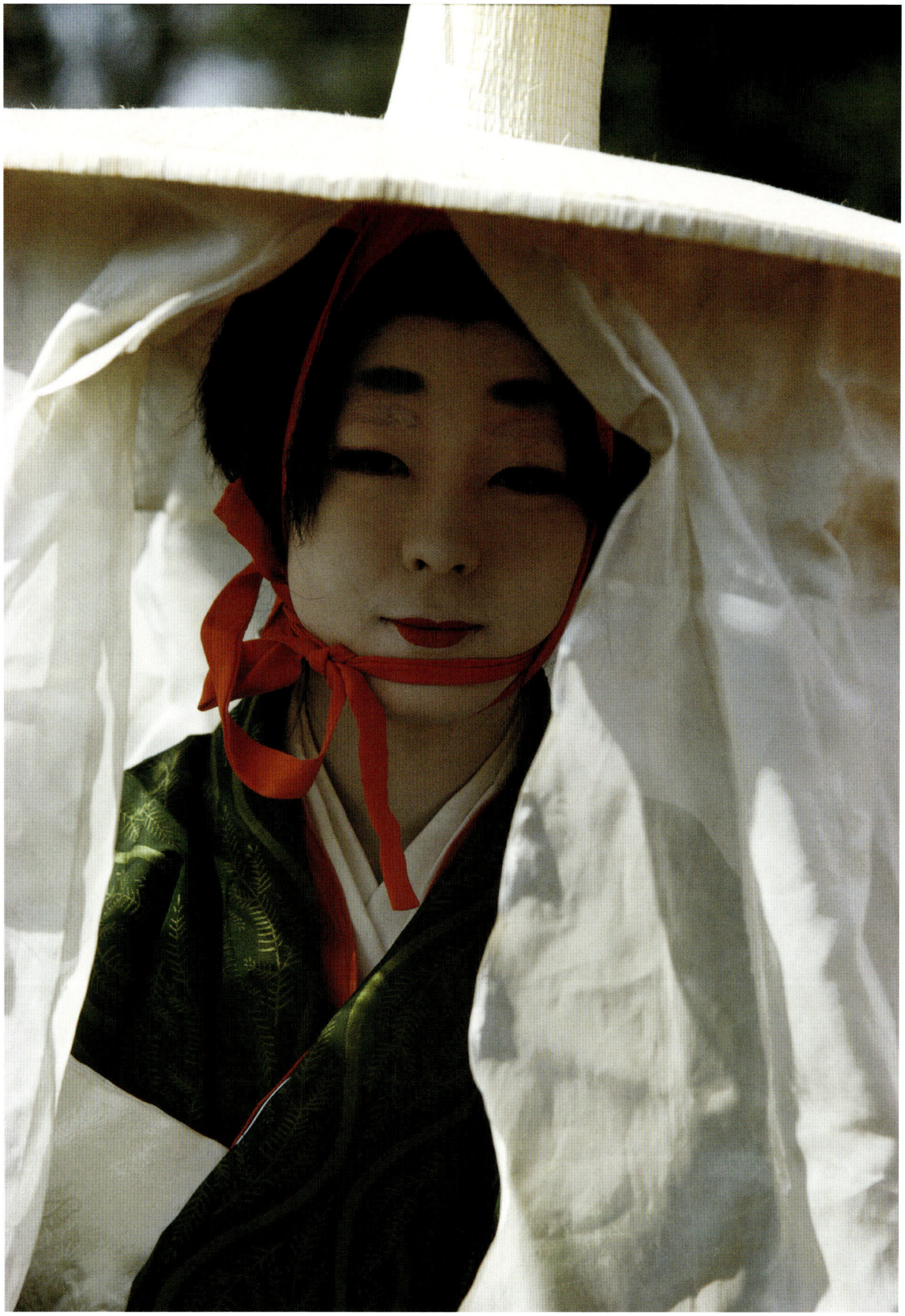

47 | Brian Brake. *Woman in Heian Period Costume, Festival of the Ages, Kyoto, Japan,* 1963. “Japan: The Modern Paradoxes”. *Life*, vol. 57, no. 11, 11 September 1964. 35mm transparency. Collection Museum of New Zealand Te Papa Tongarewa. Gift of Wai-man Lau, 2010.

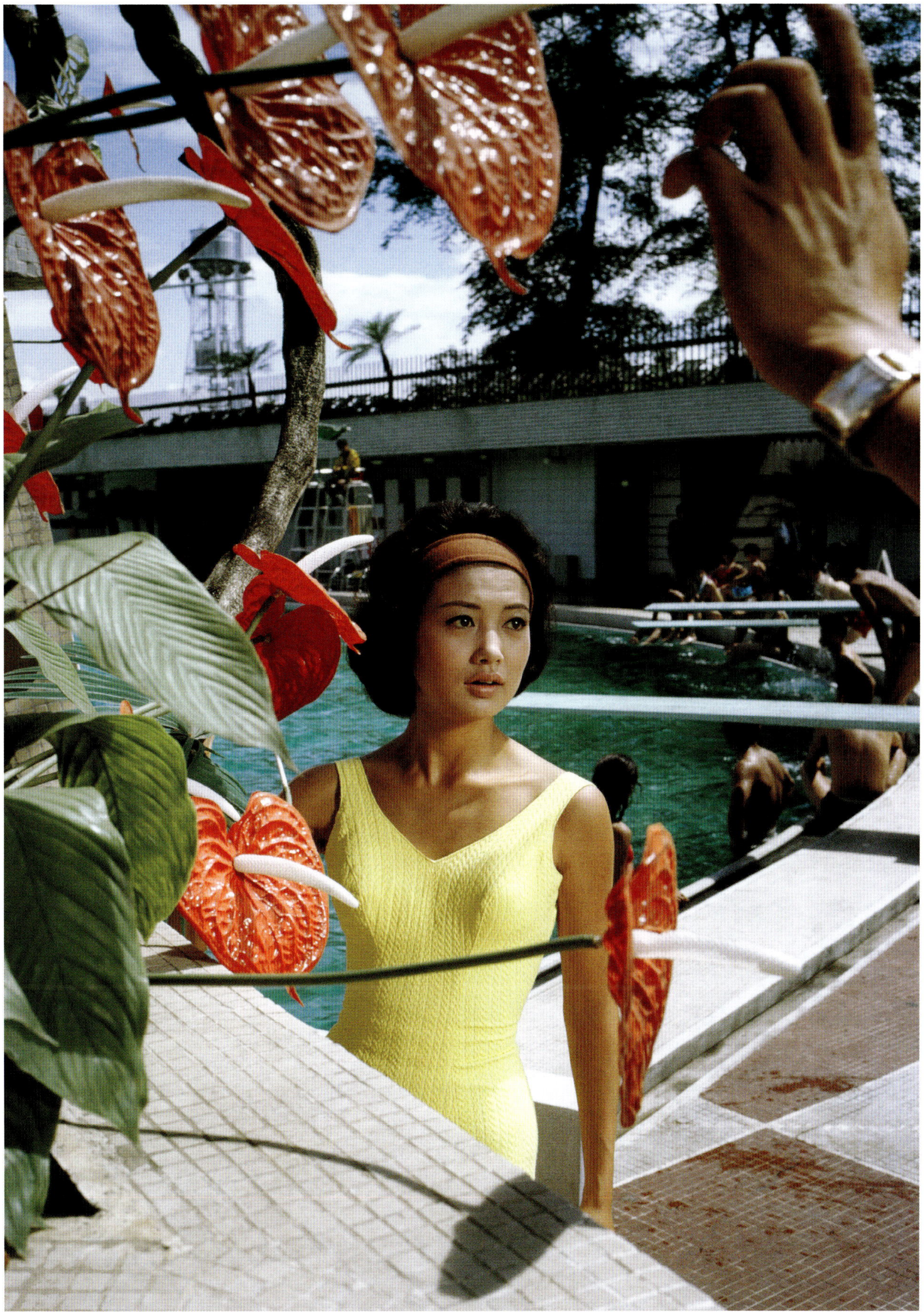

48 | Brian Brake. *Film set, Japan,* 1963. “The Universal Magic of the Movies”. *Life*, vol. 55, no. 25, December 1963. 35mm transparency. Collection Museum of New Zealand Te Papa Tongarewa. Gift of Wai-man Lau, 2001.

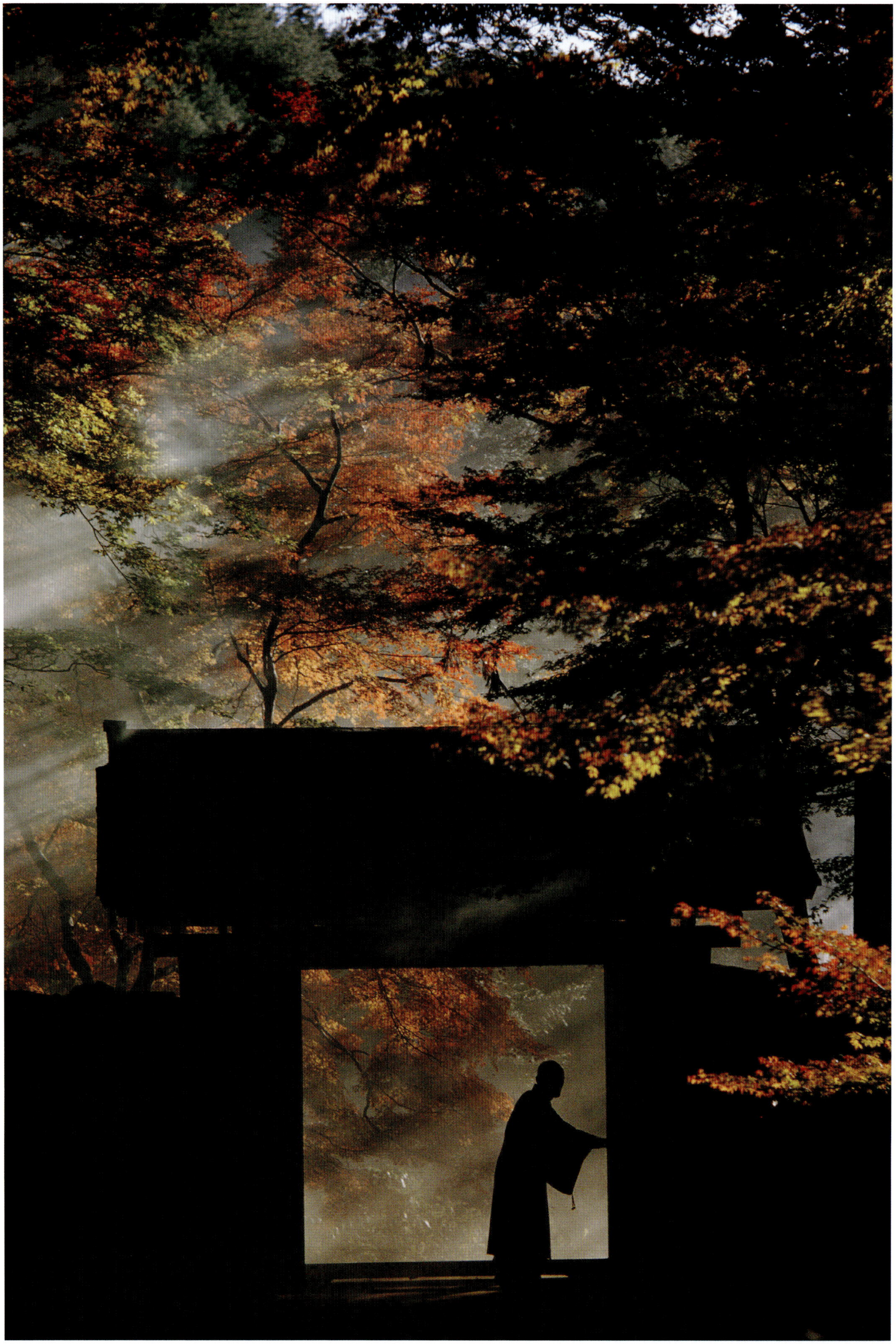

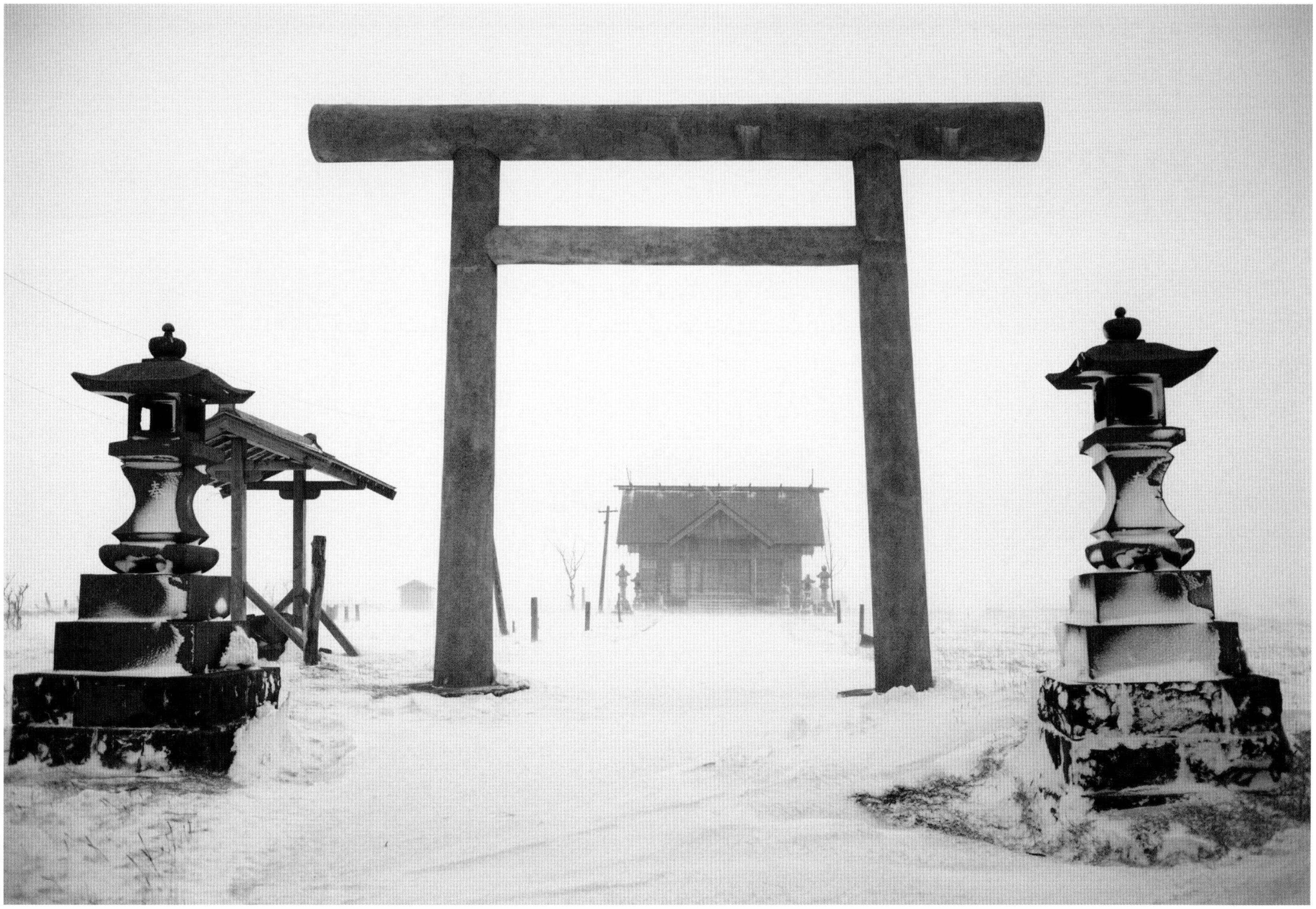

49 I Brian Brake. *Sanzen-in Temple near Kyoto, Japan,* c.1963. “Japan: The Modern Paradoxes”. *Life*, vol. 57, no. 11, 11 September 1964. 35mm transparency. Collection Museum of New Zealand Te Papa Tongarewa. Gift of Wai-man Lau, 2010.

50 I Brian Brake. *Archway in snow, Japan*. From the series: Japan, 1960s-80s. Unpublished. 35mm transparency. Collection Museum of New Zealand Te Papa Tongarewa. Gift of Wai-man Lau, 2001.

51

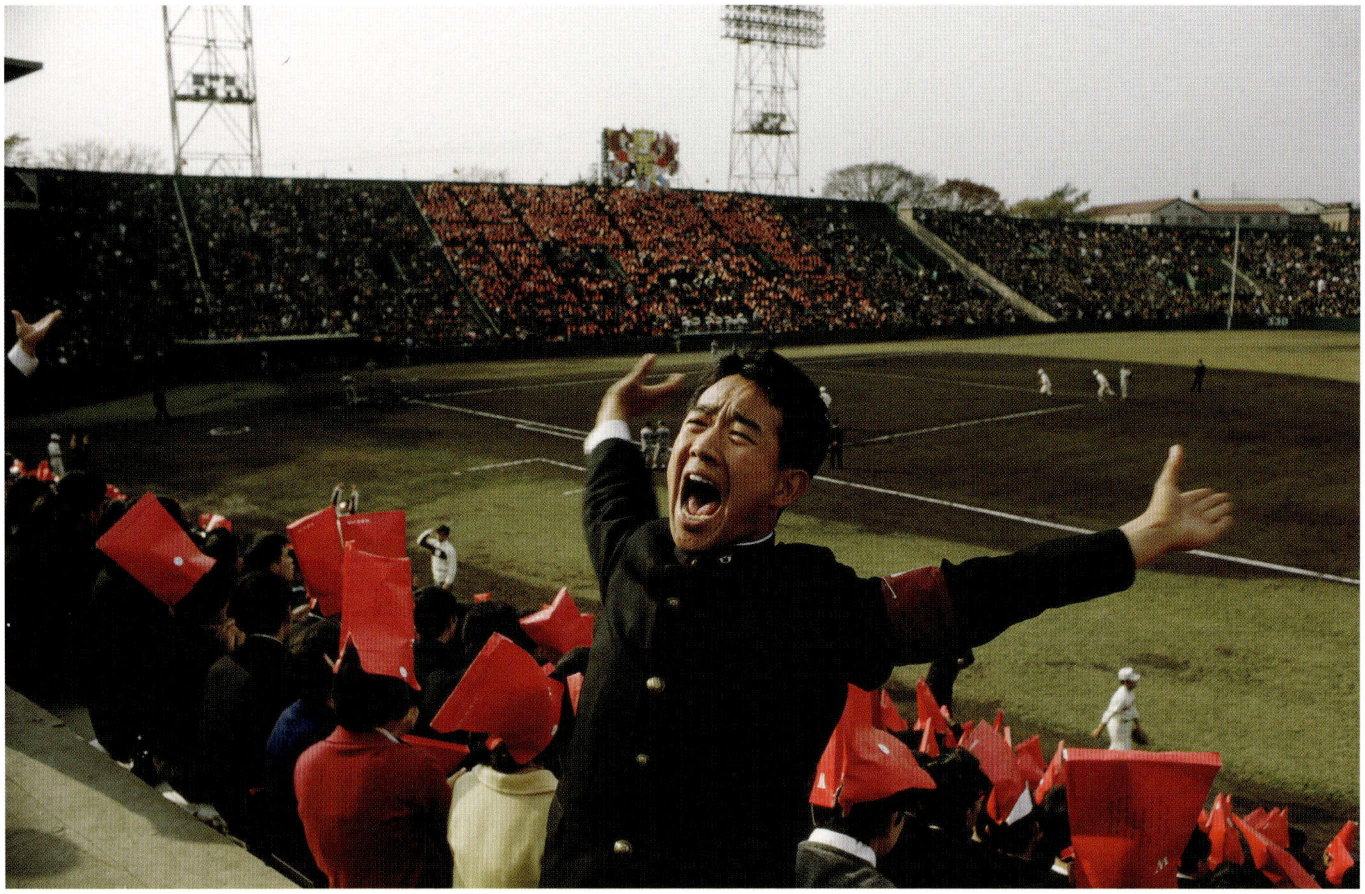

52

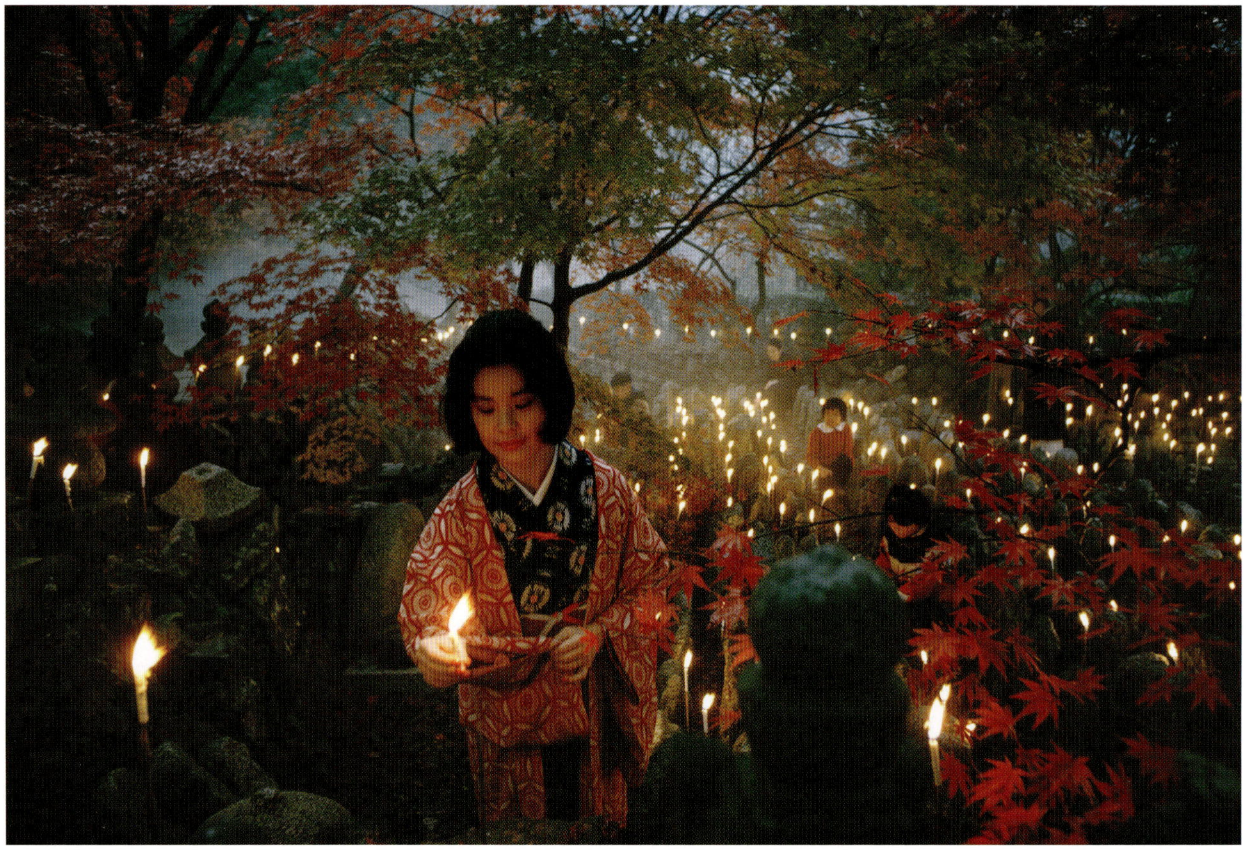

51 | Brian Brake. *Cheerleader at a Waseda University versus Keio University baseball game, Tokyo, Japan*, 1964. "Japan: The Modern Paradoxes". *Life*, vol. 57, no. 11, 11 September 1964. 35mm transparency. Collection Museum of New Zealand Te Papa Tongarewa. Gift of Wai-man Lau, 2010.

52 | Brian Brake. *Toshi Satow offering a candle—offerings to the unknown dead, Kyoto, Japan,* 1964. "Japan: The Modern Paradoxes". *Life*, vol. 57, no. 11, 11 September 1964. 35mm transparency. Collection Museum of New Zealand Te Papa Tongarewa. Gift of Wai-man Lau, 2010.

53

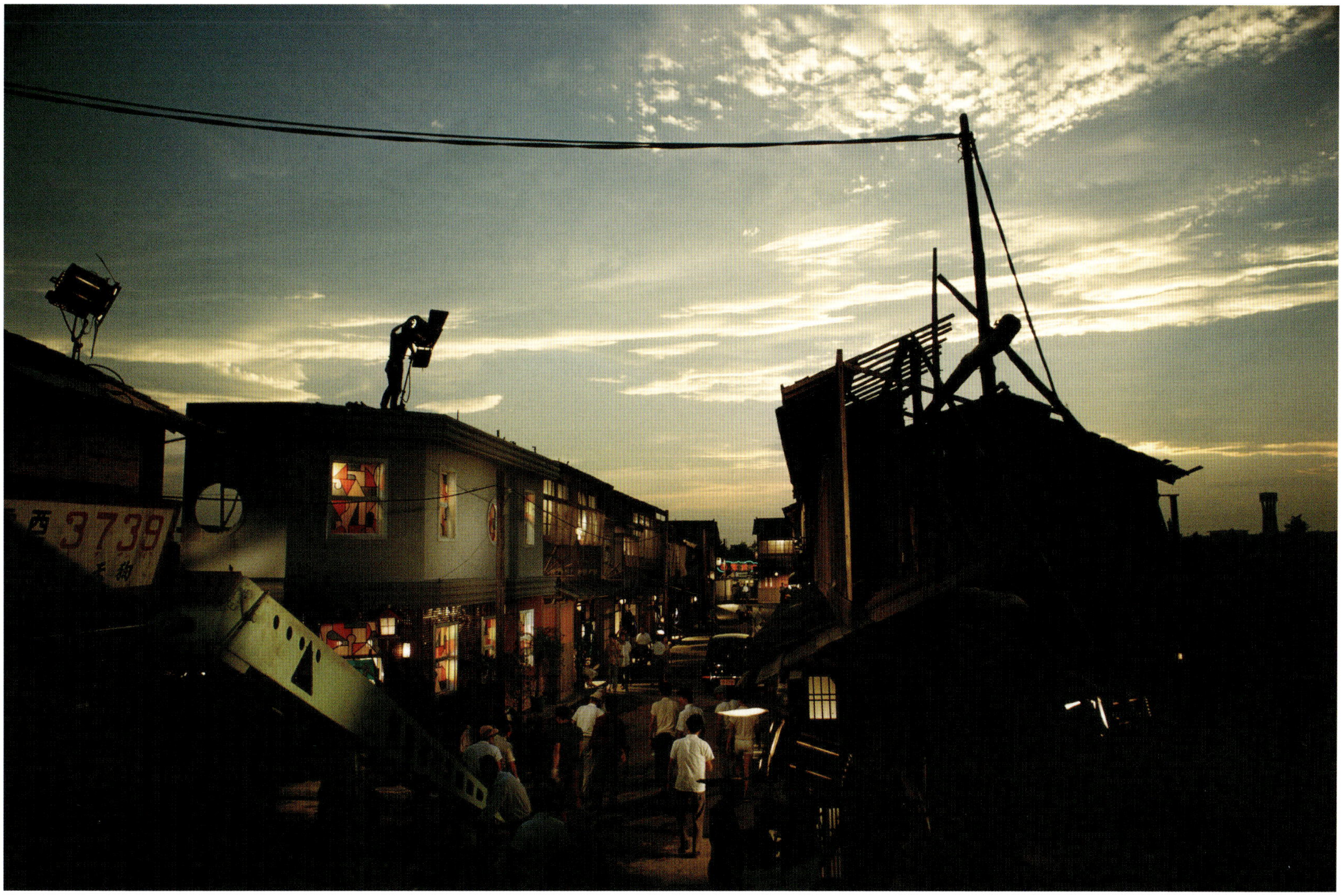

53 | Brian Brake. *Village street built for the film* Gobancho Yugiriro*, directed by Tasaka Katsutaka, Toho Studios, Tokyo, Japan,* 1963. "The Universal Magic of the Movies". *Life*, vol. 55, no. 25, December 1963. 35mm transparency. Collection Museum of New Zealand Te Papa Tongarewa. Gift of Wai-man Lau, 2001.

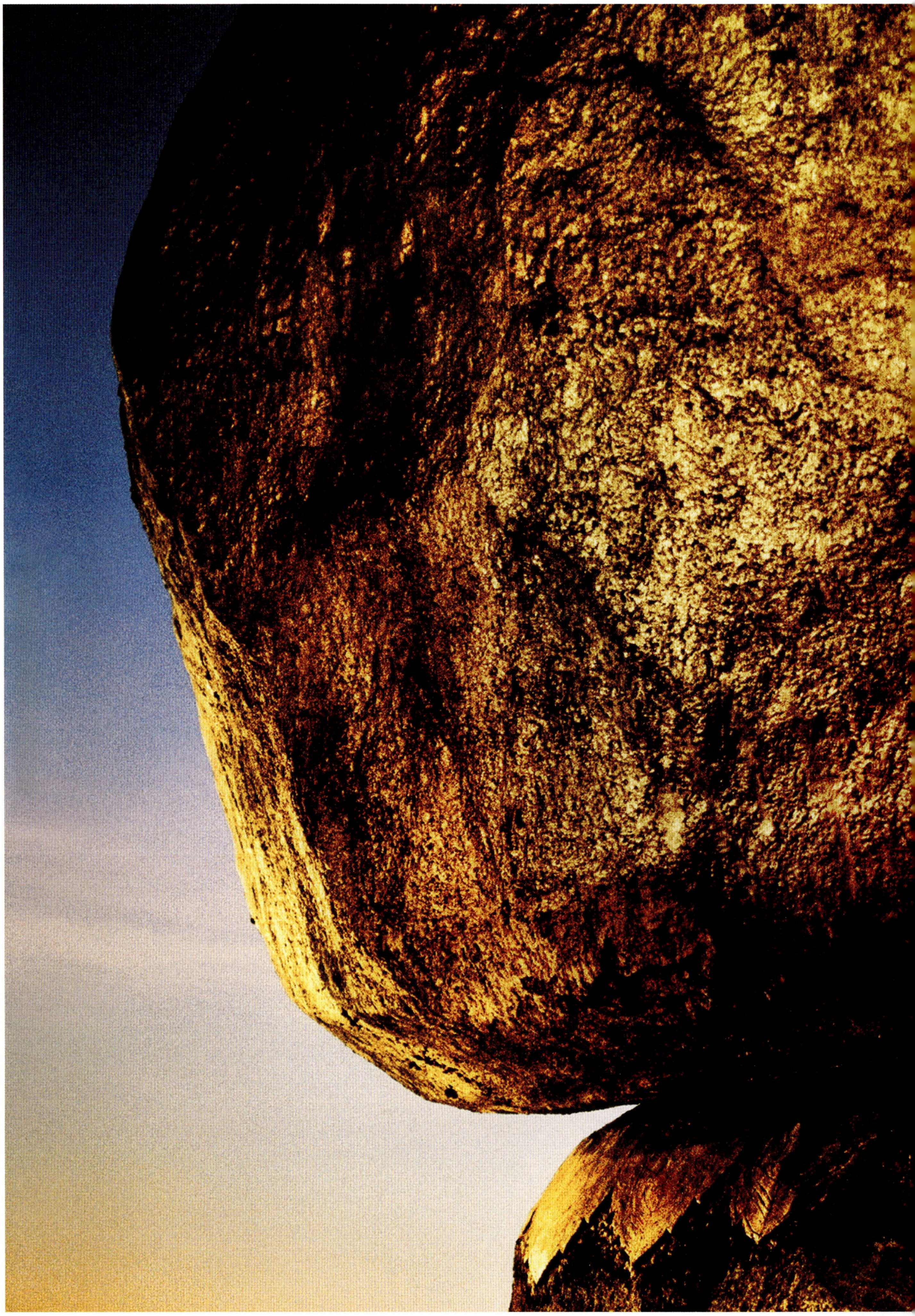

54 | Steve McCurry. *Monks praying at Golden Rock, Kyaiktiyo, Burma/Myanmar*, 1994. “Burma: The Richest of Poor Countries”. *National Geographic,* vol. 188, no. 1, July 1995. © Steve McCurry.

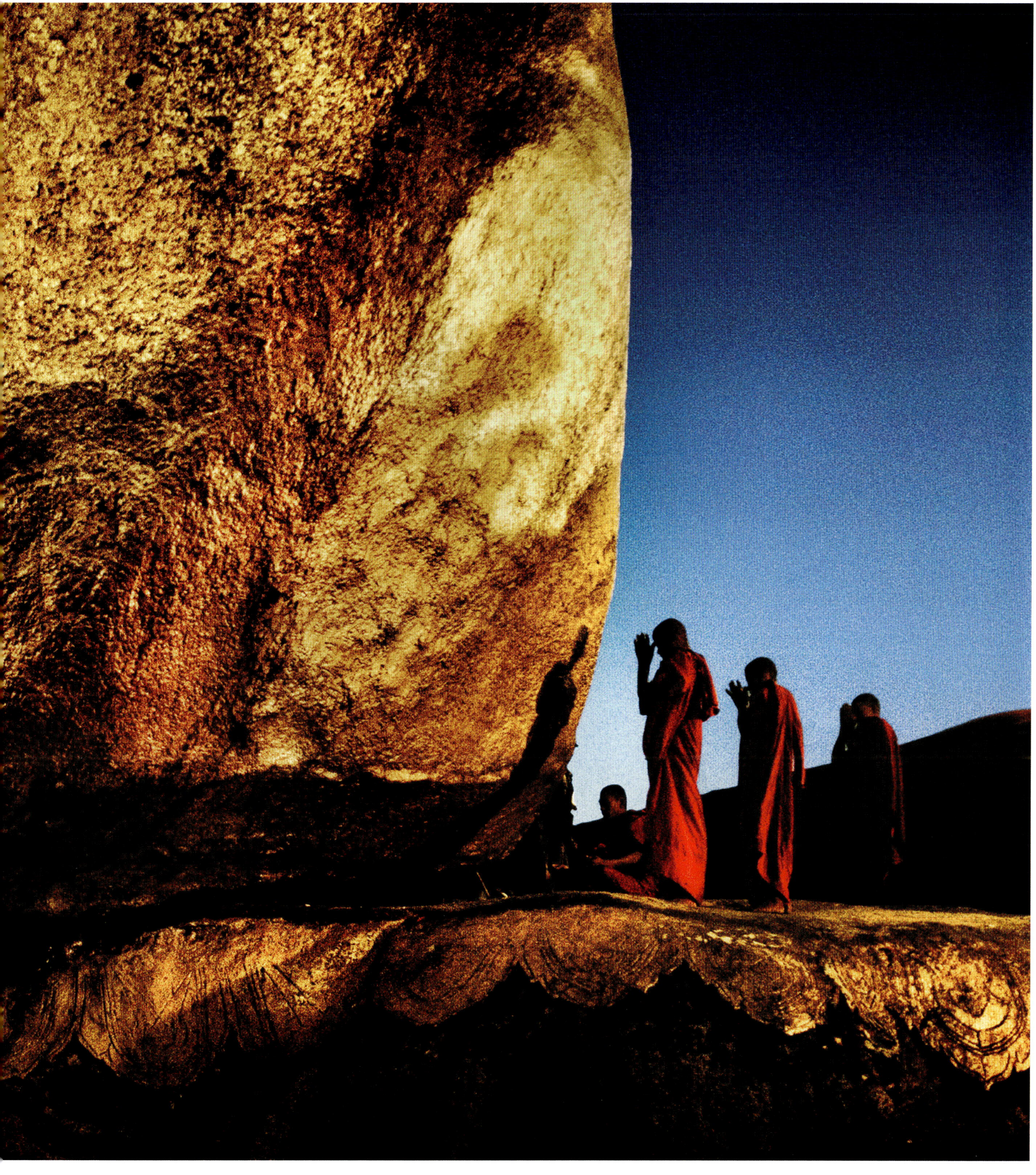

55

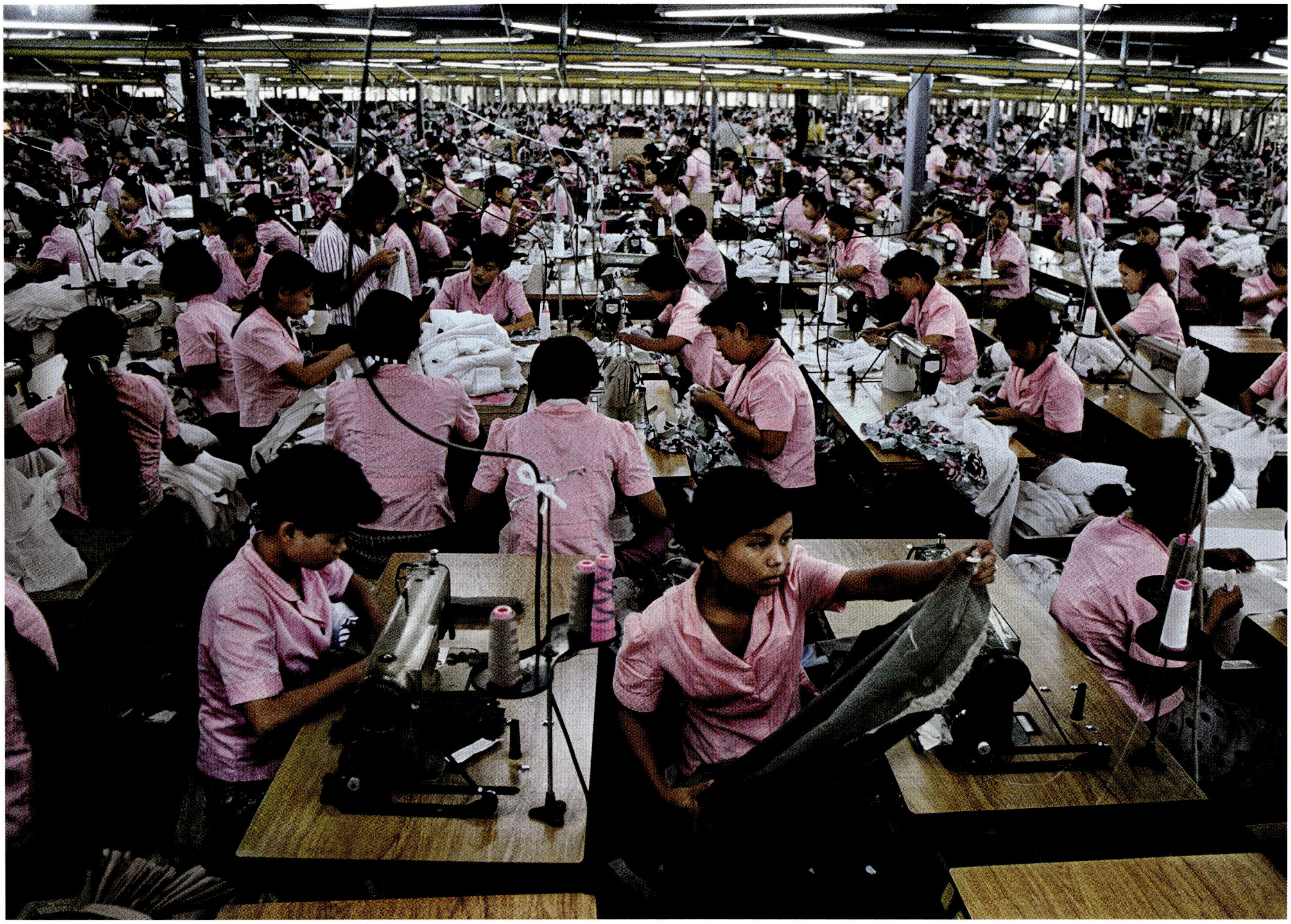

55 I Steve McCurry. *Women in a garment factory, Rangoon, Burma/ Myanmar,* 1994. *The Iconic Photographs.* London & New York: Phaidon Press, 2010. © Steve McCurry.

56

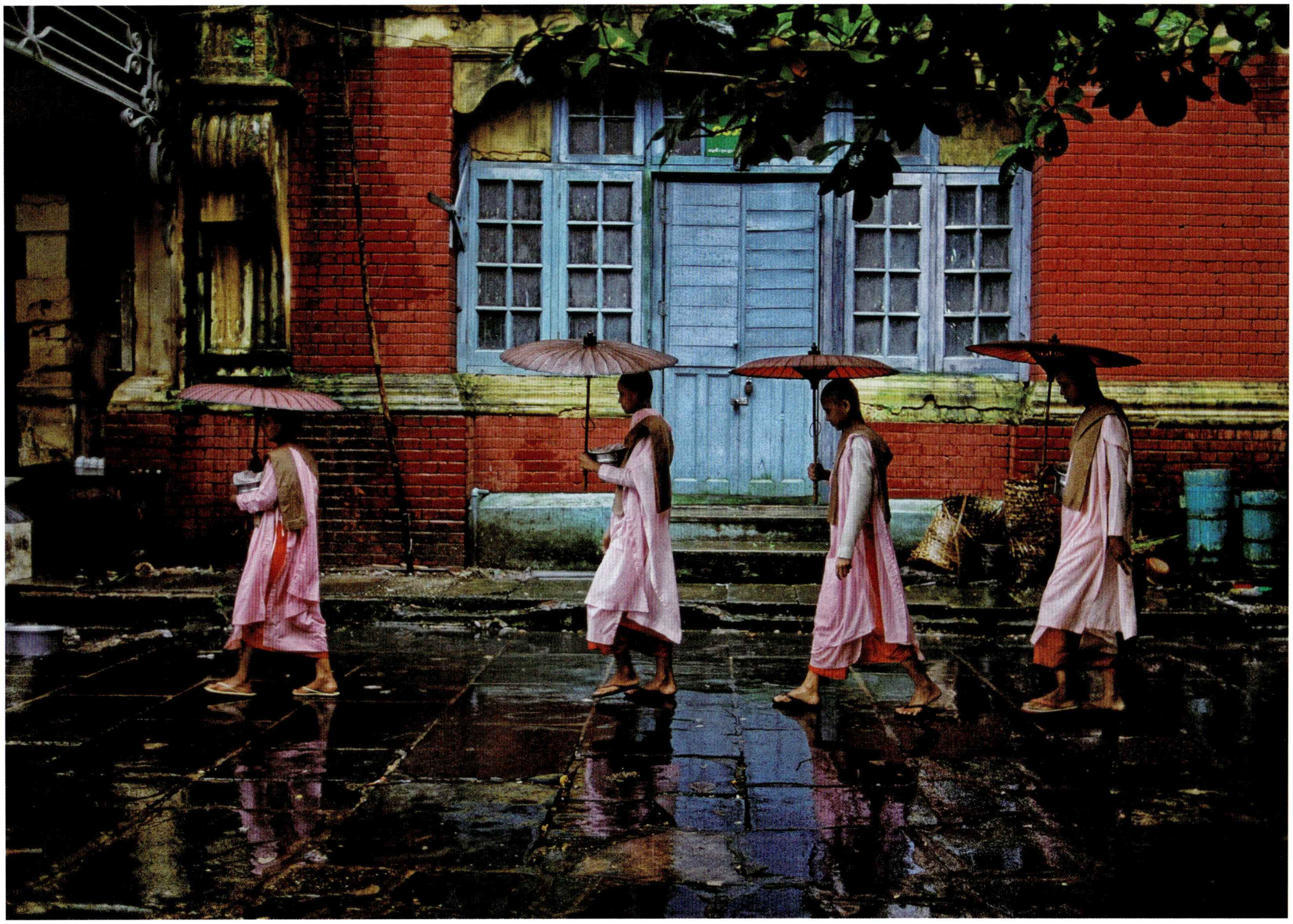

56 | Steve McCurry. *Procession of nuns, Rangoon, Burma/Myanmar,* 1994. "Buddha Rising: Out of the Monastery, Into the Living Room". *National Geographic,* vol. 208, no. 6, December 2005. © Steve McCurry.

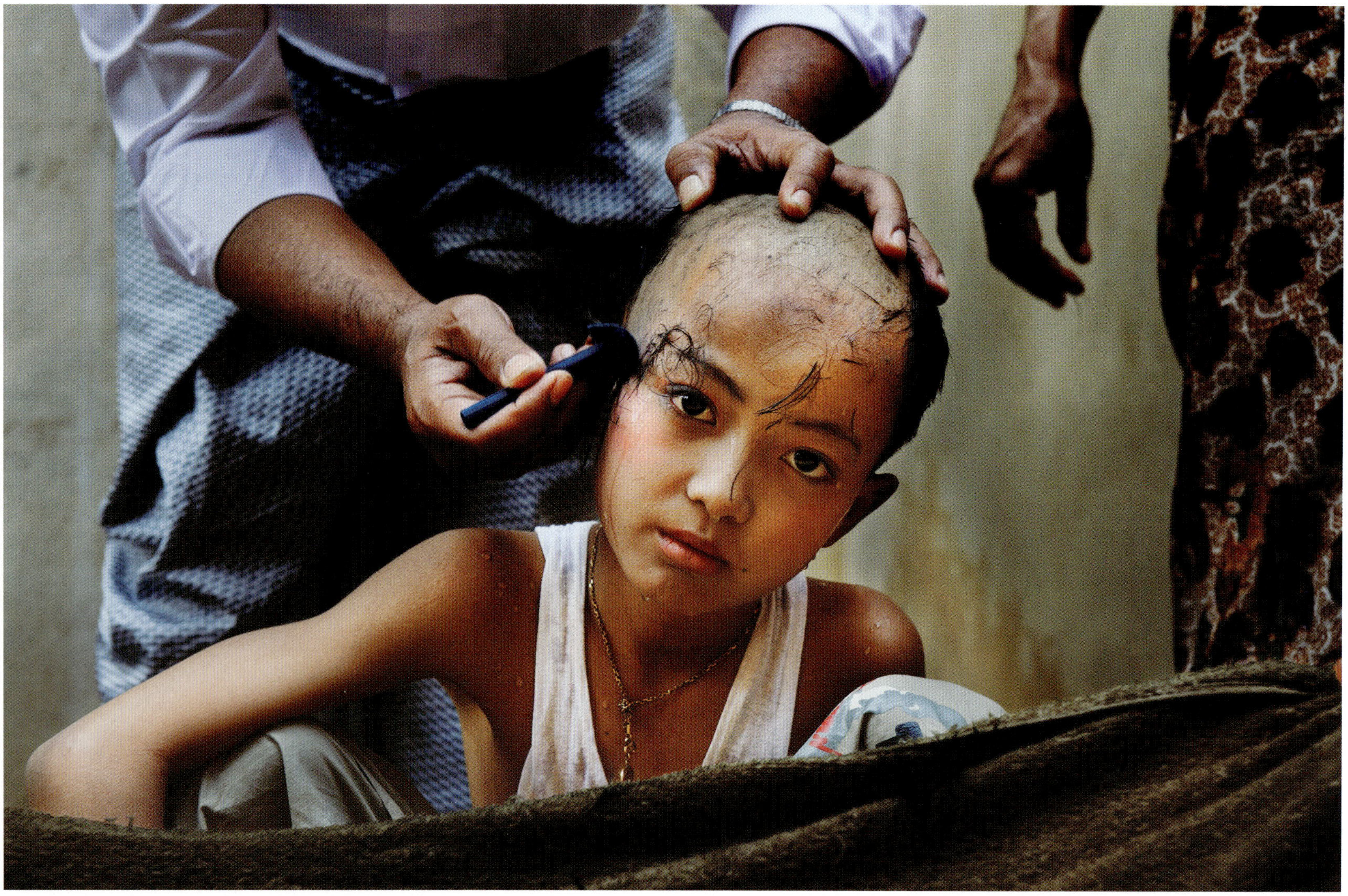

57 | Steve McCurry. *Novice getting his head shaved, Burma/ Myanmar,* 2011. Unpublished. © Steve McCurry.

58

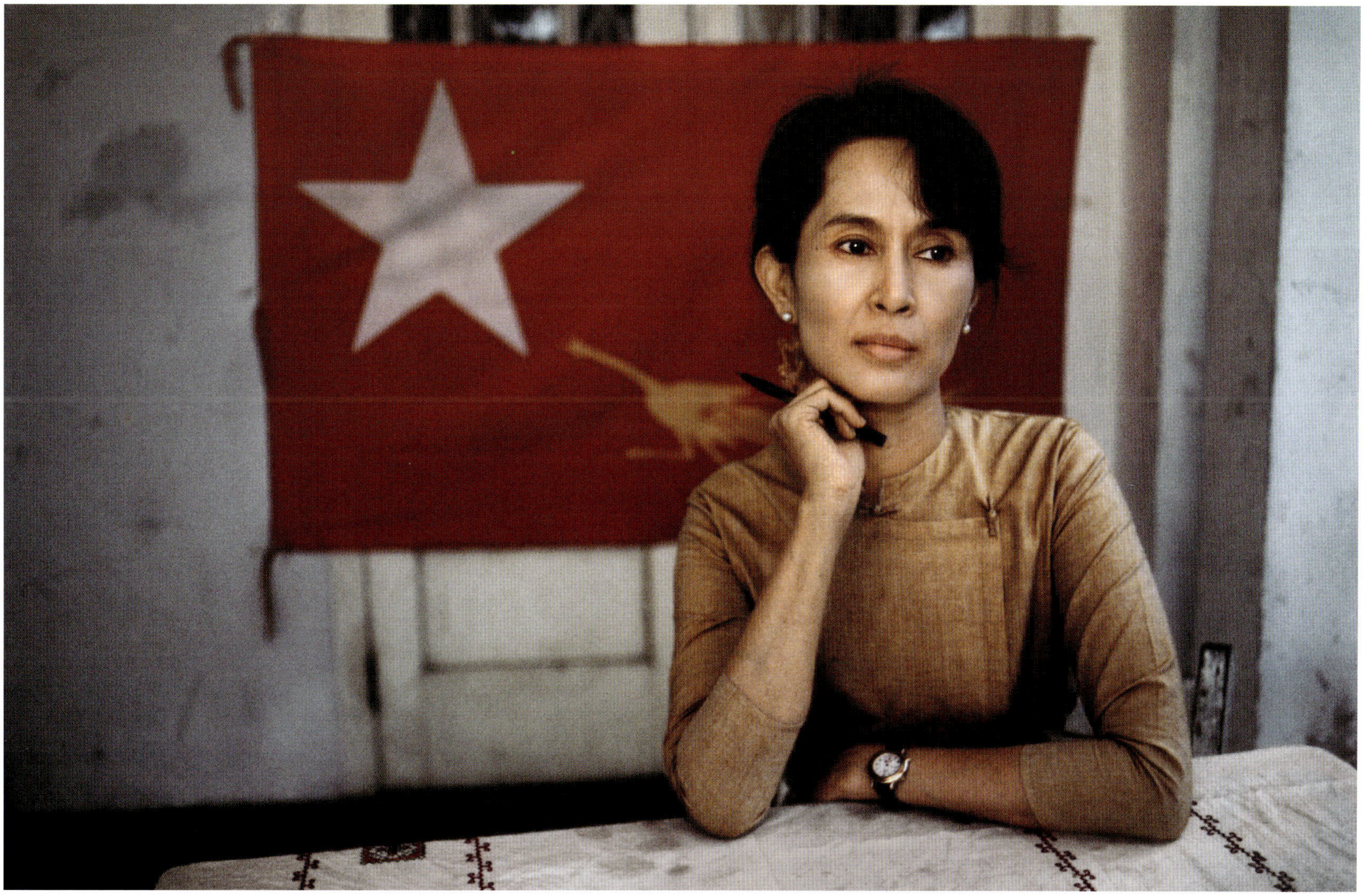

58 | Steve McCurry. *Daw Aung San Suu Kyi, Rangoon, Burma/ Myanmar,* 1995. *The Unguarded Moment*. London & New York: Phaidon Press, 2009. © Steve McCurry.

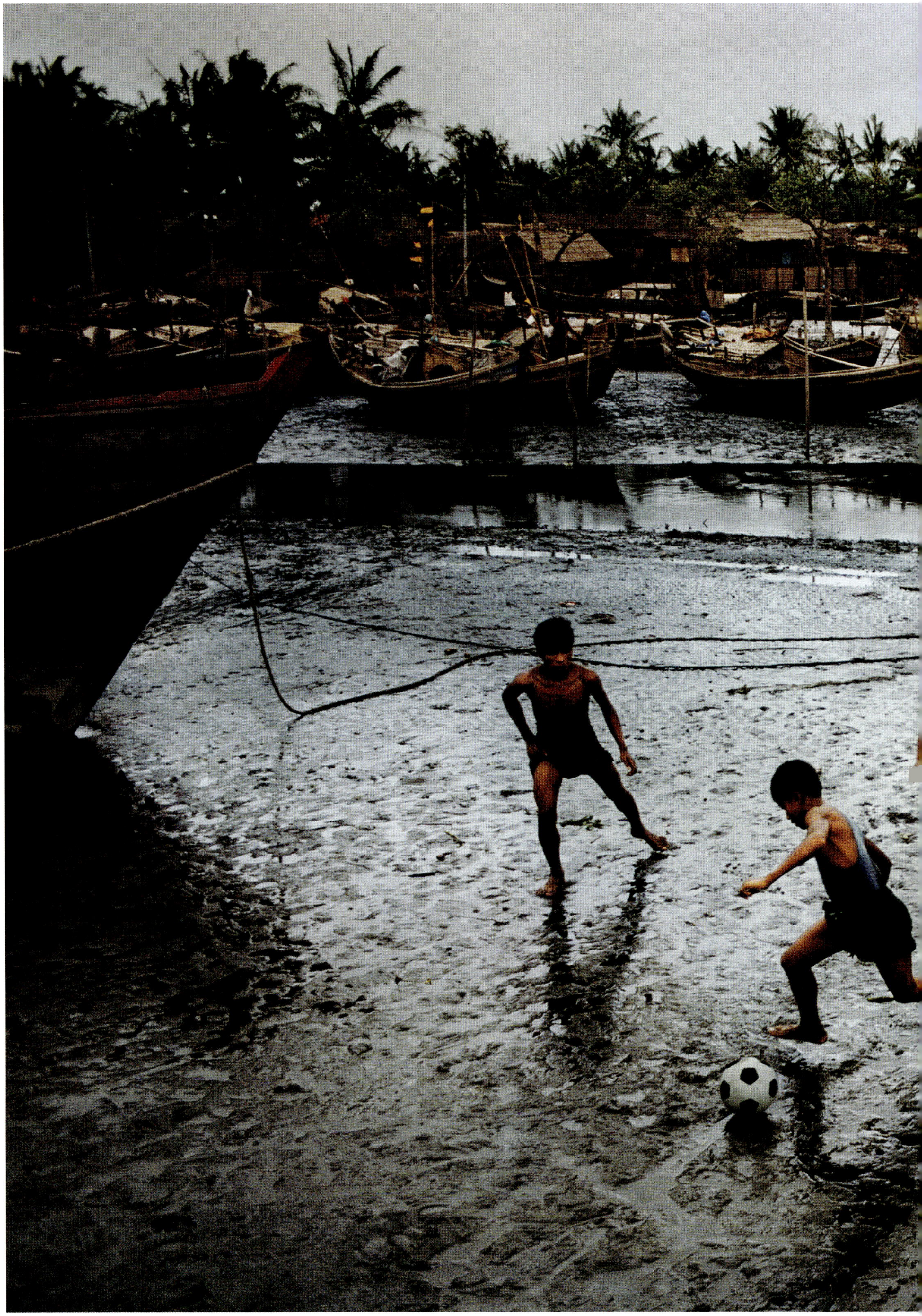

59 | Steve McCurry. *Boys playing football, Sittwe, Burma/ Myanmar,* 1994. *The Iconic Photographs*. London & New York: Phaidon Press, 2010. © Steve McCurry.

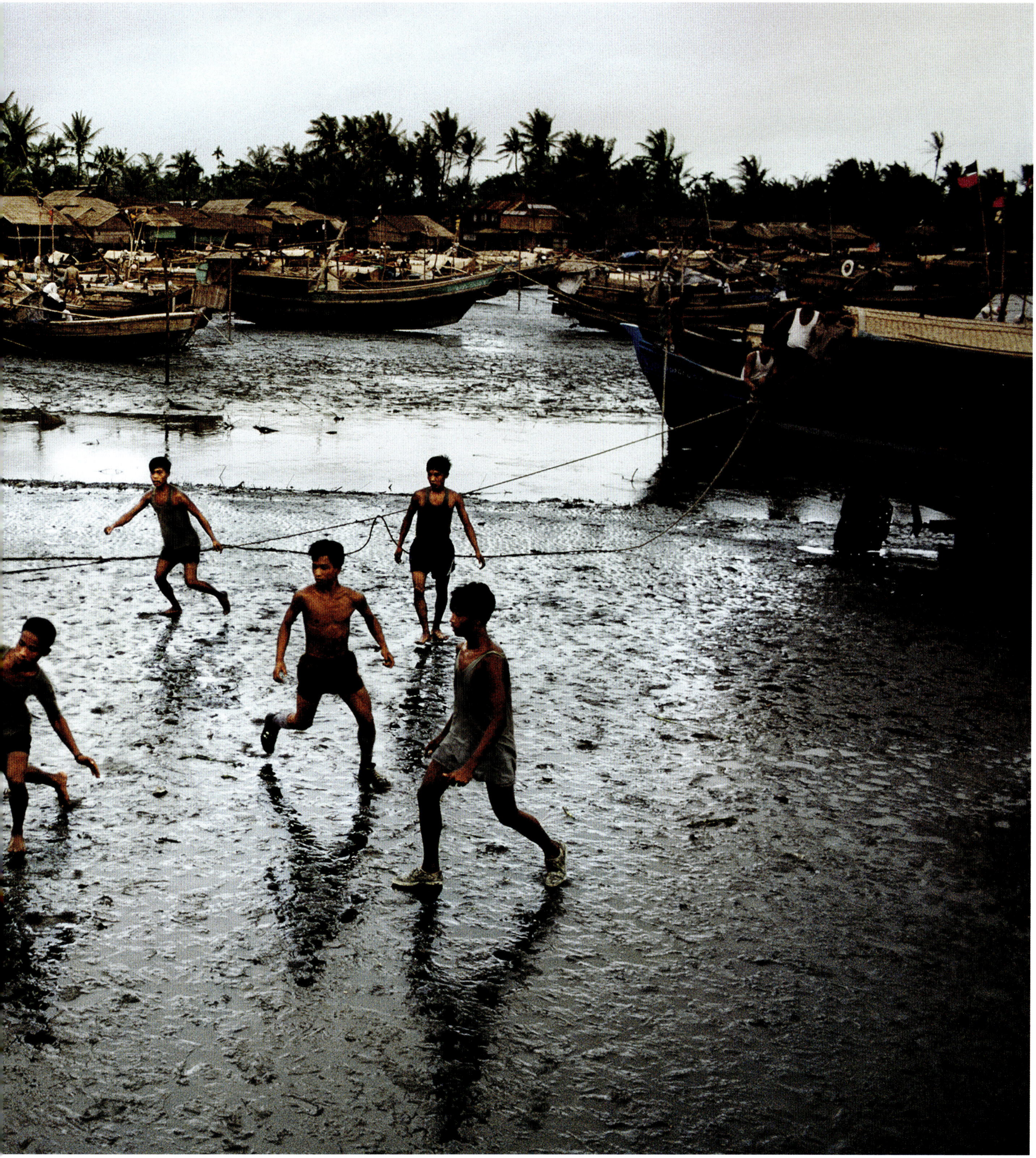

60

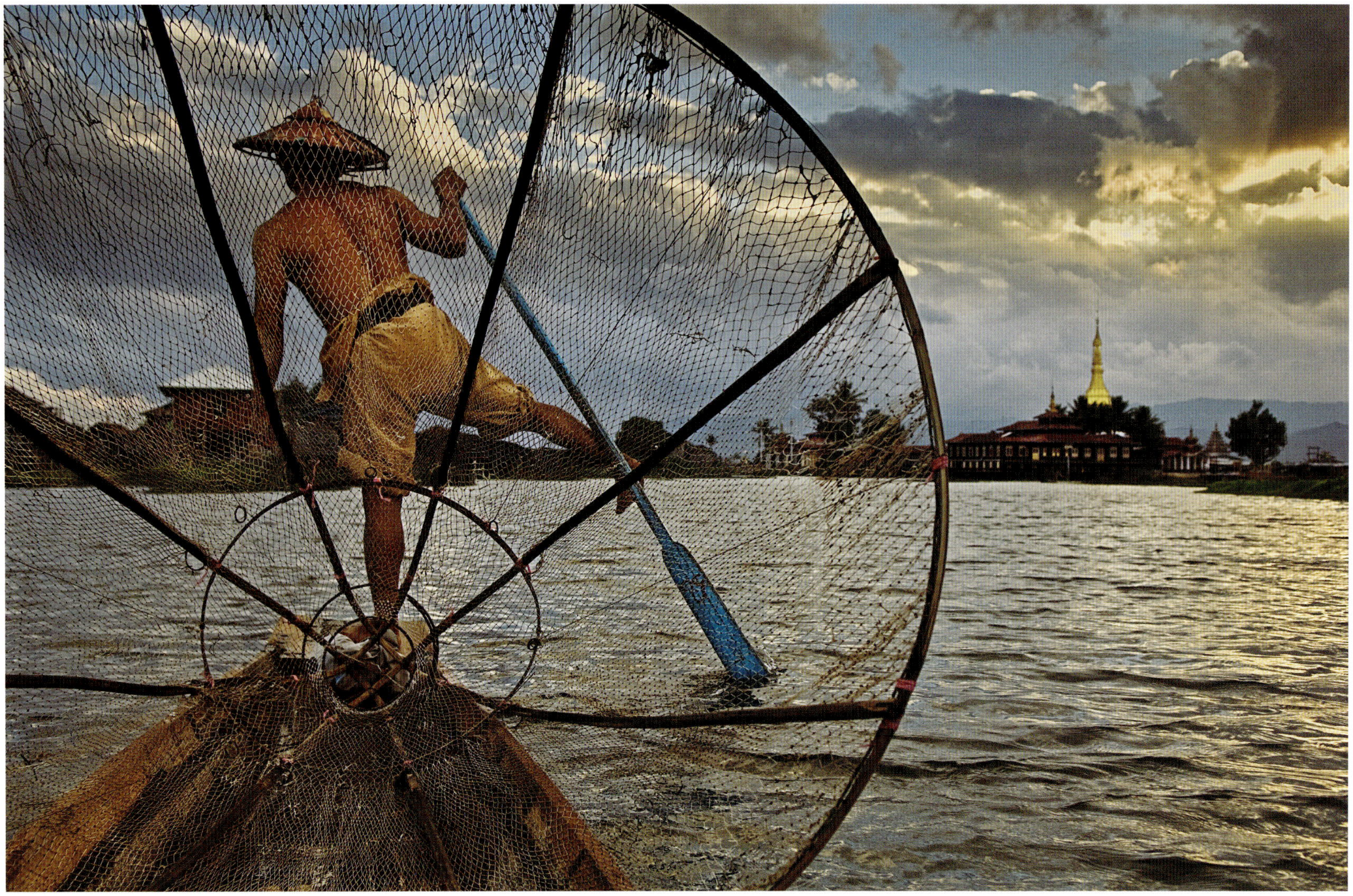

60 | Steve McCurry. *Fisherman on Inle Lake, Burma/Myanmar,* 2008. *The Iconic Photographs*. London & New York: Phaidon Press, 2010. © Steve McCurry.

61

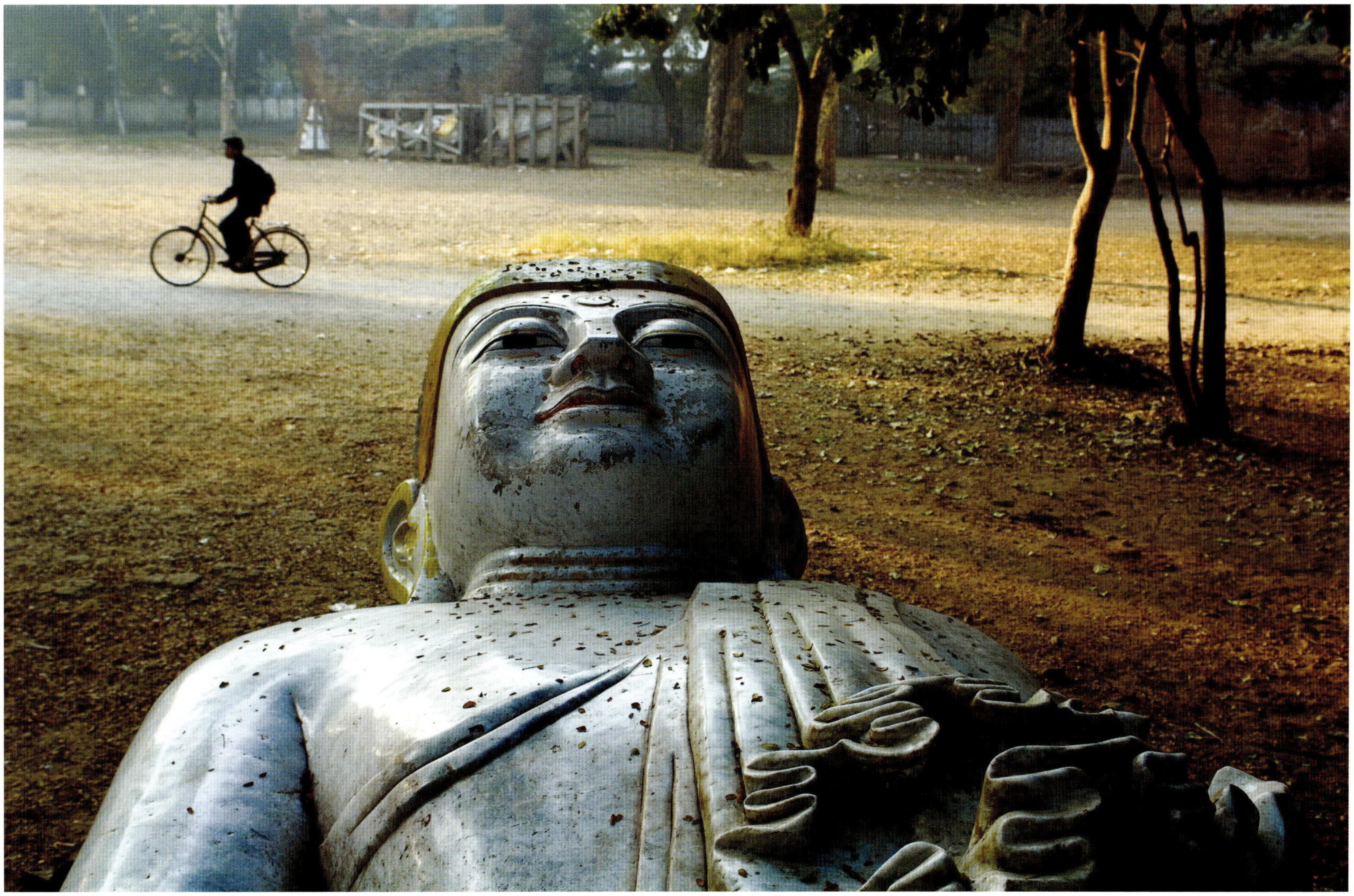

61 | Steve McCurry. *Buddha statue in Mandalay, Burma/Myanmar,* 2008. *The Unguarded Moment*. London & New York: Phaidon Press, 2009. © Steve McCurry.

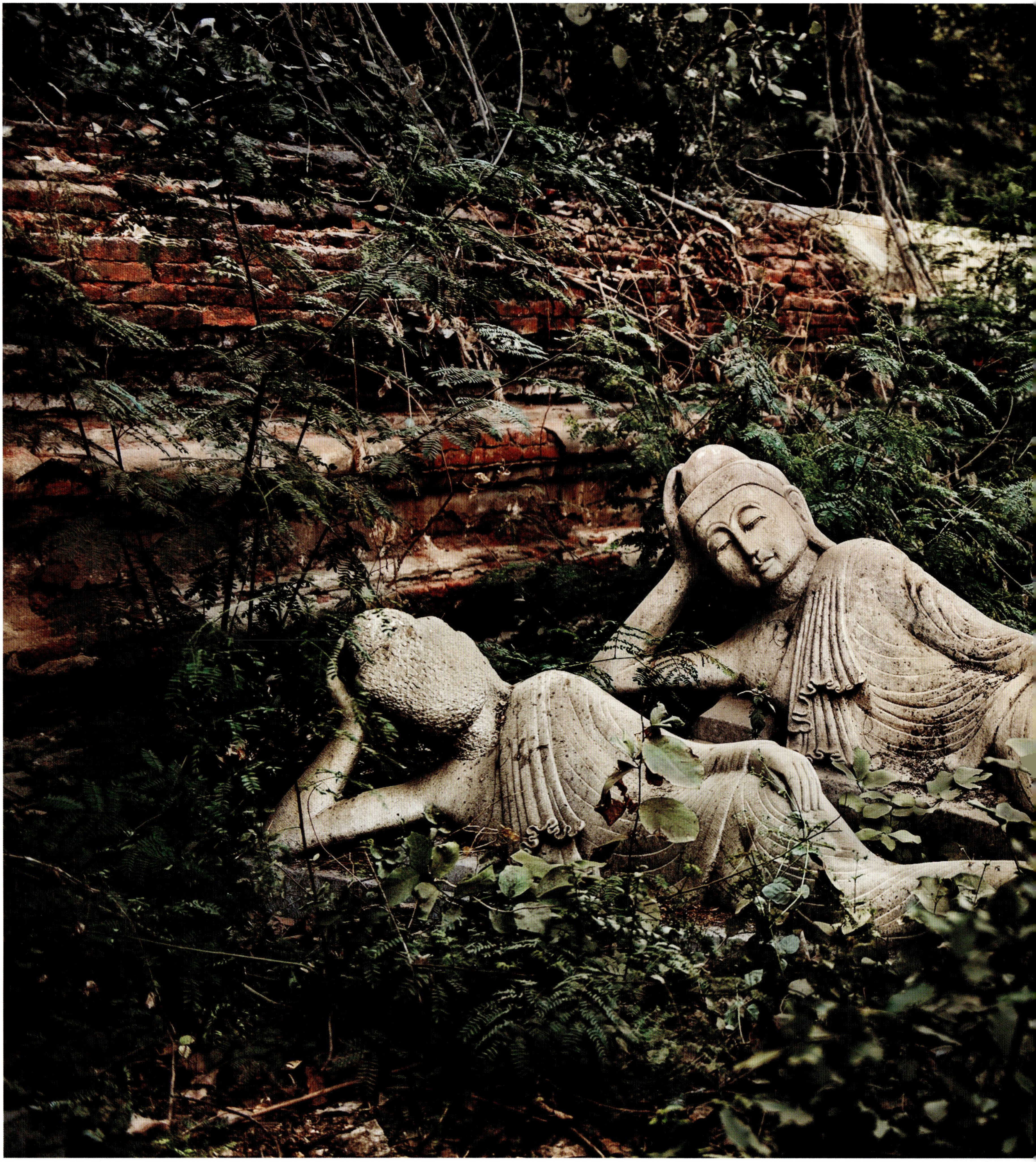

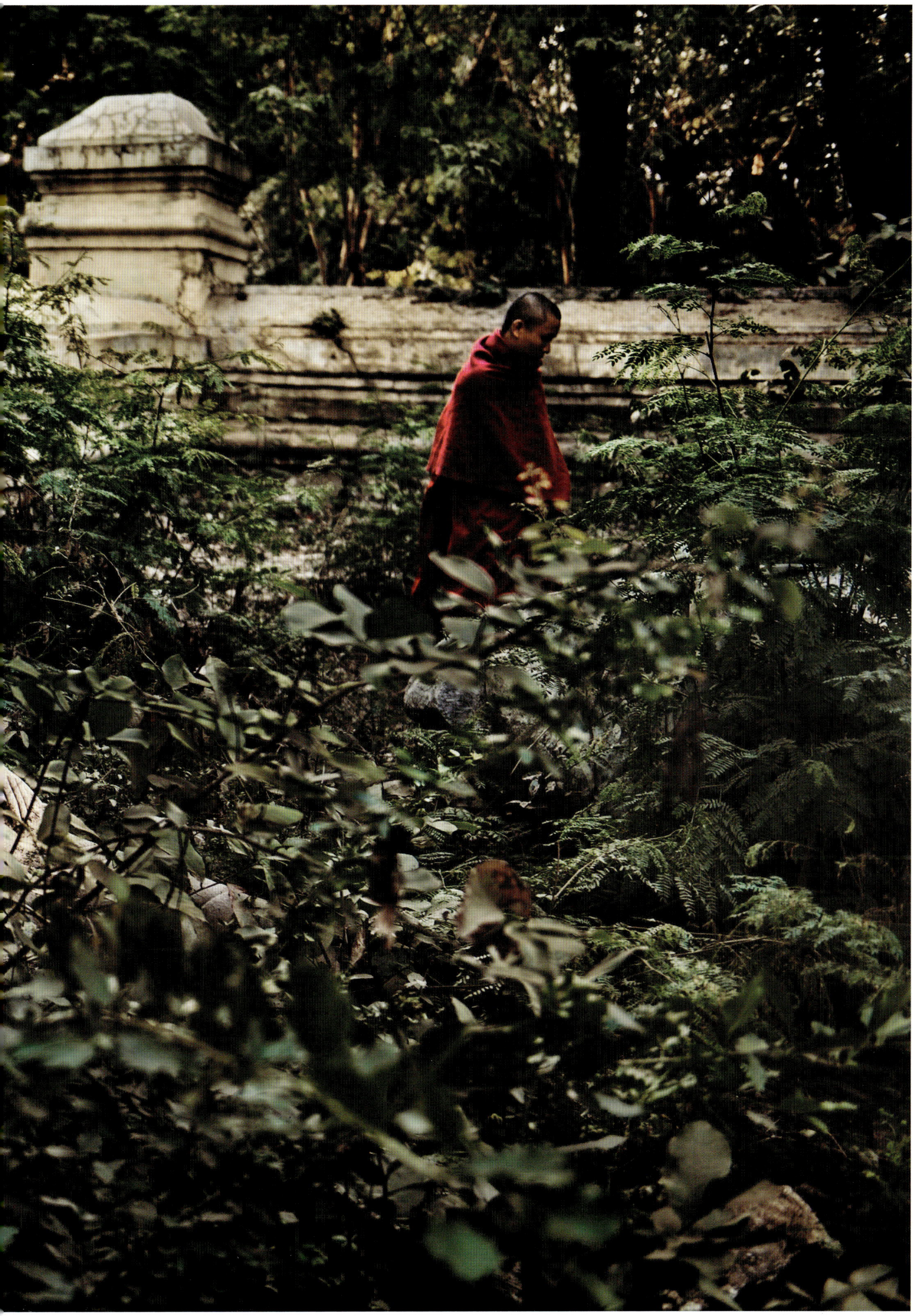

62 | Steve McCurry. *A monk walks past reclining Buddha statues, Schwedagon Pagoda, Rangoon, Burma/Myanmar,* 2010. Unpublished.

SIGNATURE STYLES

Brian Brake and Steve McCurry have both worked extensively in India, Sri Lanka, Indonesia, Thailand, the Philippines and Hong Kong. Brake had a distinct interest in China and Japan. In McCurry's case, his long-term engagement with Afghanistan is crucial, as are his treatments of Burma/Myanmar, and Tibet. In the previous sections, the exhibition focuses on their work in specific territories. In this section, however, a diverse range of locations is included.

McCurry could be speaking for both photographers when he says he wants to show "the human connection between all of us". But each photographer has distinct styles.

The portrait is central to McCurry's practice, and often his human subjects are directly engaged in the process. Nearly a third of the sixty-one photographs in his 2010 publication *Steve McCurry—The Iconic Photographs* involve eye contact with the men, women and children he was photographing. Only seven pictures in that book are without human presence. Other signature aspects of his style include strong primary colors and careful composition, but above all the sense of people's lives, circumstances and relationships.

Brake's work as a cinematographer gave him an eye for edited narratives. Grounded in pictorialism—the aesthetic that sees photography as an expressive, painterly medium—his photographs often welcome muted colors, diffused light and shadow, and the incorporation of patterns and framing devices. His human subjects are often viewed obliquely, in motion, oblivious of the camera. But his commitment to the truths of documentary storytelling is clear.

63

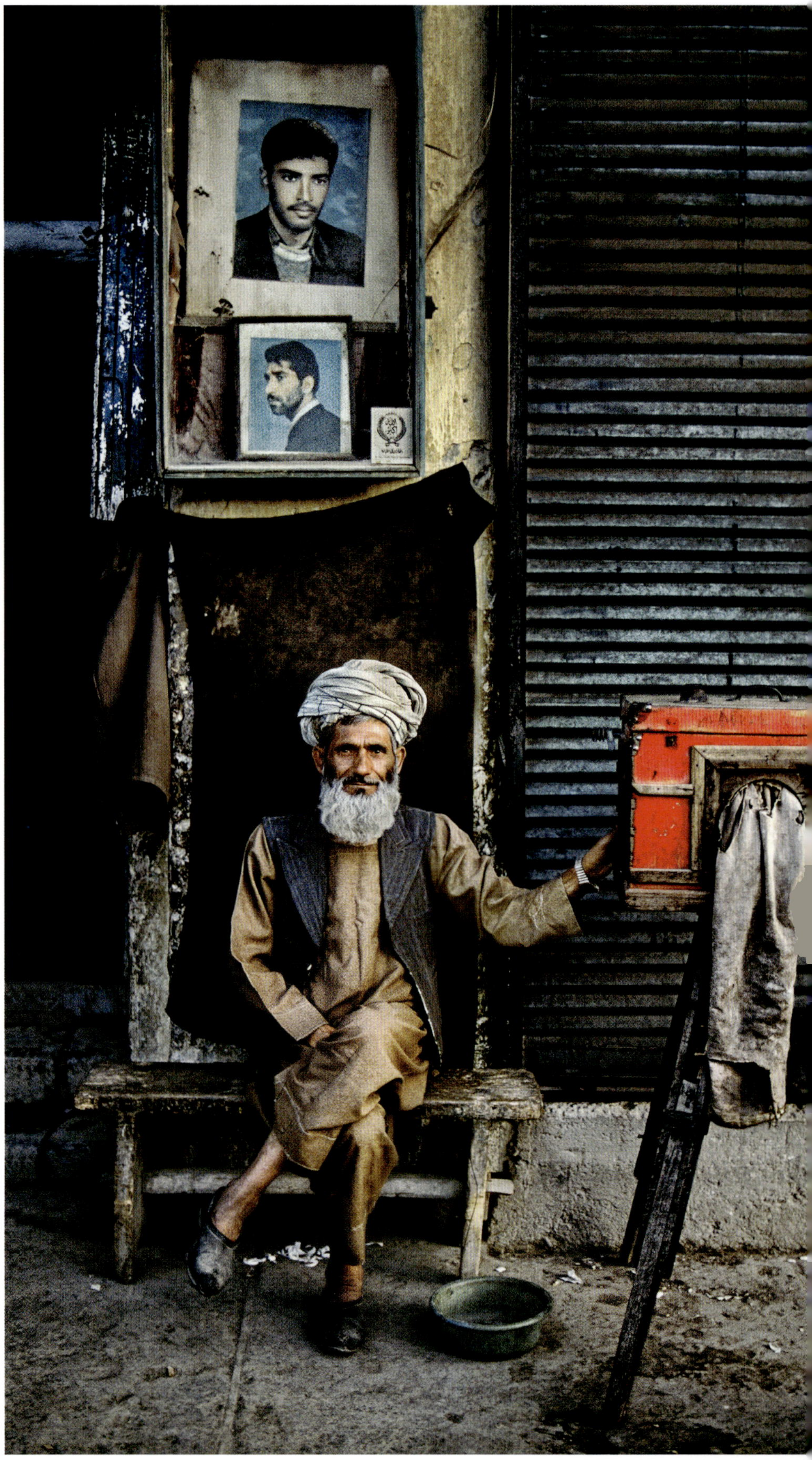

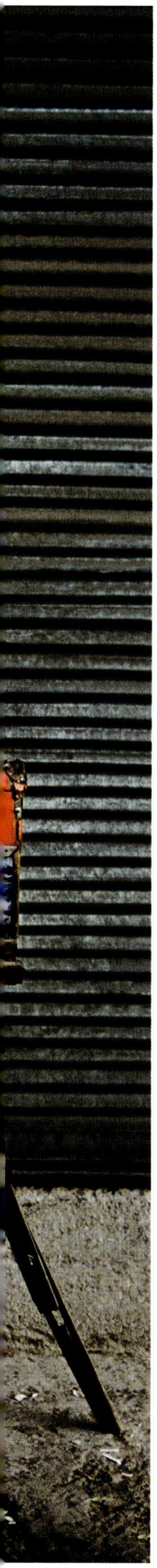

64

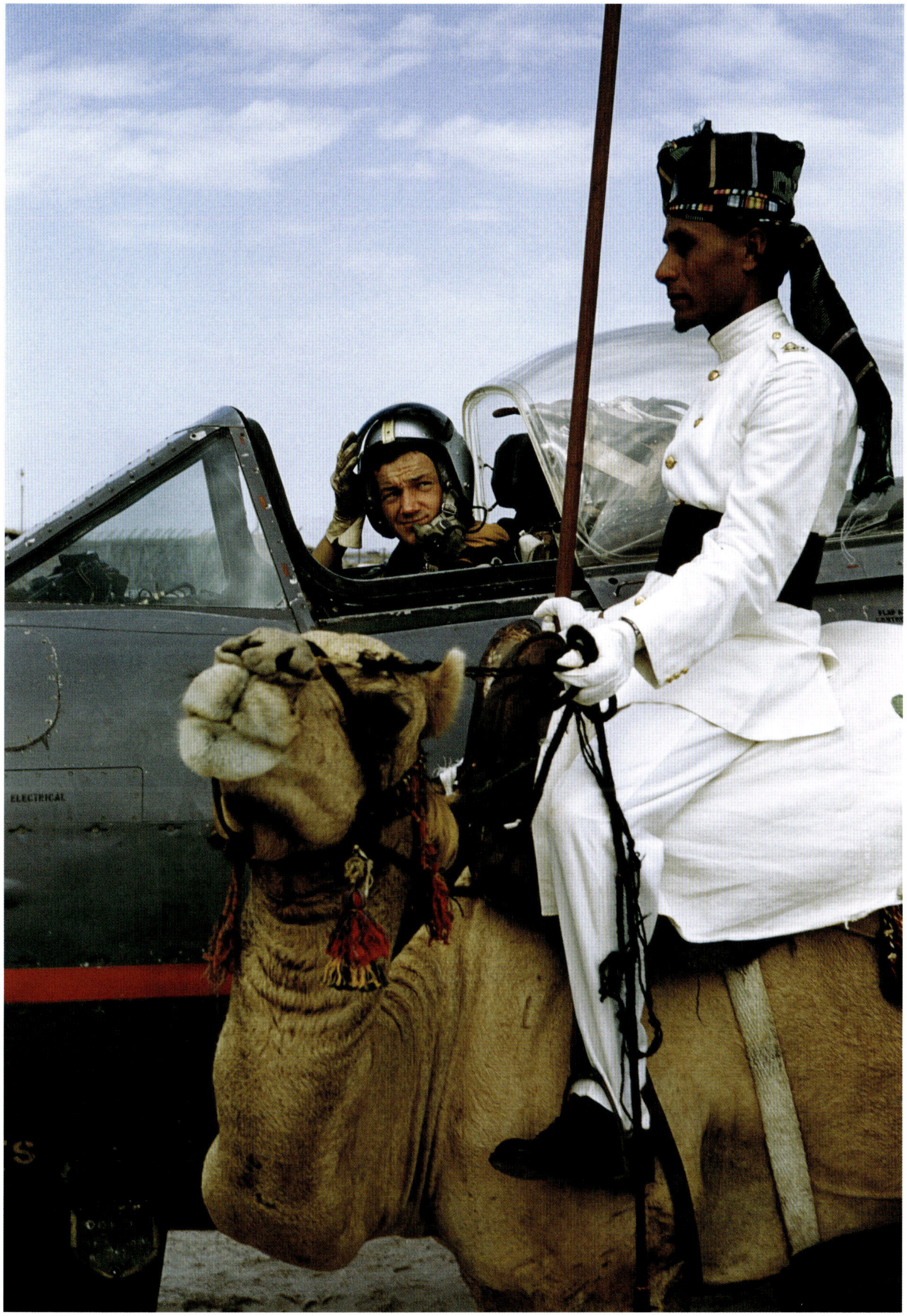

63 | Steve McCurry. *Portrait photographer, Kabul, Afghanistan,* 1992. *In the Shadow of Mountains*. London & New York: Phaidon Press, 2007. © Steve McCurry.

64 | Brian Brake. *Camel rider of the Aden Protectorate Levies beside a jet plane on the RAF airfield, Aden, Yemen,* 1956. "Along the Storied Incense Roads of Aden". *National Geographic,* vol. 111, no. 2, February 1957. 35mm transparency. Collection Museum of New Zealand Te Papa Tongarewa. Gift of Wai-man Lau, 2001.

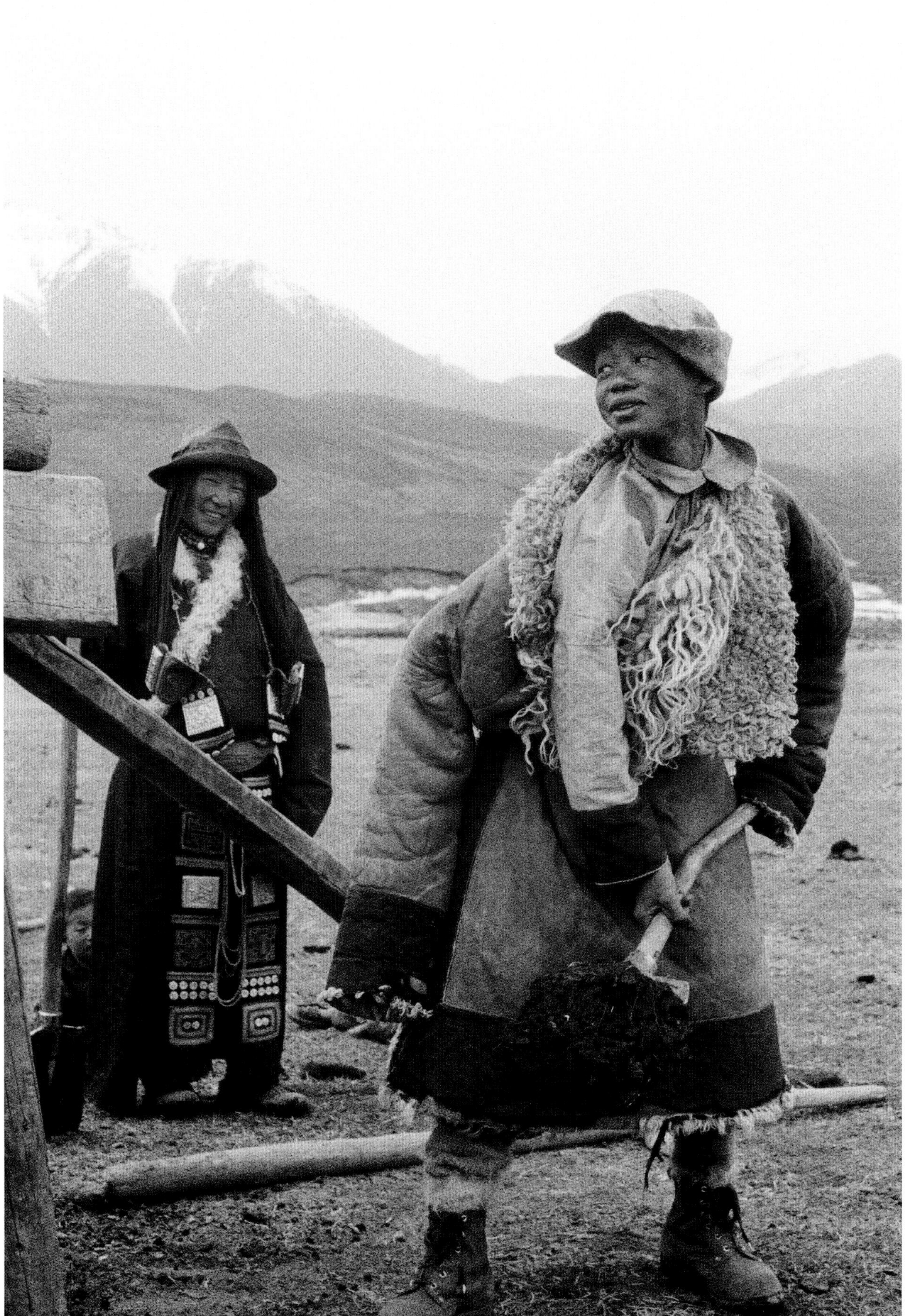

65 | Brian Brake. *Tibetan couple building a wall, Qinghai province, China,* 1957. *Brian Brake: China, the 1950s.* Wellington: Museum of New Zealand Te Papa Tongarewa, 1995. Reproduced from a 35mm black and white negative. Collection Museum of New Zealand Te Papa Tongarewa. Gift of Wai-man Lau, 2001.

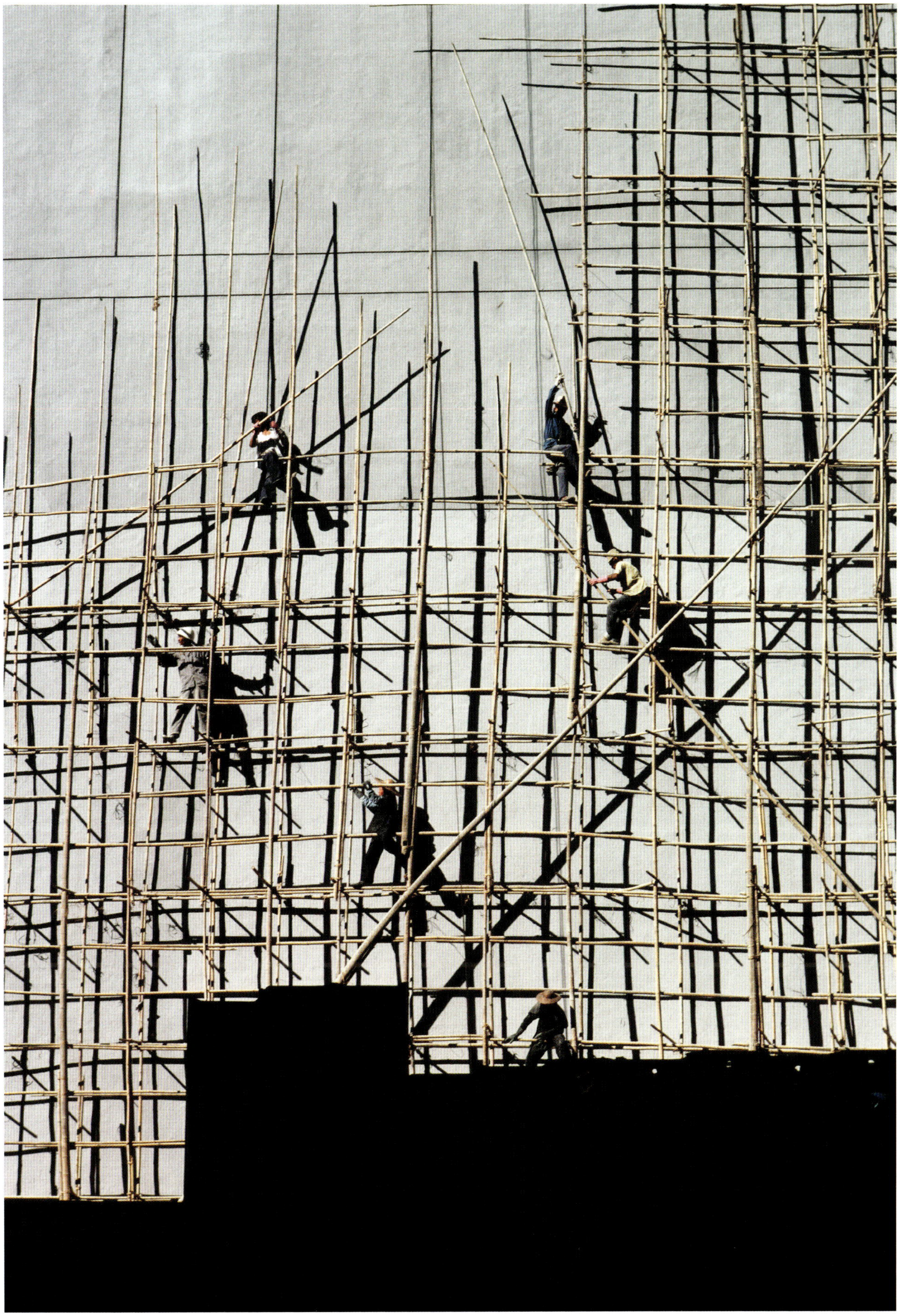

66 | Brian Brake. *Scaffolding, Hong Kong, China*, c.1976. Unpublished. 35mm transparency. Collection Museum of New Zealand Te Papa Tongarewa. Gift of Wai-man Lau, 2001.

67

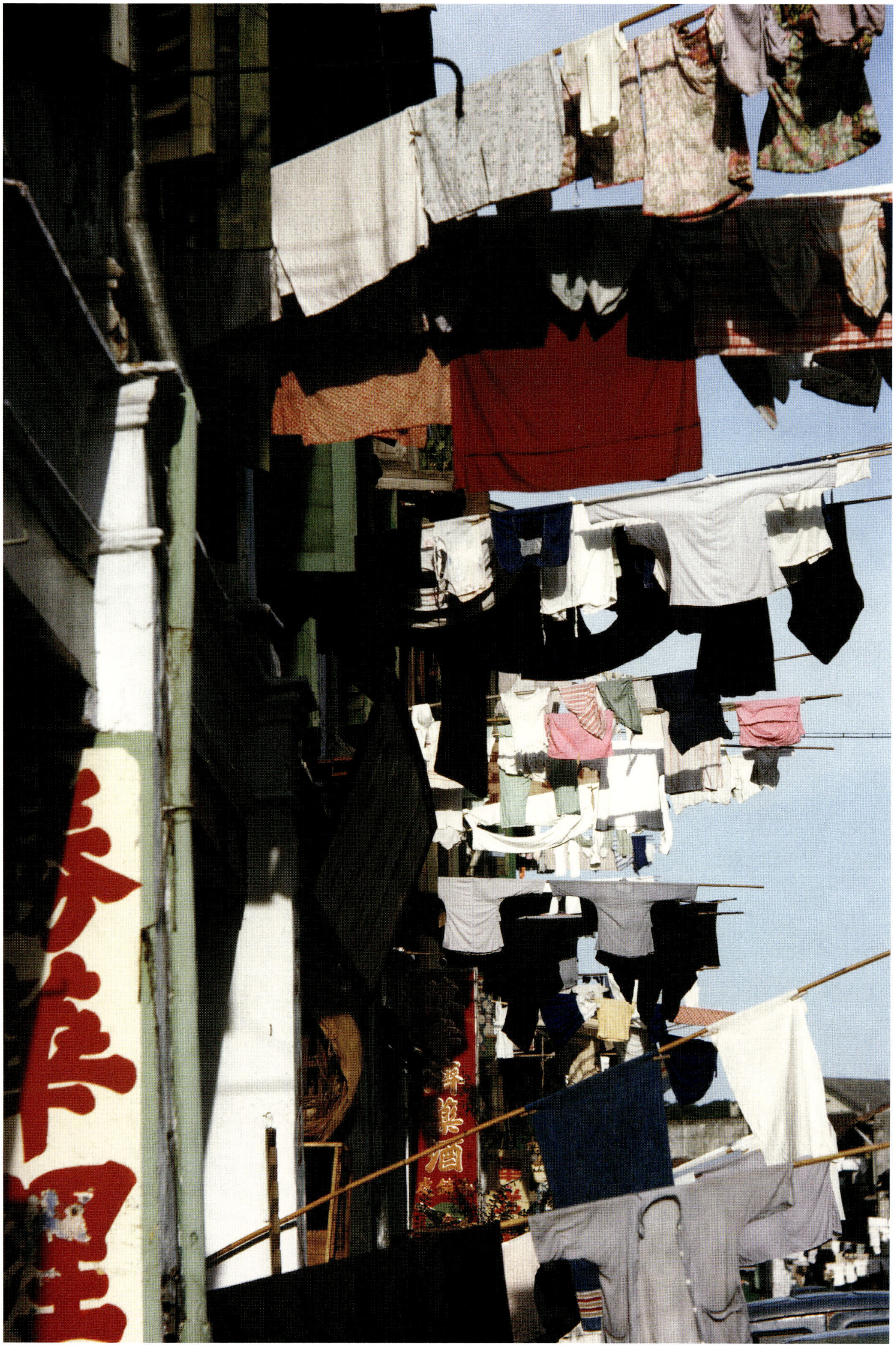

68

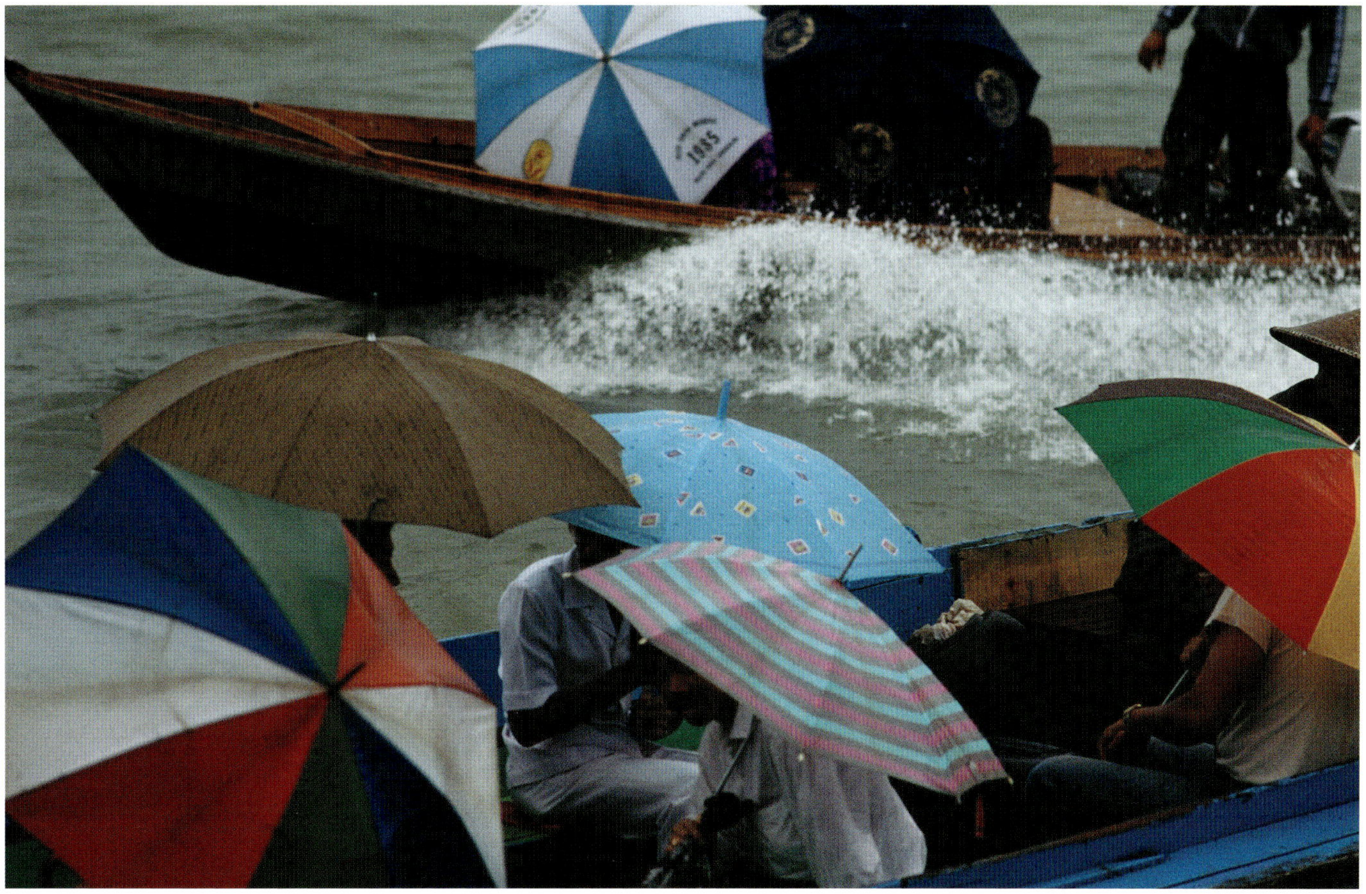

69

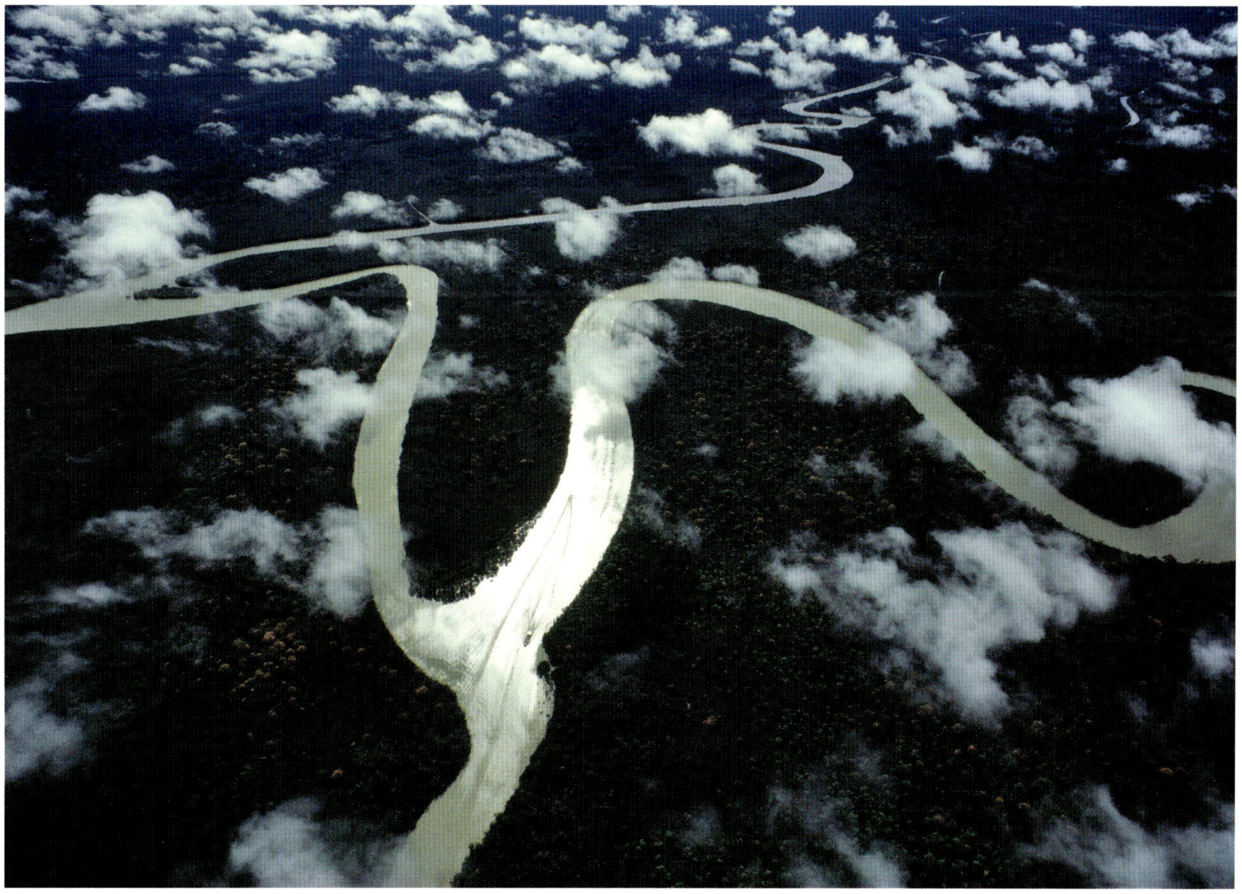

67 I Brian Brake. *Washing drying above street, Singapore,* 1963. Unpublished. 35mm transparency. Collection Museum of New Zealand Te Papa Tongarewa. Gift of Wai-man Lau, 2010.

68 I Brian Brake. *Riverboats with umbrellas, Brunei,* 1987. *Brunei Darussalam: Facts and Figures* 1987. 35mm transparency. Collection Museum of New Zealand Te Papa Tongarewa. Gift of Wai-man Lau, 2001.

69 I Brian Brake. *River, Brunei,* 1987. *Brunei Darussalam: Facts and Figures 1987.* 35mm transparency. Collection Museum of New Zealand Te Papa Tongarewa. Gift of Wai-man Lau, 2001.

70

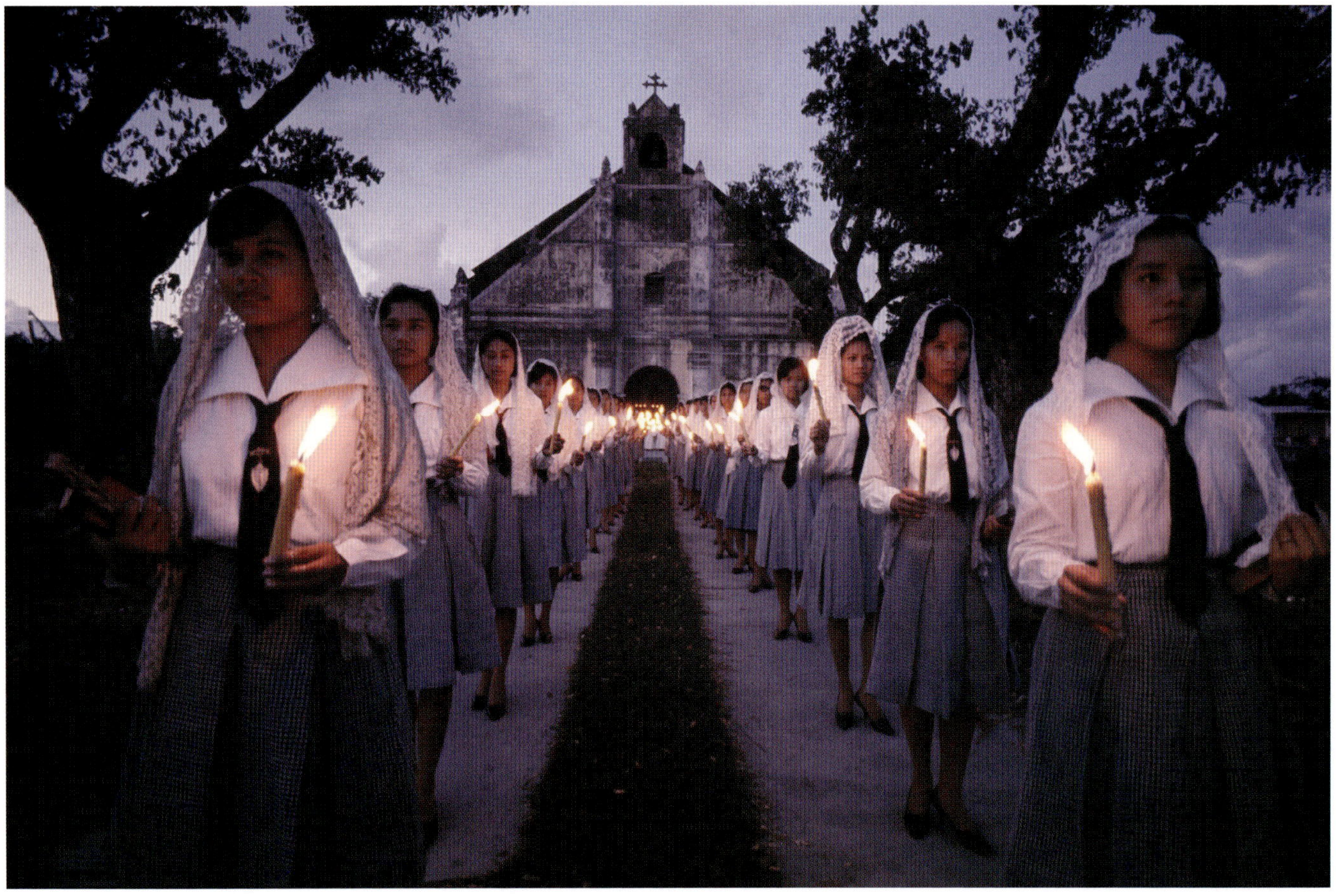

71

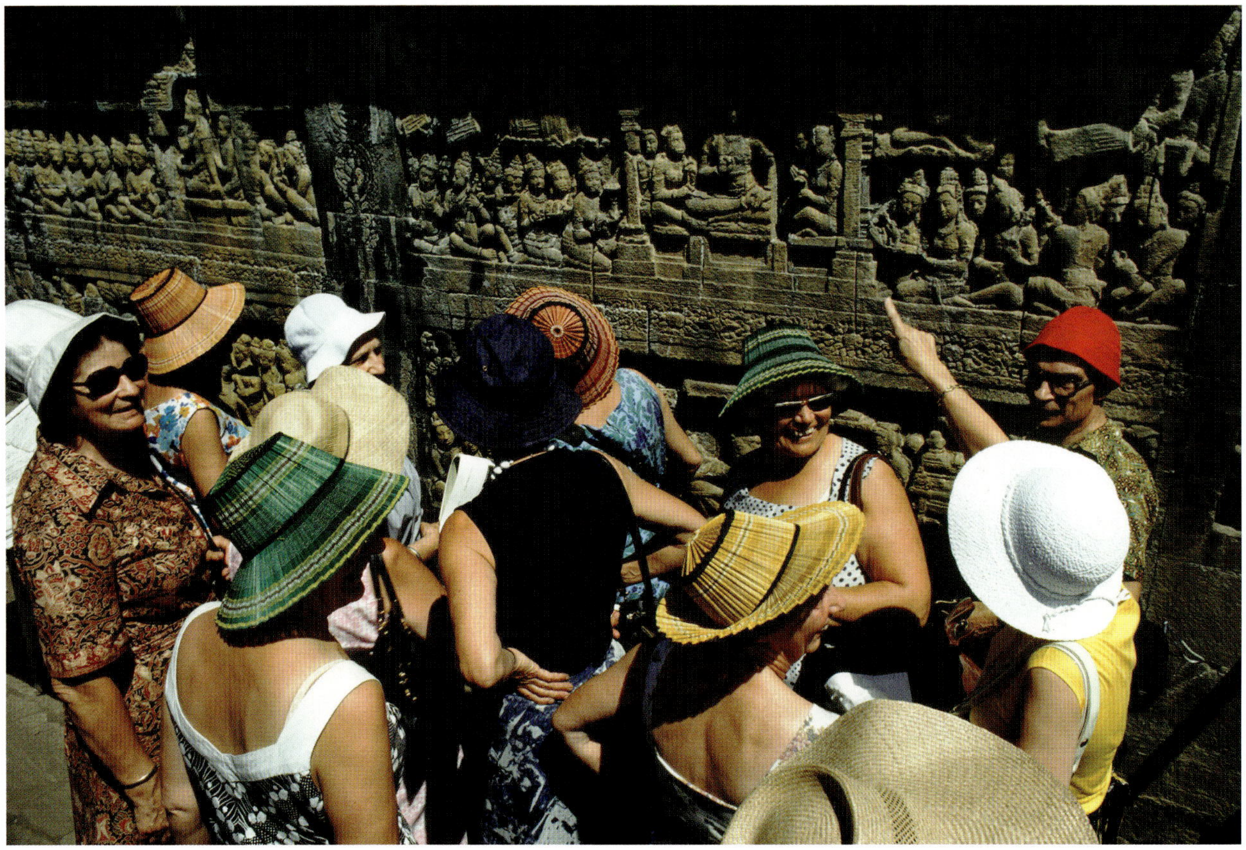

70 | Brian Brake. *Catholic church, Vihan, Northwest Luzon, Philippines,* 1965. "Brian Brake's Best of Asia". *Insight (American Express),* February/March 1984. 35mm transparency. Collection Museum of New Zealand Te Papa Tongarewa. Gift of Wai-man Lau, 2001.

71 | *Brian Brake. Tourists at the temples of Borobudur, Indonesia,* 1971. "The Cosmic Mountain: Borobudur". *India Magazine,* vol. 3, no.1, December 1982. 35mm transparency. Collection Museum of New Zealand Te Papa Tongarewa. Gift of Wai-man Lau, 2001.

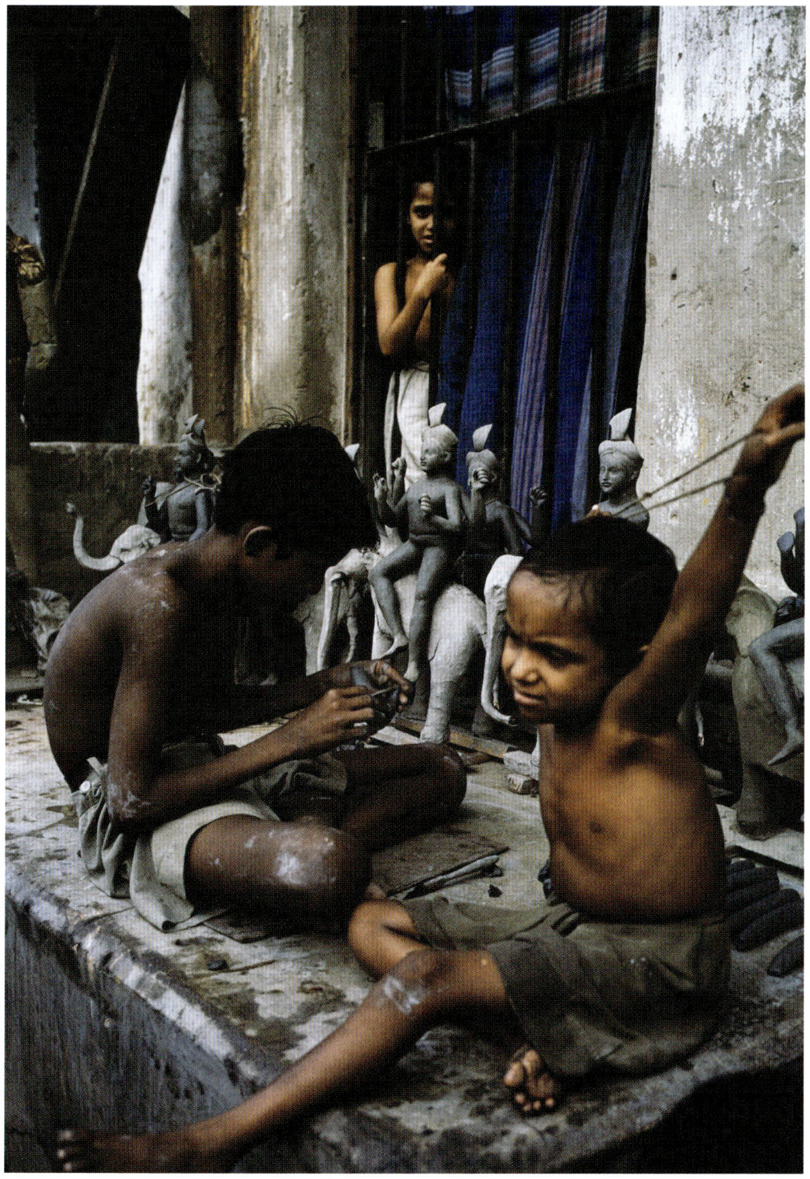

72 | Brian Brake. *Statuette maker and children, India.* From the series: India, 1960s. Unpublished. 35mm transparency. Collection Museum of New Zealand Te Papa Tongarewa. Gift of Wai-man Lau, 2001.

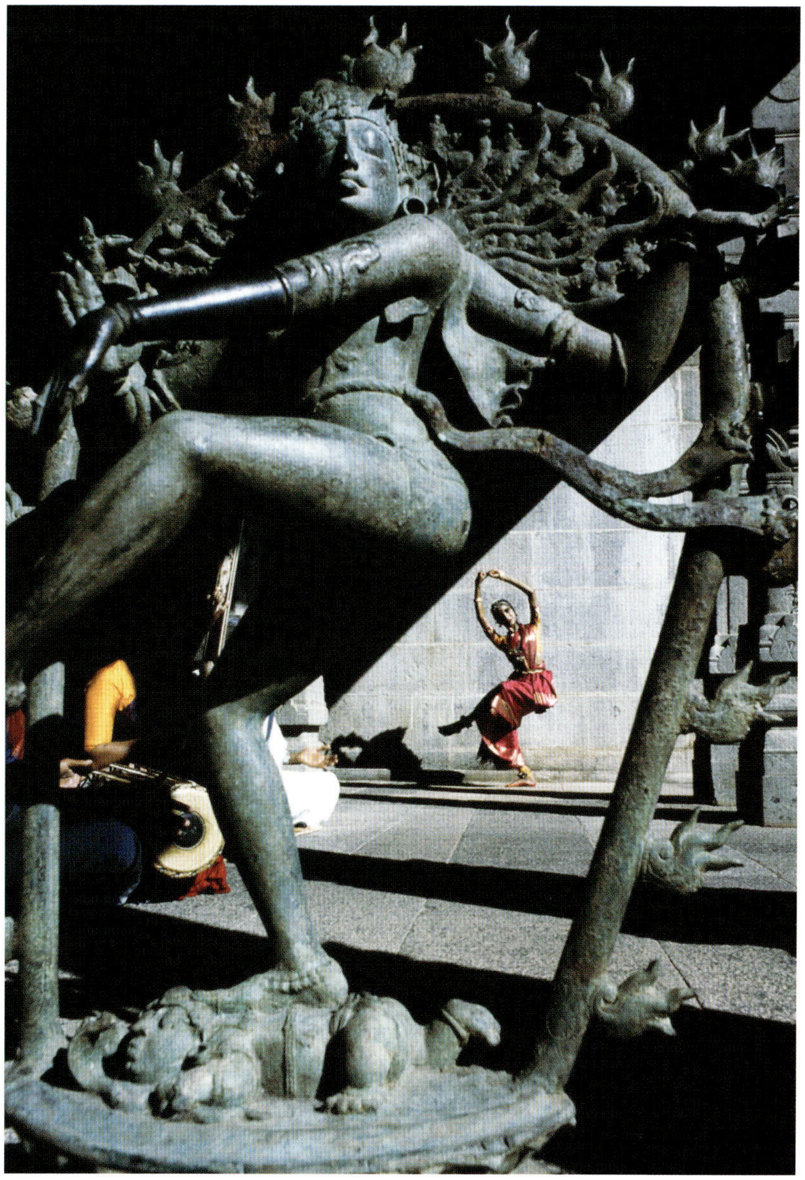

73 | Brian Brake. *Dancer performing in the Bharata Natyam style, India*. From the series: Monsoon, 1960. Unpublished. 35mm transparency. Collection Museum of New Zealand Te Papa Tongarewa. Gift of Wai-man Lau, 2001.

74 I Brian Brake. *Ruins of the ancient city of Sukhothai, Thailand.* From the series: Thailand, 1960-80. “Brian Brake’s Best of Asia”. *Insight (American Express),* February/March 1984. 4 x 5 color transparency. Collection Museum of New Zealand Te Papa Tongarewa. Gift of Wai-man Lau, 2010.

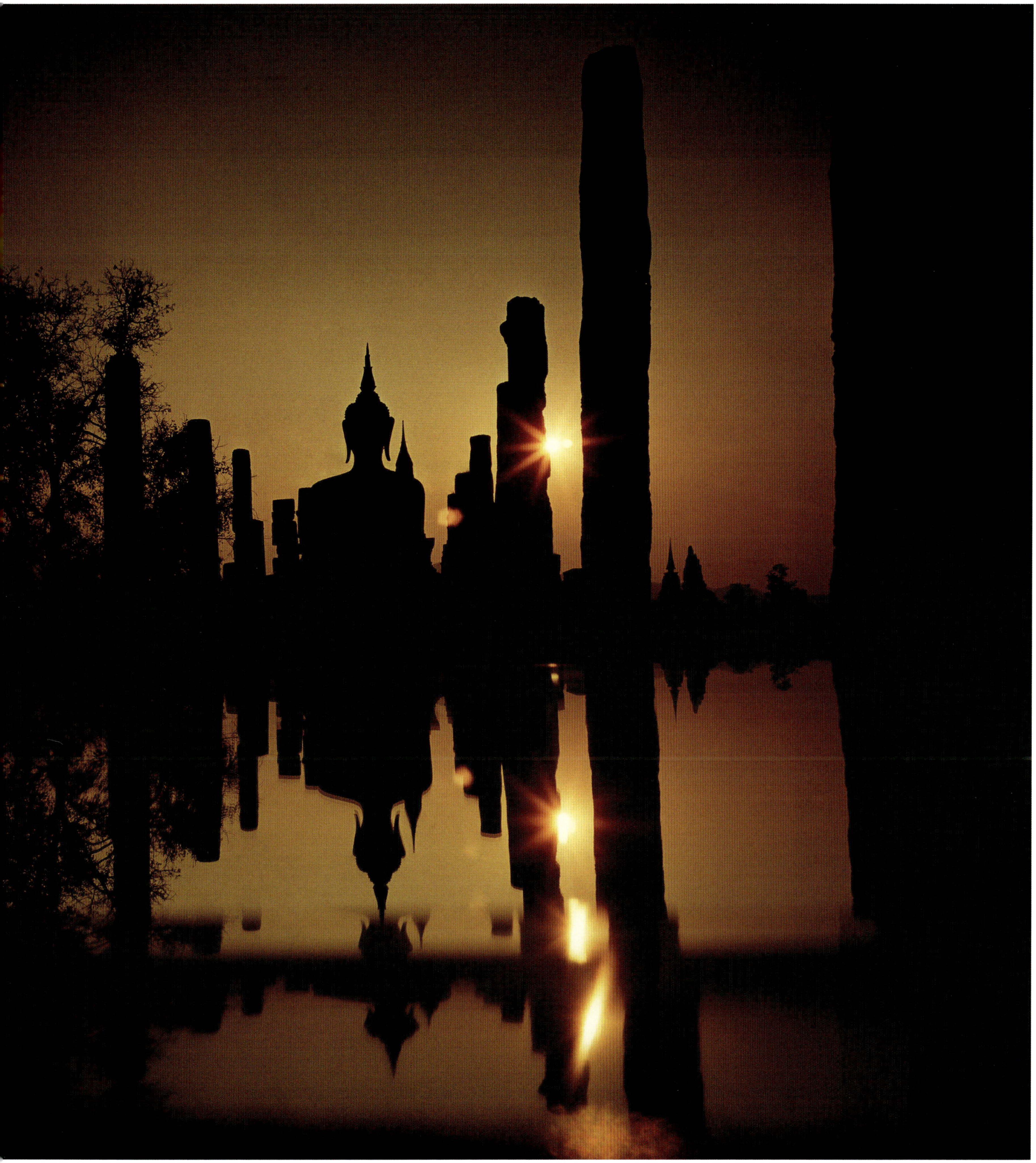

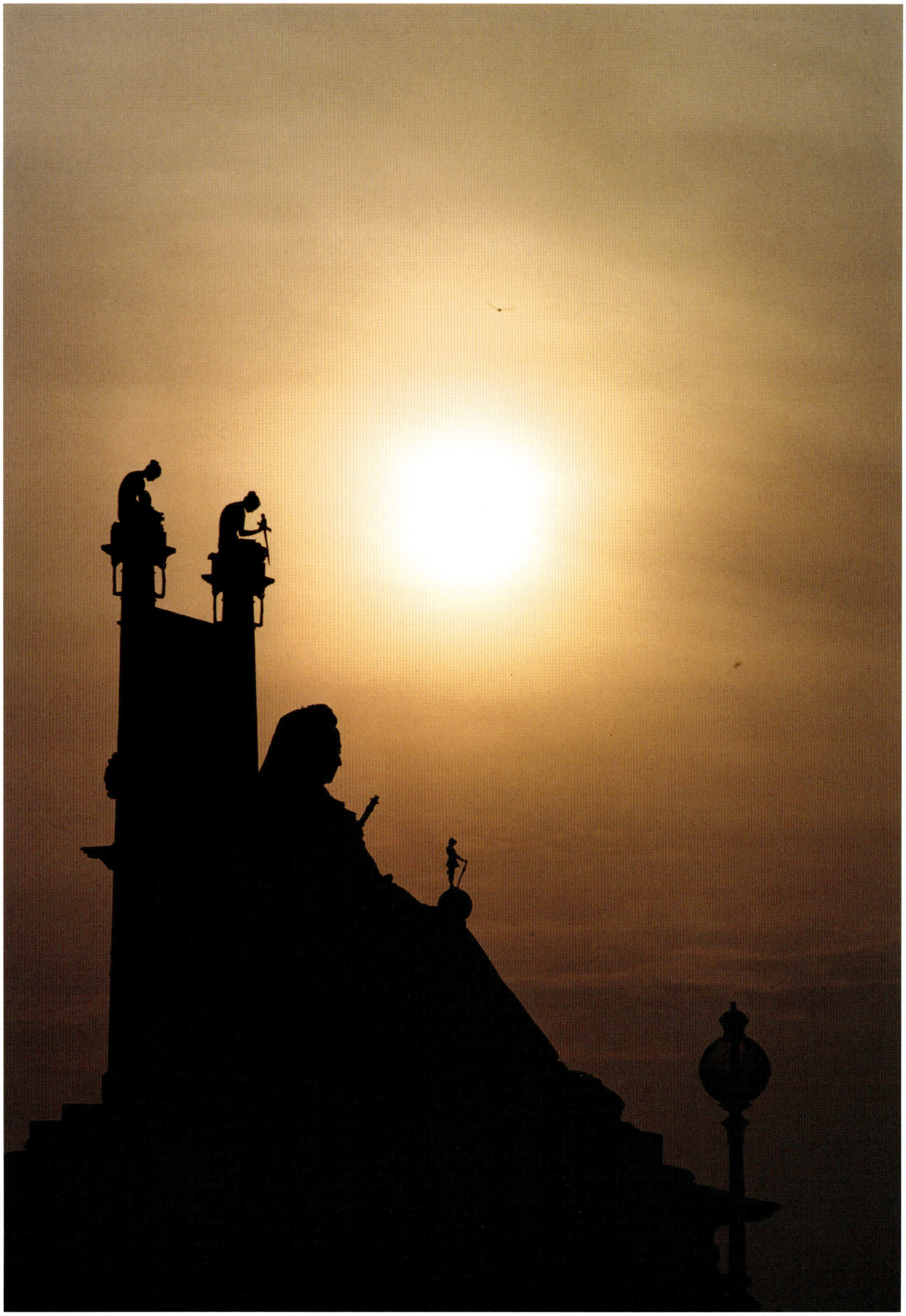

75 | Brian Brake. *Queen Victoria statue, Calcutta, India.* From the series: Monsoon, 1960. Unpublished. 35mm transparency. Collection Museum of New Zealand Te Papa Tongarewa. Gift of Wai-man Lau, 2001.

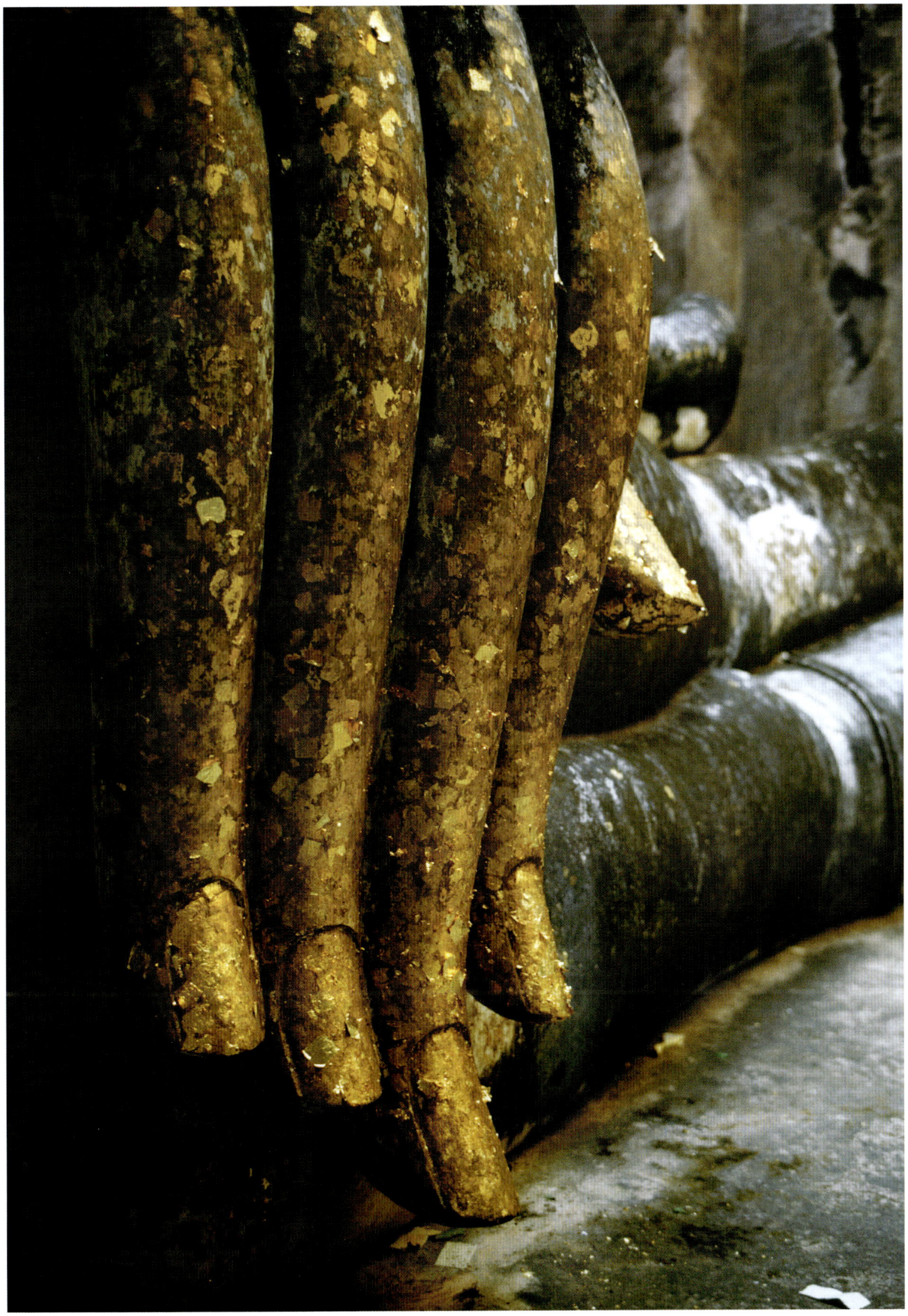

76 | Brian Brake. *Hand of the Buddha, Sukhothai, Thailand.* From the series: Thailand, 1960-80. Unpublished. 4 x 5 color transparency. Collection Museum of New Zealand Te Papa Tongarewa. Gift of Wai-man Lau, 2001.

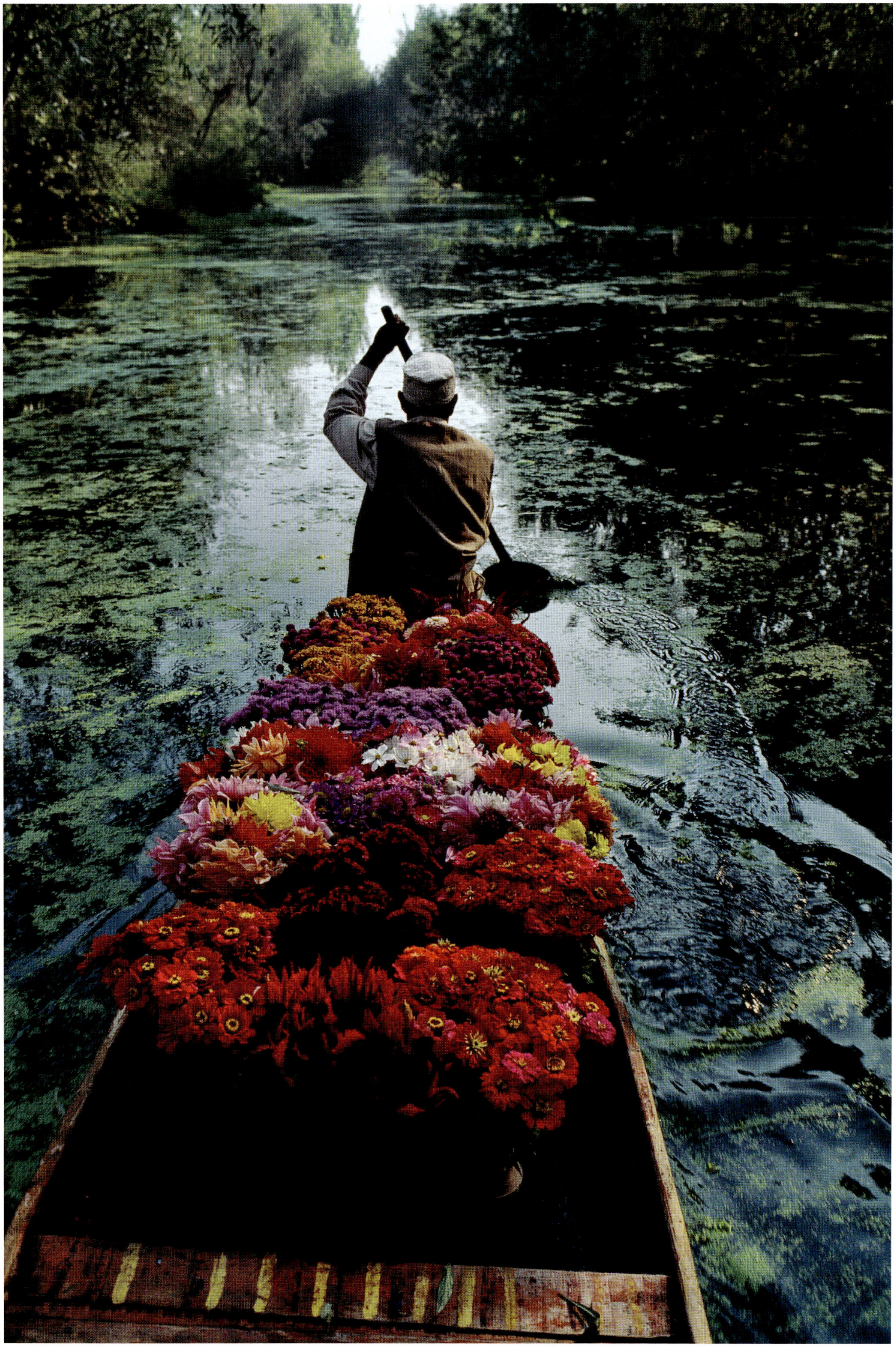

78

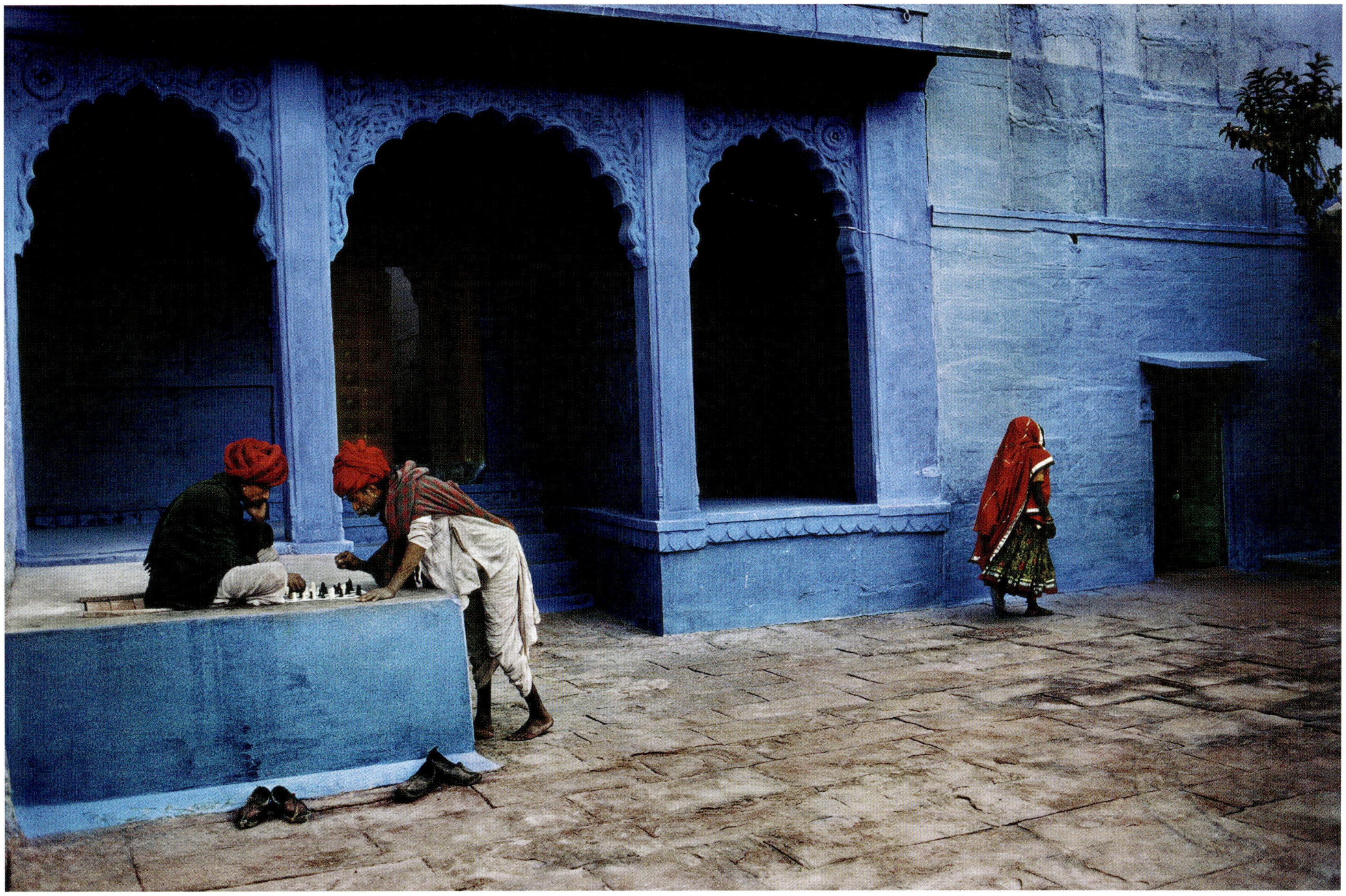

77 | Steve McCurry. *Flower seller at Dal Lake, Srinagar, Kashmir,* 1996. "Kashmir: Trapped in Conflict". *National Geographic,* vol. 196, no. 3, September 1999. © Steve McCurry

78 | Steve McCurry. *Men playing chess, Jodhpur, Rajasthan, India,* 1996. *South Southeast.* London & New York: Phaidon Press, 2000. © Steve McCurry.

79

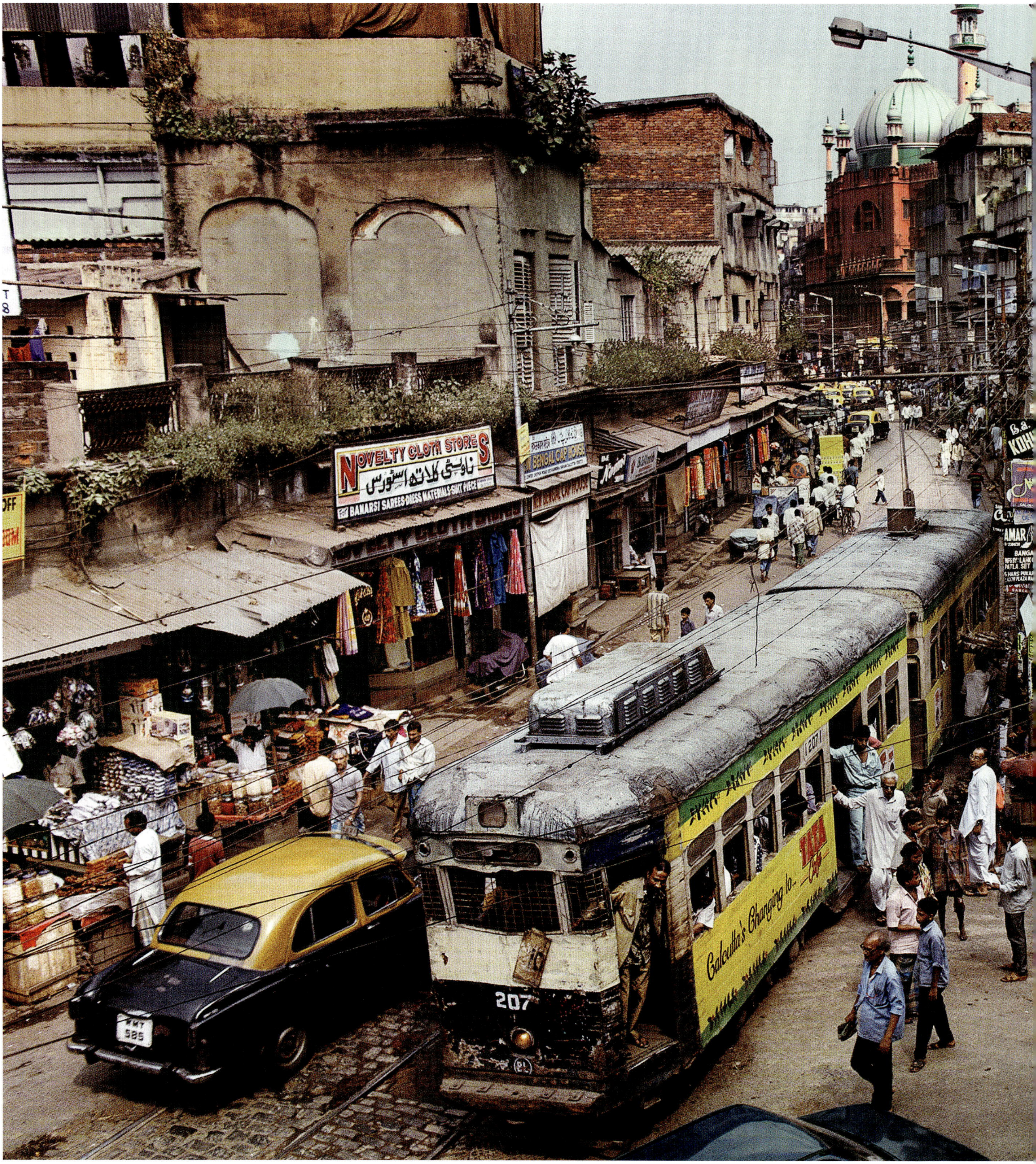
NOVELTY CLOTH STORES
BANARSI SAREES·DRESS MATERIALS·SUIT PIECE
BENGAL CAP HOUSE
Calcutta's Changing to...
TATA
207

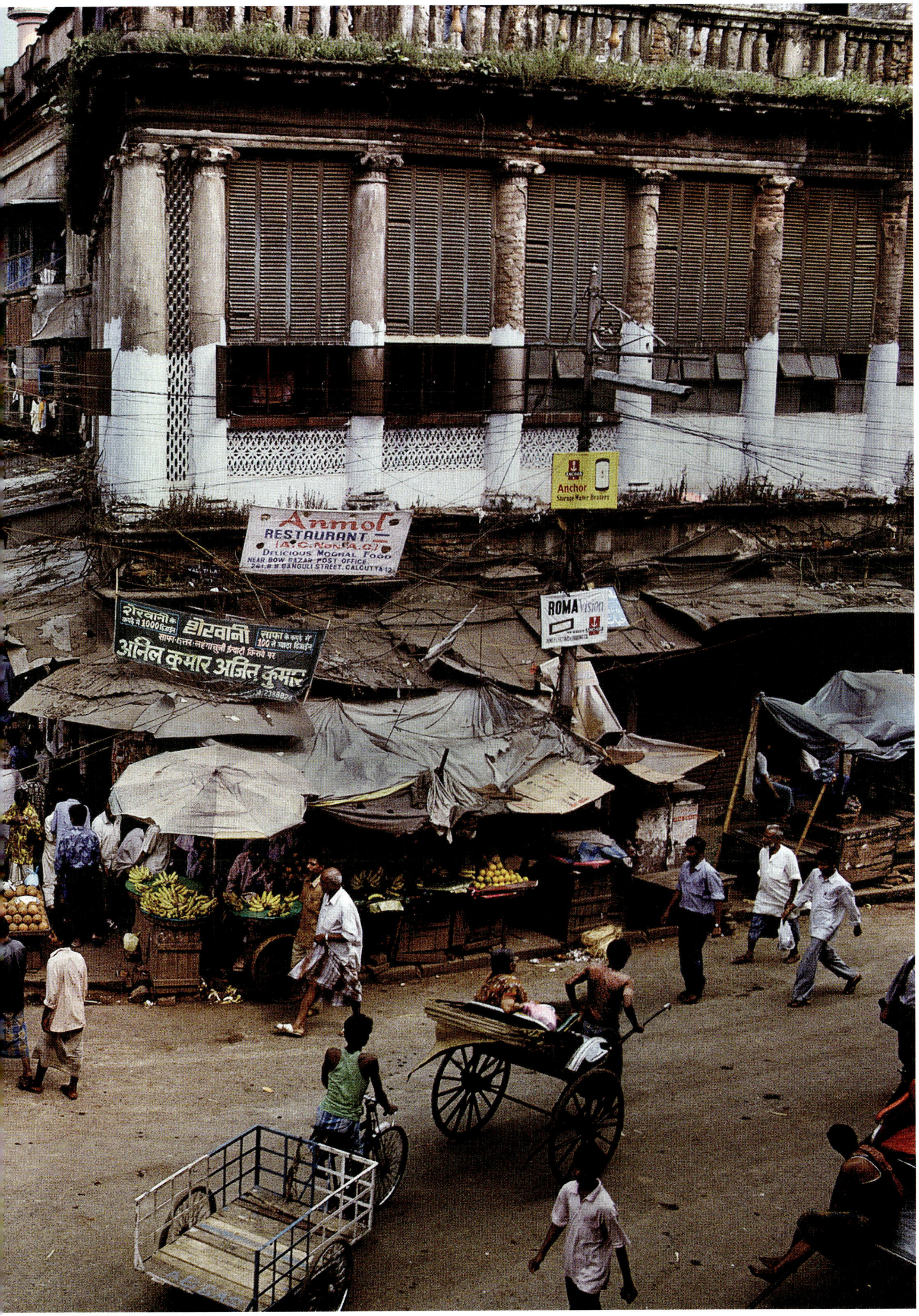

79 | Steve McCurry. *A tram, Calcutta, India,* 1996. "India: Fifty Years of Independence". *National Geographic,* vol. 191, no. 5, May 1997. © Steve McCurry.

80

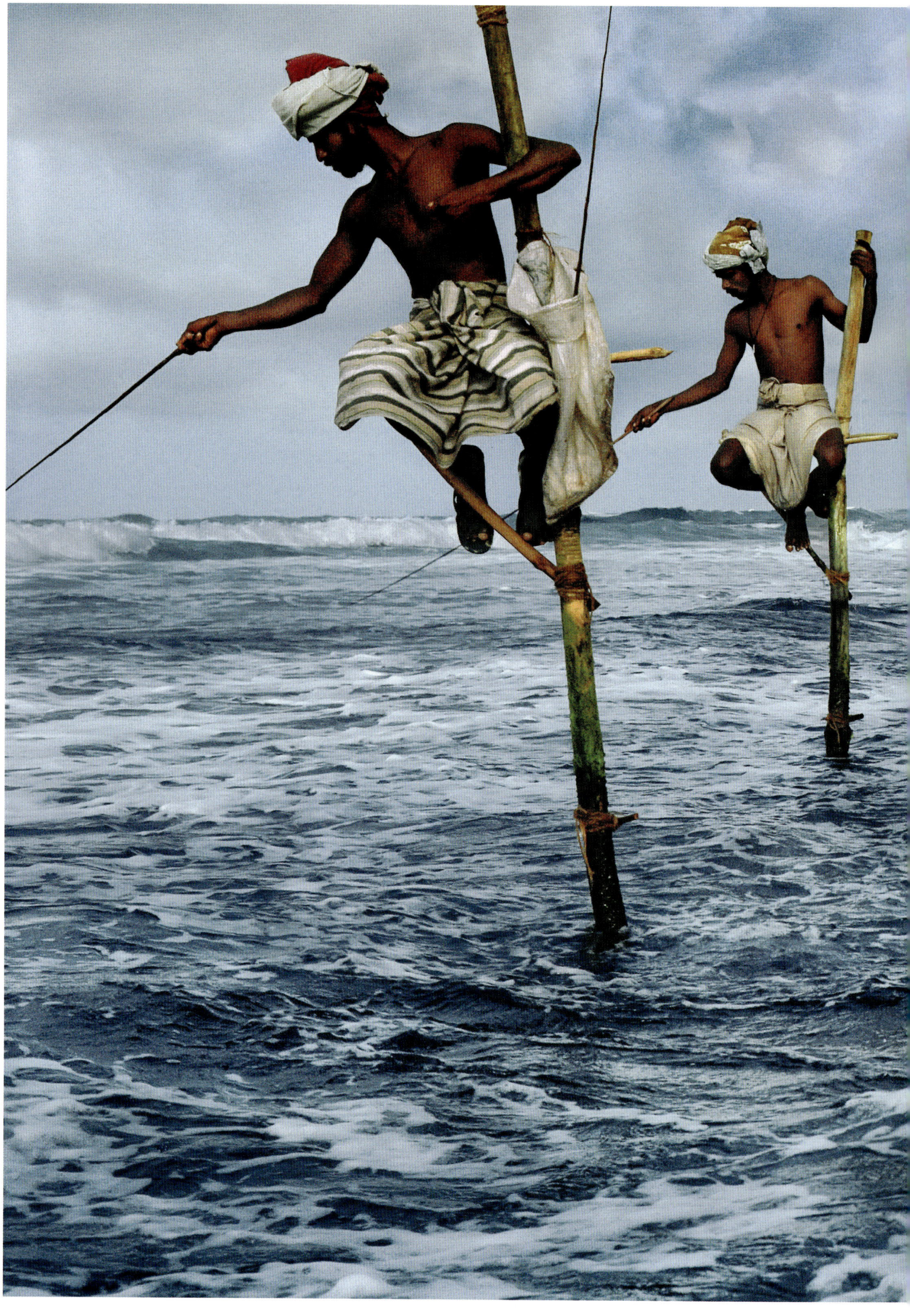

80 | Steve McCurry. *Stilt Fishermen, Weligama, Sri Lanka,* 1995. "Sri Lanka: A Continuing Ethnic War Tarnishes the Pearl of the Indian Ocean". *National Geographic*, vol. 191, no. 1, January 1997. © Steve McCurry.

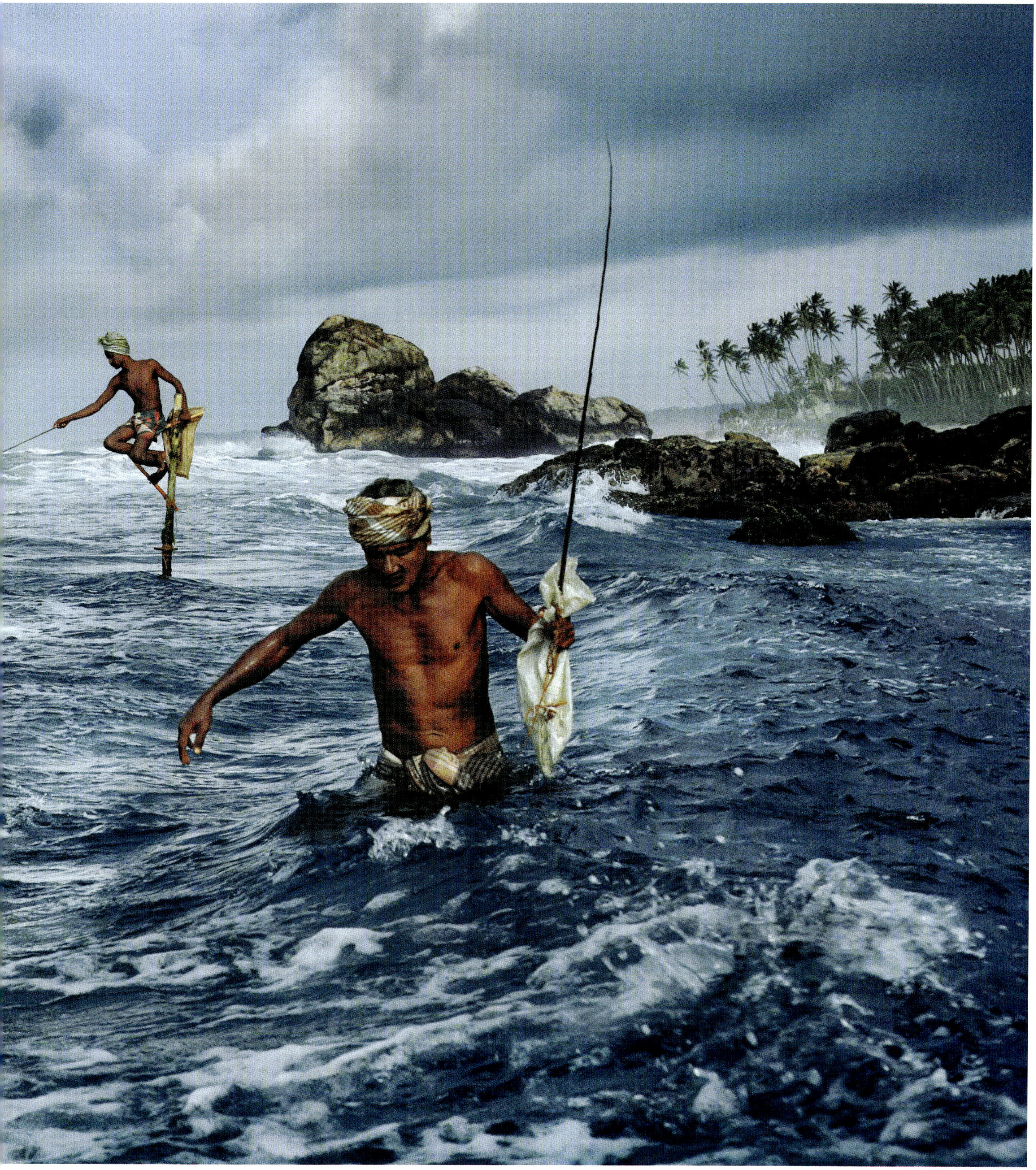

81

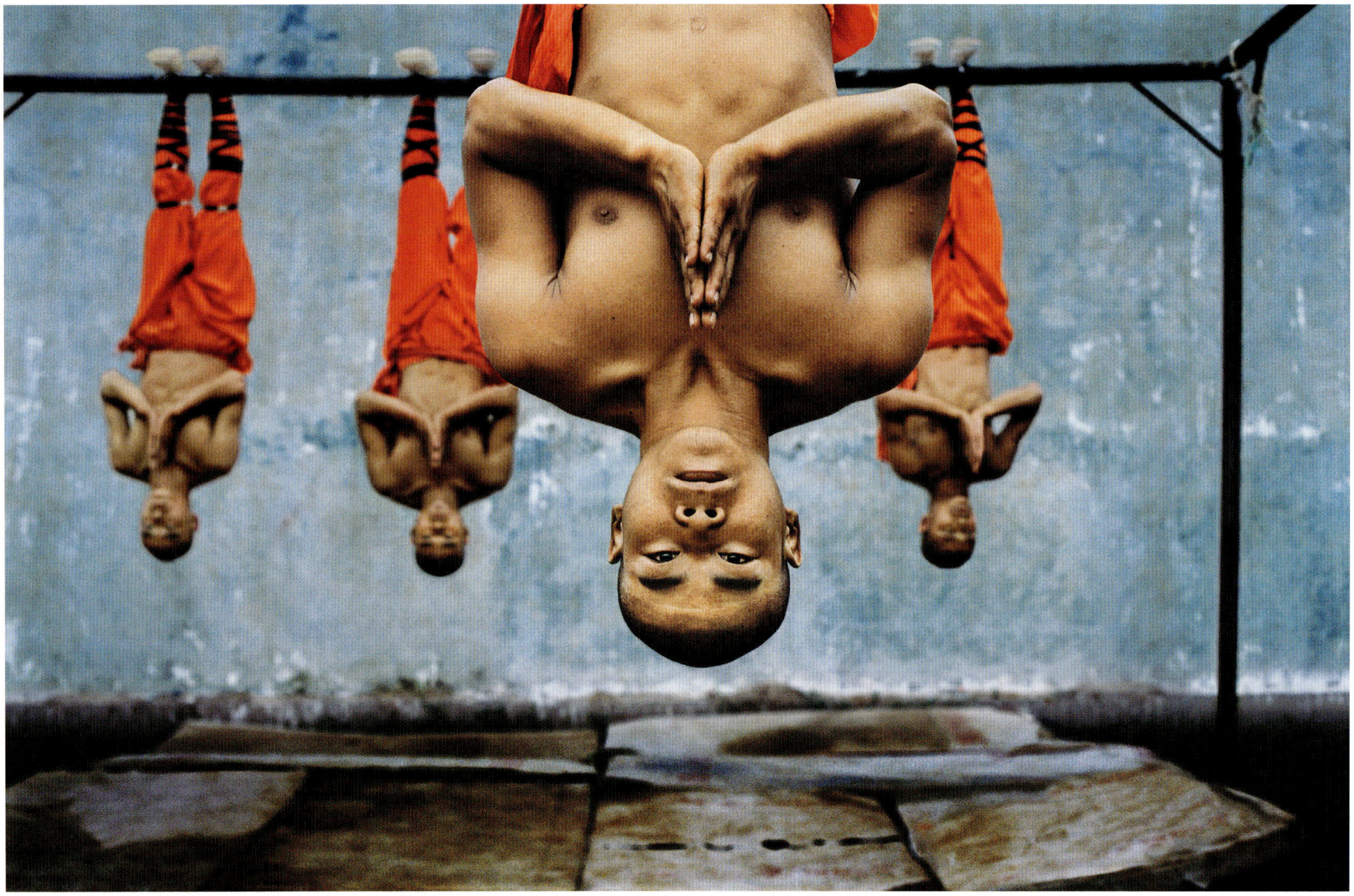

81 | Steve McCurry. *Shaolin monks training, Zhengzhou, China,* 2004. *The Iconic Photographs.* London & New York: Phaidon Press, 2010. © Steve McCurry.

82

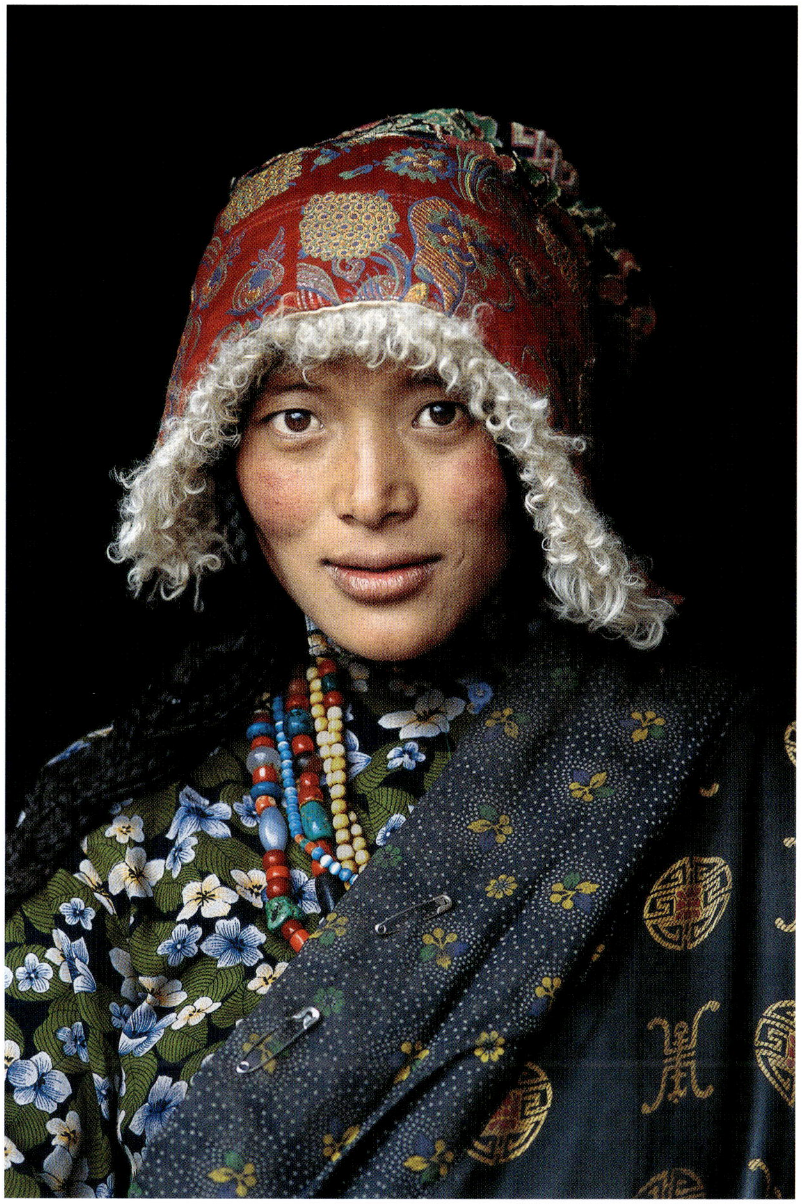

82 | Steve McCurry. *Pilgrim at a stupa, Amdo, Tibet,* 2001. *The Path to Buddha.* London & New York: Phaidon Press, 2003. © Steve McCurry.

83

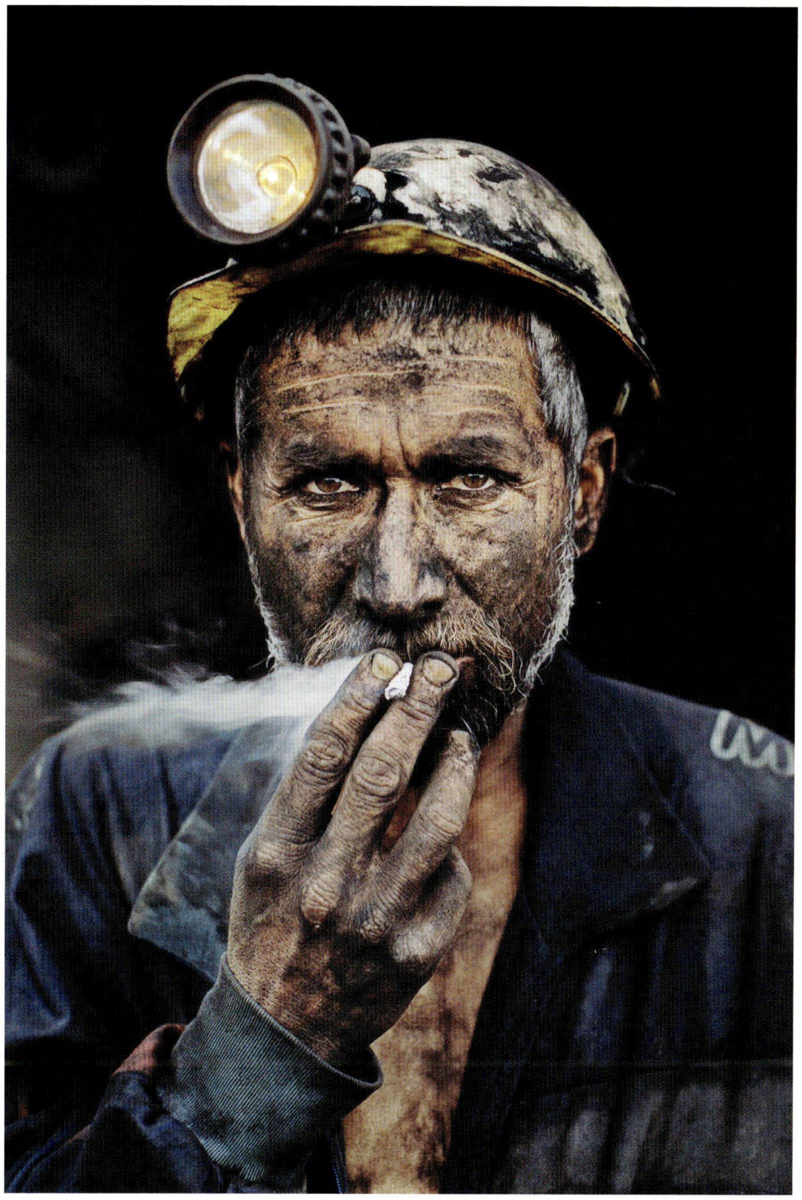

83 | Steve McCurry. *Coal miner, Pol-e Khomri, Afghanistan,* 2002. Bannon, Anthony. *Steve McCurry.* London & New York: Phaidon Press, 2005. © Steve McCurry.

84

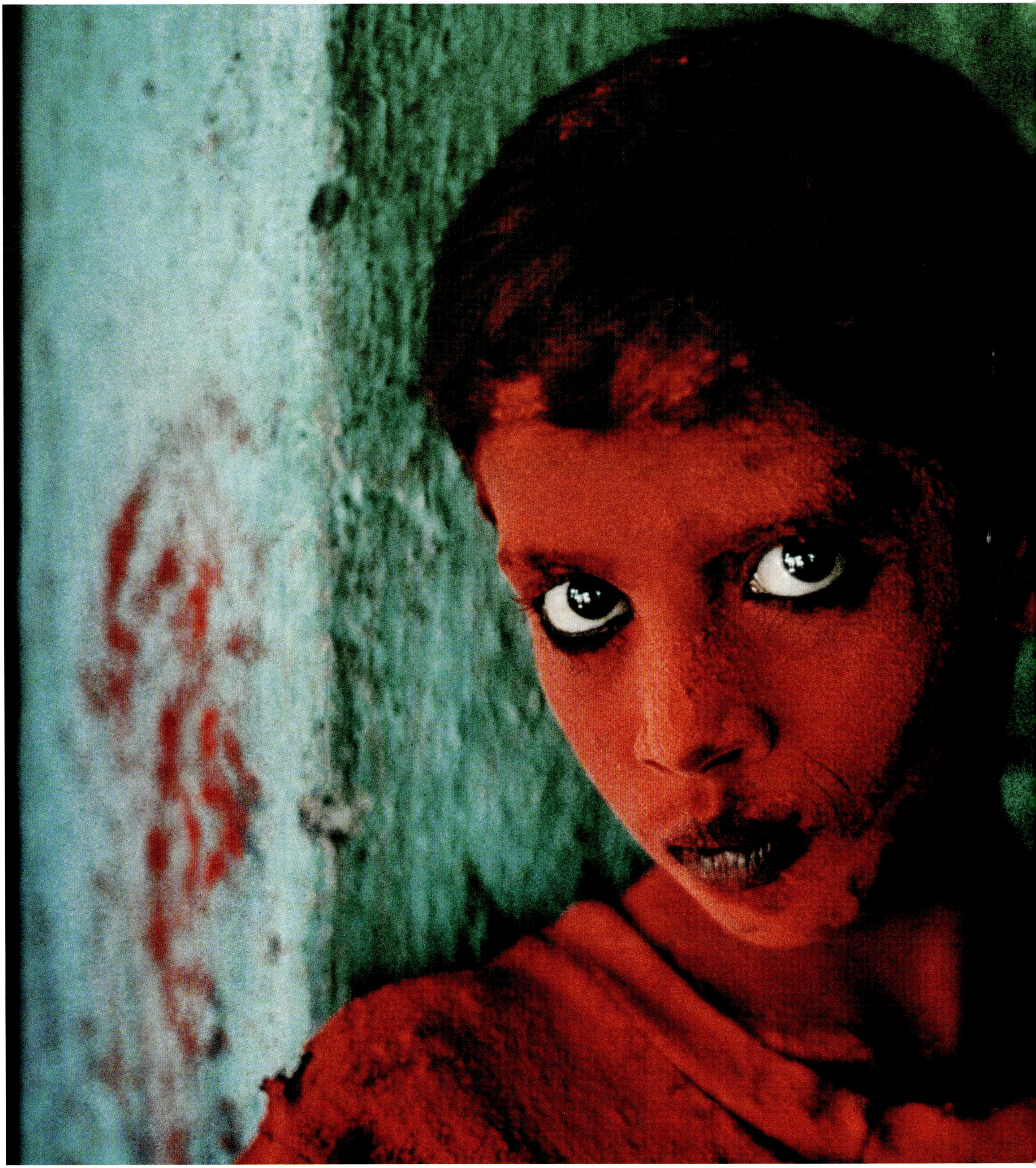

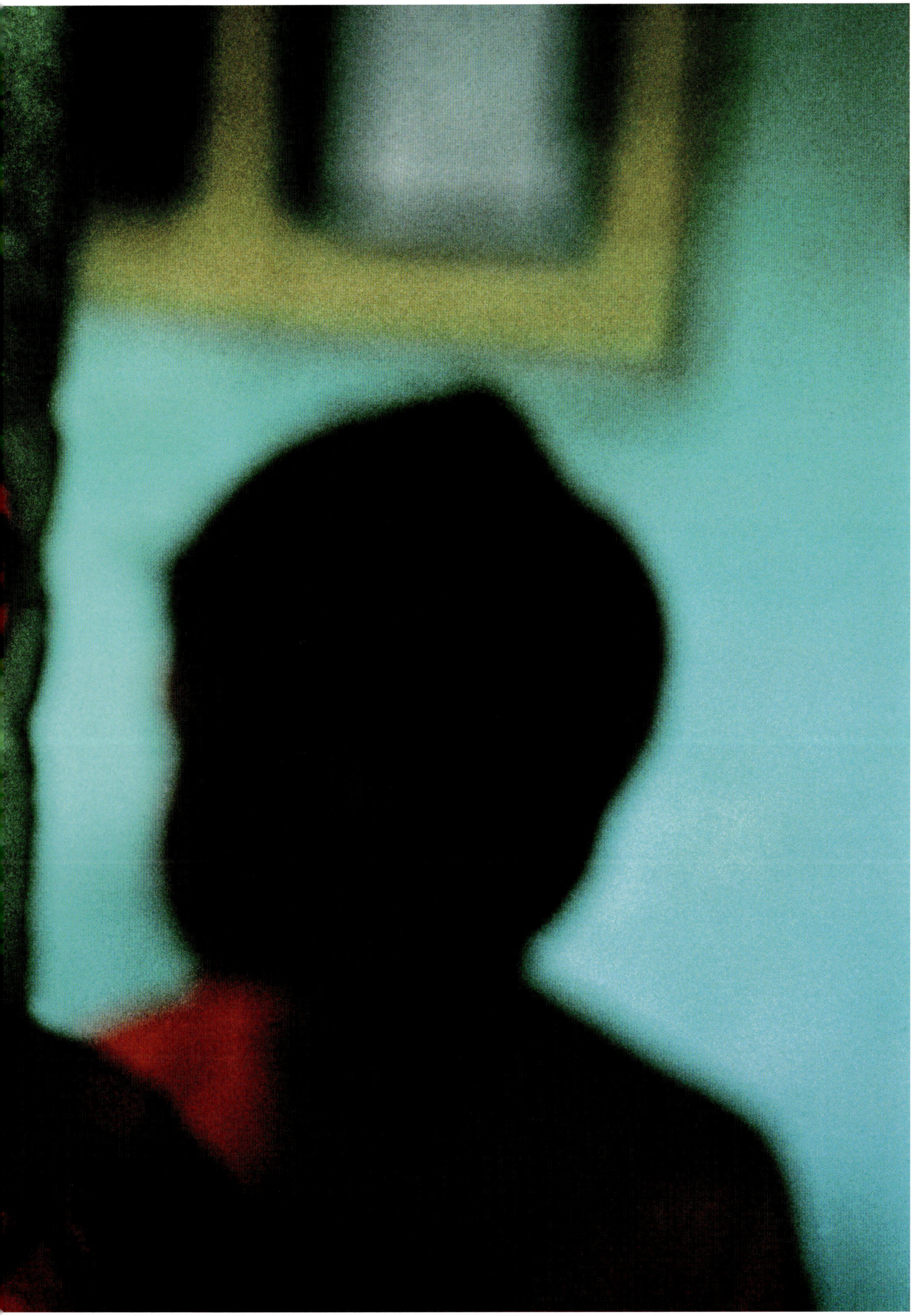

84 | Steve McCurry. *Boy at Ganesh Chaturthi festival, Mumbai, India,* 1996. "India: Fifty Years of Independence". *National Geographic,* vol. 191, no. 5, May 1997. © Steve McCurry.

85

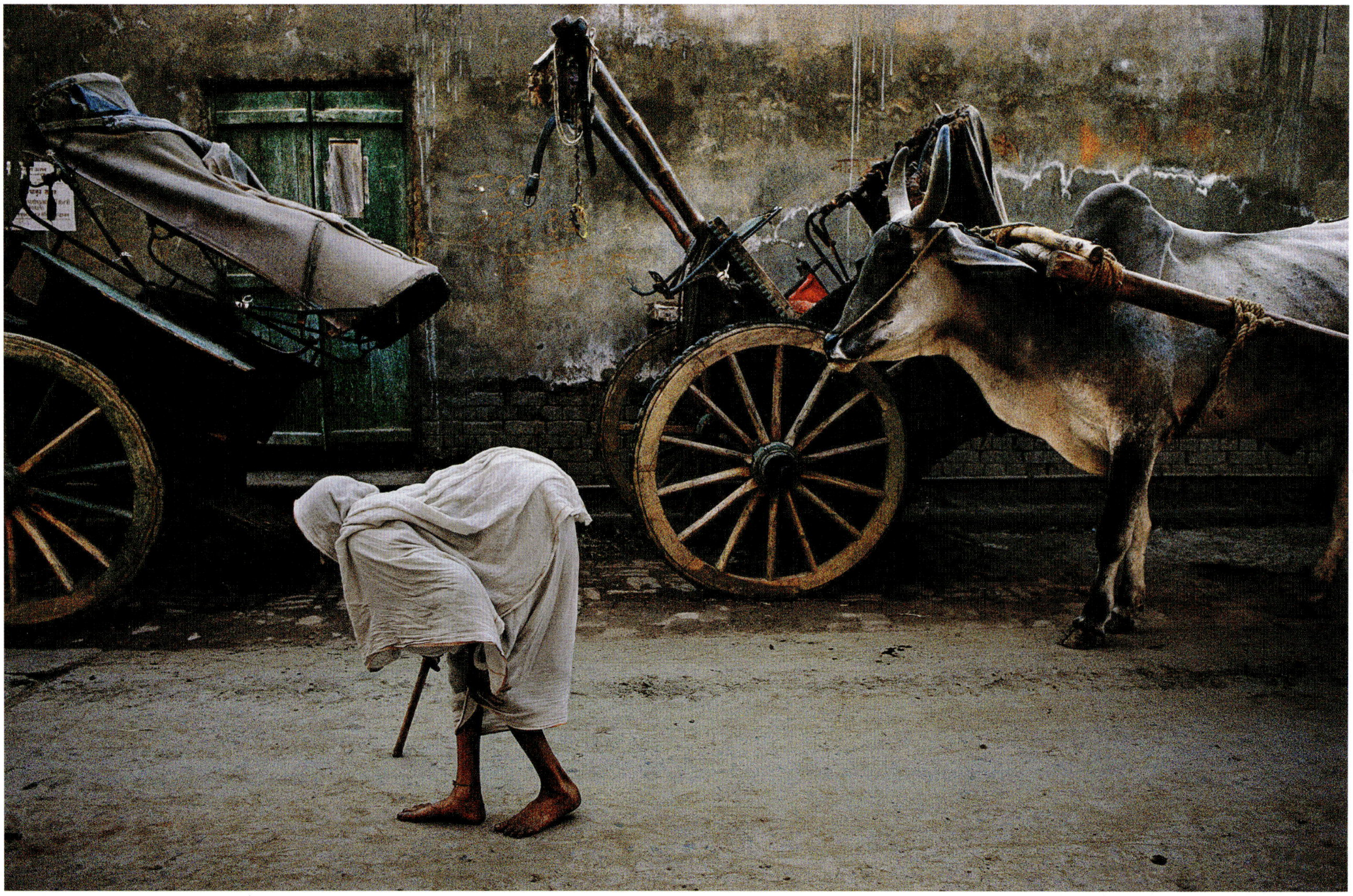

85 | Steve McCurry. *Widow returning from her ashram. Uttar Pradesh, India,* 1995. *South Southeast.* London & New York: Phaidon Press, 2000. © Steve McCurry.

86 | Steve McCurry. *Monsoon skies over Bihar, Northeast India,* 1983. *Monsoon.* New York: Thames & Hudson Ltd., 1988. © Steve McCurry.

86

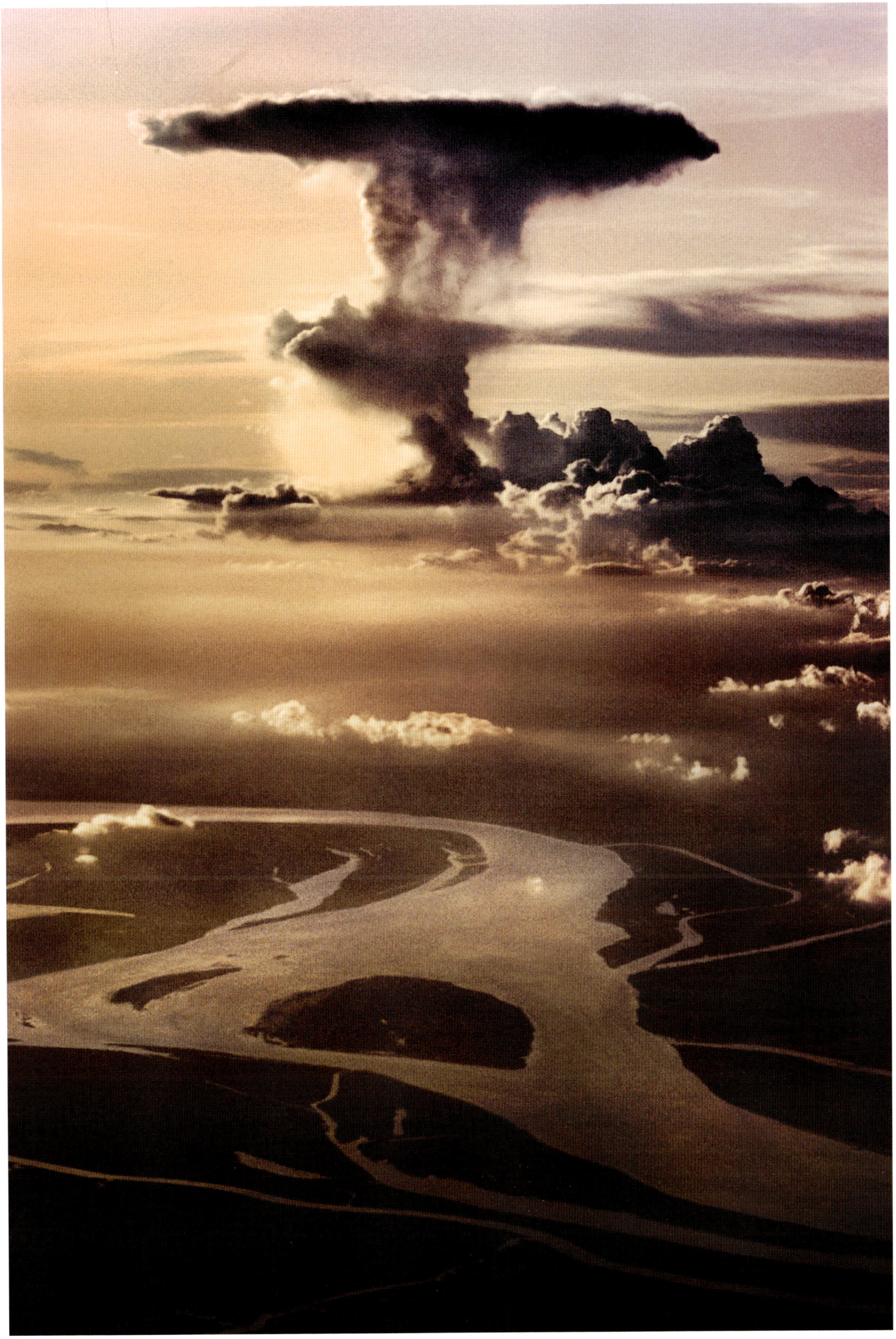

87

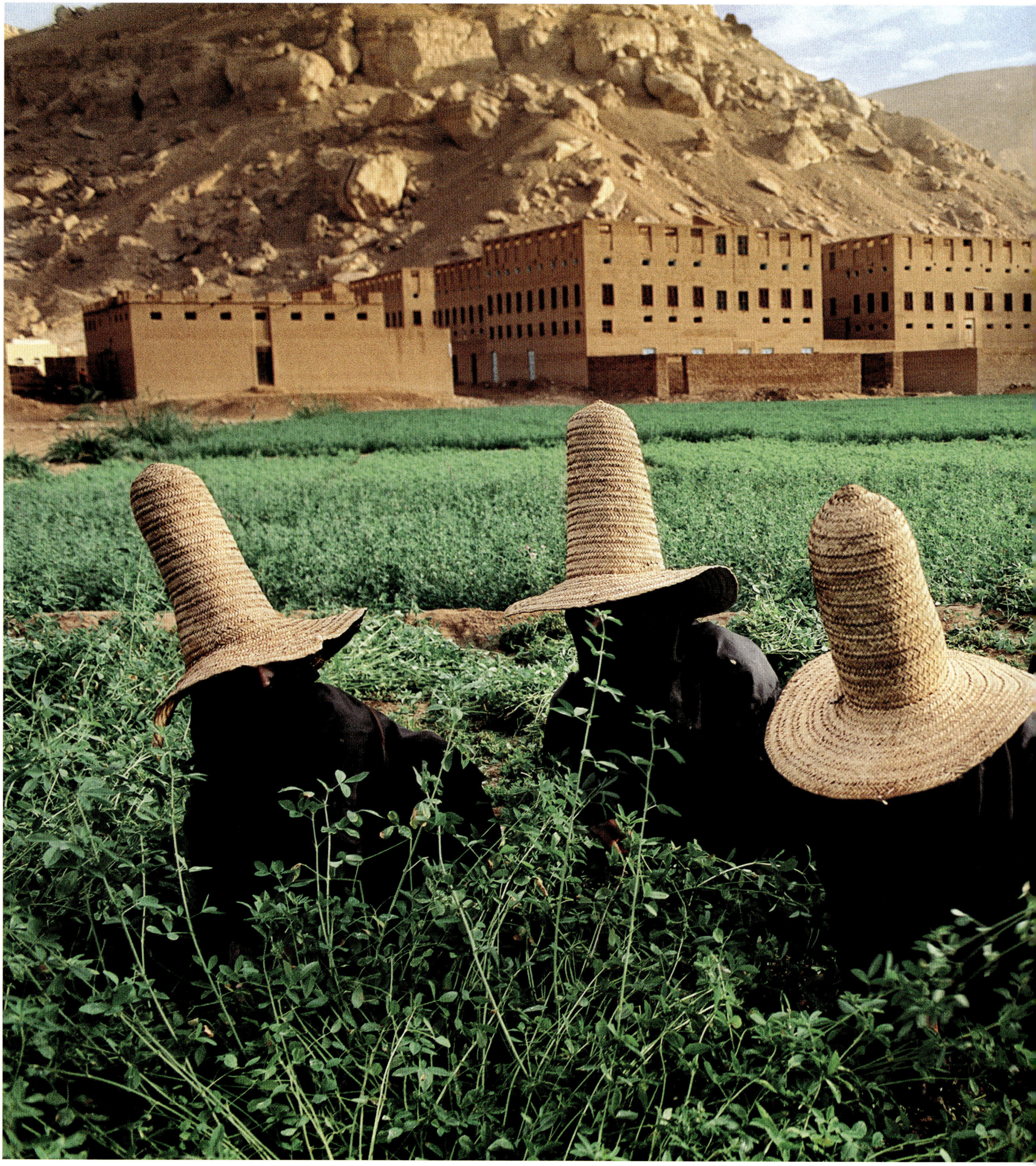

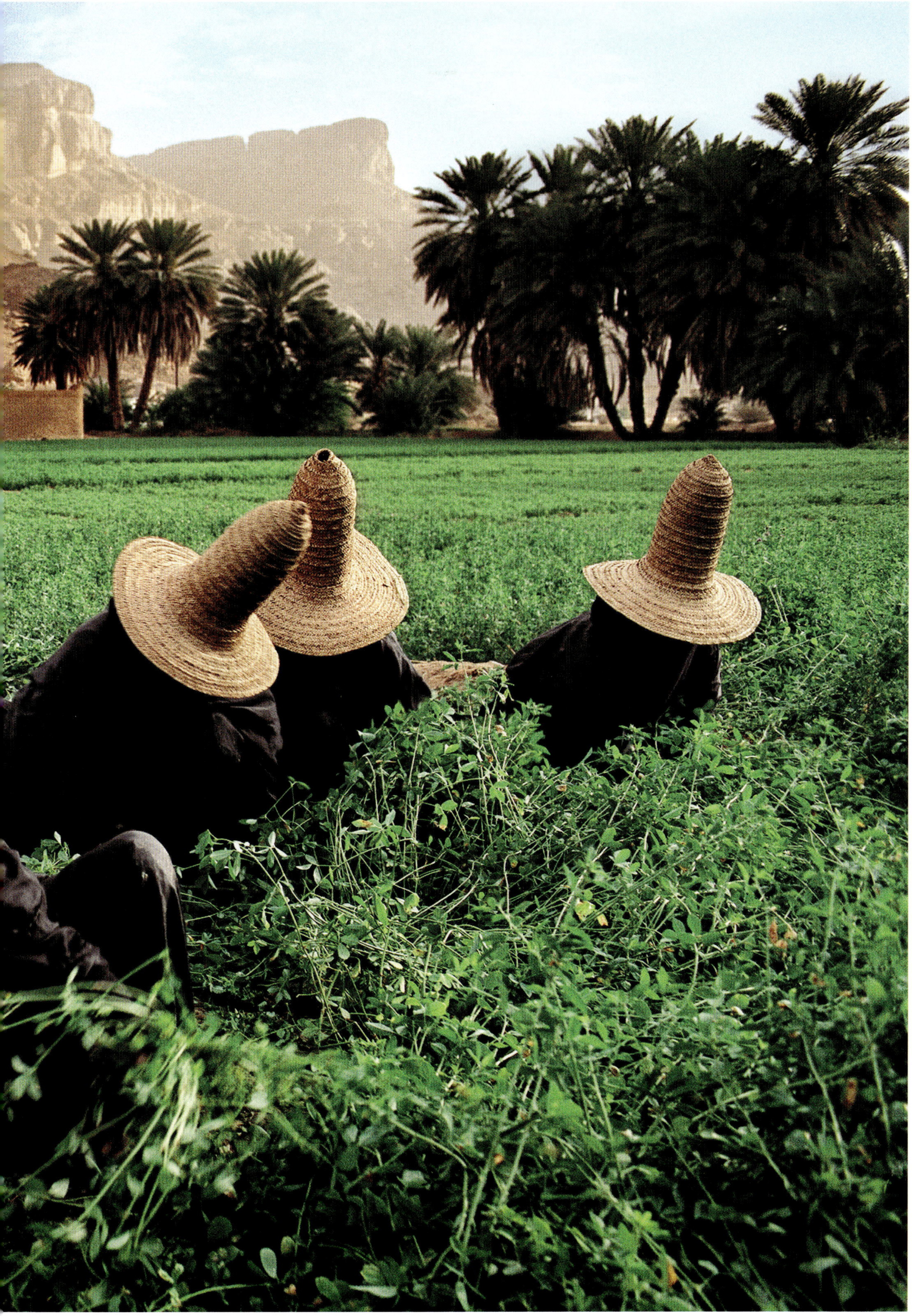

87 | Steve McCurry. *Women gather clover, Shibam, Wadi Hadhramaut, Yemen,* 1999. "Yemen United". *National Geographic*, vol. 197, no. 4, April 2000. © Steve McCurry.

"EXOTIC, ENTICING HONG KONG"

"Exotic, Enticing Hong Kong" was the title of Steve McCurry's essay in *National Geographic Traveler* (Winter 1986/87). Color spreads linked to commercial tourism promotions are familiar to us now. But when *Traveler* was launched in 1984, international air travel was in the early years. Cheaper flights following the American Airline Deregulation Act of 1978 made global tourism a growth industry. Magazine editors relied on key words like "exotic" to convey the allure of foreign destinations—especially in Asia.

McCurry's photographs of Hong Kong see past this cliché into a modern city and a society in which the colorful theatricality of Chinese Opera and the high-energy life of crowded modern streets seem to mingle. The image of a chauffeur lounging against an opulent Rolls Royce amid the bright, multi-lingual neon signages of an entertainment precinct appears at once ordinary and spectacular.

Brian Brake settled in Hong Kong in 1962, and made the city his base until 1976. In the early 1970s, competition from television caused some of the great photojournalism magazines such as *Life* to end weekly publication. Instead, many of Brake's Hong Kong photographs were collected in the book he produced with the writer Robert Elegant, *Hong Kong: Great Cities* (1977), published by Time-Life Books, the book arm of Time Inc., which produced both *Time* and *Life* magazines. Brake was fascinated by the dense patterns of Hong Kong's high-rise buildings and harbor, as well as the bustle of street markets—a world he knew not as a visitor but as a man at home in the city.

88

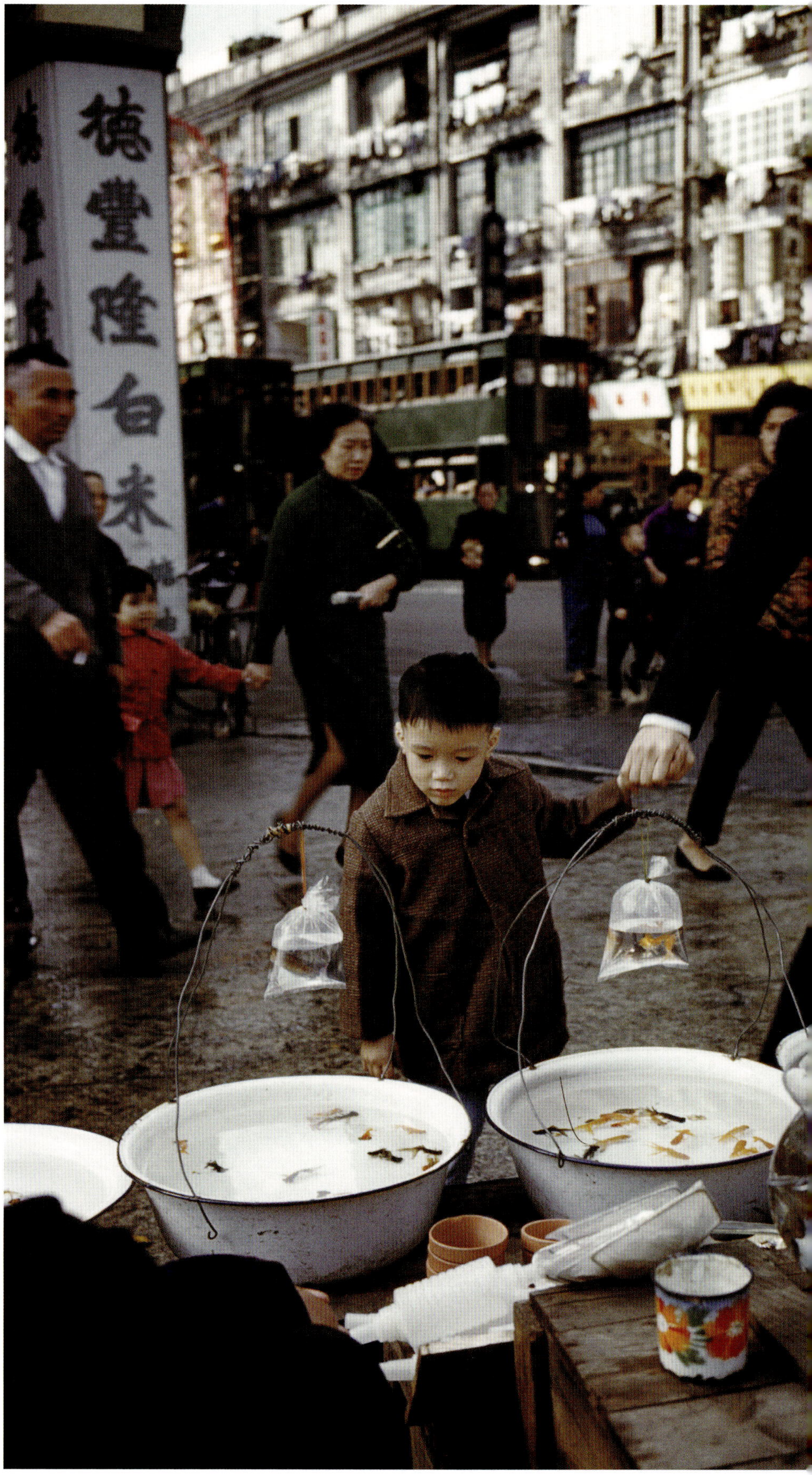

89

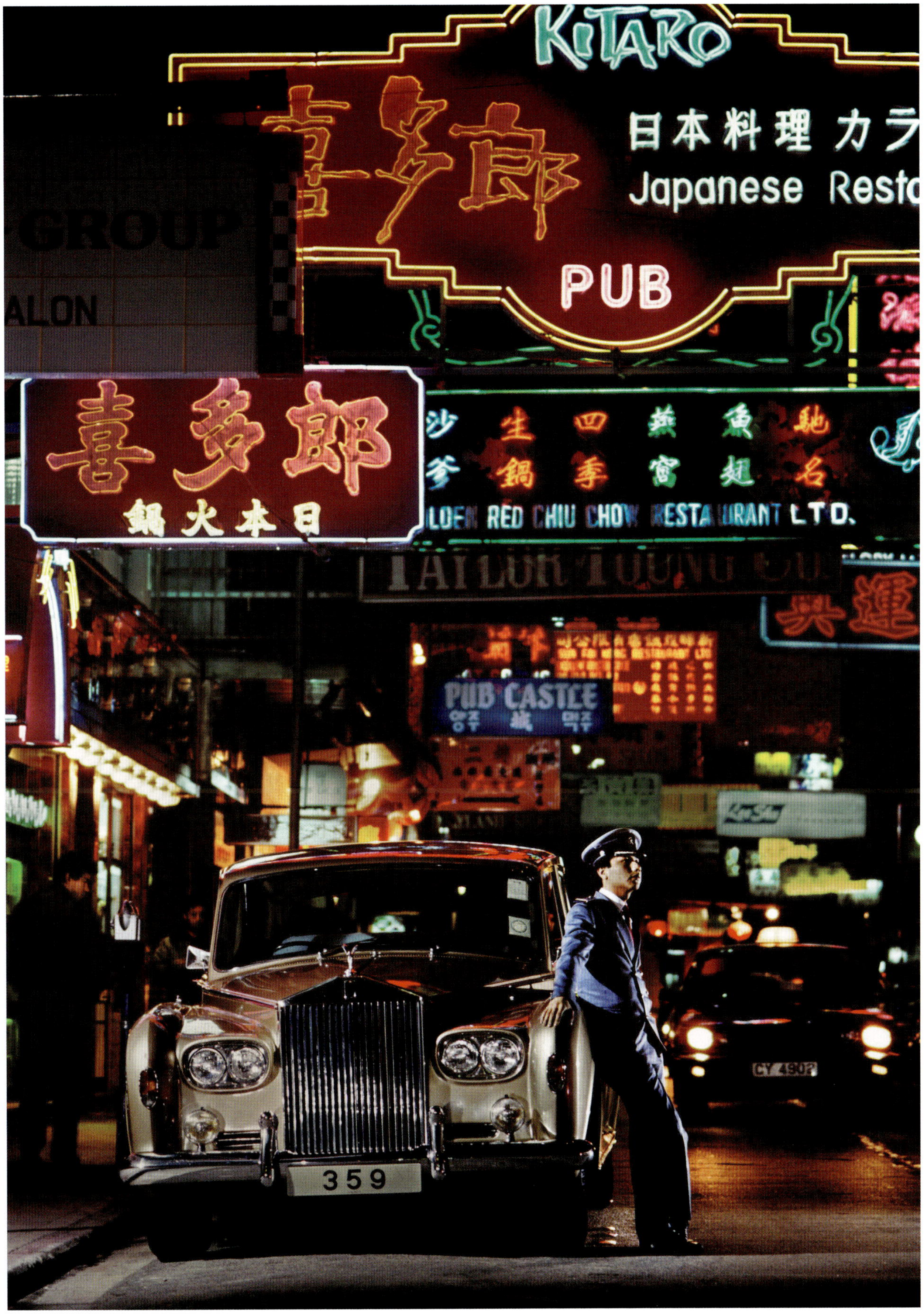

88 | Brian Brake. *Boy at goldfish stall, Hong Kong, China,* 1961. Unpublished. 35mm transparency. Collection Museum of New Zealand Te Papa Tongarewa. Gift of Wai-man Lau, 2001.

89 | Steve McCurry. *A chauffeur leans against his car, Hong Kong, China,* 1985. "Exotic, Enticing Hong Kong". *National Geographic Traveler,* vol. III, no. 4, Winter 1986/87. © Steve McCurry.

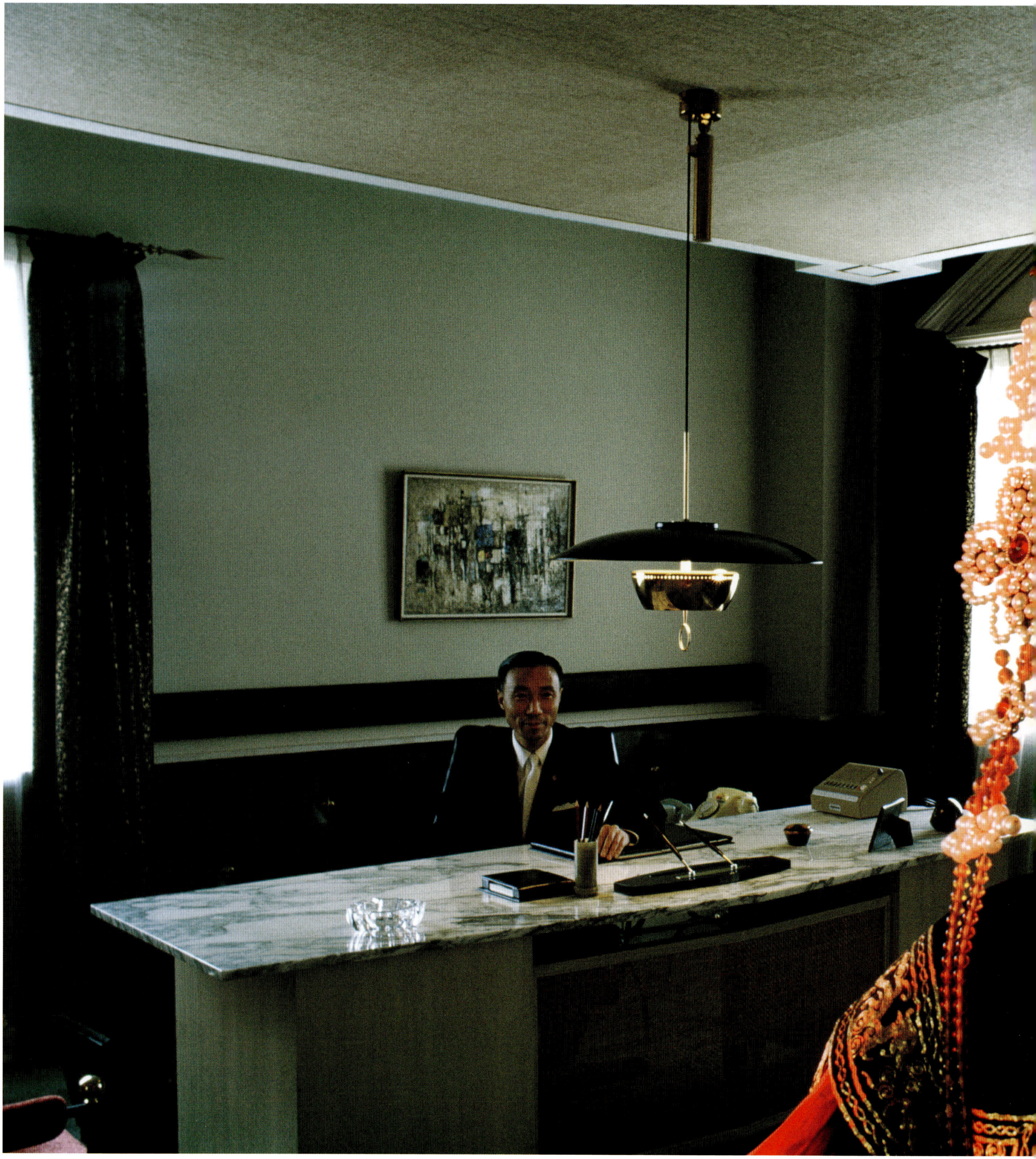

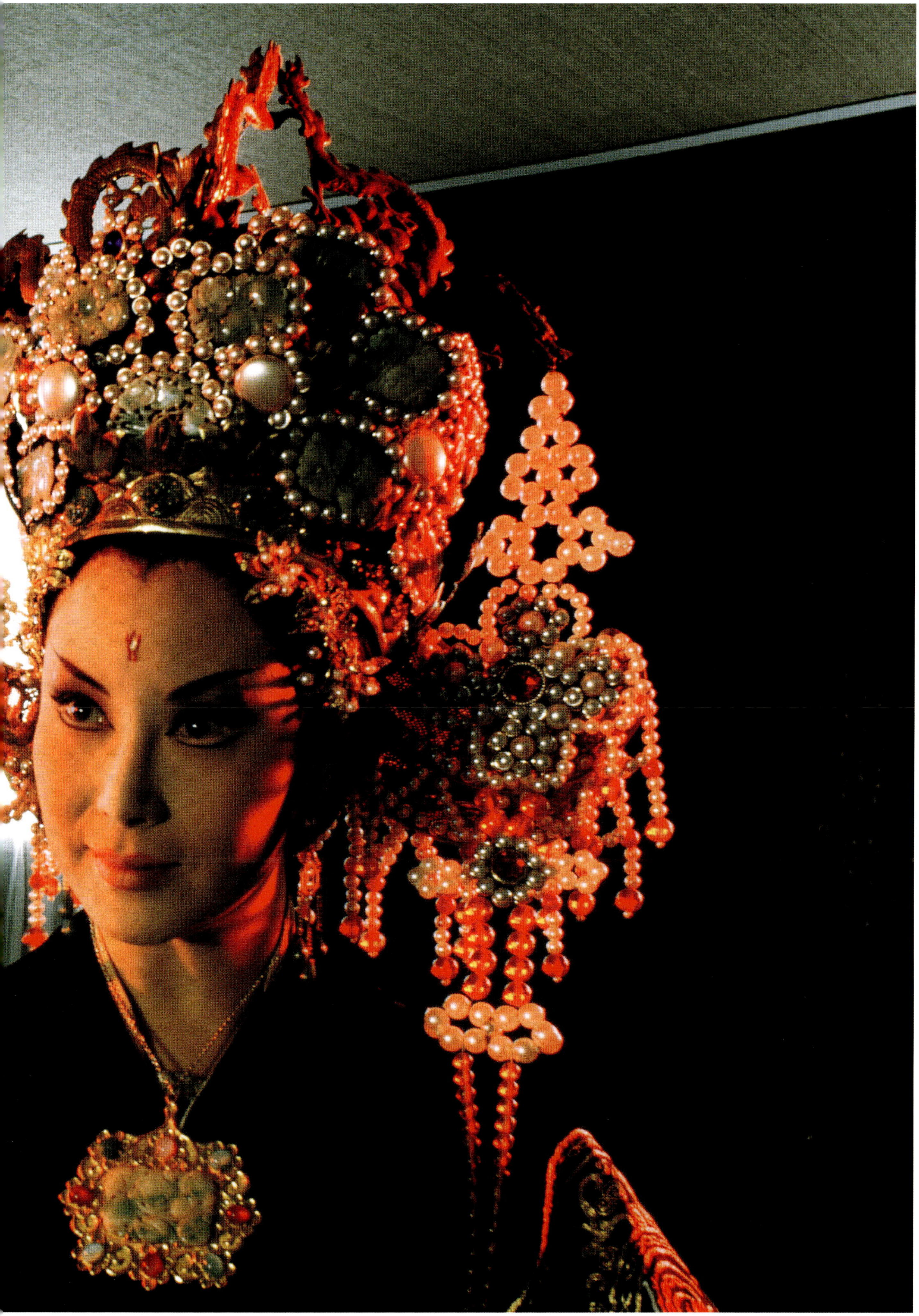

90 | Brian Brake. *Actress Li Li Hua dressed as the Empress Wu of the Tang dynasty with film producer Run Run Shaw, Hong Kong, China,* 1963. Unpublished. 35mm transparency. Collection Museum of New Zealand Te Papa Tongarewa. Gift of Wai-man Lau, 2001.

91

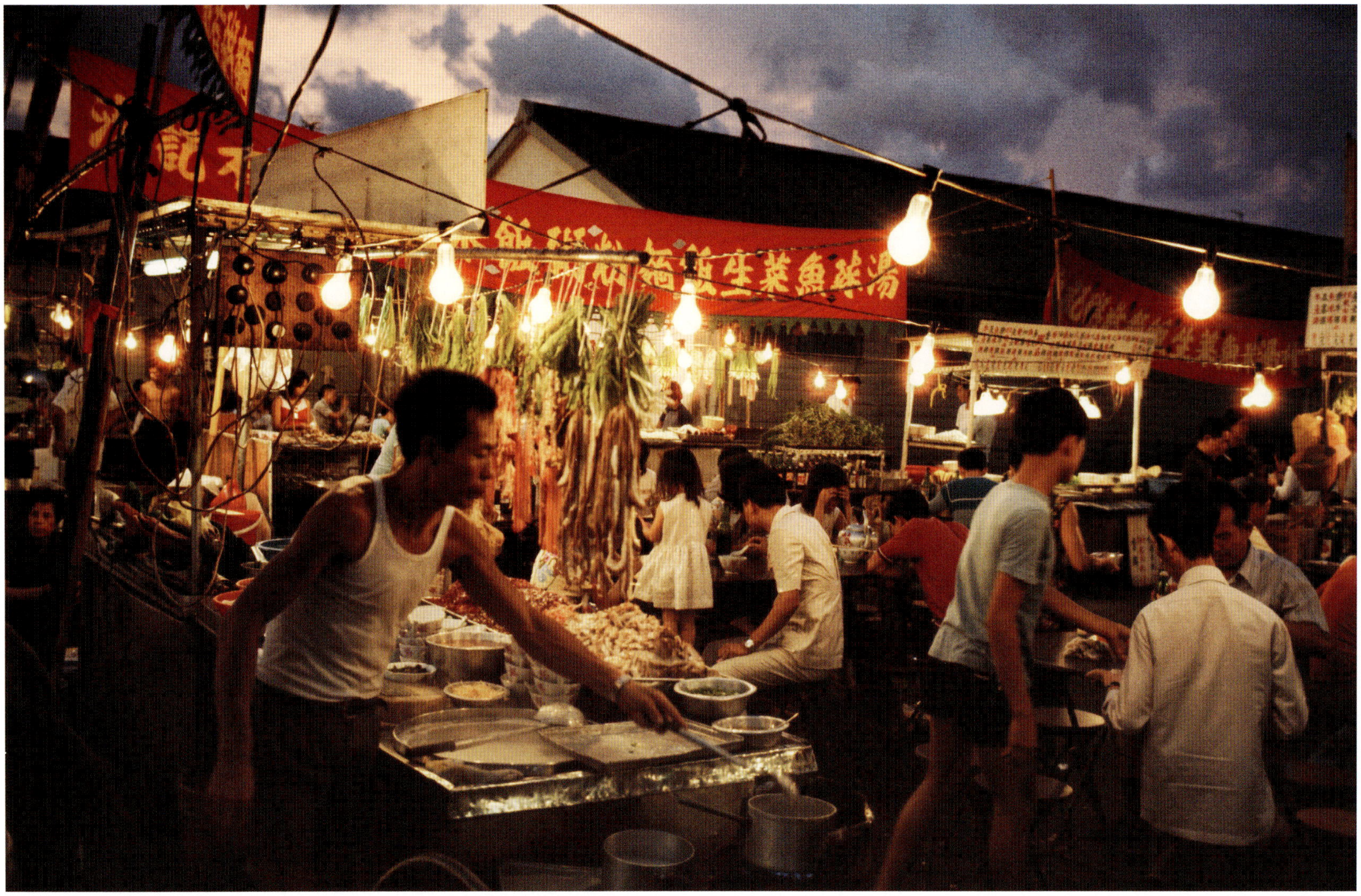

91 I Brian Brake. *Market, Hong Kong, China,* c. 1976. Unpublished. 35mm transparency. Collection Museum of New Zealand Te Papa Tongarewa. Gift of Wai-man Lau, 2001.

92

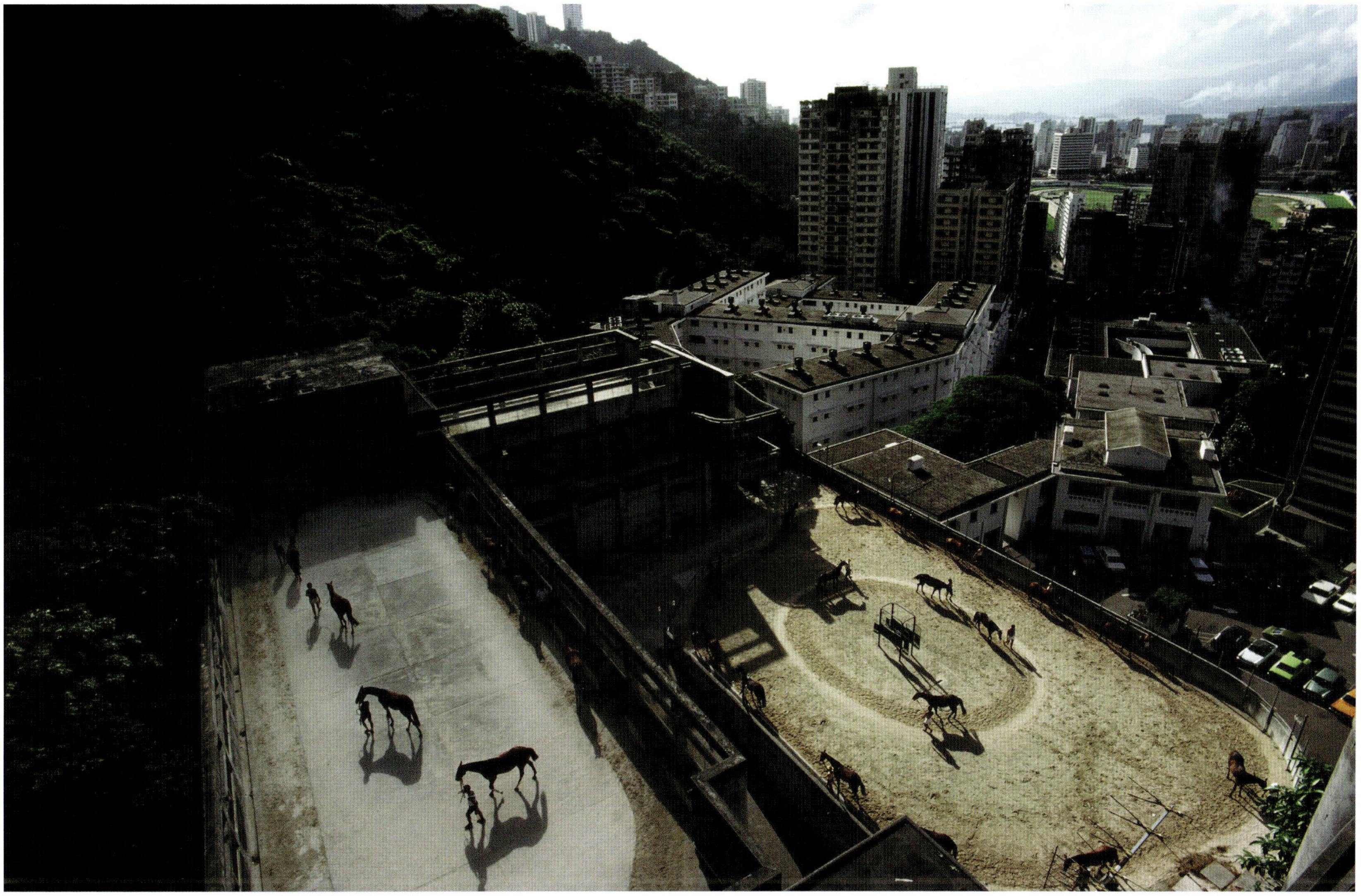

92 | Brian Brake. *Rooftop exercise yards of the Hong Kong Jockey Club, Hong Kong, China,* 1976. Brake, Brian and Robert Elegant. *Hong Kong: Great Cities*. Amsterdam: Time-Life Books, 1977. 35mm transparency. Collection Museum of New Zealand Te Papa Tongarewa. Gift of Wai-man Lau, 2001.

93

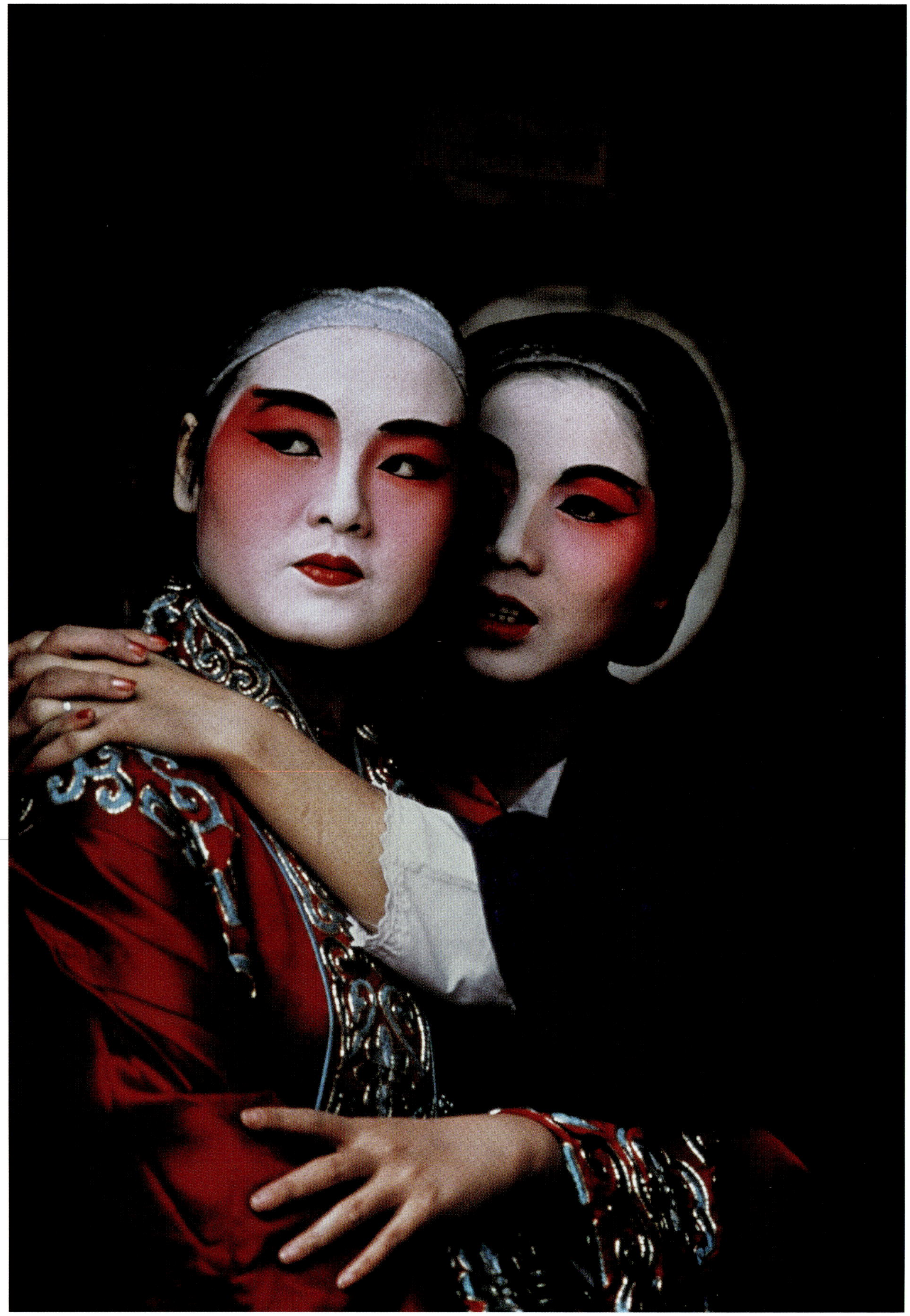

93 | Steve McCurry. *Chinese opera performers backstage, Hong Kong, China,* 1984. *Portraits*. London & New York: Phaidon Press, 1999. © Steve McCurry.

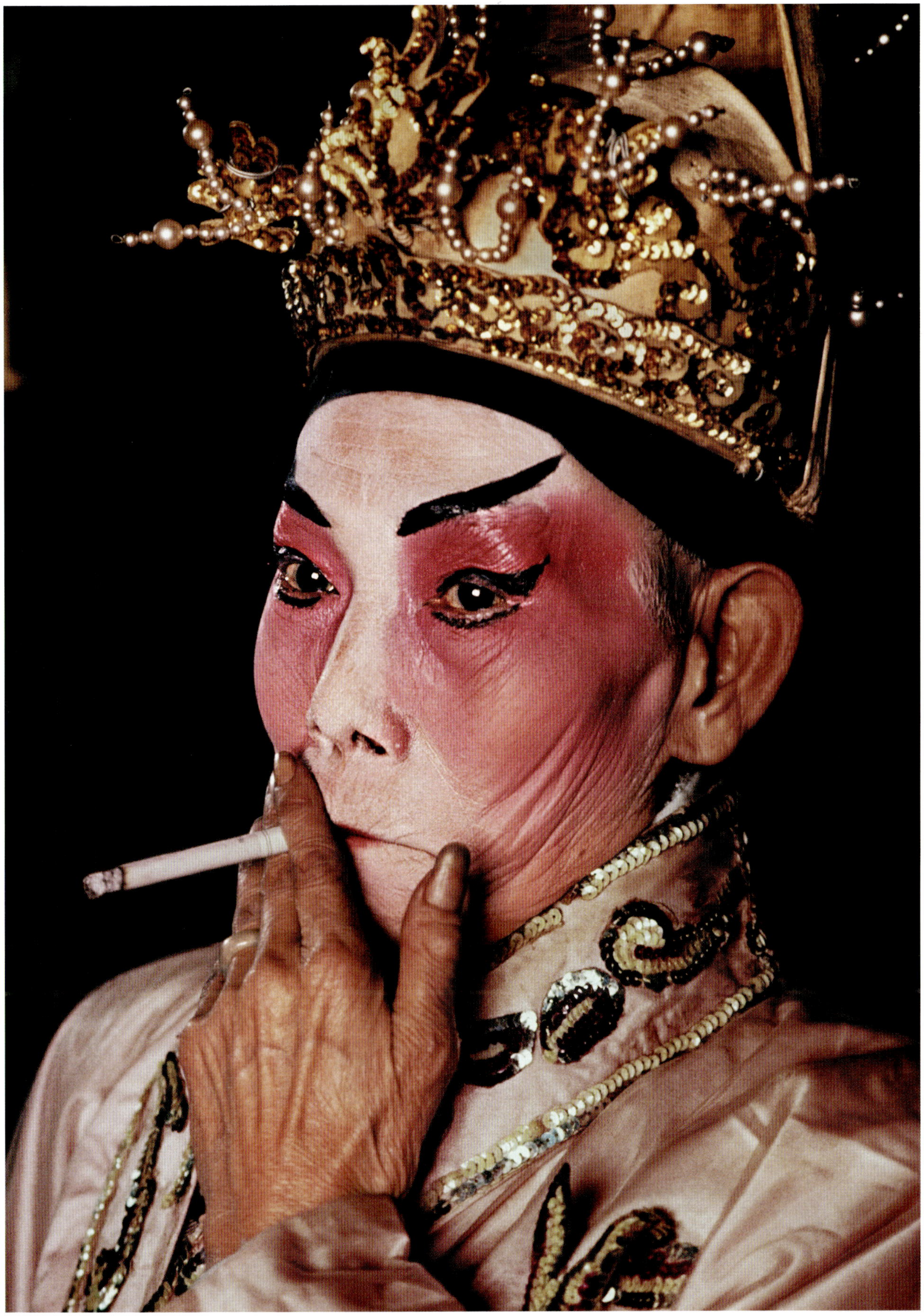

94 | Steve McCurry. *Chinese opera star at the Ming Dynasty Theatre, Hong Kong, China,* 1998. *Portraits*. London & New York: Phaidon Press, 1999. © Steve McCurry.

95

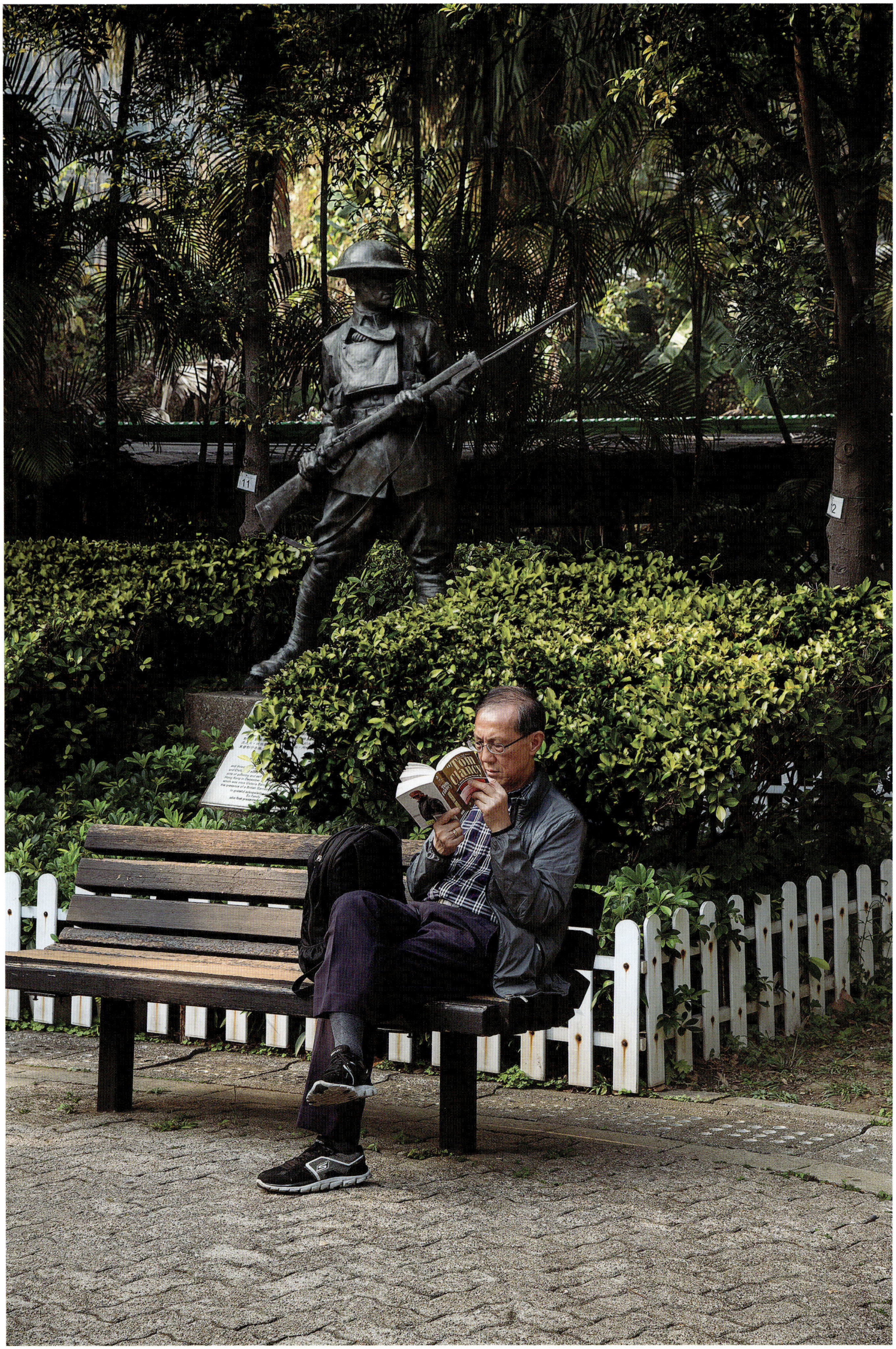

96

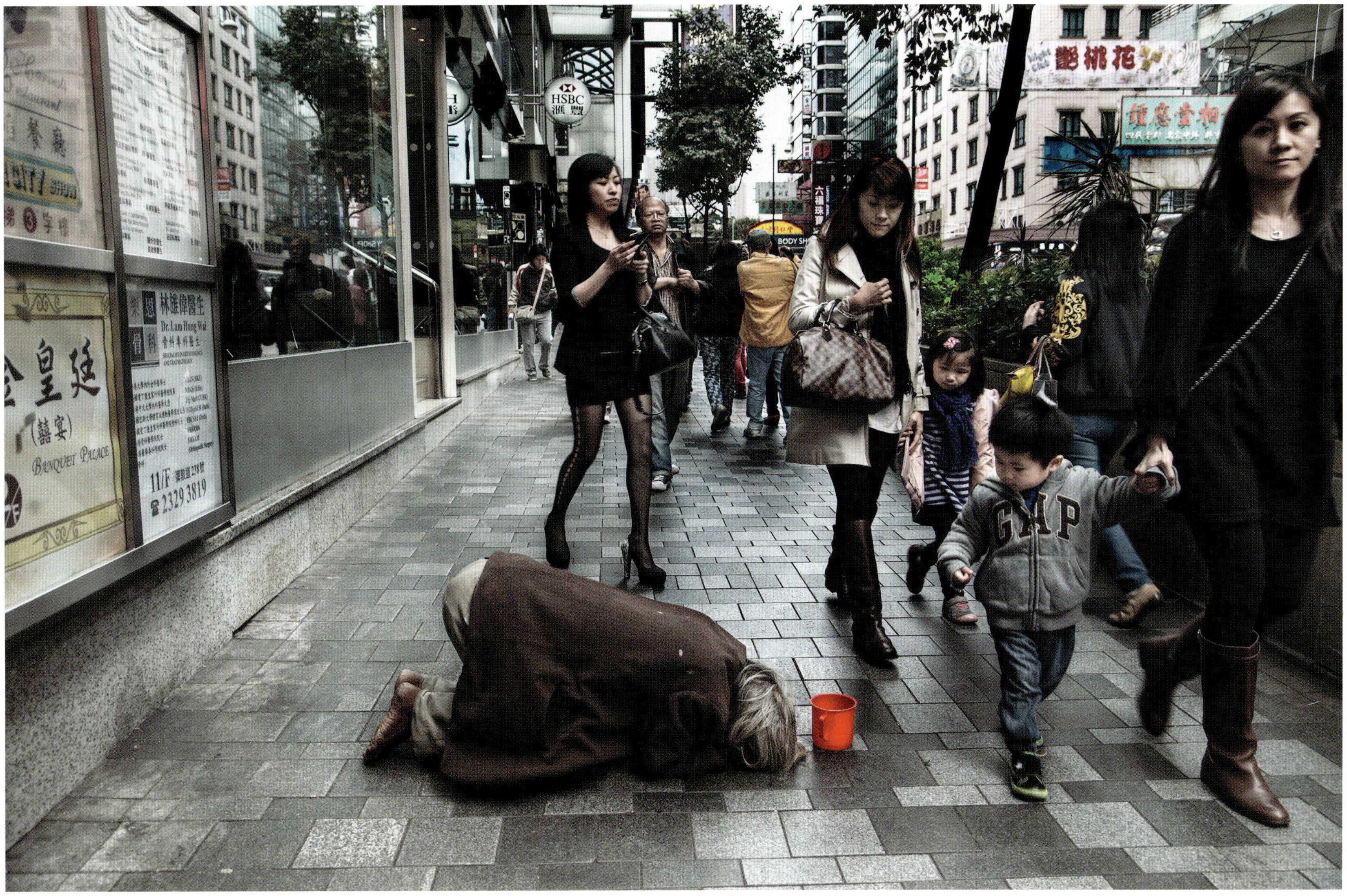

95 | Steve McCurry. *Man reading on a bench in Hong Kong, China,* 2014. Unpublished. © Steve McCurry.

96 | Steve McCurry. *People walk past a beggar on the sidewalk, Hong Kong, China,* 2014. Unpublished. © Steve McCurry.

BRIAN BRAKE: CHOOSING ASIA

Athol McCredie
Curator Photography, Museum of New Zealand Te Papa Tongarewa

Brian Brake's first contact with Asia was an incidental stop-over in Singapore in 1951 on a study trip to Europe. Coming from sparsely populated New Zealand, including boyhood years of living in a remote alpine village, the vitality and energy of its streets where people "lived, ate and died"[1] caused Brake to reassess his photography: "What jolted me out of the salon approach was the visual shock of seeing so many people having to live so close together in Singapore. My eyes started to roam, to see people, and then I had to record it."[2] He bought a Leica in Singapore, the classic camera of the photojournalist, but mainly used it to record scenic images. When he showed some of these New Zealand photographs to photojournalist Ernst Haas in 1954 he was reminded again how socially disengaged his picturesque images, born of camera club salon exhibitions, were. Haas was complimentary but wryly added, "By the way, do any people live in New Zealand?"[3]

Brake was fully galvanised this time and the resulting photographs he took on the busy streets of London helped gain him membership of the exclusive photo-agency Magnum in 1955. He was now a fledgling photojournalist in the company of leaders in the field. The following year, secure in the knowledge that Magnum would work to sell the photographs he sent back, he and his partner Nigel Cameron set off on an odyssey through Egypt, Yemen, Sri Lanka, Malaysia, Singapore, China and India. Their idealistic plan was that Cameron would write the stories and Brake take the photographs. In practice they only collaborated on one story, on Kashmir for *National Geographic*,[4] but the journey set the pattern for both of them of writing and photographing across this part of the globe, and for Brake of peripatetically criss-crossing the region for the next decade and more.

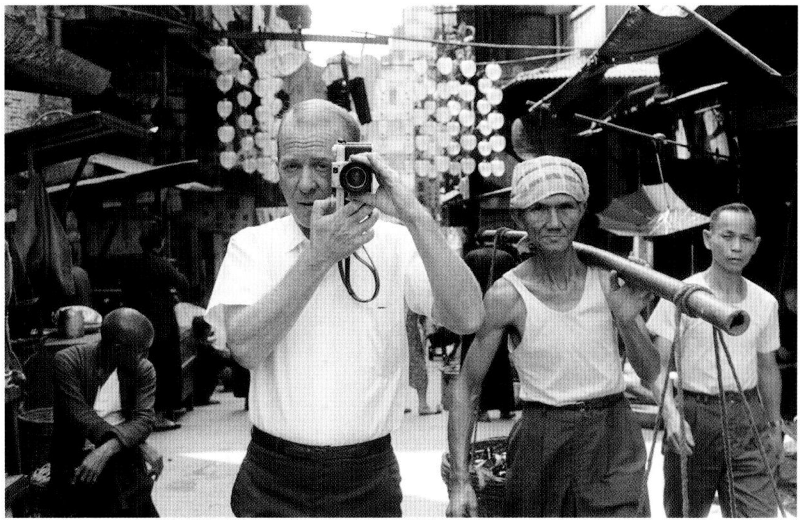

Unknown photographer. *Brian Brake in Singapore (?),* early 1960s. Reproduced from a 35mm black and white negative. Collection Museum of New Zealand Te Papa Tongarewa. Gift of Wai-man Lau, 2001.

A highlight of their travels together was three months in China in 1957, and a further significant stint for Brake there in 1959. Though accompanied by minders in the form of translators, guides and drivers, Brake and Cameron were adamant that they had access to anything they wanted to see. Brake photographed the spectacles of parades in Beijing for May Day in 1957 and the tenth anniversary of the founding of the communist state in 1959, each including the associated visits of Soviet leaders. These found ready outlets in international magazines such as *Paris Match* and *Life* (including a *Life* cover, the ultimate goal for many a photojournalist of the period). But the bulk of Brake's photographs were sympathetic images of everyday life amongst the Chinese. Cold War anti-communist sentiment

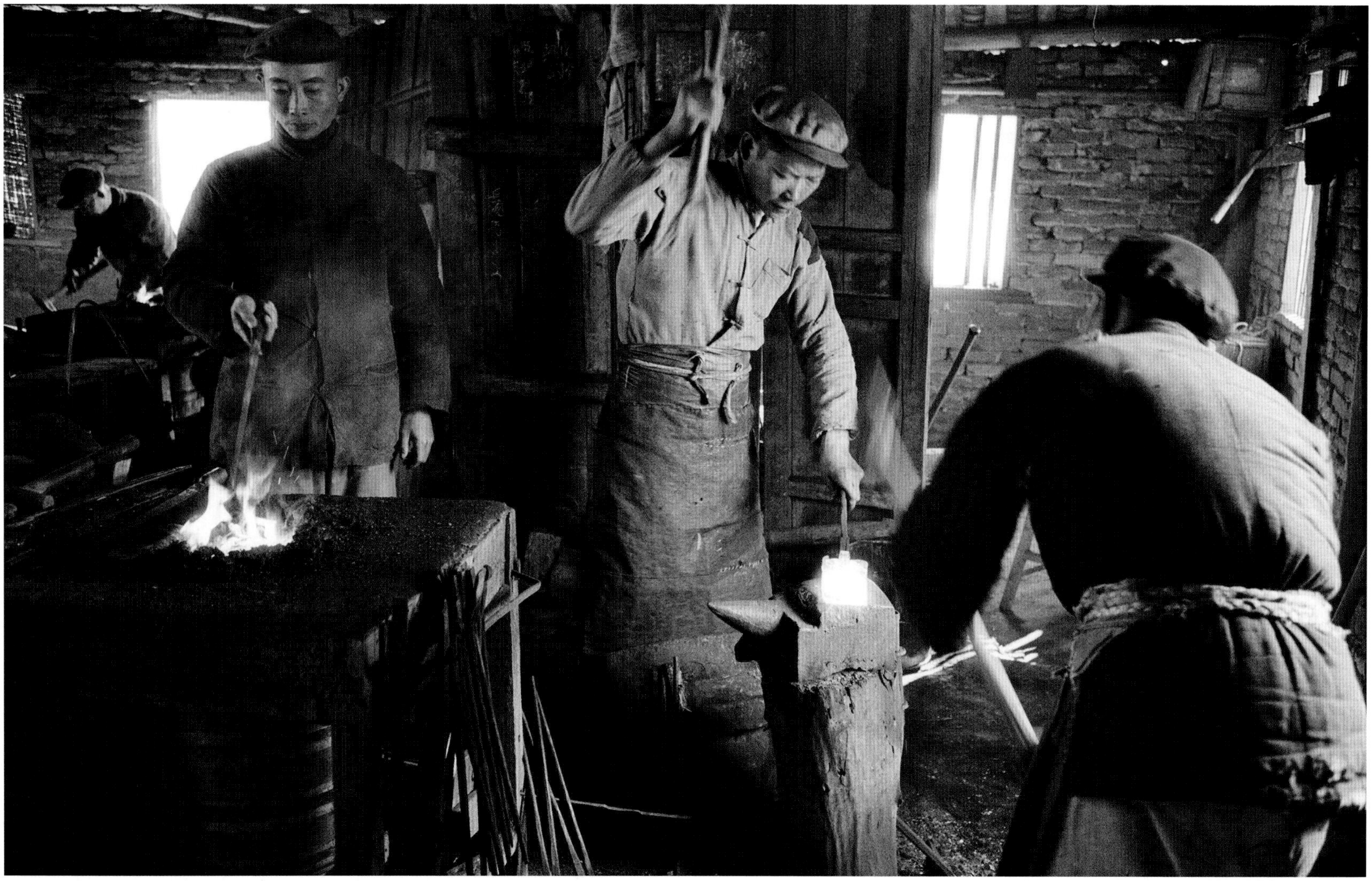

Brian Brake. *Forging iron in a commune*, 1959. Reproduced from a 35mm black and white negative. Collection Museum of New Zealand Te Papa Tongarewa. Gift of Wai-man Lau, 2001.

meant that few of these were published, yet along with the work of a handful of other foreign photographers such as the New Zealander Tom Hutchins, and Frenchmen Marc Riboud and Henri Cartier-Bresson, they capture an invaluable record of a country in a positive mood of massive reconstruction before the tragedies of the Great Leap Forward and the Cultural Revolution. During this period, Magnum's leading figure, Henri Cartier-Bresson, suggested to Brake that he choose a territory so the agency could ensure its members were globally well spread. Brake picked Asia. His work to date had mainly been there, and the monolingual photographer who was probably at a disadvantage around the Paris headquarters of Magnum found he "was more comfortable in Asian situations than in European. There wasn't the language barrier. In Asia they don't put you down if you don't understand the language—if you try and smile they're open and friendly."[5]

Cartier-Bresson's other proposition was that Brake should find a major project, something to get his teeth into. Brake nominated the monsoon weather cycle in India, a subject previously considered by others and felt too difficult to convey in photographs. Indeed, he judged his initial attempt in 1959 a failure, due to under-researching the topic. But he tried again in 1960, this time taking the trouble to get local feedback and to make the photographs reflect Indian experience: "I remember showing my monsoon pictures to some people in Calcutta. They said, 'Brian, that's not the monsoon, come with us ...' And they took me to their villages."[6] "It had to be authentic for them for it was their monsoon just as much as my interpretation."[7]

Brake's monsoon photo essay was a sensation when he showed it to European magazine editors, for it told an eternal, elemental story in a poetic manner, using color, sequence and layout—rather than a commentary text—to build and release tension that echoed the cycle of drought to rains. "The magazines fought for it like it was a news story," recalled Brake, though they had to hold off until *Life*, which had first option, published it in September 1961. Eventually it was printed in at least twelve picture magazines, each with a variant selection, and featured in a Museum of Modern Art exhibition on the photo essay in 1965.[8]

"Monsoon" marked a turning point in Brake's career. He committed to Asia by buying an apartment in Hong Kong in 1962 and basing himself there for the next fourteen years. Brake also found that his work fitted a new mood of the international picture magazines as they shifted from traditional black and white photojournalism to color reproduction and a focus on broad, thematic stories. He became acclaimed as one of the world's best magazine photographers[9] and now commanded the attention of the most prestigious magazine of all, *Life*, flagship publication of Time Inc.

Brake was never actually on *Life*'s staff, but felt he was considered "part of the family": "If you did a good job for *Life*, it simply kept on snowballing and you were given even more of a free hand all the time."[10] One of the first assignments was as contributor to a *Life* double issue on the movies, with Brake covering Asian cinema.[11] He was a natural choice for the job, as he had been a film maker himself early in his career and had already photographed on film sets in China, India and Sri Lanka. His next major shoot for *Life* was for a special Japan issue ahead of the 1964 Tokyo Olympics.[12] Now his freedom was so great that his brief from the magazine was simply to get the "feeling" of the country. In Brake's published images this became the contrast between traditional customs and modern Japanese life.

Less well known in Brake's oeuvre were a host of photo stories published in a diverse array of magazines in the late 1950s through to about 1965. These include items on Hong Kong for *Jours de France, Praline, Queen, L'Illustrazione Italiana* and *National Geographic* between 1958 and 1962, similar coverage of Kolkota for *Jours de France*, *Praline* and *Globus*; a piece on the legacy of the British Raj in India in *Paris Match* and the *Sunday Times Color Magazine* in 1962 and 1963 respectively; coverage of the Dalai Lama's flight from Tibet in *Life* in 1959; traditional Indian dance for *Horizon* in 1963; and a regular staple of stories for Hong Kong's *Asia Magazine*.

Further work on major features for *Life* occupied Brake in the mid-to-late 1960s. First was a feature in a seven-part series on the Roman Empire that required him to travel the breadth of the ancient territory. Brake again obviously pleased the magazine's editors, for he was then given the job of photographing all six parts of a series on ancient Egypt, a task that kept him busy for eighteen months over 1966 and 1967. Much of this work photographing

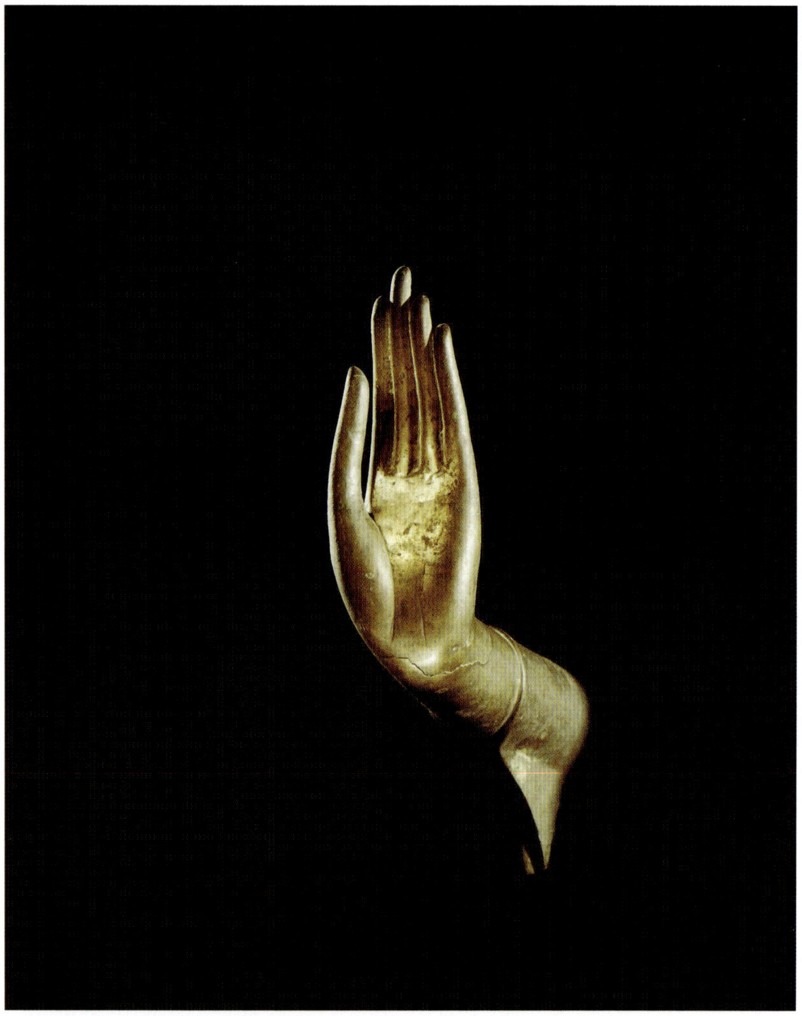

Brian Brake. *Hand from an image of the Buddha, National Museum, Bangkok, Thailand*, 1970. 127 x 102mm color transparency. Collection Museum of New Zealand Te Papa Tongarewa. Gift of Wai-man Lau, 2001.

monuments, tombs and museum pieces required a large tripod-mounted camera and studio lighting. The change in technique and subject matter heralded a shift to the next phase of his career as the picture magazines gradually folded in the face of competition from television, and he found a niche photographing Asian art objects for museum exhibition catalogues. These included, for example, *The sculpture of Thailand* for New York's Asia Society and *Form und Farbe* (on Chinese bronzes and ceramics) for the Museum für Ostasiatische Kunst in Cologne, both published in 1972. Books for museums did not provide a full time living however, so in 1970 Brake decided to revisit the craft of film making he'd learned in his early twenties at New Zealand's National Film Unit. He formed Zodiac Films in Hong Kong and spent the next five years making documentary films in Indonesia for the state owned oil company Pertamina. His best known are *Borobudur: The cosmic mountain* (1972), made to raise funds to restore the ninth century Buddhist monument in Java; and *The Ramayana Indonesia* (1974), in which dancers performing this ancient tale are filmed in the jungle and temples with a hand-held camera weaving freely amongst them as they slowly swirl about the lens.

Brake returned to live in the country of his birth in 1976 with the idea of working at a slower pace. Here he continued photographing for books on museum objects, but with New Zealand subjects, and branched out into corporate annual reports (including for Hong Kong's Jardine Matheson). He was also commissioned by Time-Life to photograph for books on Hong Kong and Sydney as part of their "Great Cities" series.[13] Now he found that the sort of crowded, cosmopolitan city that had been an eye-opening experience when first encountered in 1951, had become too familiar: "The [Hong Kong] assignment was a nightmare as I had lived in the city. I had to go around those corners that I knew so well and see everything afresh."[14] Brake's pictorial summation of Hong Kong ranged from a black and white photojournalistic mini-essay on the Tanka boat dwellers through to color aerial shots of patterns seen in the city below.

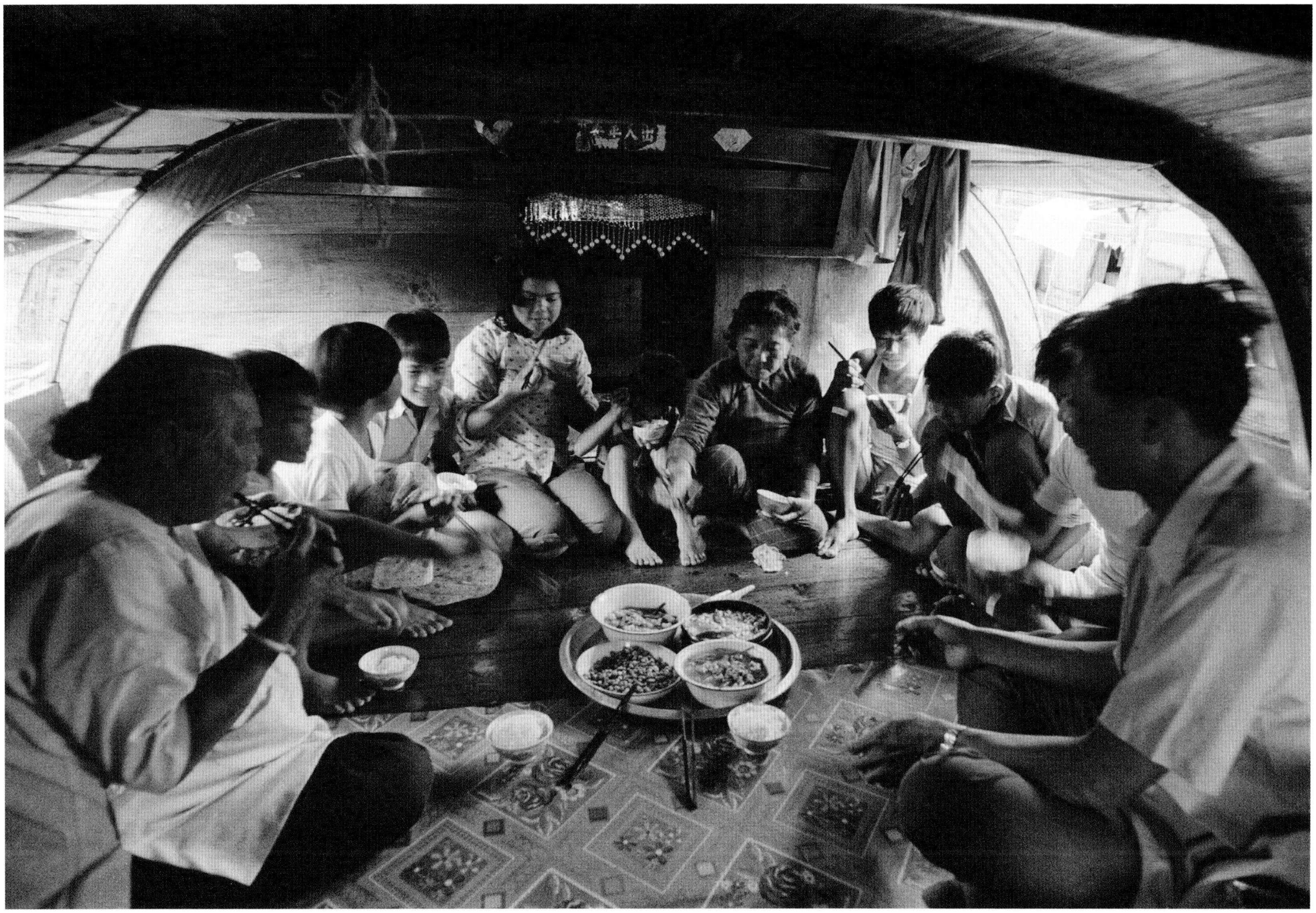

Brian Brake. *The Ma family eating a meal on their junk, Hong Kong.* Taken for *Hong Kong: Great Cities,* 1967. Reproduced from a 35mm gelatin silver black-and-white negative. Collection Museum of New Zealand Te Papa Tongarewa. Gift of Wai-man Lau, 2001.

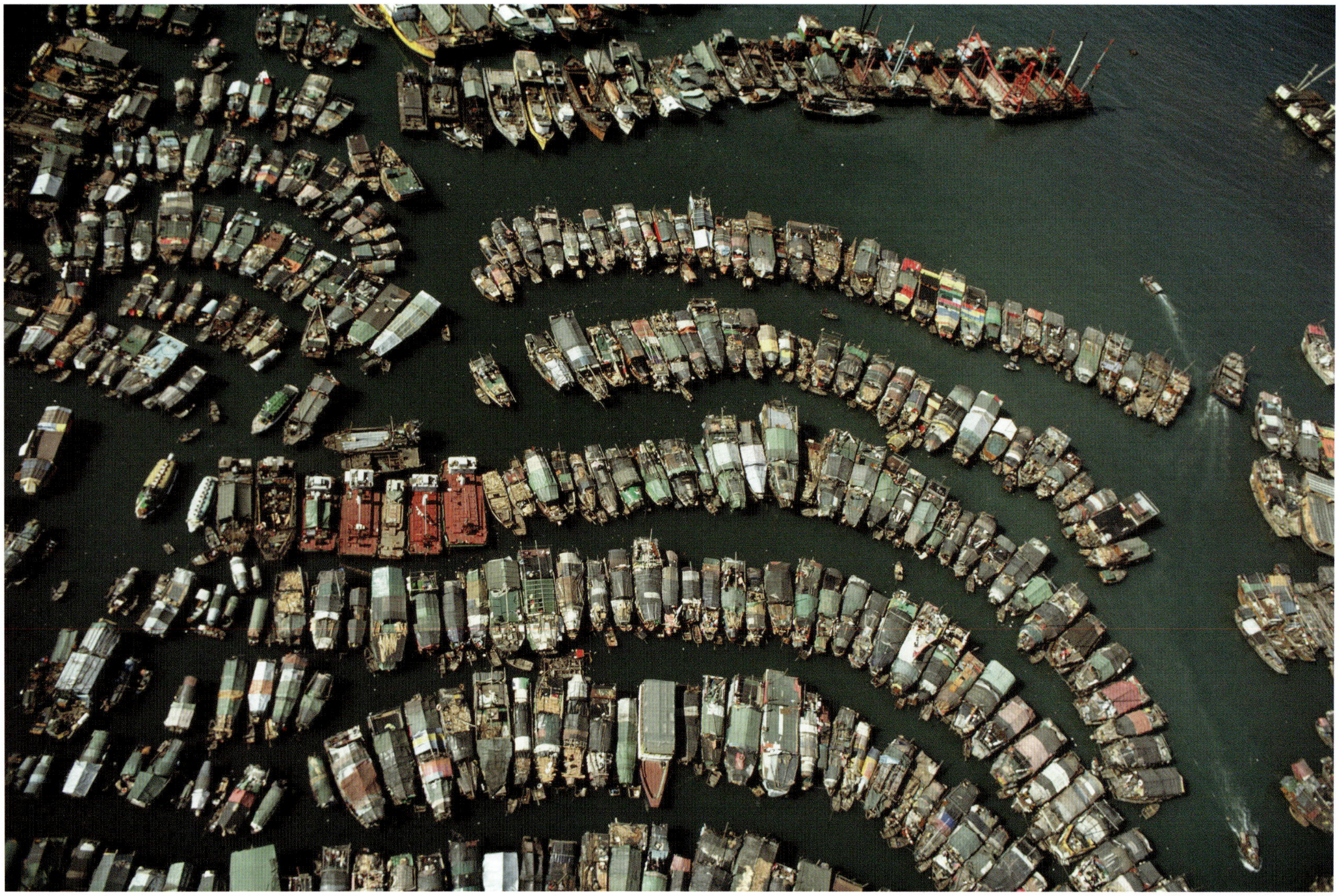

Brian Brake. *Boats on Hong Kong Harbor,* 1976. Brake, Brian and Robert Elegant. *Hong Kong: Great Cities.* Amsterdam: Time-Life Books, 1977. 35mm transparency. Collection Museum of New Zealand Te Papa Tongarewa. Gift of Wai-man Lau, 2001.

These demonstrated both the range of styles he could now draw upon and the fact that he was essentially an illustrative photographer, someone who could be relied upon to produce eye-catching images for publishers that captured a subject or theme. He was criticized on his return to New Zealand by a younger generation of newly emerged art photographers for producing "a kind of mercenary photography"[15] in which "you don't see a lot of Brian Brake coming through".[16] An individualized voice would have been largely incompatible with the requirements of mass market magazines however, and perhaps for Brake the personal aspect of his photography lay in his passion for his subject. He told a journalist that he had "loved working in Asia. The wealth of cultural heritage and history fascinated me—I could see it in the buildings and on the faces of people and I decided I wanted to impart that to the rest of the world."[17]

Biographical note

Athol McCredie is Curator of Photography at the Museum of New Zealand Te Papa Tongarewa. His many publications and exhibitions include *Brian Brake: Lens on the world* (Te Papa Press, 2010) and *New Zealand photography collected* (Te Papa Press, 2015). At Te Papa he has curated the exhibitions *Striking poses: New Zealand portrait photography* (2003), *Brian Brake: Lens on the world* (2010), *New Zealand photography collected* (2015–16) and took a lead role on the development of *Toi Te Papa: Art of the nation* (2006).

Notes

1: Brian Brake quoted in Tara Werner, "Brian Brake: Photography's distant enigma", *Metro,* vol. 6, no. 61, July 1986, p. 139.

2: David McGill, "Brian Brake: An Asian odyssey", *NZ Listener,* 10 May 1975, p. 10.

3: "Around the world in 35mm", *NZ Listener,* 11 January 1957, p. 10.

4: "The Emperor's private garden", *National Geographic,* vol. 114, no. 5, November 1958, pp. 606–47.

5: Werner, *op. cit.,* pp. 139–40.

6: Brian Brake, interview with Kathy Saunders in "Focus on New Zealand", *Kaleidoscope*, Television New Zealand, transmitted 17 May 1985 (television programme).

7: Dee Gibney, "Lens in the eye of a storm", *South China Morning Post,* 23 March 1973, p. 12.

8: There was never a fixed version of "Monsoon", and magazine editors and designers would have played a considerable role in the form it took in each case, though Brake undoubtedly exerted an influence where he could.

9: Influential editor Norman Hall of *Photography* magazine claimed that the "Monsoon" essay "ranked with the greatest achievements in photography" ("Topics: Come the rains", *Photography*, [1961], pp. 8, 10, undated tear sheet, Te Papa Archive).

10: Brian Brake cited in Craig Anthony, "Brian Brake photo-journalist", *Industrial and Commercial Photography,* May 1979, p. 19.

11: "Prodigious output of the East", *Life*, vol. 55, no. 25, 20 December 1963.

12: "The Modern Paradoxes", *Life*, vol. 57, no. 11, 11 September 1964, cover and pp. 10–23.

13: Brian Brake and Robert Elegant, *Hong Kong: Great Cities* (Amsterdam: Time–Life Books, 1977).

14: Angela Griffen, "Coming home", *Jetaway*, September–October 1983, p. 10.

15: Des Kelly, "Brian Brake: 40 photographs" (exhibition review), *PhotoForum* August–September 1976.

16: John B. Turner quoted in Werner (1986), p. 143.

17: "Brian Brake: New Zealand's master photographer in focus", *Tasman Journal*, vol. 5, no. 2, 1986, p. 10.

"THE SNAKE ON THE TABLE AND THE MERMAID ON THE WALL": STEVE MCCURRY'S ASIA

Anthony Bannon

Executive Director, Burchfield Penney Art Center

Is this not a beautiful way to begin: with Steve McCurry's *Tailor in monsoon, Porbandar, India*, 1983, an image of a man in such joy, neck-high in adversity, all to save an instrument of labors that also is a symbol of repair and restoration (plate 02 p 033)?

The happy man has found his sewing machine. With silver beard and hair, he wears the signs of life's long experience, perhaps wisdom. Though the austere image focuses solely upon him, his machine, and his reflection—The Man, the Flood, and the Machine—it also suggests narrative threads.

The picture has attributes we might identify as sacred, beginning with the old, anonymous art of stitchery—the grace of joining loose ends, of bringing things together, as with a garment or a people; even a book or a nation. With this narrative thread the viewer might weave a hope for continuity. The instrument once lost under the deluge now is found and returned. The machine and man reunite to suggest the reward of endurance and the clemency of acceptance, the tailor again with the means to make amends, to be of service in Porbandar, State of Gujarat, in Western India.

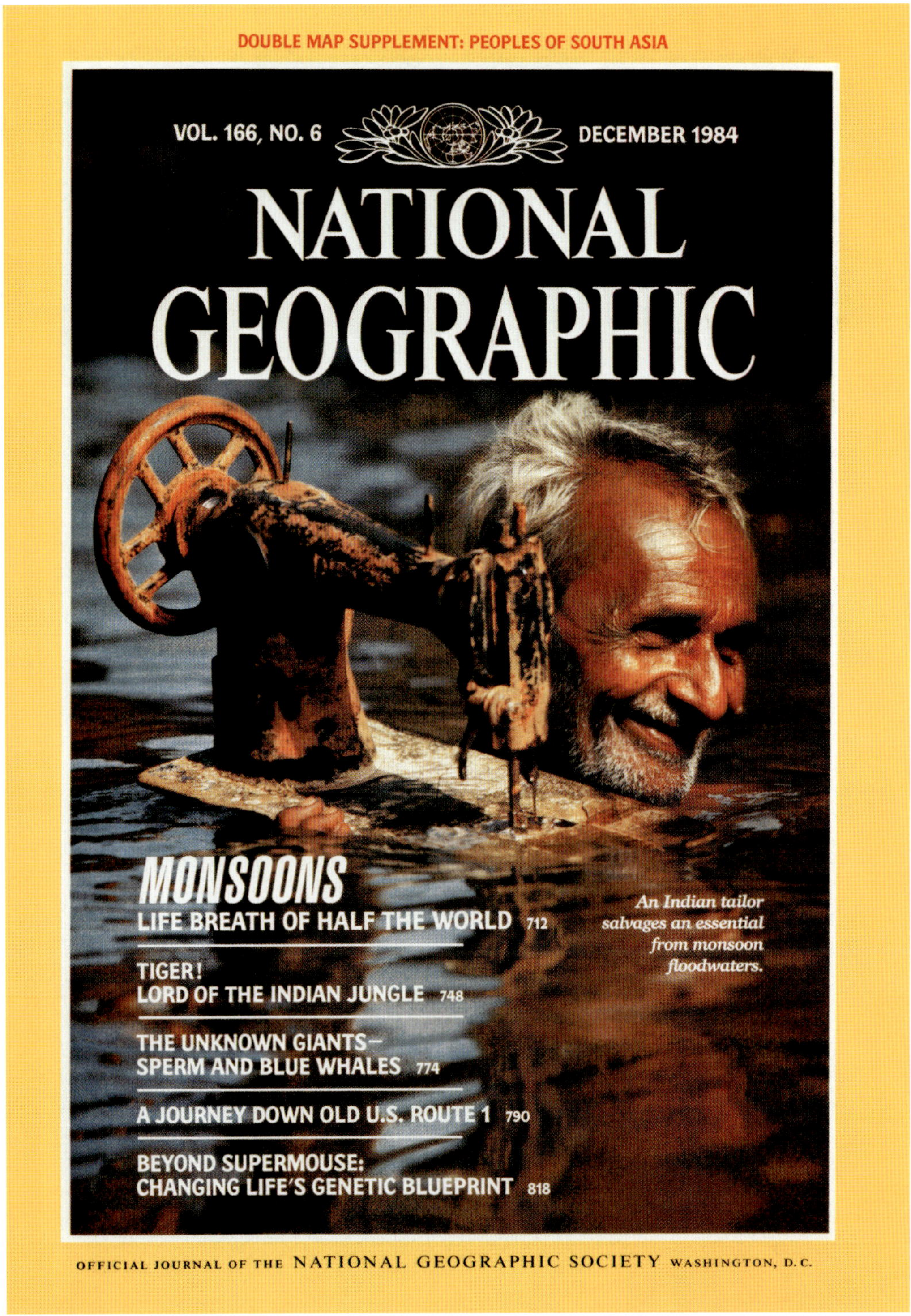

Steve McCurry. *Tailor in monsoon, Porbandar, India,* 1983. Cover, *National Geographic,* vol. 166, no. 6, December 1984. © NATIONAL GEOGRAPHIC CREATIVE.

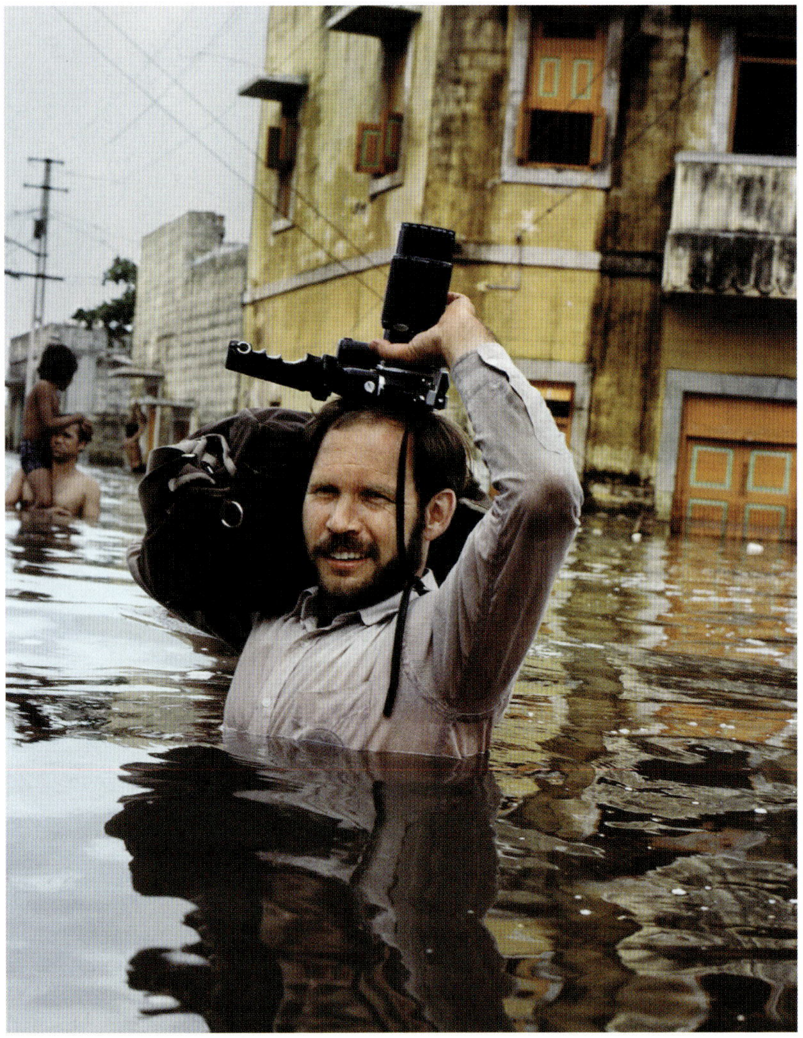

Unknown Photographer. *Steve McCurry in monsoon floods, Porbandar, India,* 1983. © Steve McCurry.

The exhibition *Picturing Asia*'s selection of nearly forty years of photographic vision by Steve McCurry proposes the variety of thin threads, so to speak, that hold a changing world together. These forty-six images thread among the millions of pictures the artist has created. His photography is vast and it is global, though he makes no secret of the fact that his soul is in East Asia, evidenced by the great body of his published works. Notably, McCurry portrays the people and their places that define what it means to live in our time—and to transform it.

McCurry's work suggests we see the tailor as among the holy ones. And there are others.

Find the father who carries his frail daughter across *A flooded street, Porbandar, India,* 1983 (plate 17 p 048) and the father in *A father and son, Rajasthan, India*, 1984, who shelters his son in the torrent, no house in sight. The boy in that rain covers his face, his eyes now blocked against the flooding of the land—and his gesture finds resonance in prayerful invocations located across the earth's many faiths and cultures (plate 15 p 046).

McCurry is known as a colorist, though for years he has pointed in another direction, asserting his allegiance to the masters of photography, such as the Americans Walker Evans and Dorothea Lange from the Farm Security Administration photography program (1935–1944); and the Hungarian-born global freelancer André Kertész (1894–1985), mentor of many, including McCurry's Magnum mentor, Henri Cartier-Bresson. These were among the men and women who have been the gatekeepers to photography's great ideas.

In the give and take between photography and painting, some may be tempted to diminish the importance of subject matter, seeing the tiny slice of time that is the province of the photograph as merely anecdotal. But McCurry's images resist separation from the life events they strive to present. They are direct, single-minded, no mistake about them. They contribute to his life-long quest for understanding. Surely color plays its role in his images, along with pattern and composition. But a photographer is not ashamed of the utility of information. Case in point:

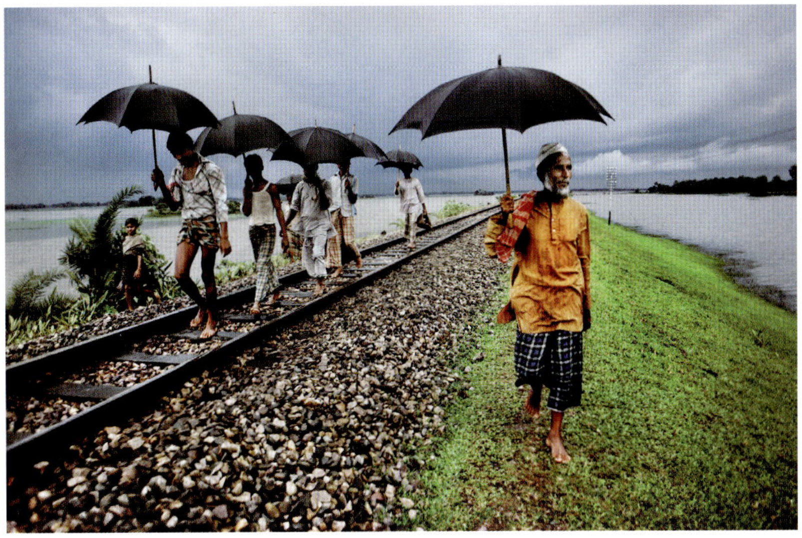

Steve McCurry. *Railway track, Bangladesh,* 1983. © Steve McCurry.

McCurry's first cluster of images in this exhibition takes up the theme of fortitude and acceptance, an inevitable, elemental struggle that will go on, life ever hanging from that tailor's thread. Men in the monsoon, for instance, are forced to go out of their way to return to their homes along the only route possible, the embankment in *Railway track, Bangladesh*, 1983 (plate 14 p 045). This trek, it is said, is a metaphor for our time alive and life's inescapable diversions. And it is fundamental to McCurry's work, also seen in the *Procession of nuns, Rangoon, Burma/Myanmar*, 1994, in the rain as well (plate 56 p 091); and seen more casually in the coincidental bicyclist passing the *Buddha statue in Mandalay, Burma/Myanmar*, 2008 (plate 61 p 097). Profoundly, the theme of fortitude and acceptance is found in the bent image of the seventy year-old *Widow returning from her ashram in Vridavan*, *Uttar Pradesh, India,* 1995, where she is commissioned to pray for others (plate 85 p 122); or in that light-struck daily trip to market by the *Flower seller at Dal Lake*, *Srinagar, Kashmir*, 1996 (plate 77 p 112).

People make do. In *Mother and child at car window, Mumbai, India*, 1993, a mother extends her palm for help, literally as an outsider, standing in the rain, petitioning as

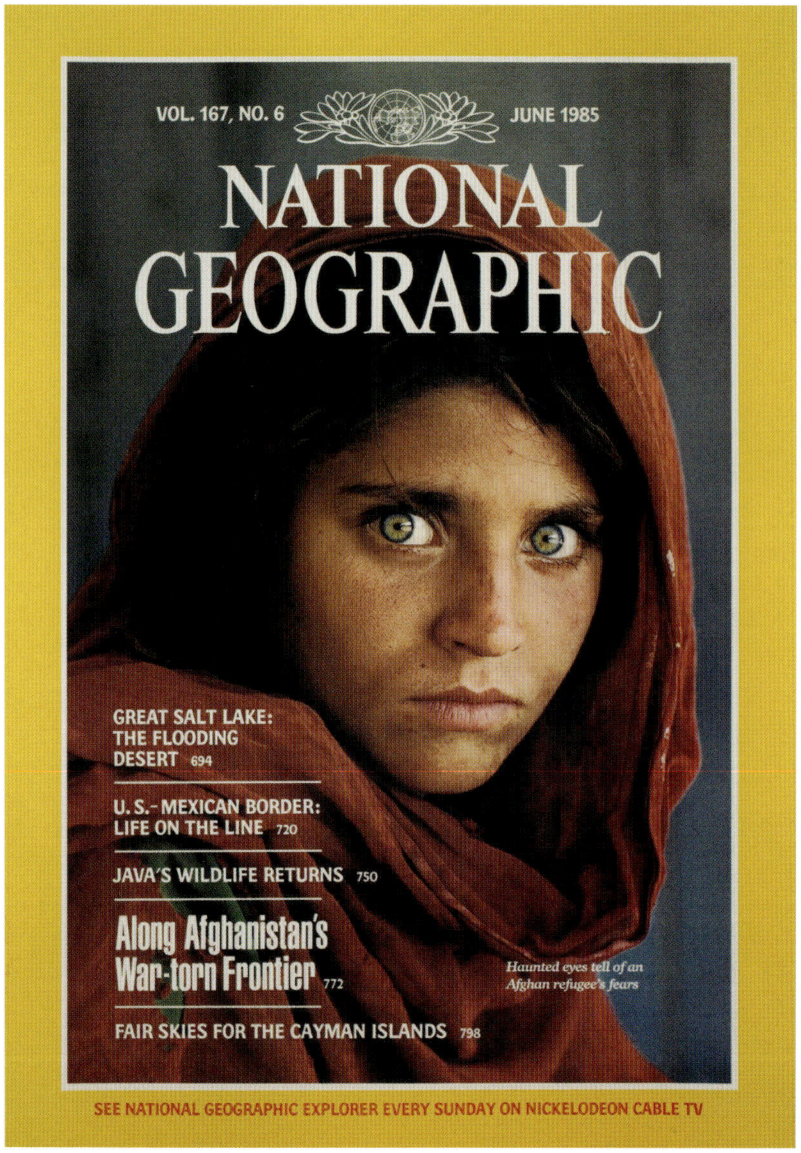

Steve McCurry. *Sharbat Gula, "Afghan Girl", at Nasir Bagh refugee camp near Peshawar, Pakistan,* 1984. Cover, *National Geographic*, vol. 167, no. 6, June 1985. © NATIONAL GEOGRAPHIC CREATIVE.

if her open hand was a blessing proffered to whomever was protected inside the vehicle (plate 13 p 045). Such gestures assert that what is true may be difficult, or what is beautiful, unpleasant. Within these moments, the viewer may discover virtue, even when it hurts.

Those women in *Dust storm, Rajasthan, India*, 1983, who moments ago were working on the highway, now form a circle, their backs to the stinging monsoon wind, facing each other as mirrors of protection (plate 12 p 044). It is the second image in a sequence of eight photographs that show the beneficence and perils of the monsoon. A telling detail: the water jugs at the women's feet are empty.

At roughly ten-image intervals in the exhibition's sequence, we encounter one of McCurry's iconic photographs; these are turning points, moving the narrative thread into new themes, for example from water and its wealth and weal to a by-now familiar sign of defiance, maintained in the face of grave national challenge. For such a transition, who can ignore the power of the twelve year-old *Sharbat Gula, "Afghan Girl", at Nasir Bagh refugee camp near Peshawar, Pakistan*, 1984—her clear-eyed endurance at the heart of turmoil (plate 20 p 052)? Her story now is legendary, although decades have passed since McCurry gained the cover of *National Geographic Magazine* on 8 June 1985 for Sharbat's image. She is the symbol of displaced youth, an image of struggling young migrant people throughout the world. Collect here the other images cited from 1983 to 1985 and total the experience of a continent and its struggle to stay alive. McCurry's contribution to global understanding is not lost in the amnesia of yesterday's stories. In this period he was recognized as the Magazine Photographer of the Year by the National Press Photographer's Association.

He also won the Oscar Rebbot Memorial Award and four awards from World Press Photographers. And he covered the Iran-Iraq War with distinction. Sharbat's gaze carries the reader forward to the *Blue Mosque*, *Mazar-i-Sharif, Afghanistan*, 1991, also in Gula's homeland, and to the swirling flock of doves symbolizing the hope for peace (plate 33 p 068). This is the same year in which McCurry covered the Gulf War in Kuwait and Iraq.

McCurry has a poet's eye for complex symbols, balancing piety with profanity, highs with lows, often in the same image—a *Father and daughter at home, Kamdesh, Afghanistan*, 1992, for instance, sitting at tea with a frightful weapon on the table with them, set as if an element among the tableware (plate 34 p 070). This scene is commonplace, McCurry told me. "You see it all the time: a father and daughter or son, tea and a gun." This was the year McCurry spent trying to make sense of Afghanistan after the war. It also is the year he joined the famed Magnum Cooperative Agency as a full member. The father's look is wary, and in her way, so is the daughter's. The artist's images weave among the fundamental needs of humankind—needs for food and drink; for safety and shelter; for family and community, and, tacitly, for esteem. Where once a meal was taken with a proper roof overhead and with one's neighbors within earshot, now the echoes of different shots are recalled with no one but a surreal cluster of people around a fire in the *Bombed townscape, Herat, Afghanistan*, 1992 (plate 38 p 074). This is a very different approach when compared to the perspectives of *A Day in the Life* (*of America*, or *Japan*, or ...)—the 1981–91 photo-book series initiated by Rick Smolan—and a long reach back to achieve again Edward Steichen's *The Family of Man* (1955) with its quote from Virgil: *What region of the earth is not*

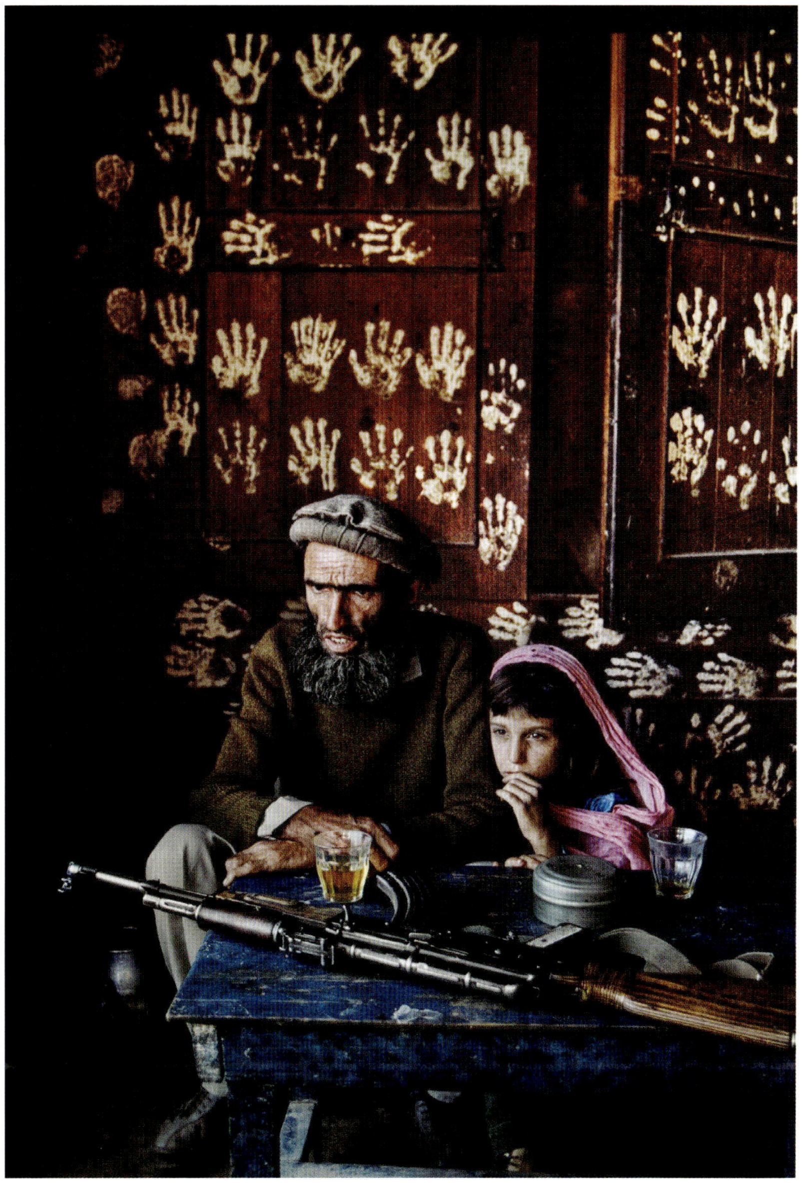

Steve McCurry. *Father and daughter at home, Kamdesh, Afghanistan,* 1992. © Steve McCurry.

full of our calamities? It is difficult to imagine this rubble at Herat, just for example. The absence of basic needs brings forward deep-seated themes, notably a tenacious will to live and find the means to say again and again, "This is what I must do." I, the *Orange seller, Kabul, Afghanistan*, 2003 (plate 35 p 071) must sell oranges from the trunk surface of a burnt-out car, and I will make do." The image requires no words. And in the same year, McCurry agreed to show nearly a hundred of these images at the largest and oldest independent museum of photography—The George Eastman House—in an exhibition organized for subsequent tour by the late Rick Hock. A subsequent cluster of books and films about his work then magnified public awareness, and the awards—from around the world—continued.

McCurry's skill with color—he says that he does not think about it—and his declarative style of composition are gifts that focus the image's purpose. For these are cultures, after all, ways of being in the world, and McCurry has taken on the task of tallying the manners through which people declare themselves—perhaps in *Asylum, Kabul, Afghanistan*, 1992, where we encounter a man in a deep trance, pondering the patterned presence of light (plate 40 p 076); or more sanguinely, threading the ironies of social change with women in burquas shopping for shoes in *Kabul, Afghanistan,* 1992 (plate 37 p 073); or a man dressed for business striding past *A ruined building, Kabul, Afghanistan*, 2002 (plate 41 p 077). Ironies abound.

McCurry's career took off after *The New York Times* published a black and white image of *Mujahideen fighters watch convoy, Nuristan, Afghanistan*, 1979, as an enemy convoy passes by, outside the frame of the picture (plate 39 p 075). He was among the first photographers on the scene in Afghanistan. *Time* magazine also ran his work and McCurry won the Robert Capa Gold Medal, awarded annually for "best published photographic reporting from abroad requiring exceptional courage and enterprise". From the beginning, McCurry takes on the theme of watchful waiting, as in *Monks praying at Golden Rock, Kyaiktiyo, Burma/Myanmar*, 1994 (plate 54 p 088); or with the *Novice getting his head shaved, Burma/Myanmar*, 2011, in commitment to the Holy Life (plate 57 p 092).

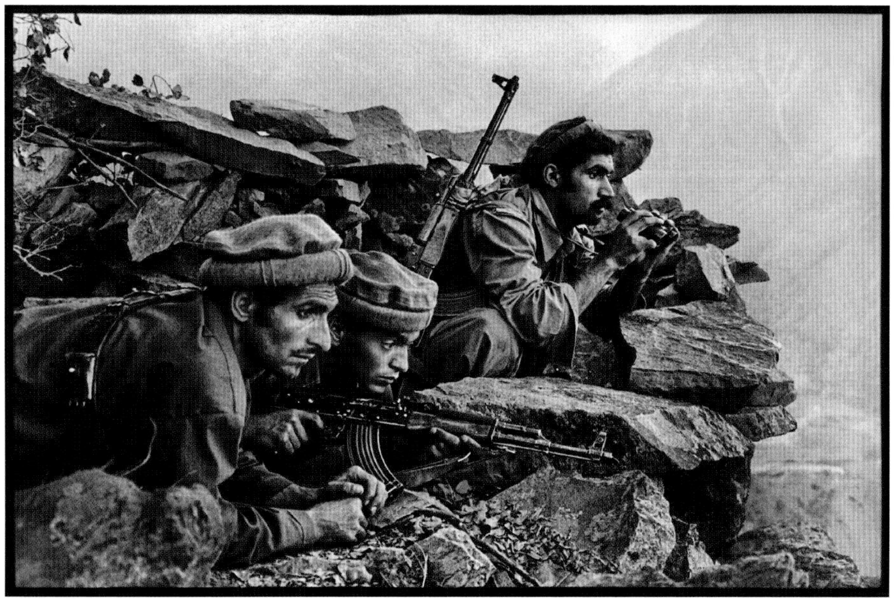

Steve McCurry. *Mujahideen fighters watch convoy, Nuristan, Afghanistan,* 1992. © Steve McCurry.

Like the great ones who preceded him in the Magnum Cooperative (particularly the founders Robert Capa, David Seymour, Cartier-Bresson and George Rodger), McCurry's strength has been the diversity of his unbridled curiosity. Thus, he finds wonder and amazement on the factory floor, where *Women in a garment factory, Rangoon, Burma/Myanmar*, 1994,

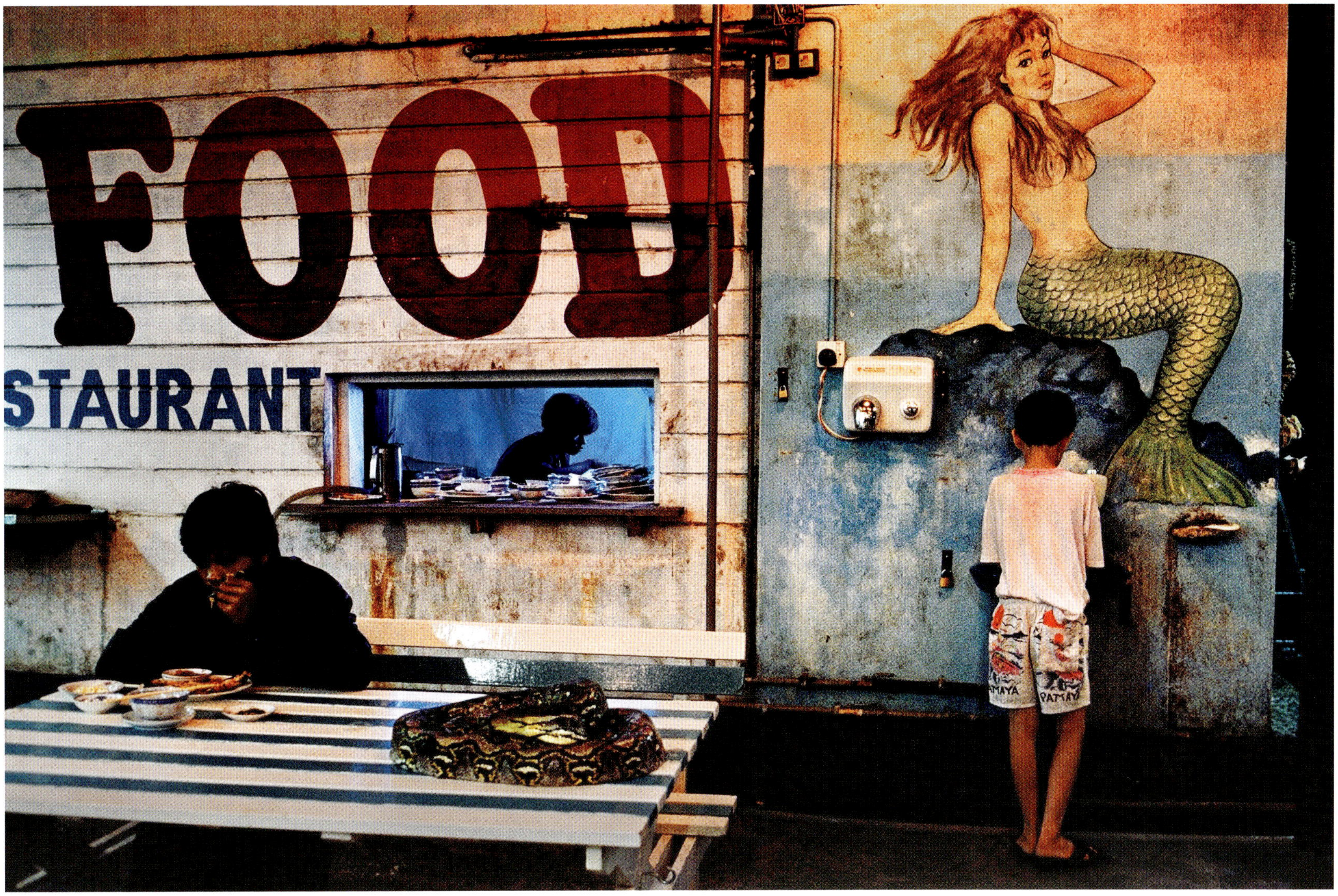

Steve McCurry. *"Food", Rangoon, Burma/Myanmar,* 1994. © Steve McCurry

wear pink uniforms like the *Procession of nuns*, although in a temple of industry (plate 56 p 091). How does the *Fisherman on Inle Lake, Burma/Myanmar*, 2008, guide his boat with his ankle (plate 60 p 096)? How do the *Stilt Fishermen, Weligama, Sri Lanka,* 1995, balance on their poles (plate 80 p 116)?

These are pictures of our time, a sampling of those that would otherwise remain unrecorded—that *Pilgrim at a stupa, Amdo, Tibet*, 2001 (plate 82 p 119), or that *Coal miner, Pol-e-Khomri, Afghanistan*, 2002 (plate 83 p 119). The labor and the games. The mundane and the melody: the snake on the table in "*Food*", *Rangoon, Burma/Myanmar* (plate 42 p 078)—and the mermaid on the wall. The stitching; the seeing, and now the saying.

Biographical note

Anthony Bannon is emeritus director at George Eastman Museum, Rochester, New York, now serving as research professor and director of the Burchfield Penney Art Center at SUNY Buffalo State, USA. He has written about Steve McCurry's photographs in *Steve McCurry* (London & New York: Phaidon Press Ltd., 2005). In 2012 Dr Bannon was awarded the J. Dudley Johnston Award for History and Criticism in Photography from the Royal Photographic Society of Great Britain.

OPENING THE DOOR

Jonathan Flaws

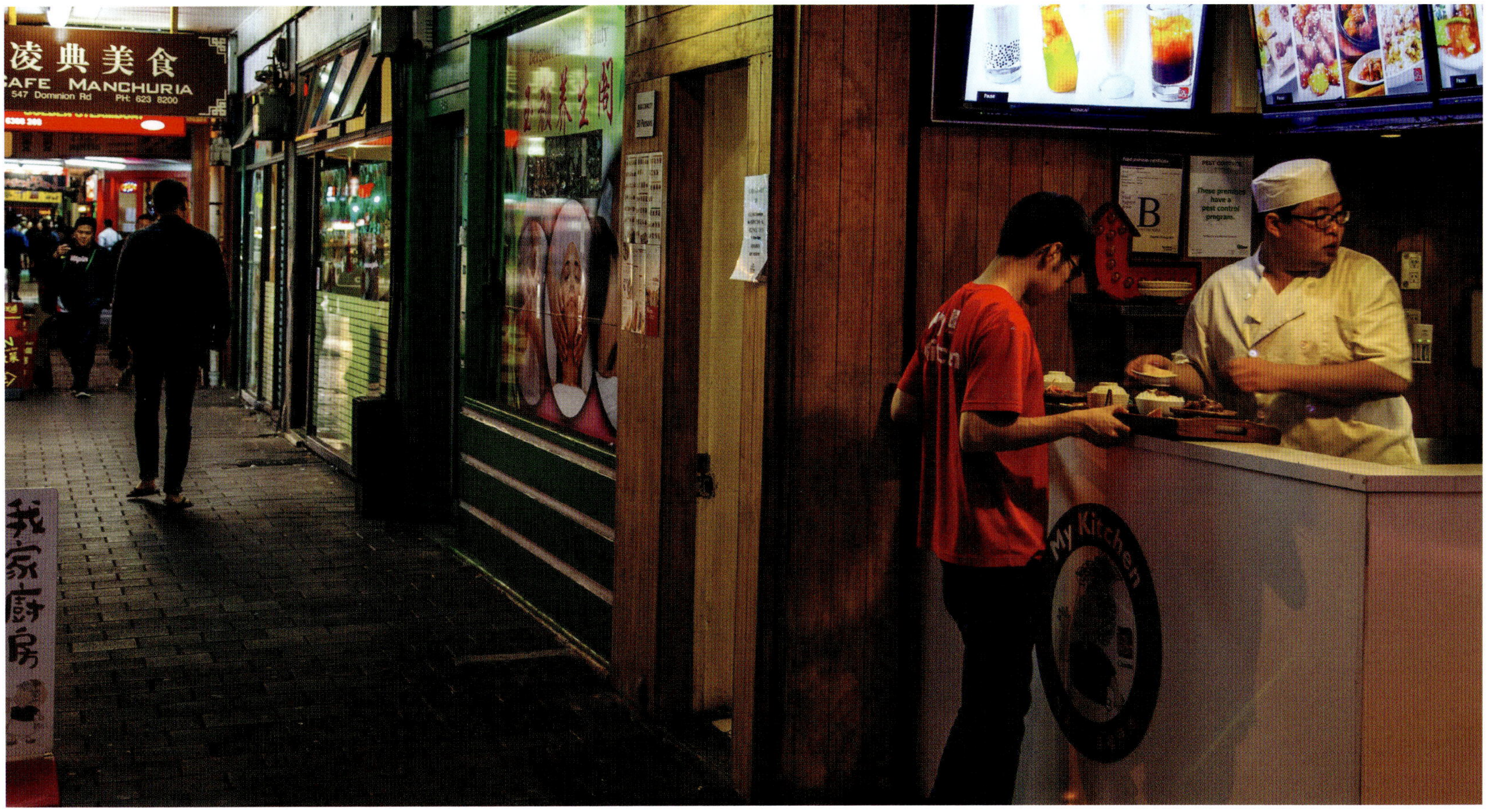

Jonathan Flaws. *Dominion Road Streetscape—My Kitchen, Auckland, New Zealand,* 2016 © Jonathan Flaws.

If I had been asked to picture Asia in 1961 I could not have done so. As a young boy living in New Zealand, I had no reference points in my environment and no experience to help me create the picture.

Today, it's not difficult. Reference points abound in the Asian streetscape along Dominion Road in the Auckland suburb of Balmoral. Now, "Dominion" and "Balmoral" are British-colonial placename ghosts among the Asian signage. In 1961, where today a Chinese server collects food to deliver to the tables upstairs for "My Kitchen", I would pack my bicycle with newspapers for the start of my before-school newspaper delivery round. What was then a newsagent-bookshop is now a Chinese kitchen.

At what is now the Wuhan café, I would park my bike and follow the warm smell of freshly baked bread through the door of the local bakery and exchange a paper for a fresh loaf of bread. As I continued my deliveries, if I was in luck, a milkman would stop and exchange a pint of milk for a newspaper and complete my traditional English breakfast on the run.

In the New Zealand of the 1960s, it was hard not to feel British. I was born a New Zealand citizen but, confusingly, I was also a British subject.[1] My parent's generation called Britain "Home"; which, for my father it was.

Historically, New Zealand had some connections with Asia through trading in sealskins in the early 1800s,[2] the Chinese goldminers in the late 1800s, and market gardeners in the 1930s and 1940s. In Dunedin, Presbyterian missionaries and doctors formed the Canton Villages Mission and founded mission stations and hospitals in Southern China.

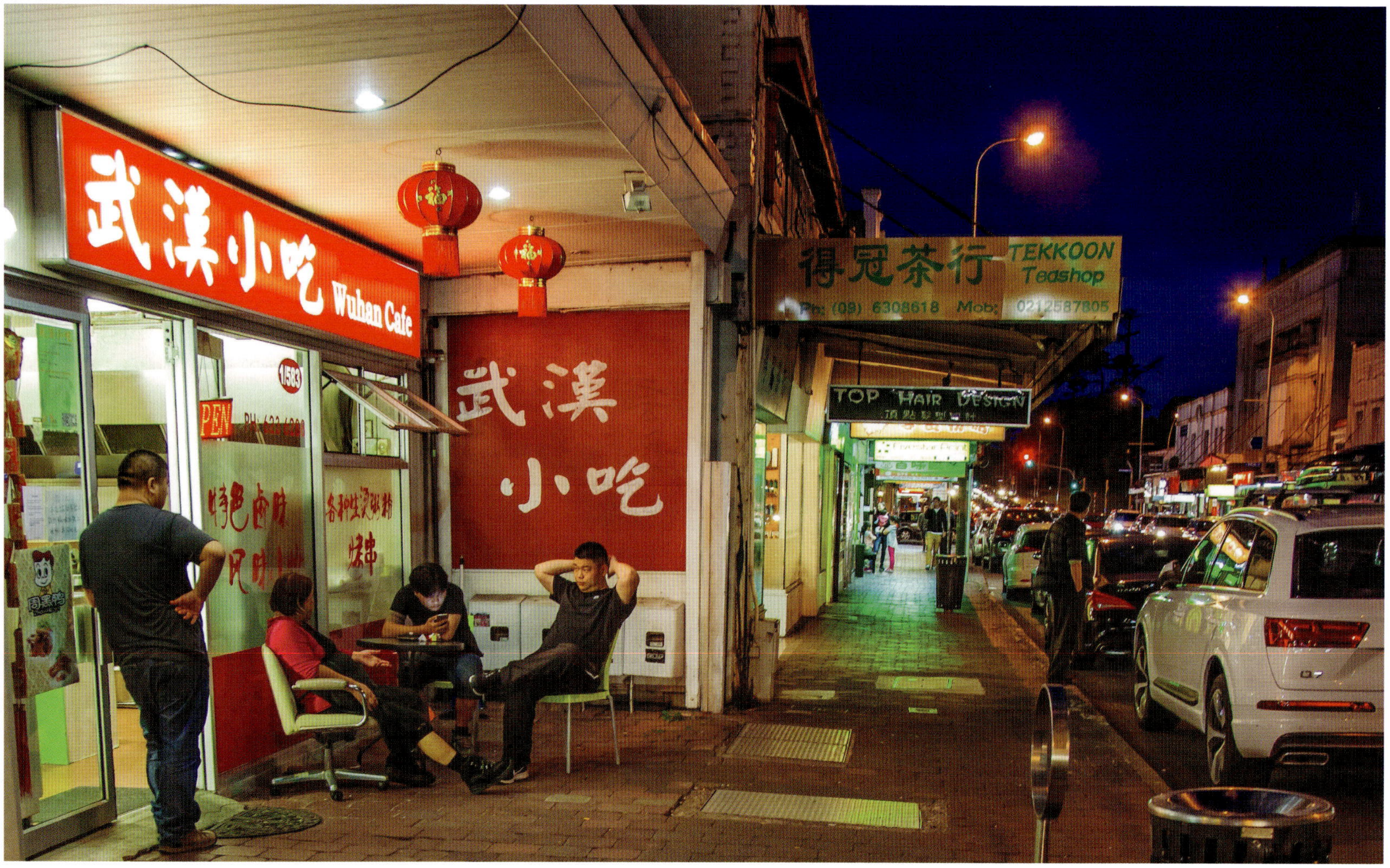

Jonathan Flaws. *Dominion Road Streetscape—Wuhan Café, Auckland, New Zealand,* 2016 © Jonathan Flaws.

Despite these connections, Asia was a mystery to me. New Zealand-born Chinese, too, found it hard to picture Asia. A colleague of mine at law school described picturing himself in history as an English knight atop an armoured steed with a lance, only to become confused when he looked in the mirror and saw the facial features of China. We were both more familiar with the history of Britain than of our own region.

I first became aware of Asia in my early teens through paper-based media. Magazines such as *Life* and *National Geographic* were an important source of information—primarily visual—and it was through these that my awareness of Asia developed.

On reflection, I can flag Brian Brake's "Monsoon" essay in the 1961 international edition of *Life* as the start of my awareness of Asia.[3] Looking back over old *Life* editions I can see now that Brake's photographic essay on the monsoon was a significant change of emphasis. Previous editions had presented photographs as adjunctive to politically motivated text.[4] In the "Monsoon" essay, politics is absent. Text and poetry emphasize and develop the photo-narrative. But the images spoke words that penetrated and remained in my memory long after the magazine was returned to the shelf.

A decade later and my wife, Mary, a geography teacher, used the "Monsoon" essay as a reference source for teaching Monsoon Asia, a topic in the curriculum. The New Zealand education system was changing focus. Mary started my collection of Brian Brake's photography when she found and purchased for me an old copy of the international 1961 edition of *Life* with "Monsoon Girl" on the cover, in a bookshop in Christchurch (plate 01 p 032).

By 1984, the text and the photographs in magazines had become synchronized. Steve McCurry's *National Geographic* narrative on a rail journey across India accompanies text by the travel writer Paul Theroux.[5] The text and the photographs no longer conflict, and we are now presented with a combined narrative on the humanity of India. McCurry was asked by *National Geographic* to photograph the monsoon. Instead of replicating Brake's work, his photographs provided a narrative on the effect of the monsoon across a wider range of Asia.[6]

McCurry then produced a stunning example of the lasting impact that can be created by the right image. His article was entitled "Along Afghanistan's War-torn Frontier", but it was his "Afghan Girl" photograph on the cover of the June 1985 issue of *National Geographic* containing the story that memory retains, not the words of the article.[7]

In 2007, I reconnected with Brake's "Monsoon" when I purchased at auction a boxed set of his photographs from the "Monsoon" essay. In the 1980s, Brake was asked by David Lange, our Prime Minister at the time of the reopening of the New Zealand High Commission in New Delhi, to create a set of prints from the monsoon series as a gift from New Zealand to India. He also decided to experiment with creating a smaller boxed set of the same prints for commercial sale. Sadly, he died before he could commercialize the set.

Television and video have largely replaced print as our primary means of information. In September 1997, the first

National Geographic Channels were launched in the United Kingdom, Europe and Australia. *National Geographic*'s 2013 television documentary on McCurry's last roll of Kodachrome film not only triggered my memory of his magazine photographs but connected Brake and McCurry for me.[8] Their images in magazines had helped shift my focus from Britain to Asia in a way that the New Zealand education system had not.

The documentary led me to acquire my second boxed set of photographs—this time from Steve McCurry—a collection of photographs from his last roll of Kodachrome, including the now iconic portrait of the Rabari elder with the hennaed beard.[9] When I collected the photographs from McCurry in New York, I suggested the concept of a combined exhibition with Brian Brake. This was the first step on the path to *Picturing Asia: Double Take* at the Asia Society's Old Victoria Barracks gallery in Hong Kong.

This exhibition showcases the "double-take" Brake and McCurry narrative on Asia. Although the full scope of their respective work spans the globe, each will be especially remembered for their work in Asia. In curating this exhibition, Ian Wedde has enabled the two photographers to engage in a conversation about this complex, fascinating, diverse range of peoples and cultures. Viewers have the opportunity to join this conversation—to bring to it narratives based on their own experiences and demographics. These will include not only stories like mine, in which I was enabled to picture Asia by two great photographers; but also the stories of people from Asia, looking at the ways in which they are represented here.

Whereas once I felt like a bewildered outsider peering through a distorting taxi window at an unknown world, I have at the very least, through the images of these two photographers, been enabled to open an imaginative door, step into the rain, and take a breath of Asia.

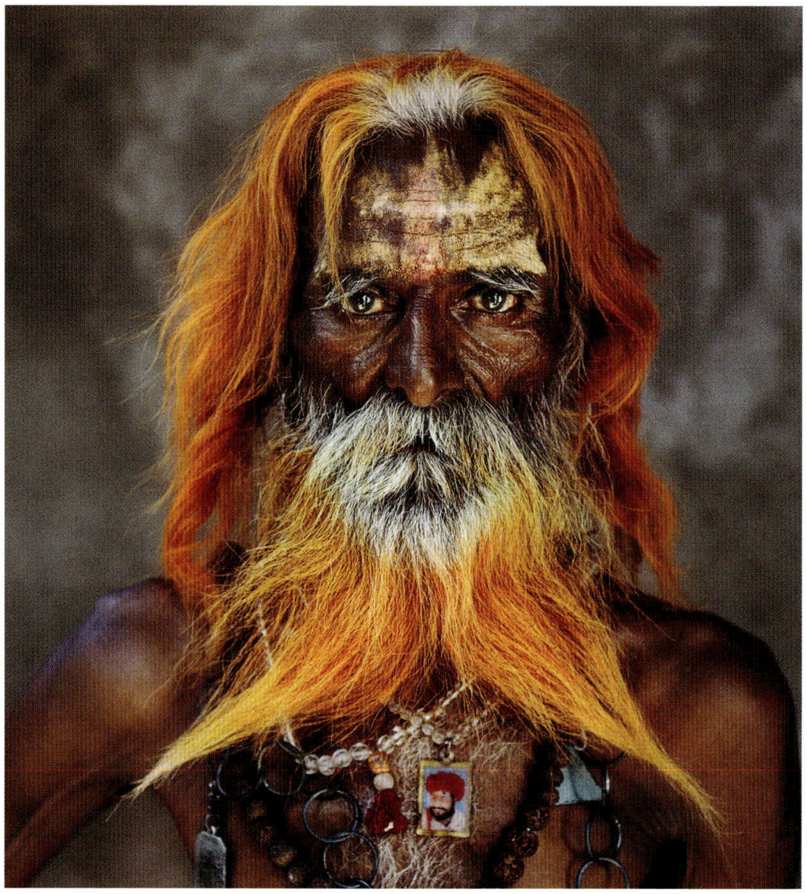

Steve McCurry. *Rabari Tribal Elder, Rajasthan, India,* 2010. © Steve McCurry.

Biographical note

Jonathan Flaws is one of the initiators of *Picturing Asia: Double Take*. He is a New Zealand lawyer and collector of art with an emphasis on photography.

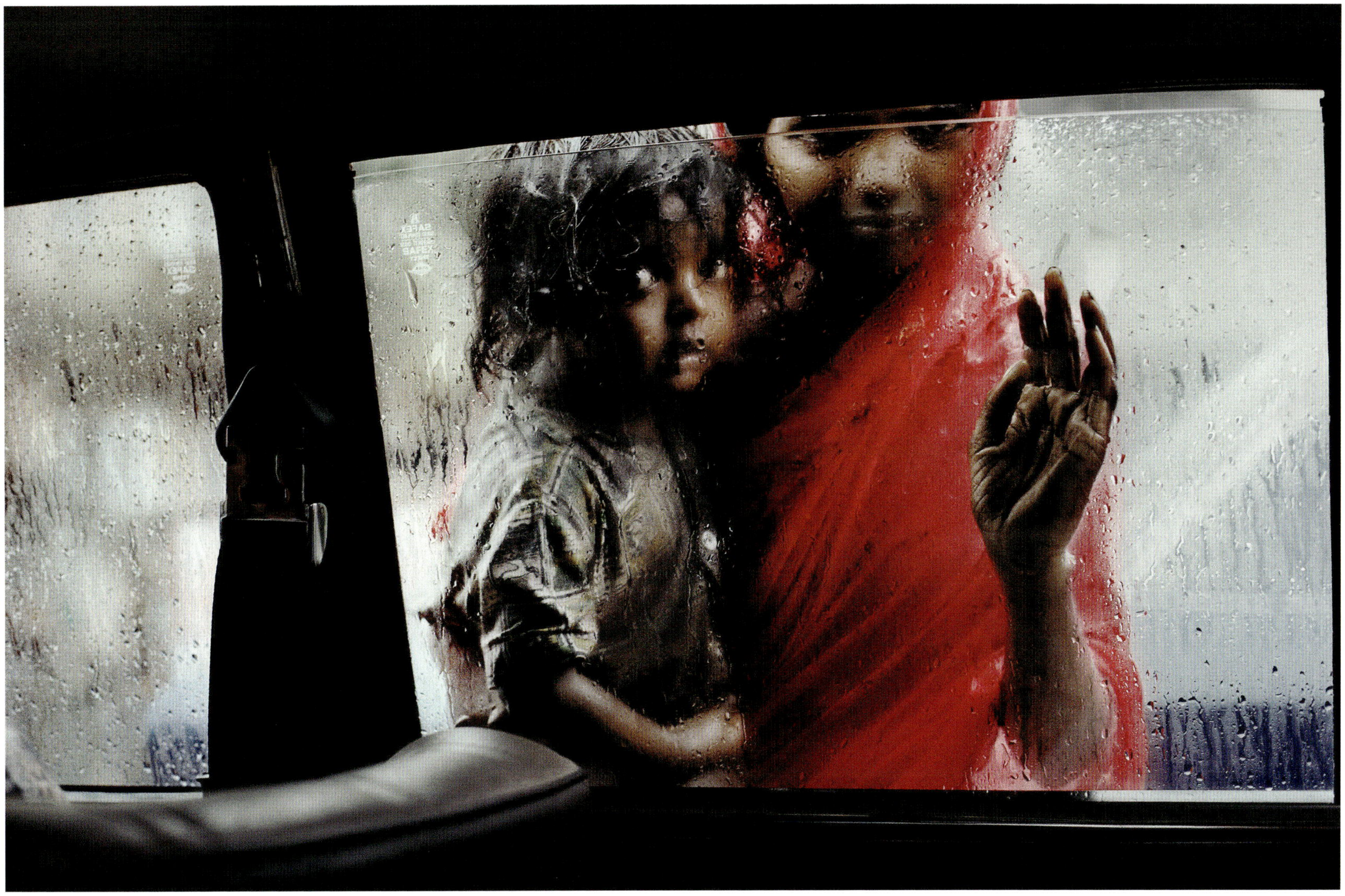

Steve McCurry. *Mother and child at car window, Mumbai, India,* 1993. © Steve McCurry.

Notes

1: The British Nationality and New Zealand Citizenship Act 1948 declared that everyone born in New Zealand after the Act commenced (1 January 1949) was a New Zealand citizen by birth. But it also provided that by virtue of that citizenship the person was also a British subject.

2: http://www.teara.govt.nz/en/asia-and-new-zealand/page-1. Accessed 10 May 2016.

3: "Monsoon", *Life International*, vol. 31, no. 11, 20 November 1961, cover and pp. 42–55. Fourteen photographs of the monsoon in India.

4: For example, "Dalai Lama's Welcome", *Life,* vol. 46, no. 18, 4 May 1959, cover and pp. 26–33. Seventeen photographs of the Dalai Lama's arrival in India from Tibet; and "Big show, no glow for K in Red China", *Life,* vol. 47, no. 16, 19 October 1959, cover and pp. 32–39. Sixteen photographs of the tenth anniversary celebrations in Beijing.

5: "By Rail Across the Indian Subcontinent", *National Geographic* vol. 165, no. 6, June 1984, cover and pp. 696–743. Thirty-four photographs of train journeys across India.

6: "Monsoons—Life breath of half the World", *National Geographic,* vol.166, no. 6, December 1984, cover and pp. 712–47. Twenty-six photographs of monsoon rains across Asia and Australia.

7: "Along Afghanistan's War-torn Frontier", *National Geographic*, vol. 167, no. 6, June 1985, cover and pp. 772–97. Twenty-two photographs on the impact of the conflict in Afghanistan.

8: *National Geographic,* "The Last Roll of Kodachrome". Video documentary uploaded 3 July 2015 to https://www.youtube.com/watch?v=S_2XFAw1qtg.

9: "A Rabari Tribal Elder", frame 15, "The last roll of Kodachrome," June 2010. View at http://www.vanityfair.com/culture/photos/2011/02/last-kodachrome-slide-show-201102_old#11.

PICTURING ASIANS

Evans Chan
Film Director

In a world ruled by photographic images, all borders ("framing") seem arbitrary. Anything can be separated, can be made discontinuous ... conversely, anything can be made adjacent to anything else.[1]

—Susan Sontag

By nature, photography is born of a raiding into—a rupture of—the flow of time. A moment, once snapped and frozen, can no longer be connected to anything else associated with the event, the same building, the same scenery, or even the same person. Similarly, a modern nation state, born of its unique history, is of course separate, distinct, different from all other—even neighboring—countries, regardless of its terrestrial belonging to a certain designation, such as Asia. As one walks through this visually striking exhibition, *Picturing Asia: Double Take*, one shouldn't forget that "Asia" is historically more a Euro-cultural concept than a physical entity. There is no logical geographic separation between Asia and Europe, and even Africa is separated from Asia merely by the man-made Suez Canal.[2]

According to one list, there are fifty-eight countries in "Asia" including Armenia, Israel, Iran, Syria and unrecognized states such as Taiwan and Palestine.[3] On another list, Russia, which straddles Asia and Europe, is included.[4] Interestingly, even though in the eighteenth century the Russians disputed the originality of using the Urals to demarcate Europe from Asia by the Swedish geographer Philip Johan von Strahlenberg in his map of 1725, they were pleased to be recognized, geographically, as Europeans rather than Asians. As such, the defining moment of Asia in its modern, Strahlenbergian, inception carried with it a sense of disfavor, in tandem with a growing European pride arising from the expansion of Europe during the Age of Discovery between the fifteenth and eighteenth centuries. According to the ancient geography of Ptolemy, the boundary of a much smaller Europe didn't extend beyond the Black Sea.[5]

Though photography wouldn't become viable until 1839, the emerging conception of a modern Asia coincided with Johann Heinrich Schulze's experimentation with silver nitrates, which laid the very foundation for the invention of photography. With consumer-level digital imaging taking off towards the turn of the last millennium, we may well have entered what has been called a "post-photographic" age. But unless one insists on the materiality of film, photos are all around us, more important, more obsession-inducing than ever—notably in social media. The mobile phone's photographic function has brought about a selfie-izaton of everyday life. And the latest tablet—iPad Air 2 at time of writing—trumpets its bigger capacity for storing more snapshots, its higher-resolution screen for viewing better HD photos.

If photography, as Sontag suggested, can fragmentize any phenomenon, it also makes everything and anything being adjacent possible. Today we can see that the Edward Steichen-curated *Family of Man* exhibition of 1955 suggested a narrative about the triumph of "globalization"—an achieved common, planetary humanity via photography, the implication of which caused Roland Barthes to decry the emptiness of the exhibition's simplistic, de-historicized "humanism".[6]

This leads us to the current exhibition. No doubt, *Picturing Asia: Double Take* does make far-flung "Asian" nations adjacent. I remember several years ago, as a jury member of the Singapore Film Festival, I was astonished to find a Turkish entry in the Asian competition film section, when Turkey had been campaigning to join the European Union. The film's amicable representative later told me, jokingly, that Turkey wouldn't mind having it both ways. I recall this anecdote to underscore the strangeness of finding my idea of Asian-ness, as a Hong Kong-raised New Yorker, being challenged by Turkey. Indeed, it's a bit startling to see McCurry's own 1979 career-launching photo of the Mujahideen fighters in Afghanistan in the same exhibition that also features Brake's photo of some washing hung outside the apartment window of a sunny Singapore in the 1960s.

Billed as a "Double Take", this exhibition doesn't pretend to be conjuring "The Family of Asia" or of Asians. The photos on view represent the visual sense of curiosity and benign cosmopolitanism of two gifted photographers, Steve McCurry and the late Brian Brake. Neither Brake nor

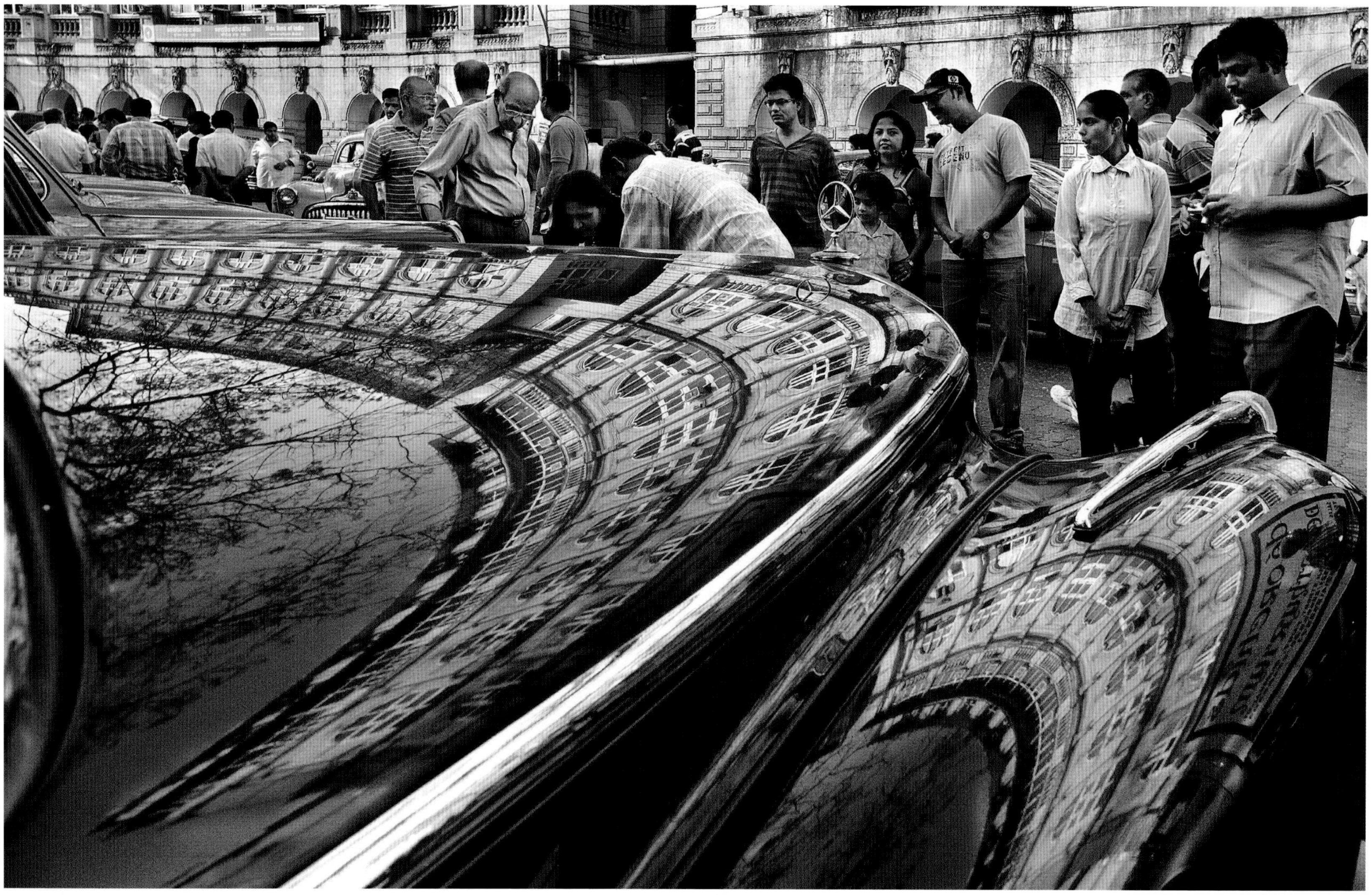

Raghu Rai, *INDIA. Mumbai. Enthusiasts at a vintage-car rally at Harniman Circle.* 2010. © Raghu Rai/Magnum Photos.

McCurry, despite the latter's early career, are known as war photographers as such. But the weight of history is felt, especially in McCurry's photos. His idea of the Afghan people's ability to endure almost anything seems to define his corpus to a large extent. Yes, it applies to the *Orange seller, Kabul, Afghanistan*, 2003 (plate 35 p 071) in war-ravaged Kabul, but most profoundly to the iconic *Sharbat Gula, "Afghan Girl", at Nasir Bagh refugee camp near Peshawar*, *Pakistan*, 1984 (plate 20 p 052) whose steely gaze and posture are haunting indeed. And probably no less in his *Flower Seller at Dal Lake, Srinagar, Kashmir,* 1996 (plate 77 p 112), the *Dust storm, Rajasthan, India*, 1983 (plate 80 p 116), or, if you will, the portrait of a young, poised Aung San Suu Kyi (plate 58 p 093), who has in the intervening years become a global hero for her political survival. Aung may now be open to criticism about her indifference to the treatment of the Muslim Rohingyas in Myanmar, but the vicissitudes of history form a narrative, not a photo, unless the photographer is interested in following up on the subject.

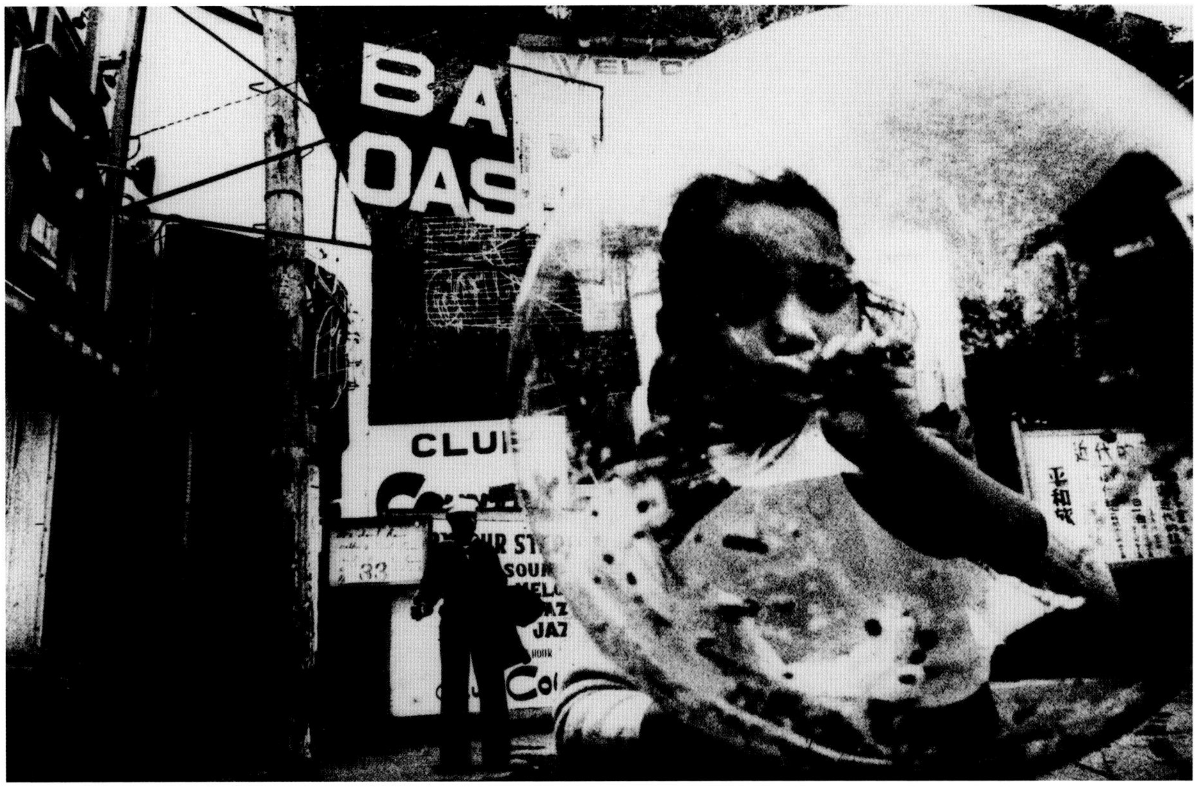

Shōmei Tōmatsu, Yokosuka from the series *Chewing Gum and Chocolate,* 1959. Gelatin silver print.
© Shōmei Tōmatsu - INTERFACE / Courtesy of Taka Ishii Gallery Photography / Film.

One pronounced feature linking both photographers is their penchant for evoking Eastern/Asian spirituality, from Thailand to Indonesia to Myanmar, India and more. The idea of "endurance" naturally calls forth the reality of hardship. And the common ground underlining both photographers' work in this exhibition is their portfolios of the monsoon season in India. One can see "endurance" as subtly allied to religious "faith", and McCurry's view of the monsoon as a cycle of catastrophe and rebirth certainly references Hindu mythology. The centrality of Indra, the Hindu god of rain, in the Indian psyche was illustrated as recently as 2012 when a mischievous legal notice was sent to Lord Indra, asking Him to explain within three days why adequate rains did not arrive in the Hardoi district during the monsoon.[7] How can a photographer overstate the importance of Indra, or the monsoon, when the Lord is the crucial weather mechanism that delivers fresh water to the Indian subcontinent? The rain-drenched close-up face of Brake's "*Monsoon girl" (Aparna Das Gupta)*, 1960 (plate 01 p 032) is lit up by a radiant, sensuous smile; while McCurry's *Tailor in monsoon*, *Porbandar, India*, 1983 (plate 02 p 033) shows an elderly man, with only his head and sewing machine above water, also smiling. Endurance, joy, spirituality: a compelling narrative chord.

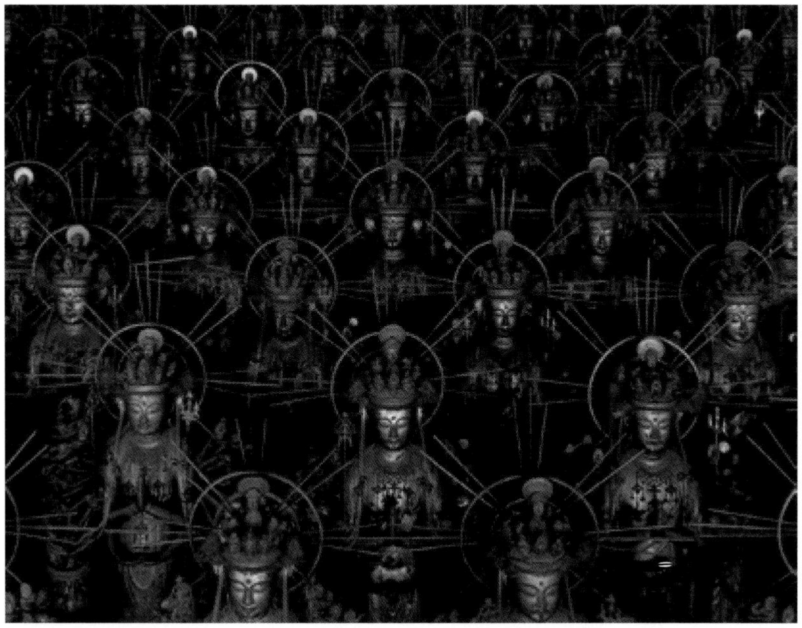

Hiroshi Sugimoto. *Hall of Thirty Three Bays/Sanjusangendo 020* (1995). © Hiroshi Sugimoto, courtesy Fraenkel Gallery, San Francisco.

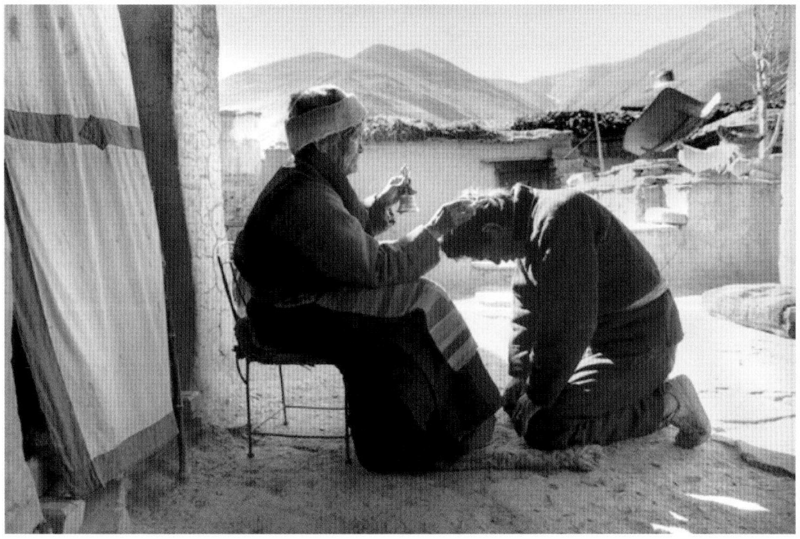

Lu Nan. *Chongye, Lhoka* (An oracle Pemayangin, 78 years, chants to heal the ill). © Lu-Nan/Magnum Photos.

However, such a religiously inflected, joyous view of India could be of lesser interest to a native Indian photographer such as Raghu Rai, whose many boldly perspectival photos are about the complex negotiation between tradition and modernity within an ancient civilization.[8]

And Brake's gorgeous portraits of Japanese temples, monuments and memorial rituals are not often the concerns of adventurous Japanese photographers either. For instance, Shomei Tomatsu's *Chewing Gum and Chocolate* photographs of post-occupation Japan 1959-78,[9] or Hiromi Tsuchida's *Hiroshima* (1985)[10] are both pointed responses to U.S. imperialism and war atrocities. Even in the case of Hiroshi Sugimoto's series of Buddha statues at Kyoto's Sanjūsangen-dō, while the photos may convey a consoling, uplifting spirituality, they also schematize the enduring, quasi-military, awe-inspiring might of pre-modern Japan.[11] Of course, exotic locations such as Tibet will often contain spiritual subjects. Both Brake and McCurry photographed Tibet. And within the Magnum collective, other than McCurry, the Japanese Hiroji Kubota[12] and the Chinese Lu Nan have all ventured into Tibet.[13]

During the heroic days of photojournalism—notably the Vietnam War years—the photos of the napalmed girl Phan Thị Kim Phúc by Nick Ut in 1972, Ron Haeberle's of the My Lai Massacre in 1968, and Malcolm Browne's of the self-immolated Vietnamese monk Thích Quang Duc in 1963 contributed to the end of an unwinnable American war. Thereafter, the backlash has been the tight control of disturbing images depicting U.S. military ventures. In that mirror image of censorship, direct or indirect, photos of self-immolated Tibetan monks within China since 2009 are rarely seen, and those outside China, such as in Nepal and India, seldom puncture the media spheres. If McCurry's pictures of Tibet are supposed to be paying homage to the resilience of Tibetan Buddhism under pressure, with recent news about the persecution of the Rohingya Muslims by the Buddhist majority, his pictures of the Myanmar Buddhas actually indict the assumed innocence and nobility of spirituality.

Brake was attracted to patterns and structures, for example in his photograph of riverboats in Brunei with colored umbrellas (*Riverboats with umbrellas, Brunei*, 1987—plate 68 p 105)—a teleological or quasi-religious sense of aesthetic order. Another Brake photo also shows a grouping of umbrellas—this one has a direct association with spirituality—one of his famous "Monsoon" images. Though not included in this exhibition, the Jagannath Festival photograph exerted a major impact on a young McCurry, who copied into his notebook the *Life* photo essay caption (*Life*, September 8, 1961): "Brake's Monsoon: 'A black sea of open umbrellas surges around the hilltop temple of Jagannath (Orissa), Lord of the Universe …'"[14]

In both the Brunei and Jagannath photos, umbrellas are used to shield against the elements. In the latter, umbrellas are in the hands of worshippers. Fast forward to the end of 2014—during a seventy-nine-day Occupation known as the Umbrella Movement that broke out in Hong Kong, umbrellas became self-protective gear, as much against pepper spray and tear gas canisters as sun or rain—as well as symbols of rebellion.

The massive movement demanded the fulfillment of an internationally notarized promise of universal suffrage made by Beijing during Hong Kong's transition from British to Chinese rule in 1997. One wonders how Brake, who lived in Hong Kong between 1962 and 1976, would have reacted to the intricate patterns of umbrellas—at times in physical confrontation with armed police—the myriad cell phone lights in the waving hands of protesters, and the proliferation of art works during the umbrella occupation. Such images, seen for almost three months on global TV, are a far cry from his celebratory scenes of China from the 1950s, some of which may hew too closely to officially prescribed visuals as exemplified by his *May Day celebrations, Tiananmen Square, Beijing, China*, 1957 (plate 32 pp 066-067). They are also a far cry from images of modern Asian/Chinese/Hong Kong materialism in Brake's image of the Hong Kong Jockey Club (*Rooftop exercise yards of the Hong Kong Jockey Club*, 1976—plate 92 p 131), or McCurry's *People walk past a beggar on the sidewalk*, which was taken in 2014, the Umbrella Movement year (plate 96 p 135).

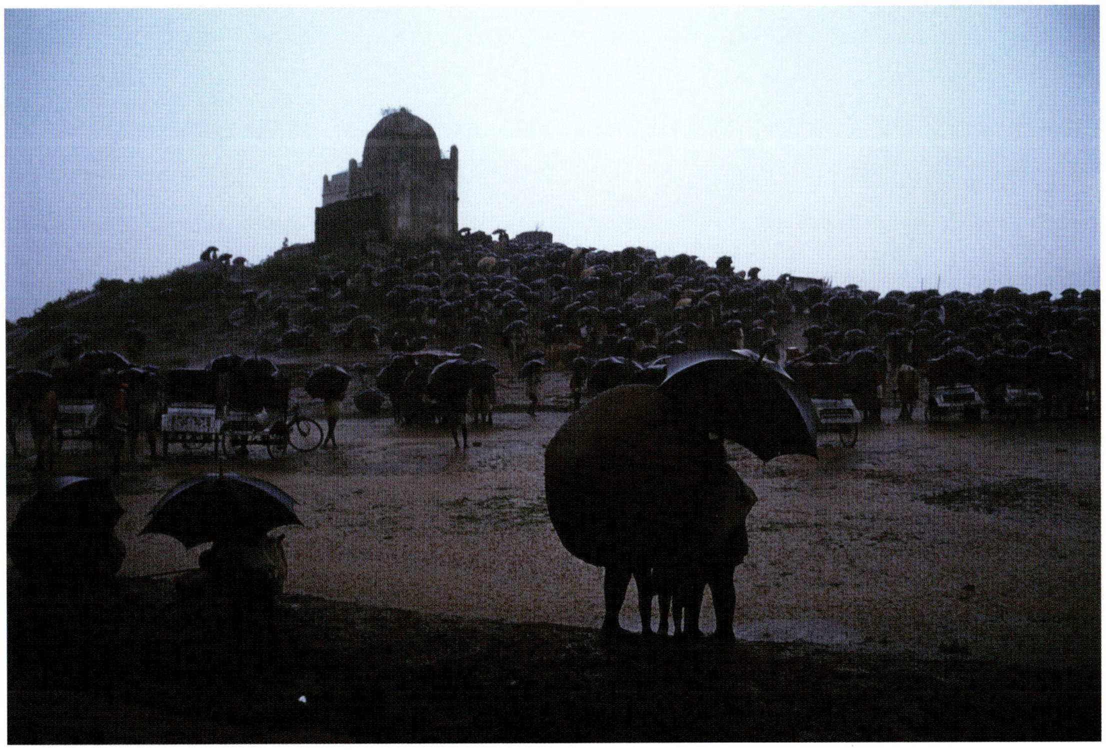

Brian Brake. *August. The Jagganath Festival at the height of the monsoon, Ranchi, South Bihar.* 35mm color transparency. Collection Museum of Te Papa Tongarewa. Gift of Wai-man Lau, 2001.

The vicissitudes of history form a narrative, not a photo, unless the photographer is interested in following up on the subject. In Brake's case, the idea of following up only heightens one's sense of human mortality—

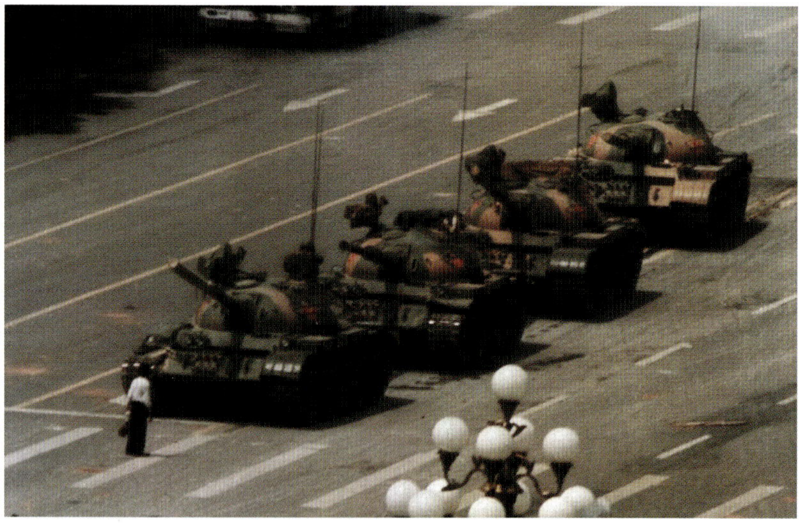

Jeff Widener. *Tank Man,* 1989. © AP/Jeff Widener.

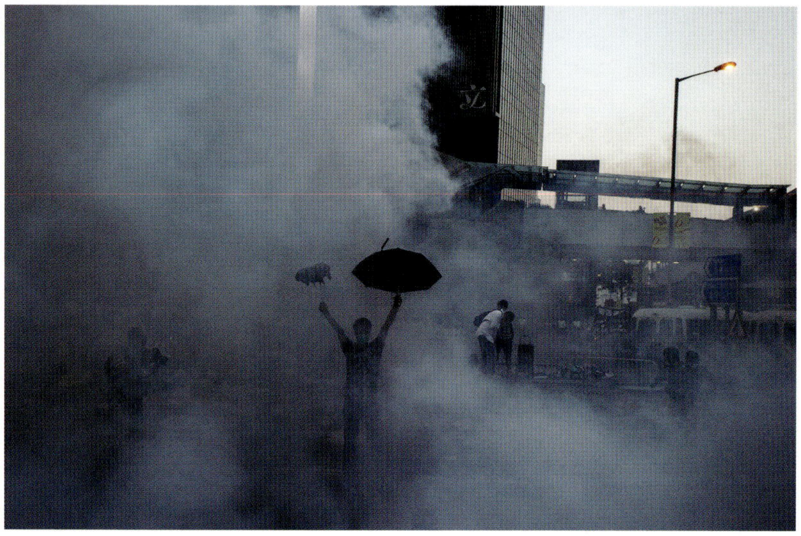

Xaume Olleros, The Umbrella Man, 2014 © Xaume Olleros.

itself a "rupturing of time". Brake's and McCurry's photographs remind us that there have been changes, some tremendous and some less so, shaking every "Asian" country since their photos were taken.

Some of the most memorable images from Asia in the last half-century were not taken by well-known photographers like Brake and McCurry. I'm thinking of Nick Ut's photo of the napalmed Phan Thị Kim Phúc; Jeff Widener's Tiananmen Square *Tank Man* (1989); and now the *Umbrella Man* (2014) by Xaume Olleros, the Spanish-born and Hong Kong based photographer.

As was the case with Widener's *Tank Man*, Olleros was not the only photographer around to have captured the image of the iconic figure/scene. For example, the Hong Kong native PH Yang has filmed not only the tear-gassing scenes during police attacks on protesters on September 28, 2014, but also the movement's one-month anniversary commemoration, and the many artworks that sprang up during the occupation—the "Umbrella Man" sculpture, the chalk mural on the traffic-free, occupied Harcourt Road, as well as the animation character inspired by Japanese manga master Hayao Miyazaki's "Totoro"—now seen holding a yellow umbrella.[15] Sontag has criticized *The Family of Man*'s humanist ideal for denying "the determining weight of history—of genuine and historically embedded differences, injustices and conflicts."[16] *Picturing Asia* doesn't attempt to be "The Family of Asia" that includes a "Family of China" sub-section, therefore one should enjoy the human affirmation offered by two outstanding photographers, whose purview extends beyond "Orientalist" exoticism—their visions also encompass cool and loving portraits of Asian urbanism, as well as compassionate depictions of the down-trodden in Asia. But of course any attempt to "picture Asia" will benefit from the perspectives of insiders and younger practitioners—some of whose names I've mentioned.

Photography both records and displaces reality. Walter Benjamin asserted that photography "has succeeded in transforming even abject poverty … into an object of enjoyment … it is one of its political functions to renew from within—that is, fashionably, the world as it is."[17] Diverse Asian peoples have certainly endured; but many of them have also looked beyond the cycles of nature and war—that is, beyond what Barthes called the uncritical acceptance of "naturality".[18] Finding "the world as it is" no longer acceptable, they are struggling to gain political control over their own destinies. And they have certainly found comradeship in the visual dissemination of their causes. Let's hope we can retain Benjamin's faith that some ardent practitioners—from the classical era of leftist Magnum-style documentary photography to the current age of peoples' photography—continue to raid the flow of time, to rupture the seemingly necessary "natural" continuity of this world, to search for the "spot where in the immediacy of that … moment the future nests so eloquently."[19]

I'd like to thank Arif Dirlik, Russell Freedman, Marina Heung, Mette Hjort and Ian Wedde for their feedback and comments on this essay.

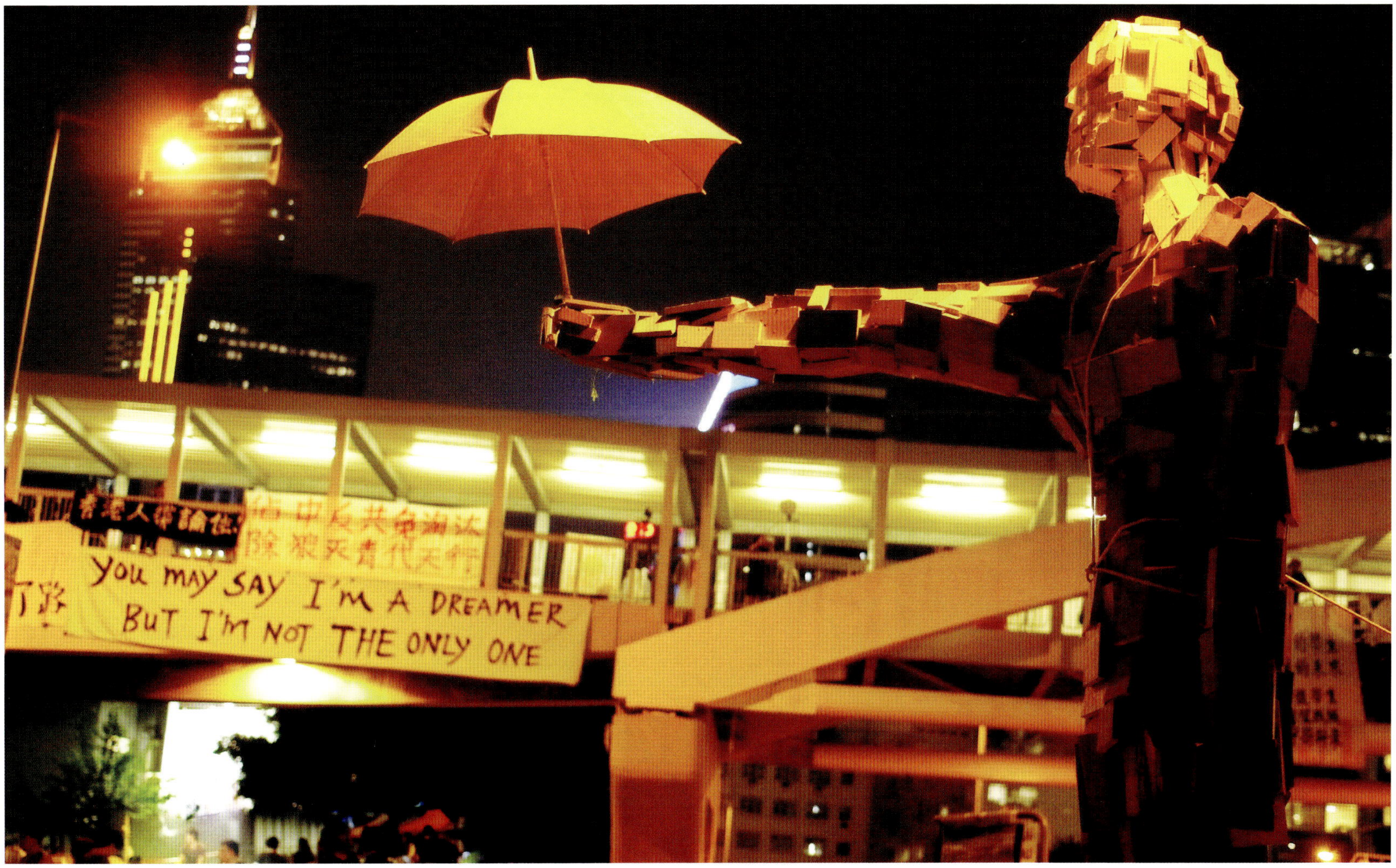

P H Yang. *Umbrella Man Sculpture*, 2014. The 'Umbrella Man' of Occupy Central in Hong Kong, immortalized on the cover of Time magazine as the iconic symbol of the Umbrella Movement, has materialized at the center of the protest zone at Admiralty as a three-meter tall statute holding a yellow umbrella. / 22 year-old artist, Milk, said he was inspired by a picture of an Occupy protester holding an umbrella over a policeman to protect the officer from the rain and is a symbol of peace. © P H Yang Photography I phyang.org

Biographical note

Evans Yiu Shing Chan (www.evanschan.com) is a critic, playwright, librettist and an independent filmmaker. Chan's four narrative features and eight documentaries include *The Map of Sex and Love* (2001), *Sorceress of the New Piano* (2004), and *Datong: The Great Society* (2011). His directorial debut *To Liv(e)* (1991) was named by *Time Out* as one of the 100 Greatest Hong Kong Films. A critical anthology about his work, *Postcolonalism, Diaspora, and Alternative Histories: The Cinema of Evans Chan* was published by the Hong Kong University Press in 2015. Evans Chan lives between Hong Kong and New York.

Notes

1. Susan Sontag, *On Photography* (New York: Dell Publishing, 1979), p. 22.

2. http://accessscience.com/content/asia/054800. Accessed January 31, 2016.

3. http://www.ranker.com/list/the-countries-in-asia/best-world-journeys?page=2. Accessed 4 February 2016.

4. https://en.wikipedia.org/wiki/List_of_sovereign_states_and_dependent_territories_in_Asia. Accessed 4 February 2016.

5. Larry Wolff, *Inventing Eastern Europe: The Map of Civilization on the Mind of the Enlightenment* (Palo Alto: Stanford University Press, 1994), pp. 152–54.

6. See Roland Barthes' essay "The Great Family of Man" in *Mythologies*, trans. by Richard Howard and Annette Lavers (New York: Hill and Wang, 2012), pp. 196–99.

7. http://timesofindia.indiatimes.com/city/lucknow/Anything-is-possible-in-UP-Notice-to-lord-Indra-for-no-rains/articleshow/15391332.cms. Accessed 4 April 2016.

8. Raghu Rai (born 1942) began his career as a photojournalist in 1966. An exhibition of his work in Paris in 1971 led Henri Cartier-Bresson to nominate him to join Magnum Photos in 1977. He may be best known for his 1984 and 2001 Bhopal portfolios, which resulted in the book *Exposure: Portrait of a Corporate Crime—Photographs of Bhopal by Raghu Rai* (Amsterdam: Greenpeace, 2002).

9. Shōmei Tōmatsu (1930–2012) featured in the groundbreaking *New Japanese Photography* exhibition in 1974 at the Museum of Modern Art, New York and is best known for *Chewing Gum and Chocolate* (2014), his subtle yet biting series about the long shadow cast by American victory on post-WWII Japan.

10. Hiromi Tuschida, *Hiroshima* (Tokyo: Kosei Publishing Co., 1985). Kosei Publishing Co. is a conspicuously Buddhist-oriented, peace-activist publisher. Tsuchida (born in Fukui Prefecture, Japan, 1939) received the Ina Nobuo Award in 1978 for his work about Hiroshima and the aftermath of the atomic bomb.

11. Born in Tokyo in 1948, Hiroshi Sugimoto moved to New York in 1974. His use of an 8×10 large-format camera and his acknowledgements of Man Ray and Duchamp have made him one of the cosmopolitan presences in the international photographic scene. He created the *Sanjūsangen-dō* ("Hall of Thirty-Three Bays") series in Kyoto in 1995, focusing on 1,000 life-size, gilded wooden bodhisattvas from the twelfth and thirteenth centuries.

12. Hiroji Kubota (born in Tokyo, 1939) trained as an assistant to Cornell Capa. He covered the U.S. presidential election in 1968, Ryūkyū islands (before their return to Japan) in 1972, Saigon in 1975, North Korea in 1978, and China in 1979–85, and the U.S.A. again in 1988–92. Like McCurry, Kubota also photographed the "Golden Rock" at Shwe Pyi Daw in Myanmar, sixteen years before McCurry, in 1978.

13. Lu Nan (born in Beijing, 1962) is one of the greatest social activist documentary photographers of our time. Among his photographic subjects are mental asylums in China and prison camps in Myanmar.

14. In Brake's posthumous book *Monsoon* (Auckland: David Bateman, 2007) this photograph is captioned *August. The Jagannath Festival at the height of the monsoon, Ranchi, South Bihar.*

15. See also *PH Yang Photography*: "Umbrella Festival 2015: Blossoms Everywhere", at phyang.org.

16. Sontag, *op. cit.*, p. 33.

17. See Walter Benjamin's essay, "The Author as Producer", in *Selected Writings Vol II, Part II 1931-1934*, ed. by Michael W. Jennings, Howard Eiland and Gary Smith; trans. by Rodney Livingstone et al. (Cambridge, MA: Belknap/Harvard, 1999), p. 775.

18. Barthes, *op. cit.*, p. 198.

19. See Benjamin's essay, "Little History of Photography", *op. cit.*, p. 510.

SELFIES FIRST

Kristy Soo and Ashley Nga-sai Wu
Assistant Curators

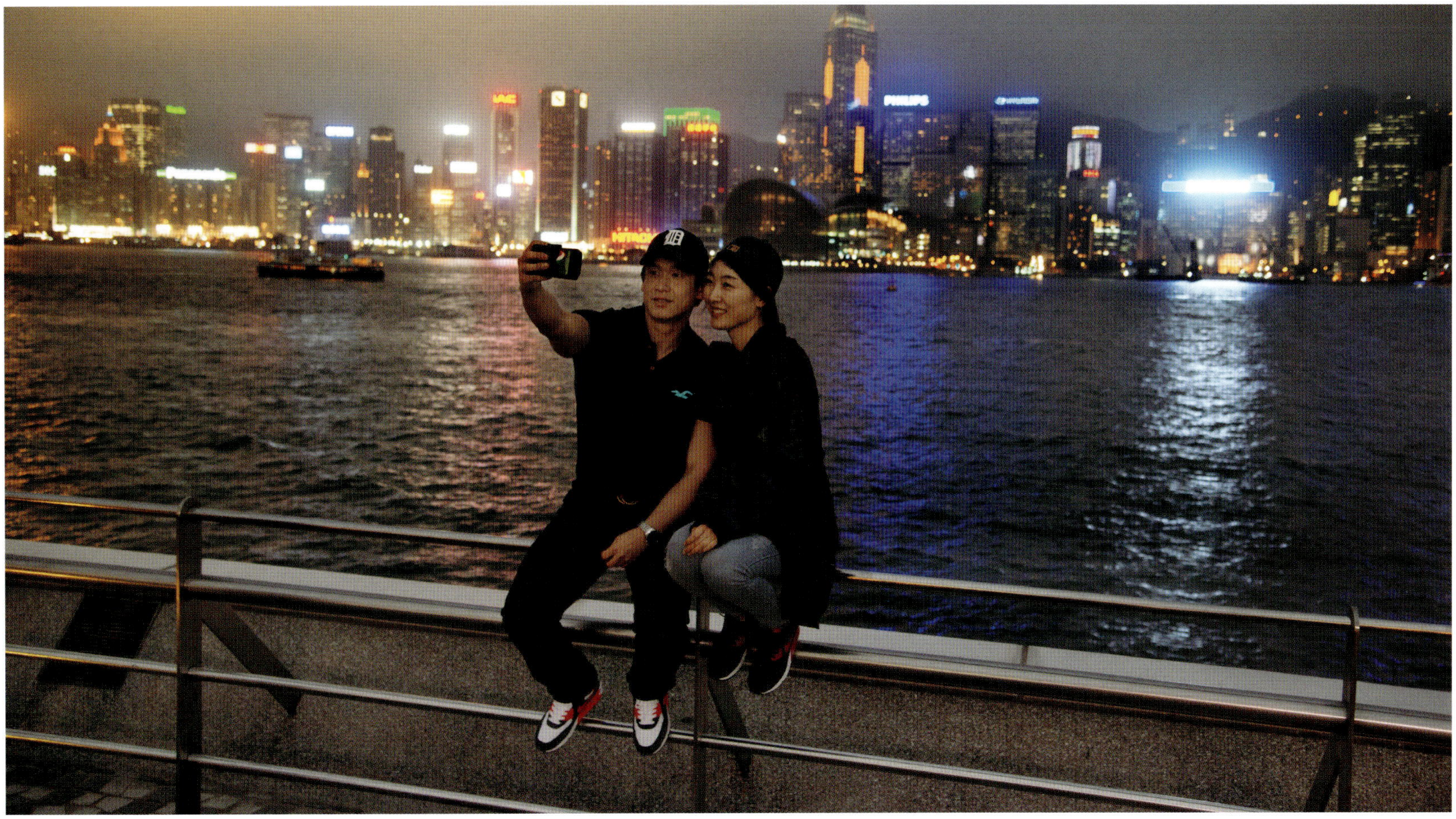

Steve McCurry. *Couple taking a photograph, Hong Kong,* 2014 © Steve McCurry

In 2014, Steve McCurry took a photo of a young couple getting a "selfie" against the glittering backdrop of Hong Kong's night-time cityscape, thus capturing an everyday act of the digital generation. McCurry's picture looks simple and no doubt the selfie taken by the young couple did, too. But looking into this image we may find more than meets the eye. In Hong Kong photography was once considered a hobby of "spendthrifts",[1] but is now a daily essential. The first camera phone, produced by Sharp, was sold in Japan not long ago in 2000.[2] In less than two decades, a mobile phone without an integrated camera has become unthinkable. Since Facebook was made available to the public in 2006, photo-sharing applications like Instagram and Snapchat, coupled with camera phones, enable and prompt users to share photos on their own social media accounts. Private individuals now have unparalleled autonomy to represent themselves—with a few taps and wipes a photo is taken and published online.

This essay surveys the impact, both personal and social, of such a democratization of digital photography and its dissemination, with an emphasis on how this plays out in the context of the Umbrella Movement, the mass pro-democracy protest and occupation that took place in Hong Kong in 2014, the year McCurry took his photograph of the young Hong Kongers getting their selfie. We look at how this proliferation of images mashes together the selfie and what used to be called photojournalism; how the "self" in "selfie" might also be an activist; how this relates—or does not—to the great tradition of photojournalism represented by Steve McCurry and, earlier, by Brian Brake.

On a personal level, digital photography offers a powerful way to connect people with the aid of social media. As distinct from its traditional film-based predecessor, the speedy circulation of a digital photograph is facilitated by the ease of its duplication. Private individuals take advantage of this to keep pace with what is happening in today's fast moving world, especially that of their friends. The Pew Research Center's study *Teens, Social Media and Technology Overview 2015* found that teens appreciate how photo-sharing social media keep them in the loop with friends.[3] This is indeed what most of these platforms are designed for, with keywords such as "connect" and "share" appearing time and again in their mission statements. The "add friend" button of Facebook reflects a yearning for human connection. On the site, a group photo does more than preserve a happy moment from oblivion, as posting it online and tagging your friends are public affirmations of this clique's friendship.[4] Users are also allowed to direct their own semi-public story by actively feeding information to their friends. For instance, Snapchat encourages users to stay in touch by sending ephemeral snaps that could become chained content automatically shared with the user's contact list. As a result, digital photography, through various social networks, has developed a new system to denote relationship dynamics and display affections.

However, once a photo is shared on social media, it is subjected to peer gaze. Social media has shaped a world where the private is on public display, in which a person's popularity is then quantified and affirmed in the units of "likes" prompted by a photo shared, and "followers" who anticipate updates. This has tempted users, driven by vanity, to put up a façade. Many pursue these social media currencies by fabricating an electronic second life through photographs. In 2015, Argentinian-born artist Amalia Ulman demonstrated how readily people accept falsified photographs on social media with her Instagram performance *Excellences and Perfections*.[5] Having scripted the story of an artsy, provincial girl who moved to Los Angeles for the first time, the photos of her performed lavish lifestyle, such as selfies in posh settings, extravagant dinners, and breast augmentation, were gone along with as representations of reality by her willing online audience. Ulman's performance is an extreme, ironic example of how social networks are virtual spaces infiltrated by fictions—or with lies and distortions, if you will—made believable by photography's reputation for reproducing a moment in time exactly as it was.

In fact, the "truth value" of photography has long been debated. Brian Brake's "Monsoon girl" (plate 01 p 032) was controversial in the context of photojournalism, as it was a staged photoshoot with a model. Some believed he had violated a fundamental rule of documentary photography's truth-telling, others argued that he still captured the essence of the Indian monsoon experience.[6] While it is sometimes hard to come to terms with the hiatus between photographs and the reality they are supposed to mirror, our generation, born in the 1990s, is less outraged to discover that certain photos have been manipulated. Nowadays, any Instragrammer can beautify their images easily by adding filters, and tamper with the interpretation of them through captions and hashtags. Numerous softwares such as Photoshop and Meitu are handy editing tools to flatter an image. Altered photographs gratify both the subject who wants to change, fantasize or perform alternative identities, genders or histories; and viewers interested in identity-bending.

These two issues—the easy dissemination of photographs, and the potential to generate misleading content—collided during the Umbrella Movement in Hong Kong. The collision was brought about by regular social media users exercising their full editorial rights, their democratic right to freedom of expression.

As a pro-democracy political action, the Umbrella Movement demonstrated how digital photography and its circulation on social networks bring a city together, and may even make the world "feel a little bit smaller".[7] It is no exaggeration to say that photo-sharing online fuelled the Umbrella Movement on 28 September 2014 and brought city-dwellers closer to each other. As images of pepper spray and tear gas in the Admiralty neighbourhood of Hong Kong went viral online, enraged citizens rushed into the district and eventually occupied it. The photograph and social media, employed as press tools, operated by appealing directly to an audience's emotions, consequently mobilizing like minds—as did Steve McCurry's poignant 1984 image of the "Afghan Girl", Sharbat Gula, with her "intense, haunted look" (plate 20 p 052).[8] Like "Afghan Girl", images of the Umbrella Occupation won wide international support. However, the individual freedom exercised by social media users to express and distribute their views is compromised in classic photojournalism modes due to the print media's diminished immediacy, lower accessibility, and potential censorship (or self-censorship). This is truer than ever at a time when Hong Kong's traditional media are suffering from an integrity crisis—many of the city's publications and TV stations are owned by local tycoons who, wary of jeopardizing their ties and interests in the mainland, go to great lengths to maintain a conservative editorial line.

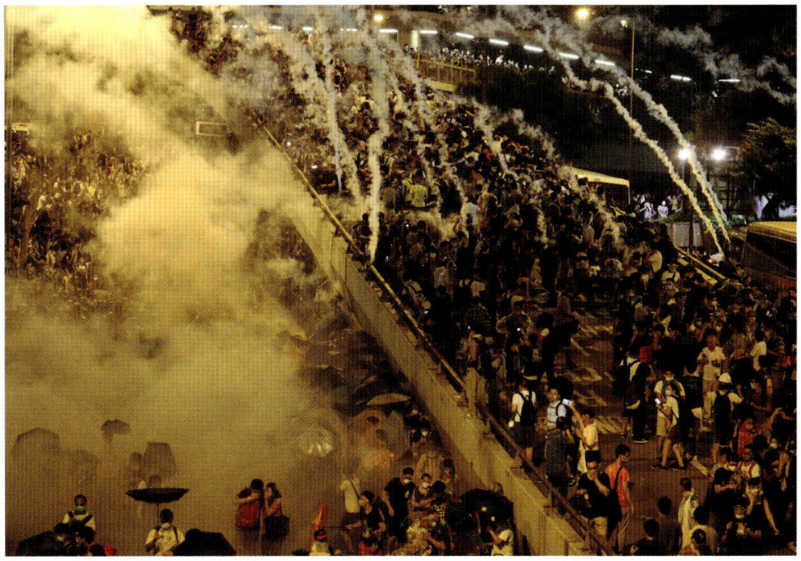

Aaron Tam: *Police fire tear gas upon pro-democracy demonstrators near the Hong Kong government headquarters on September 28, 2014.* Police fired tear gas as tens of thousands of pro-democracy demonstrators brought parts of central Hong Kong to a standstill Sunday, in a dramatic escalation of protests that have gripped the semi-autonomous Chinese city for days. AFP Photo/Aaron Tam © AFP.

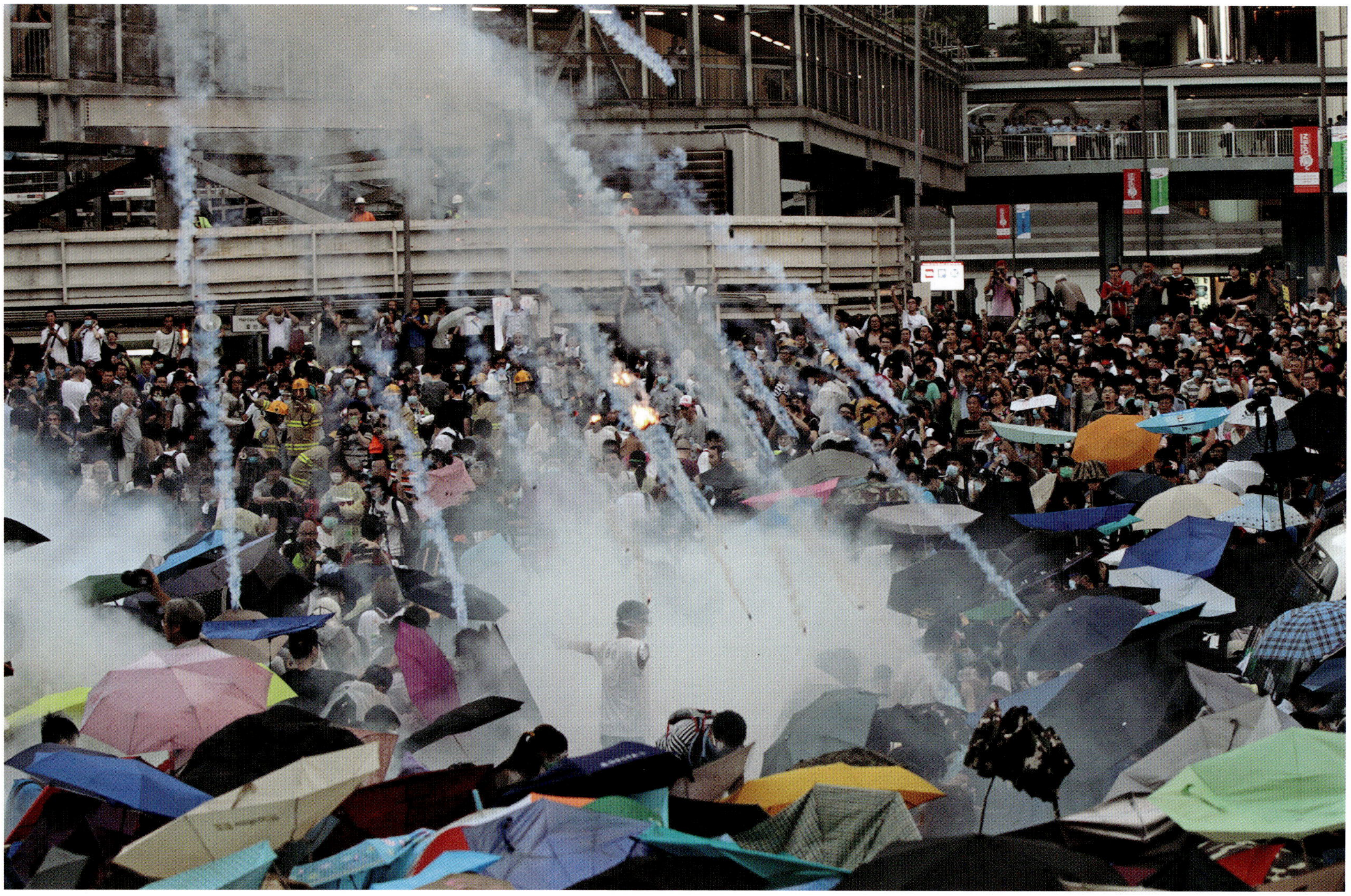

Police firing one of the first of the eighty-seven tear gas canisters since 6:00 pm, 28 September, 2014. © AFP/Wally Santana.

Operating at a personal, intimate level, the photographs on social networks also helped Hong Kongers, especially those active participants in the Movement, to receive first-hand and timely updates on the protest's development and on their friends' whereabouts and safety. These photographs by private citizens offered more than factual reports. Sharing them on personal social media accounts meant they were taken as expressions of political positions. Such positions came to be color-coded—different colored ribbons and umbrellas united people who supported the same cause (yellow ribbon for pro-students and protestors; blue ribbon in favour of the authority and police force), subsequently forming online groups that exchanged information to maintain the Movement's momentum.

These photographic vehicles also ensured the news transcended geographical boundaries. A global public managed to follow the Movement's development through shared photographs, which even brought about rallies in support of the protest in over sixty-four cities worldwide.[9] Coverage of the event spread rapidly, and images of it have now been documented in perpetuity. Today, simply by searching #umbrellarevolutionhk on Instagram, one can instantly browse an assortment of images taken during the Movement, serving as an historical record from a diverse pool of witnesses.

While photographs can wield tremendous communal power, they may also interrupt life as much as they document and share it; nor do they always reveal the motives of the photographer. Long before the invention of Instagram, Susan Sontag commented that photo-taking essentially involves imposing a camera between ourselves and our experiences, and as a consequence has become one of the principal devices for legitimizing experience.[10] Photographs offer indisputable evidence that "the trip was made, the program was carried out, and the fun was had."[11] When online identities are at stake and an experience is measured by its display value, a photograph is not necessarily a declaration of a socio-political stance, nor a reliable representation of a moment, let alone a truth. Photography's power to interrupt action and life was apparent during the last days of the Umbrella Movement.

"VA", a first aider stationed in Admiralty, said the Occupy zones saw resurging numbers of people on the eve of the announced clearance date. Yet a lot of protestors returned merely to capture this last moment for their online profile, instead of taking actual action to defend and continue the Occupation.[12] An ironic reversal of what Sontag called a photographer's "non-intervention"[13] occurred—participants withdrew themselves from the protest to assume roles as non-intervening photographers. They became bystanders of their own Movement, lamenting its end before that happened, imprinting themselves, or themselfies, on a history from which they had withdrawn as active participants. In such instances, we become so obsessed with demonstrating and legitimizing our own lives and presences that we prioritize these secondary experiences—"See? I was there!"—over the primary ones.

Whether we take photographs to stay in touch with our friends, to freeze a moment of our lives, or to send a political message, it is undeniable that digital photography has become an inseparable part of our lives, impacting on our interpersonal relationships and our identities, and on how we participate as witnesses, on a scale unimaginable in the era of magazine photojournalism. It is easy to make fun of people—especially Asians, according to the Tumblr blog "Pictures of Asians Taking Pictures of Food"[14]—taking pains to get Instagrammable food photos, including standing on chairs to "let the camera eat first". But in less trivial matters such as those that decide a city's fate, the contemporary obsession with photo-taking and sharing—what the Pew report characterizes as a "frenzy of access"[15]—is no laughing matter. It involves a collision of values and effects, best characterized perhaps as the selfie-ization of communal activism. In 2014, when Steve McCurry took his idyllic photograph on the bank of Hong Kong harbour, his young couple may have been experiencing simultaneously the pleasure of sharing a precious moment with their friends, and the alienation narrated in Amalia Ulman's delusional *Excellences and Perfections.*

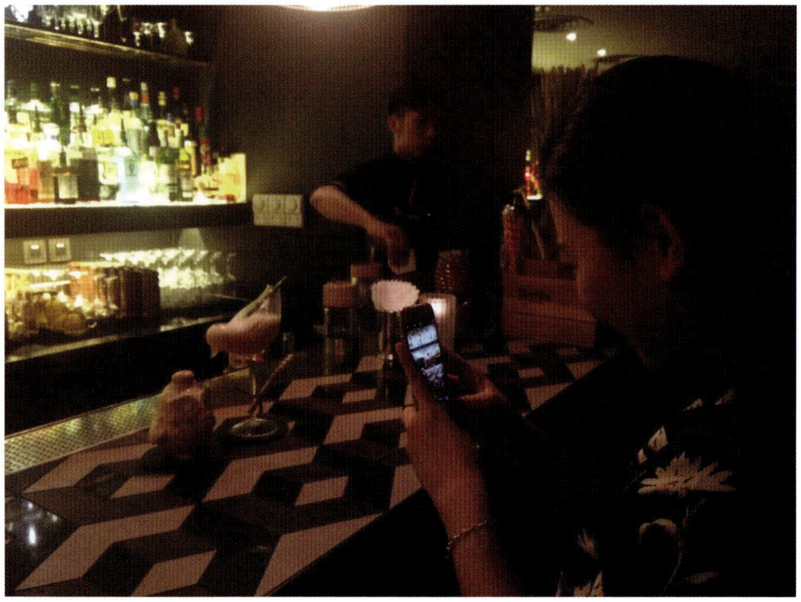

A young Hong Kong woman taking photos of cocktails with her iPhone 6S. Image by the author from 2016.

Biographical note

Kristy Soo is an Assistant Curator at Chantal Miller Gallery, Asia Society Hong Kong Center, where she has worked on exhibitions including *Bat Cave: Treasures of the Day and Creatures of the Night* (2015), *Shahzia Sikander: Apparatus of Power* (2016), *Shen Wei: Dance Strokes* (2016) and *Picturing Asia: Double Take—The Photography of Brian Brake and Steve McCurry* (2016).

Ashley Nga-sai Wu is an Assistant Curator at Chantal Miller Gallery, Asia Society Hong Kong Center. Exhibitions she has worked on include *Temple, Scrolls, and Divine Messengers: Archaeology of the Land of Israel in Roman Times* (2014); *Life is Only One: Yoshitomo Nara* (2015); *Bat Cave: Treasures of the Day and Creatures of the Night* (2015), *Shahzia Sikander: Apparatus of Power* (2016), *Shen Wei: Dance Strokes* (2016) and most recently *Picturing Asia: Double Take—The Photography of Brian Brake and Steve McCurry* (2016).

Notes

1: *Vision Beyond, Hong Kong Art Photography 1900–2000* (Hong Kong: Hong Kong Heritage Museum, 2001), catalogue, p. 3.

2: Sharp, "Industry's First Camera-Equipped Mobile Phone <J-SH04>," http://www.sharp-world.com/corporate/info/his/only_one/item/t34.html. Accessed 24 May 2016.

3: Amanda Lenhart, *Teens, Social Media and Technology Overview 2015* (Washington, D.C.: Pew Research Center, 9 April 2015), http://www.pewinternet.org/2015/04/09/teens-social-media-technology-2015/. Accessed 13 April 2016.

4: John Berger, *Understanding a Photograph* (London: Penguin UK, 2013), p. 54.

5: Amalia Ulman [amaliaulman], Instagram, https://www.instagram.com/amaliaulman/?hl=en. Accessed 5 April 2016.

6: *Brian Brake, Lens on the World*, ed. by Athol McCredie (Wellington: Te Papa Press, 2010), p. 175.

7: blog.instagram.com, 22 September 2015, http://blog.instagram.com/post/129662501137/150922-400million. Accessed 5 May 2016.

8: Steve McCurry, *Untold, the Stories Behind the Photographs* (New York: Phaidon Press Inc., 2013), p. 75.

9: Rishi Iyengar, "Global Support Pours In for Hong Kong Democracy Protest," http://time.com/3444225/hong-kong-democracy-protests-global-support/. Accessed 24 May 2016.

10: Susan Sontag, *On Photography* (London: Penguin Books Ltd., 2008), pp. 5–7.

11: *Ibid.*, p. 9.

12: "VA", Personal Interview, 18 May 2016.

13: Sontag, *op. cit.,* p.12.

14: *Pictures of Asians Taking Pictures of Food*, Tumblr, http://picsofaznstakingpicsoffood.tumblr.com/, Accessed 16 May 2016. See also *TimeOut Kuala Lumpur*, http://www.timeout.com/kuala-lumpur/restaurants/camera-eats-first-is-instagram-changing-the-way-we-eat. Accessed 5 May 2016.

15: Pew Research Center, *op. cit.,* p.1. Accessed 13 April 2016.

BRIAN BRAKE BIOGRAPHY AND PLATES IN ALPHABETICAL ORDER

Brian Brake (1927–1988) was New Zealand's best known photographer, celebrated for both his international photojournalism and definitive images of the landscape and cultural objects of New Zealand.

Brake began working as an apprentice in a portrait studio in the late 1940s in New Zealand. He was then employed as a cameraman and director at the government's National Film Unit, working on documentaries from 1948 to 1954. He became an expert in color cinematography and learned how to assemble individual shots into a story, both of which he brought to play in his later work as a photojournalist.

Brake's career began in earnest when he moved to London in 1954. Within a year he was a nominee member of the famous Paris-based photo agency Magnum, propelling him into the life of a globetrotting photojournalist. His first significant published photographs were of Pablo Picasso and Jean Cocteau at a bullfight in southern France and featured in *Life*, *Paris Match* and *Sunday Graphic* in 1955.

In 1956 he embarked upon an extended global journey through the Middle East, Sri Lanka, India and South East Asia, taking photographs for Magnum. This was interrupted by three months in China in 1957, where he was one of the few Western photographers to document the massive changes the country was undergoing following the Revolution. It was followed up by a further exclusive visit in 1959 covering the tenth anniversary celebrations of the founding of the People's Republic of China.

Brake's most famous photographs were taken in 1960, when he shot the "Monsoon" series in India. This work was seen around the world in at least twelve major picture magazines, including *Life, Paris Match* and *Epoca.* His photograph *Monsoon girl*, of a young woman ecstatically raising her face to the first rains, became a world-famous image. The "Monsoon" photo essay was a landmark in magazine photography for its exclusive use of color, its epic theme, and its poetic narrative flow that worked on its own visually, without an accompanying text.

The success of "Monsoon" led to several large assignments for *Life* magazine in the 1960s, including one on the Asian film industry, and another for a special issue on Japan before the 1964 Tokyo Olympics. For *Life* magazine it was a time of grand projects, big budgets and an increasing use of color. Brake was perfectly suited, and spent much of the mid-1960s working on an extended series for *Life* on the Roman Empire and ancient Egypt.

As the international picture magazines succumbed to the impact of television from the late 1960s Brake moved to taking studio photographs of Asian art objects for museum publications. He also set up a Hong Kong-based film company in 1970 and made a series of documentary films in Indonesia.

In 1976 Brake returned to New Zealand to live and concentrated on further museum-style books—now on New Zealand topics—as well as corporate annual reports, travel publications and books on Sydney and Hong Kong. Although many New Zealanders knew of his international fame, he was also acclaimed locally for his best-selling 1963 book, *New Zealand: Gift of the Sea*, which set a new, sophisticated standard for picture books on the country. His return enabled him to work on an updated version, eventually published in 1990, two years after his death. His long-held ambition to produce a book on the "Monsoon" series was also only completed posthumously (in 2007), and in 2010 the Museum of New Zealand Te Papa Tongarewa published a survey of his life's work, *Brian Brake: Lens on the World*.

01

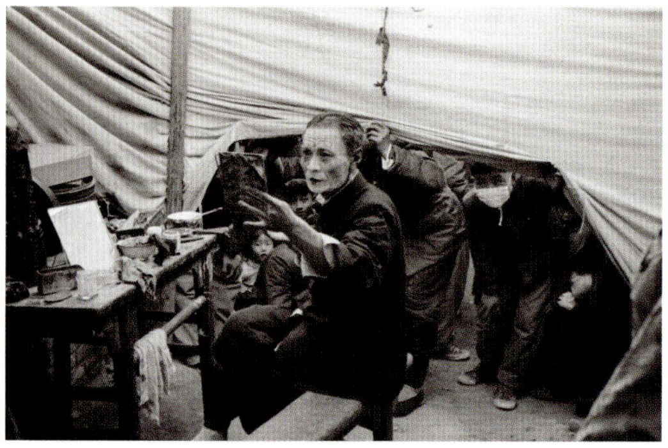

02

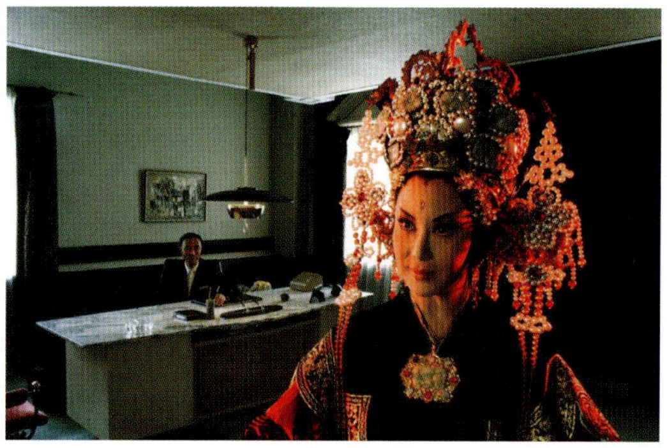

03

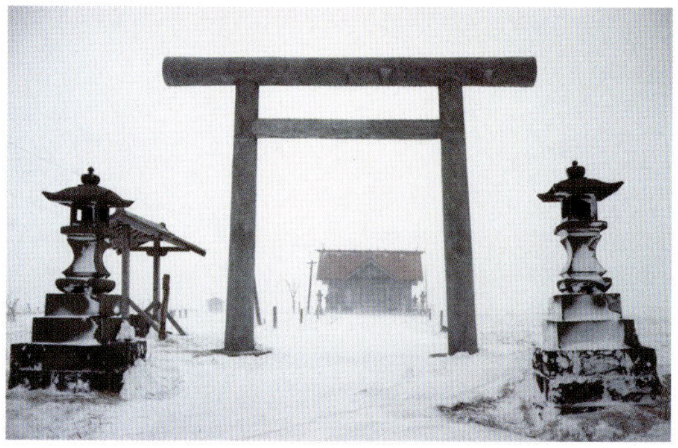

04

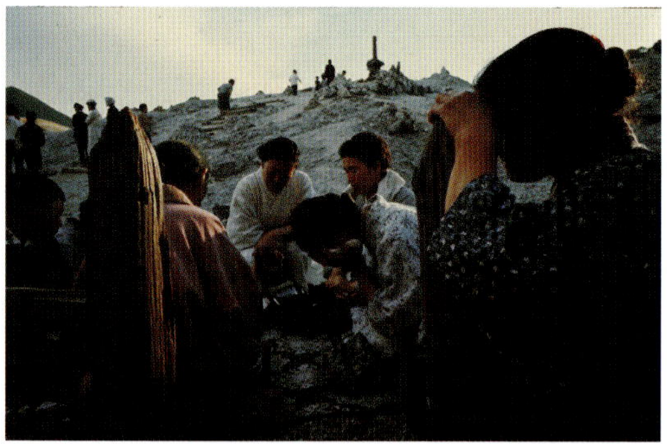

05

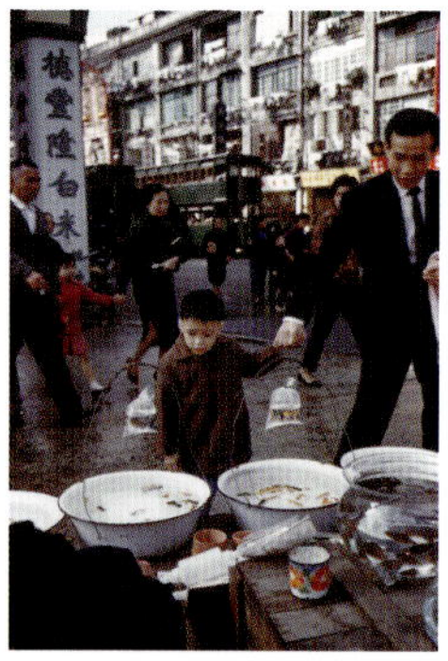

06

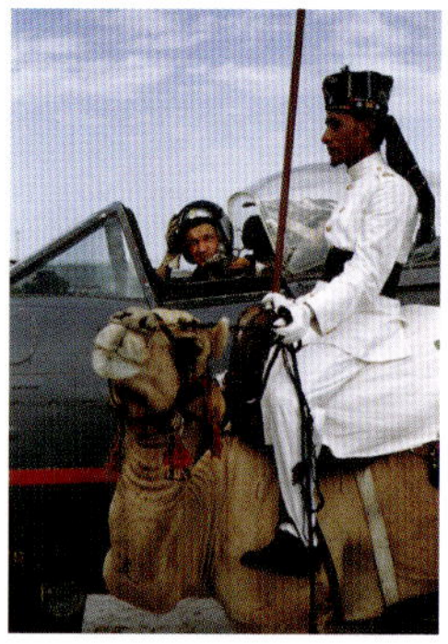

01 I *Actor applying make-up, street opera troupe, Beijing, China,* 1957. *Brian Brake: China, the 1950s*. Wellington: Museum of New Zealand Te Papa Tongarewa, 1995. Reproduced from a 35mm black and white negative. Collection Museum of New Zealand Te Papa Tongarewa. Gift of Wai-man Lau, 2001.

Plate 26
Making Reputations
Page 059

02 I *Actress Li Li Hua dressed as the Empress Wu of the Tang dynasty with film producer Run Run Shaw, Hong Kong, China*, 1963. Unpublished. 35mm transparency. Collection Museum of New Zealand Te Papa Tongarewa. Gift of Wai-man Lau, 2001.

Plate 90
"Exotic, Enticing Hong Kong"
Page 129

03 I *Archway in snow, Japan*. From the series: Japan, 1960s-80s. Unpublished. 35mm transparency. Collection Museum of New Zealand Te Papa Tongarewa. Gift of Wai-man Lau, 2001.

Plate 50
Ancient and Modern
Page 085

04 I *Blind Japanese women claiming to be mediums gather once a year in Northern Honshu, Japan*. From the series: Japan, 1960s-80s. Unpublished. 4 x 5 inch color copy transparency. Collection Museum of New Zealand Te Papa Tongarewa. Gift of Wai-man Lau, 2010.

Plate 45
Ancient and Modern
Page 081

05 I *Boy at goldfish stall, Hong Kong, China*, 1961. Brake, Brian and Robert Elegant. *Hong Kong: Great Cities.* Amsterdam: Time-Life Books, 1977. 35mm transparency. Collection Museum of New Zealand Te Papa Tongarewa. Gift of Wai-man Lau, 2001.

Plate 88
"Exotic, Enticing Hong Kong"
Page 126

06 I *Camel rider of the Aden Protectorate Levies beside a jet plane on the RAF airfield, Aden, Yemen,* 1956. "Along the Storied Incense Roads of Aden". *National Geographic*, vol. 111, no. 2, February 1957. 35mm transparency. Collection Museum of New Zealand Te Papa Tongarewa. Gift of Wai-man Lau, 2001.

Plate 64
Signature Styles
Page 101

07

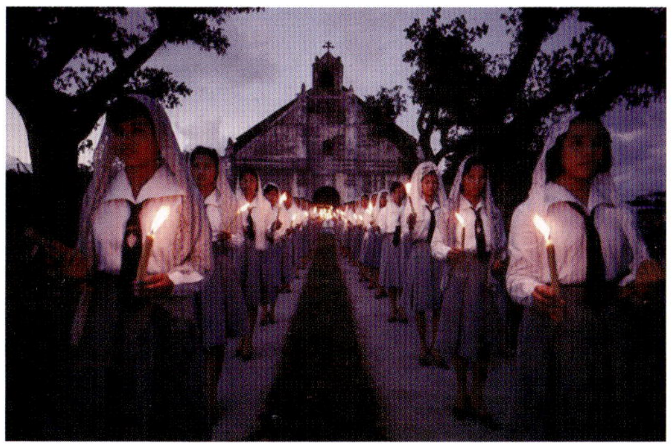

08

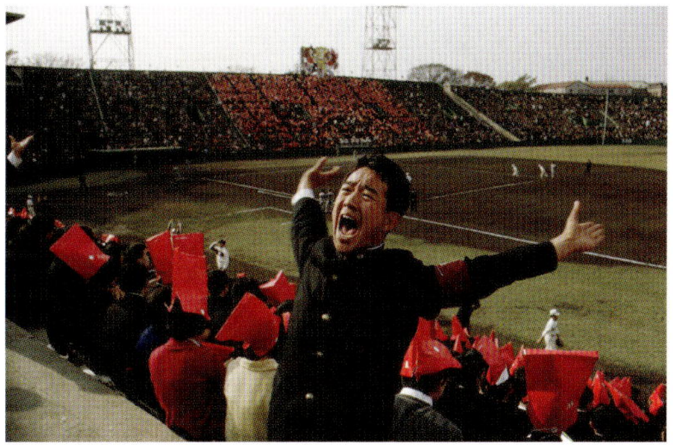

09

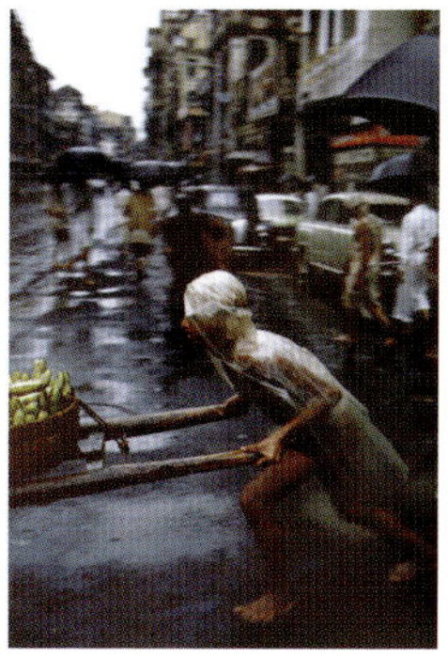

10

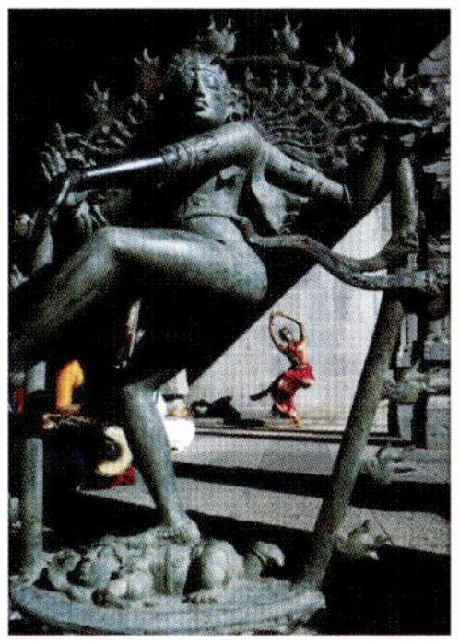

11

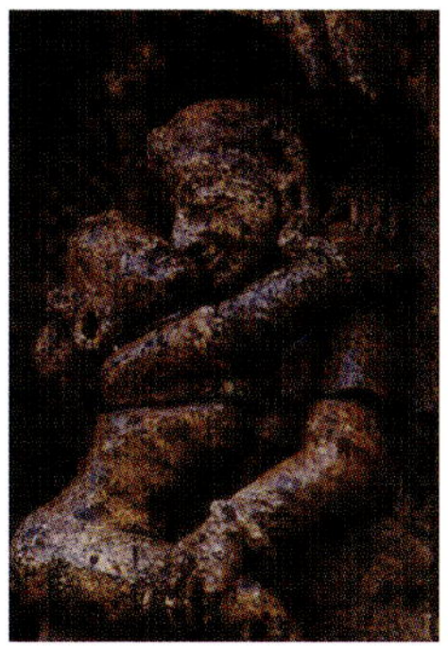

12

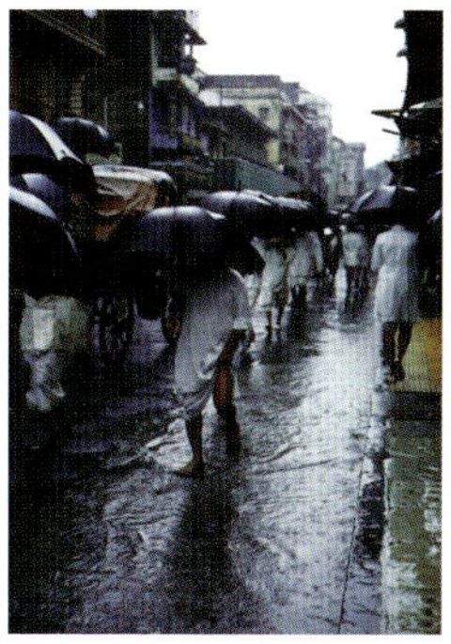

07 | *Catholic church, Vihan, Northwest Luzon, Philippines*, 1965. "Brian Brake's Best of Asia". *Insight (American Express),* February/March 1984. 35mm transparency. Collection Museum of New Zealand Te Papa Tongarewa. Gift of Wai-man Lau, 2001.

Plate 70
Signature Styles
Page 106

08 | *Cheerleader at a Waseda University versus Keio University baseball game, Tokyo, Japan,* 1964. "Japan: The Modern Paradoxes". *Life*, vol. 57, no. 11, 11 September 1964. 35mm transparency. Collection Museum of New Zealand Te Papa Tongarewa. Gift of Wai-man Lau, 2010.

Plate 51
Ancient and Modern
Page 086

09 | *Crawford Market, Mumbai, India*. From the series: Monsoon, 1960. "Monsoon". *Life*, Vol. 51, No. 10, September 8, 1961. 35mm transparency. Collection Museum of New Zealand Te Papa Tongarewa. Gift of Wai-man Lau, 2001.

Plate 06
Monsoon Meeting
Page 037

10 | *Dancer performing in the Bharata Natyam style, India*. From the series: Monsoon, 1960. Unpublished. 35mm transparency. Collection Museum of New Zealand Te Papa Tongarewa. Gift of Wai-man Lau, 2001.

Plate 73
Signature Styles
Page 107

11 | *Erotic sculpture in the Sun Temple, Konarak, India*. From the series: Monsoon, 1960. *Brian Brake – Monsoon*. Auckland: David Bateman, 2007. 35mm transparency. Collection Museum of New Zealand Te Papa Tongarewa. Gift of Wai-man Lau, 2001.

Plate 08
Monsoon Meeting
Page 039

12 | *"Every street runs like a river", Mumbai, India*. From the series: Monsoon, 1960. *Brian Brake – Monsoon*. Auckland: David Bateman, 2007. 35mm transparency. Collection Museum of New Zealand Te Papa Tongarewa. Gift of Wai-man Lau, 2001.

Plate 05
Monsoon Meeting
Page 036

01

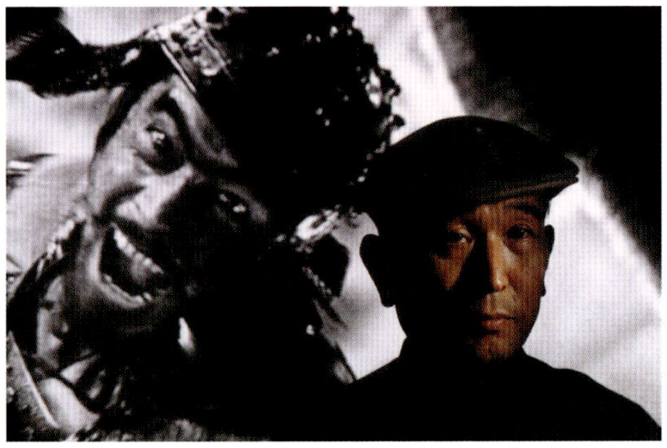

02

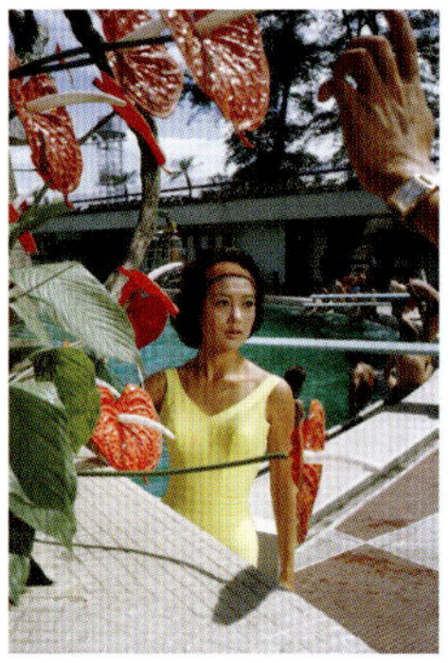

03

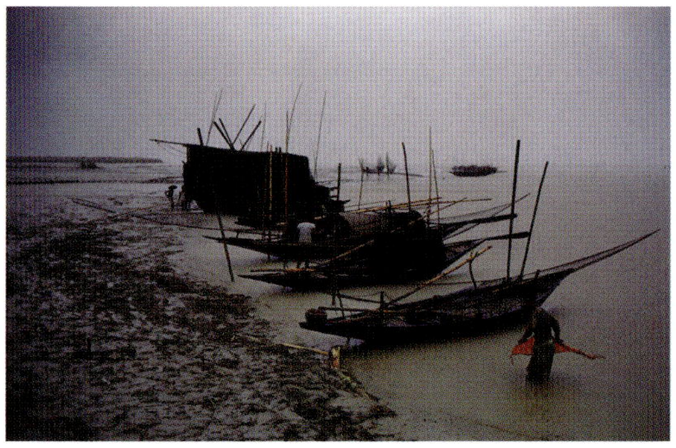

04

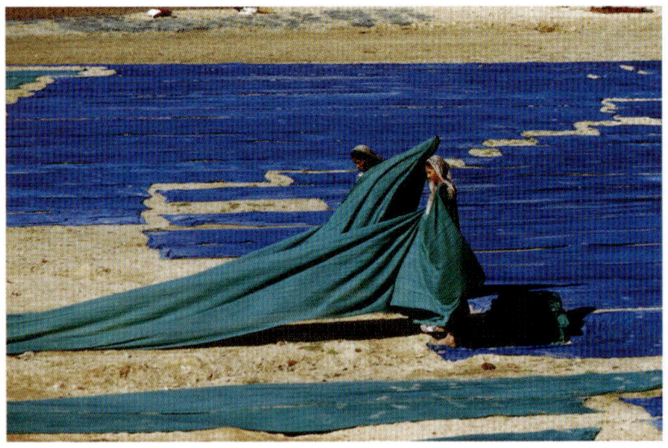

05

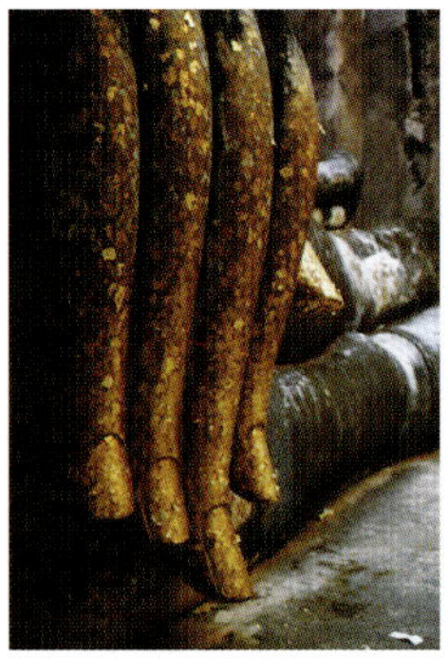

06

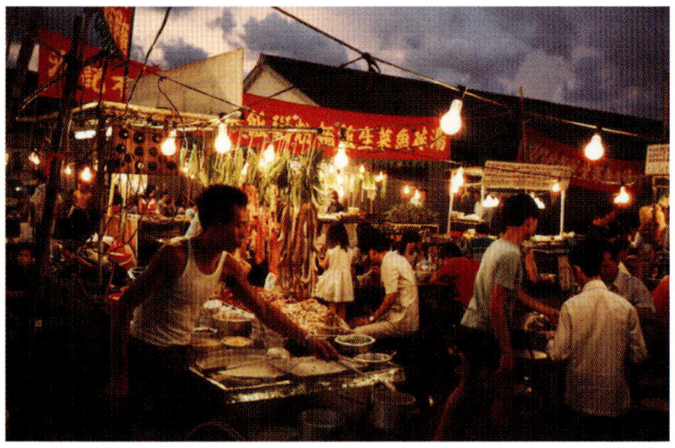

01 I *Film director Akira Kurosawa standing before an image of his principal star, Toshiro Mifune, Tokyo, Japan*, 1963. “The Universal Magic of the Movies”. *Life*, vol. 55, no. 25, December 1963. 35mm transparency. Collection Museum of New Zealand Te Papa Tongarewa. Gift of Wai-man Lau, 2001.

Plate 43
Ancient and Modern
Page 079

02 I *Film set, Japan,* 1963. “The Universal Magic of the Movies”. *Life*, vol. 55, no. 25, December 1963. 35mm transparency. Collection Museum of New Zealand Te Papa Tongarewa. Gift of Wai-man Lau, 2001.

Plate 48
Ancient and Modern
Page 083

03 I *Fishermen on the Padma River at Nimitia, West Bengal, India*. From the series: Monsoon, 1960. *Brian Brake – Monsoon*. Auckland: David Bateman, 2007. 35mm transparency. Museum of New Zealand Te Papa Tongarewa. Gift of Wai-man Lau, 2001.

Plate 09
Monsoon Meeting
Page 040

04 I *Gathering dyed cloth on the banks of the Sabarmati River, Ahmedabad, India,* 1958. *Brian Brake: 40 Photographs.* Lower Hutt: Dowse Art Gallery, 1976. 35mm transparency. Collection Museum of New Zealand Te Papa Tongarewa. Gift of Wai-man Lau, 2001.

Plate 11
Monsoon Meeting
Page 042

05 I *Hand of the Buddha, Sukhothai, Thailand*. From the series: Thailand, 1960-80. Unpublished. 4 x 5 color transparency. Collection Museum of New Zealand Te Papa Tongarewa. Gift of Wai-man Lau, 2001.

Plate 76
Signature Styles
Page 111

06 I *Market, Hong Kong, China*, c. 1976. Brake, Brian and Robert Elegant. *Hong Kong: Great Cities*. Amsterdam: Time-Life Books, 1977. 35mm transparency. Collection Museum of New Zealand Te Papa Tongarewa. Gift of Wai-man Lau, 2001.

Plate 91
“Exotic, Enticing Hong Kong”
Page 130

07

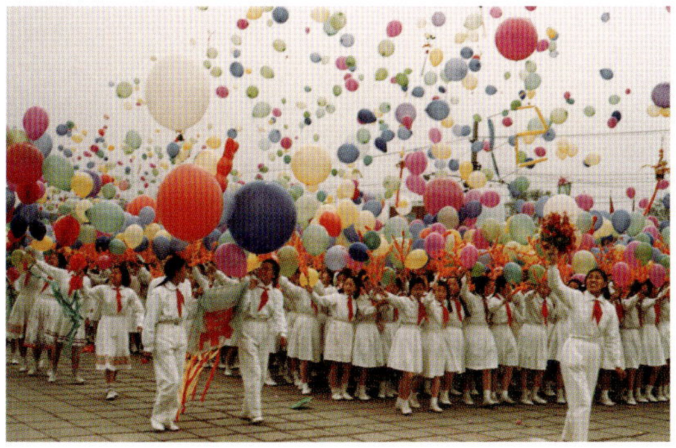

08

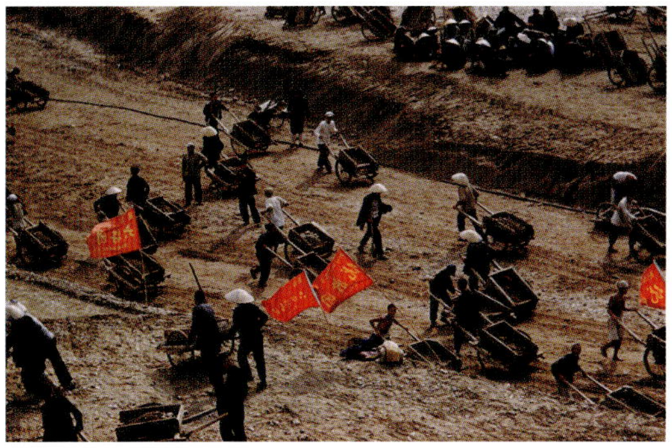

09

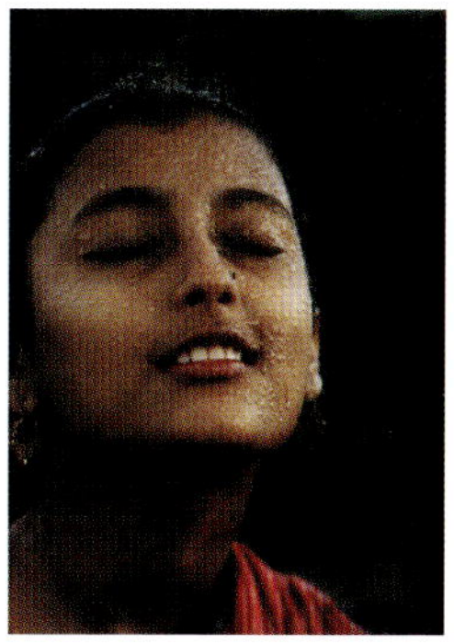

10

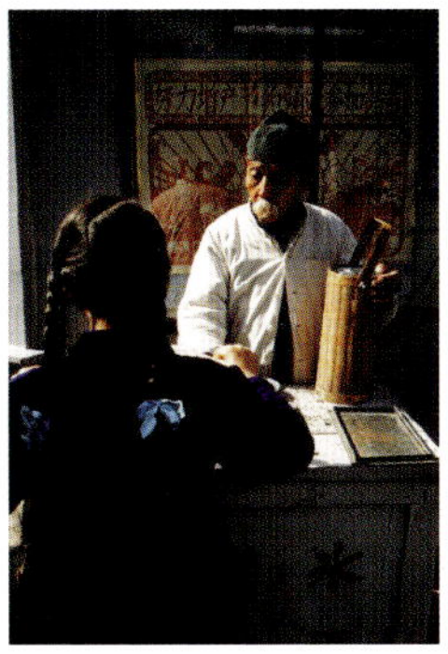

11

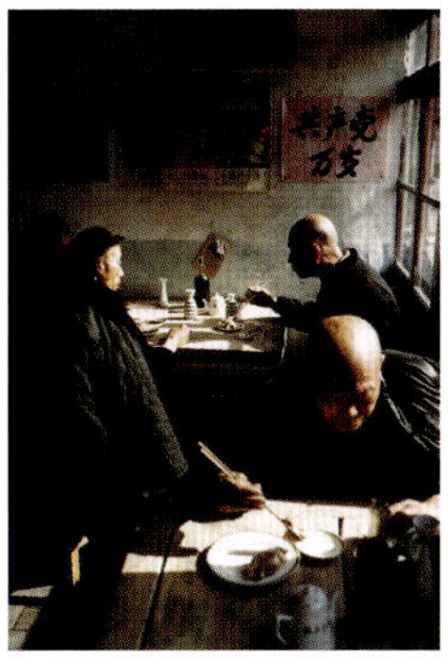

12

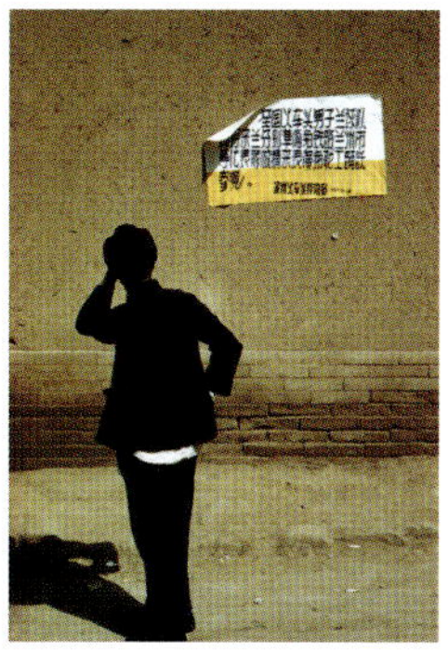

07 I *May Day celebrations, Tiananmen Square, Beijing, China*, 1957. McCredie, Athol, ed. *Brian Brake: Lens on the World*. Wellington: Te Papa Press, 2010. 35mm transparency. Collection Museum of New Zealand Te Papa Tongarewa. Gift of Wai-man Lau, 2001.

Plate 32
Making Reputations
Page 067

08 I *Miyun reservoir construction, near Beijing, China,* 1959. Variant in *Brian Brake: China, the 1950s*. Wellington: Museum of New Zealand Te Papa Tongarewa, 1995. 35mm transparency. Collection Museum of New Zealand Te Papa Tongarewa. Gift of Wai-man Lau, 2010.

Plate 27
Making Reputations
Page 060

09 I *"Monsoon girl" (Aparna Das Gupta), India*. From the series: Monsoon, 1960. "Monsoon". *Life*, vol. 51, no.10, 8 September, 1961. 35mm color transparency. Collection Museum of New Zealand Te Papa Tongarewa. Gift of Wai-man Lau, 2001.

Plate 01
Monsoon Meeting
Page 032

10 I *Old man selling popsicle to a girl, Beijing, China*, 1959. Variant in *Brian Brake: China, the 1950s.* Wellington: Museum of New Zealand Te Papa Tongarewa, 1995. 35mm transparency. Collection Museum of New Zealand Te Papa Tongarewa. Gift of Wai-man Lau, 2010.

Plate 21
Making Reputations
Page 053

11 I *Pedi-cab drivers in a restaurant in Liulichang Street, Beijing, China*, 1957. *Brian Brake: China*, the 1950s. Wellington: Museum of New Zealand Te Papa Tongarewa, 1995. 35mm transparency. Collection Museum of New Zealand Te Papa Tongarewa. Gift of Wai-man Lau, 2001.

Plate 29
Making Reputations
Page 062

12 I *Poster for a basketball match, Lanzhou, China*, 1957. *Brian Brake: 40 Photographs.* Lower Hutt: Dowse Art Gallery, 1976. 35mm transparency. Collection Museum of New Zealand Te Papa Tongarewa. Gift of Wai-man Lau, 2001.

Plate 22
Making Reputations
Page 054

01

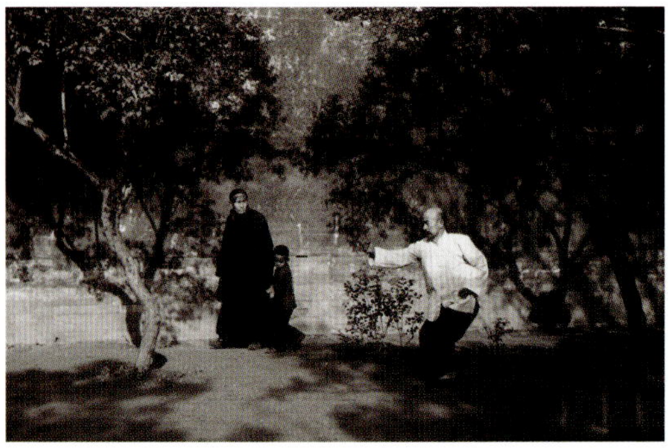

02

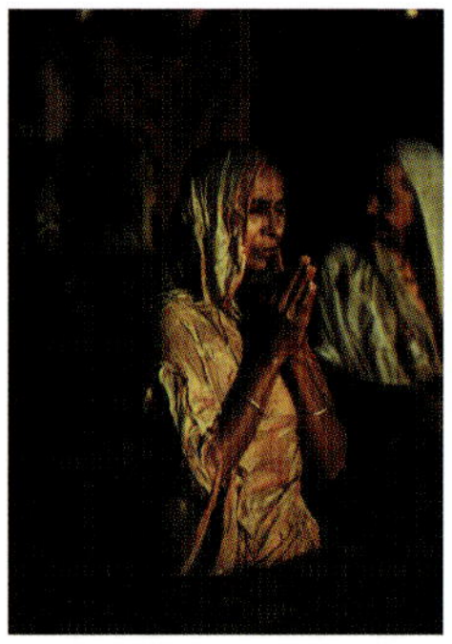

03

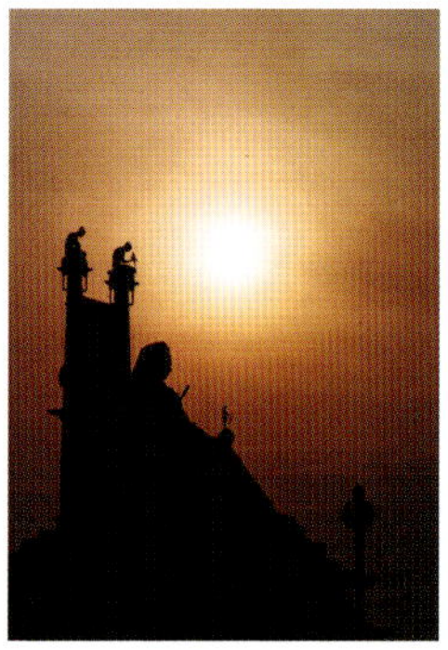

04

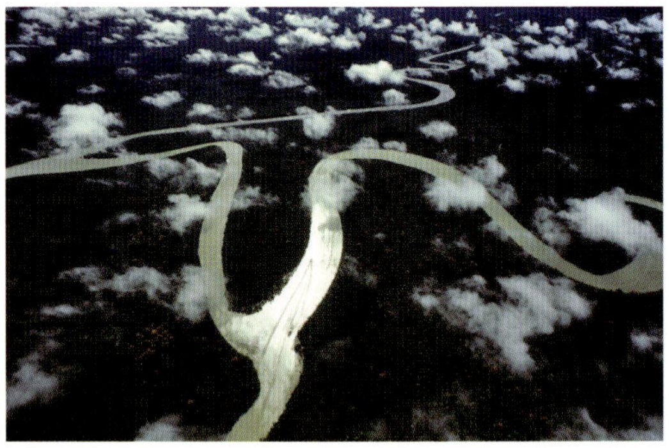

05

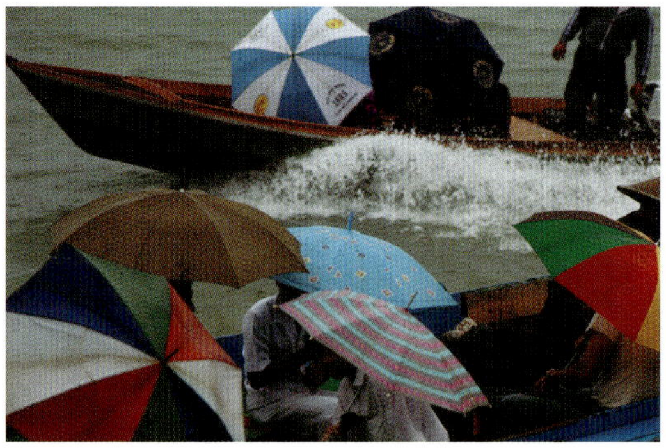

06

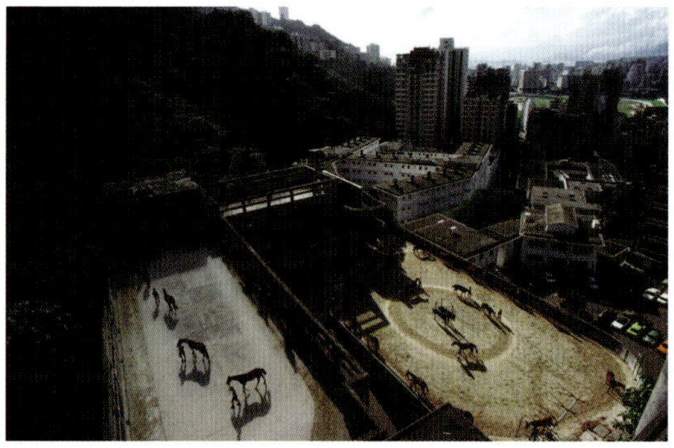

01 | *Practising taijiquan by the palace wall, Beijing, China*, 1957. *Brian Brake: China, the 1950s*. Wellington: Museum of New Zealand Te Papa Tongarewa, 1995. Reproduced from a 35mm black and white negative. Collection Museum of New Zealand Te Papa Tongarewa. Gift of Wai-man Lau, 2001.

Plate 25
Making Reputations
Page 058

02 | *Praying in the holy Ganges, Benares, India*. From the series: Monsoon, 1960. "Monsoon". *Life*, vol. 51, no. 10, 8 September, 1961. 35mm transparency. Collection Museum of New Zealand Te Papa Tongarewa. Gift of Wai-man Lau, 2001.

Plate 04
Monsoon Meeting
Page 035

03 | *Queen Victoria statue, Calcutta, India*. From the series: Monsoon, 1960. Unpublished. 35mm transparency. Collection Museum of New Zealand Te Papa Tongarewa. Gift of Wai-man Lau, 2001.

Plate 75
Signature Styles
Page 110

04 | *River, Brunei*, 1987. *Brunei Darussalam: Facts and Figures 1987*. 35mm transparency. Collection Museum of New Zealand Te Papa Tongarewa. Gift of Wai-man Lau, 2001.

Plate 69
Signature Styles
Page 105

05 | *Riverboats with umbrellas, Brunei*, 1987. *Brunei Darussalam: Facts and Figures 1987*. 35mm transparency. Collection Museum of New Zealand Te Papa Tongarewa. Gift of Wai-man Lau, 2001.

Plate 68
"Exotic, Enticing Hong Kong"
Page 105

06 | *Rooftop exercise yards of the Hong Kong Jockey Club, Hong Kong, China*, 1976. Brake, Brian and Robert Elegant. *Hong Kong: Great Cities*. Amsterdam: Time-Life Books, 1977. 35mm transparency. Collection Museum of New Zealand Te Papa Tongarewa. Gift of Wai-man Lau, 2001.

Plate 92
Signature Styles
Page 131

07

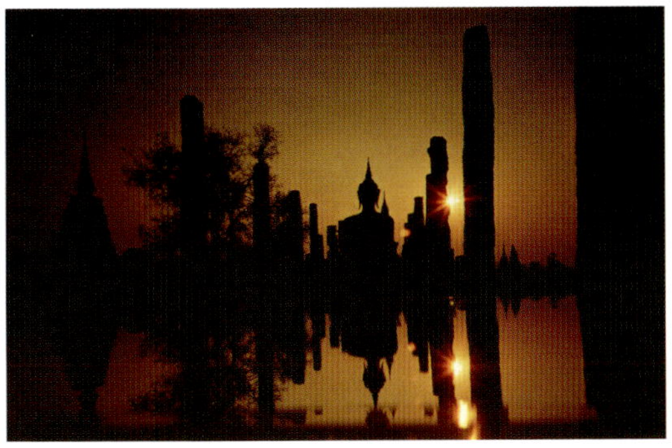

08

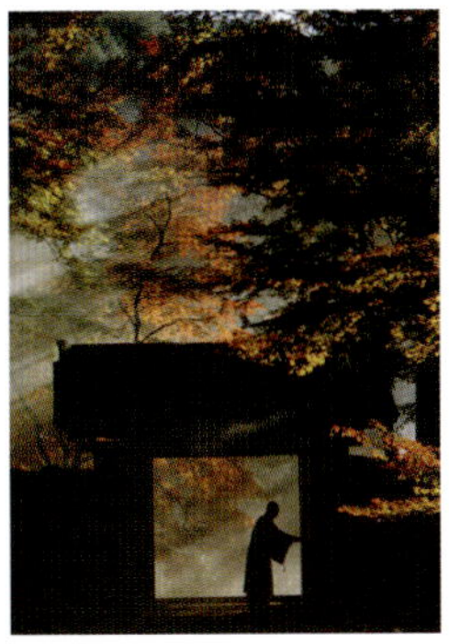

09

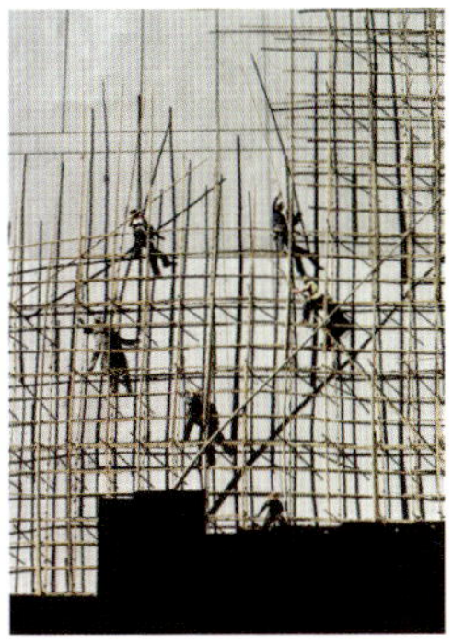

10

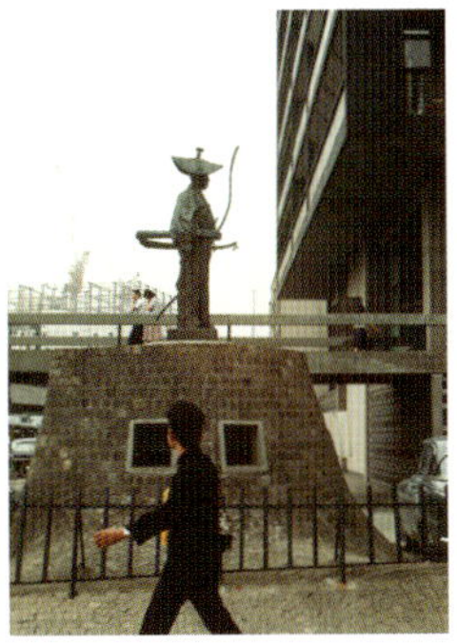

11

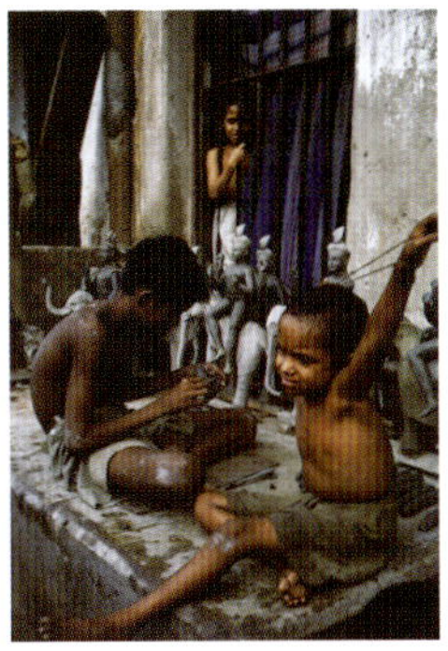

12

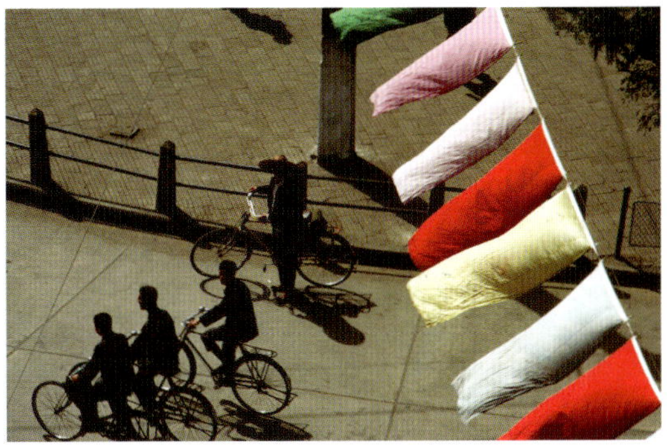

07 I *Ruins of the ancient city of Sukhothai, Thailand.* From the series: Thailand, 1960-80. "Brian Brake's Best of Asia". *Insight (American Express)*, February/March 1984. 4 x 5 color transparency. Collection Museum of New Zealand Te Papa Tongarewa. Gift of Wai-man Lau, 2010.

Plate 74
Signature Styles
Page 108

08 I *Sanzen-in Temple near Kyoto, Japan*, c.1963. "Japan: The Modern Paradoxes". *Life*, vol. 57, no. 11, 11 September 1964. 35mm transparency. Collection Museum of New Zealand Te Papa Tongarewa. Gift of Wai-man Lau, 2010.

Plate 49
Ancient and Modern
Page 084

09 I *Scaffolding, Hong Kong, China*, c.1976. Unpublished. 35mm transparency. Collection Museum of New Zealand Te Papa Tongarewa. Gift of Wai-man Lau, 2001.

Plate 66
Signature Styles
Page 103

10 I *Sculpture, Kanto, Japan.* From the series: Japan, 1960s-80s. Unpublished. 35mm transparency. Collection Museum of New Zealand Te Papa Tongarewa. Gift of Wai-man Lau, 2001.

Plate 44
Ancient and Modern
Page 080

11 I *Statuette maker and children, India.* From the series: India, 1960s. Unpublished. 35mm transparency. Collection Museum of New Zealand Te Papa Tongarewa. Gift of Wai-man Lau, 2001.

Plate 72
Signature Styles
Page 107

12 I *Street flags, Beijing, China.* From the series: China, 1957-59. Unpublished. 35mm transparency. Collection Museum of New Zealand Te Papa Tongarewa. Gift of Wai-man Lau, 2001.

Plate 28
Making Reputations
Page 061

01

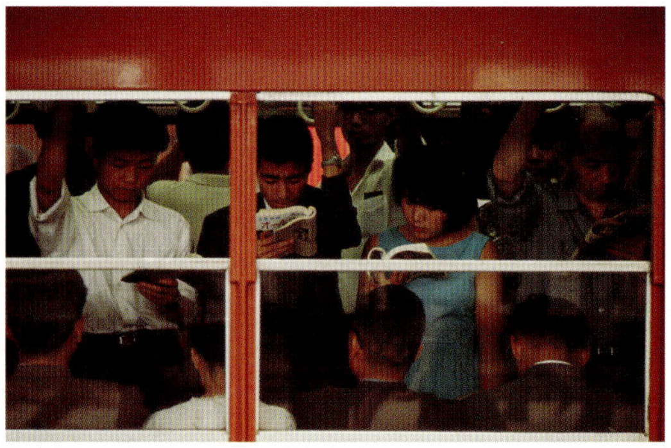

02

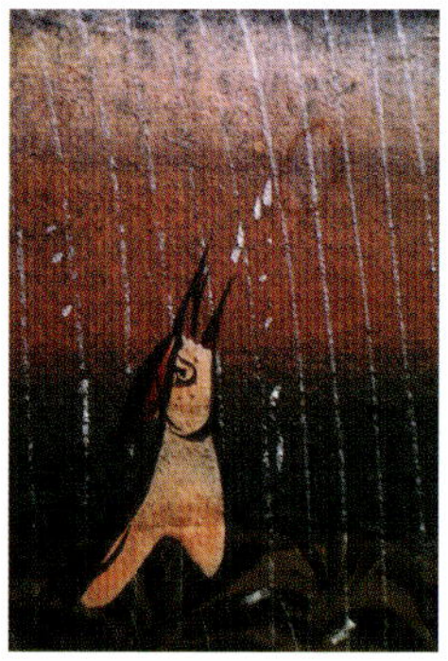

03

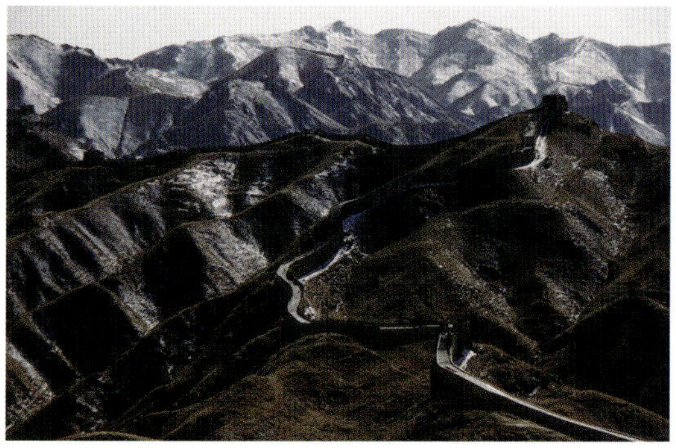

04

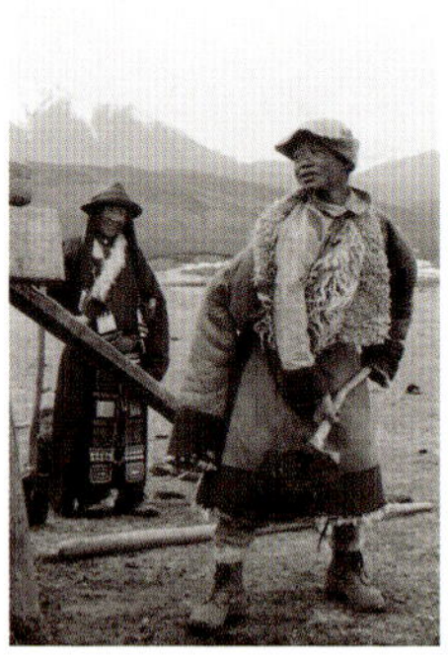

05

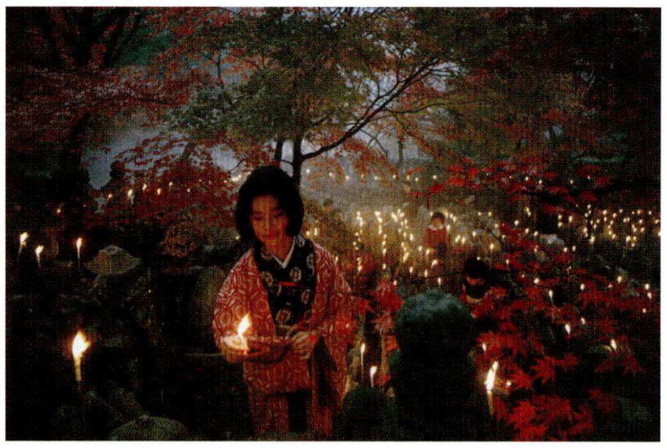

06

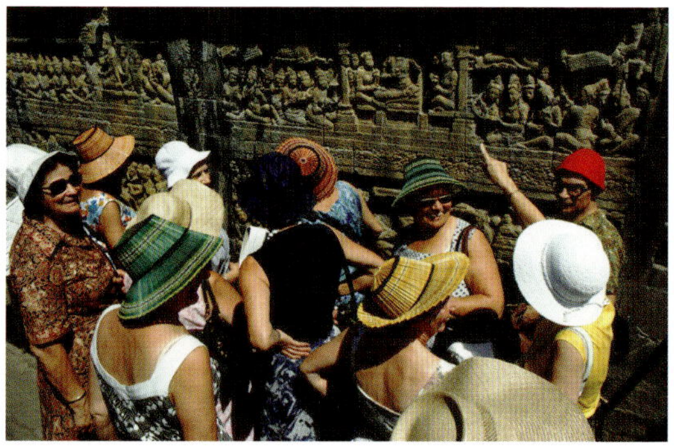

01 | *Subway, Tokyo, Japan,* 1964. "Japan: The Modern Paradoxes". *Life,* vol. 57, no. 11, 11 September 1964. 35mm transparency. Collection Museum of New Zealand Te Papa Tongarewa. Gift of Wai-man Lau, 2001.

Plate 46
Ancient and Modern
Page 081

02 | *The chatak bird (detail from a miniature), India.* From the series: Monsoon, 1960. *Brian Brake – Monsoon.* Auckland: David Bateman, 2007. 35mm transparency. Collection Museum of New Zealand Te Papa Tongarewa. Gift of Wai-man Lau, 2001.

Plate 10
Monsoon Meeting
Page 041

03 | *The Great Wall, Chuyun Kuan, China,* 1957. *Brian Brake: China, the 1950s.* Wellington: Museum of New Zealand Te Papa Tongarewa, 1995. 35mm transparency. Collection Museum of New Zealand Te Papa Tongarewa. Gift of Wai-man Lau, 2001.

Plate 31
Making Reputations
Page 064

04 | *Tibetan couple building a wall, Qinghai province, China,* 1957. *Brian Brake: China, the 1950s.* Wellington: Museum of New Zealand Te Papa Tongarewa, 1995. Reproduced from a 35mm black and white negative. Collection Museum of New Zealand Te Papa Tongarewa. Gift of Wai-man Lau, 2001.

Plate 65
Signature Styles
Page 102

05 | *Toshi Satow offering a candle—offerings to the unknown dead, Kyoto, Japan,* 1964. "Japan: The Modern Paradoxes". *Life,* vol. 57, no. 11, 11 September 1964. 35mm transparency. Collection Museum of New Zealand Te Papa Tongarewa. Gift of Wai-man Lau, 2010.

Plate 52
Ancient and Modern
Page 086

06 | *Tourists at the temples of Borobudur, Indonesia,* 1971. "The Cosmic Mountain: Borobudur". *India Magazine,* vol. 3, no. 1, December 1982. 35mm transparency. Collection Museum of New Zealand Te Papa Tongarewa. Gift of Wai-man Lau, 2001.

Plate 71
Signature Styles
Page 106

07

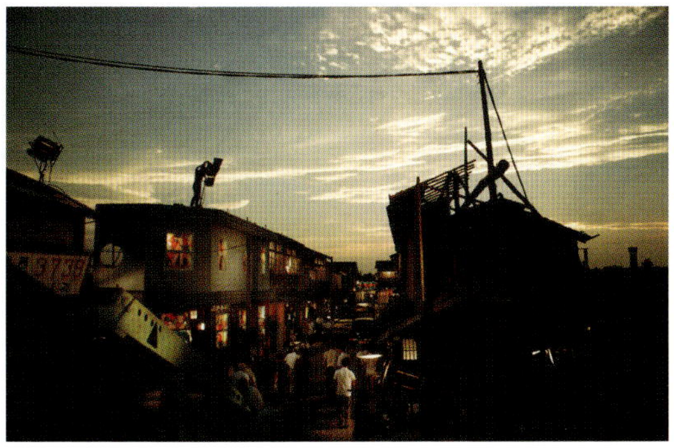

08

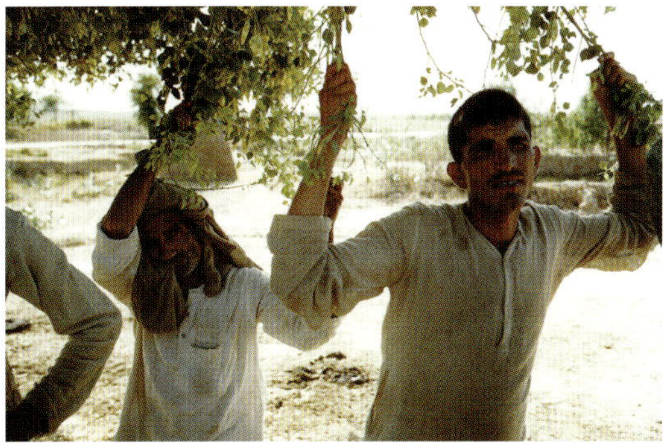

09

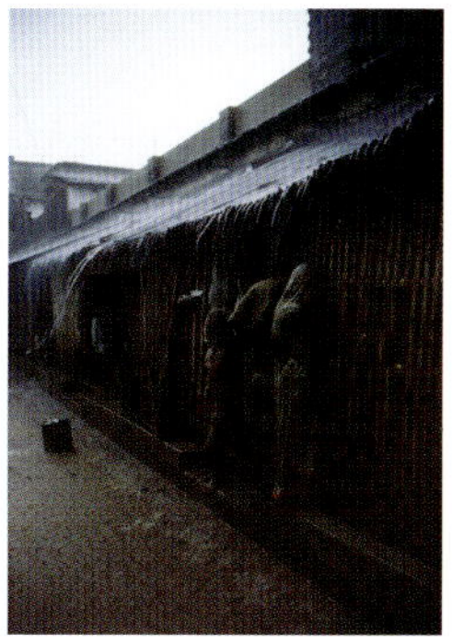

10

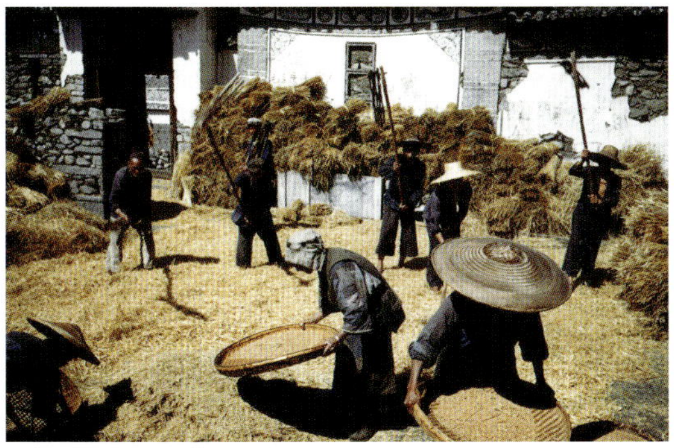

11

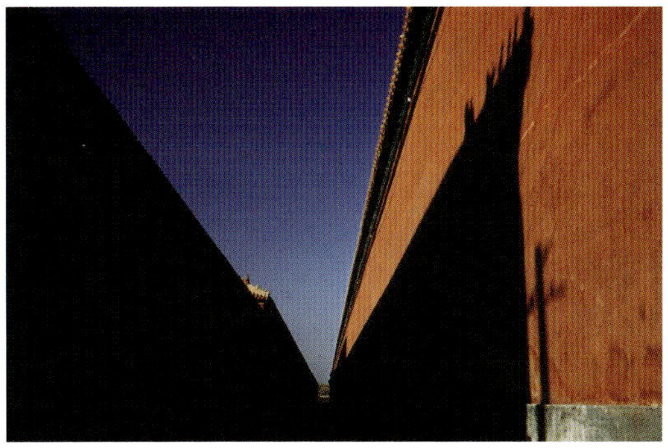

12

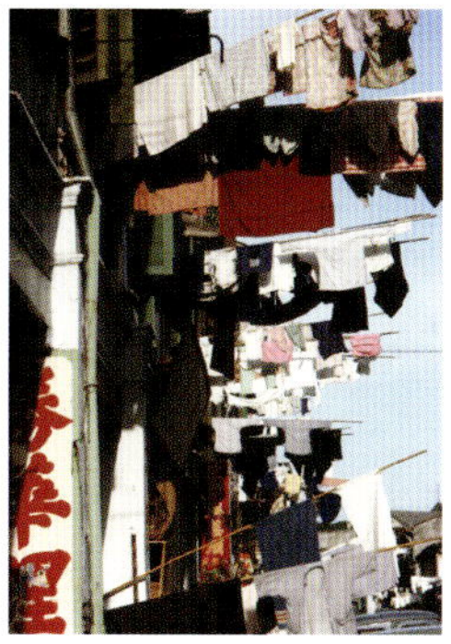

07 I *Village street built for the film* Gobancho Yugiriro, *directed by Tasaka Katsutaka, Toho Studios, Tokyo, Japan*, 1963. "The Universal Magic of the Movies". *Life*, vol. 55, no. 25, December 1963. 35mm transparency. Collection Museum of New Zealand Te Papa Tongarewa. Gift of Wai-man Lau, 2001.

Plate 53
Ancient and Modern
Page 087

08 I *Villagers in the shade of a tree during the afternoon heat, Punjab, India.* From the series: Monsoon, 1960. *Brian Brake – Monsoon.* Auckland: David Bateman, 2007. 35mm transparency. Collection Museum of New Zealand Te Papa Tongarewa. Gift of Wai-man Lau, 2001.

Plate 03
Monsoon Meeting
Page 034

09 I *Villagers shelter from torrential rain, Nimitia, West Bengal, India.* From the series: Monsoon, 1960. "Monsoon". *Life,* vol. 51, no. 10, 8 September, 1961. 35mm transparency. Collection Museum of New Zealand Te Papa Tongarewa. Gift of Wai-man Lau, 2001.

Plate 07
Monsoon Meeting
Page 038

10 I *Villagers threshing, Tali-Sakwan, Yunnan, China,* 1959. *Brian Brake: China, the 1950s.* Wellington: Museum of New Zealand Te Papa Tongarewa, 1995. 35mm transparency. Collection Museum of New Zealand Te Papa Tongarewa. Gift of Wai-man Lau, 2001.

Plate 24
Making Reputations
Page 056

11 I *Walls of the Forbidden City, Beijing, China,* 1957. *Brian Brake: China, the 1950s.* Wellington: Museum of New Zealand Te Papa Tongarewa, 1995. 35mm transparency. Collection Museum of New Zealand Te Papa Tongarewa. Gift of Wai-man Lau, 2001.

Plate 30
Making Reputations
Page 063

12 I *Washing drying above street, Singapore,* 1963. Unpublished. 35mm transparency. Collection Museum of New Zealand Te Papa Tongarewa. Gift of Wai-man Lau, 2010.

Plate 67
Signature Styles
Page 104

01

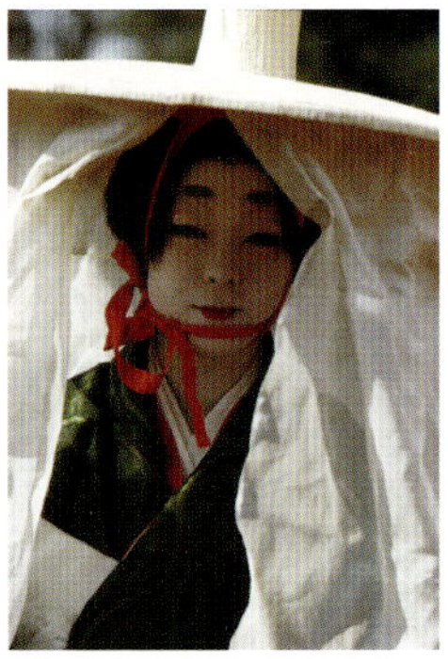

02

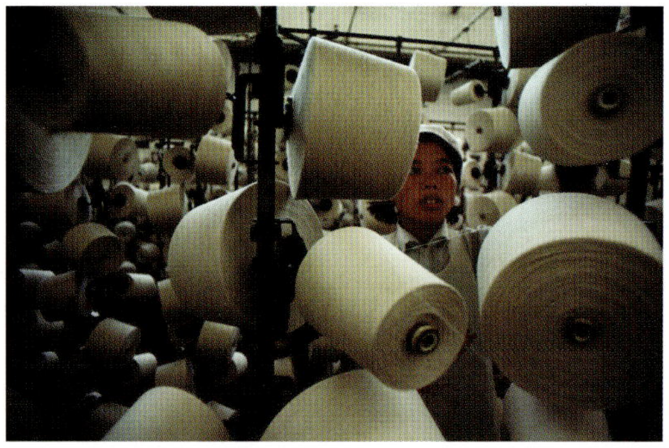

01 I *Woman in Heian Period Costume, Festival of the Ages, Kyoto, Japan,* 1963. "Japan: The Modern Paradoxes". *Life,* vol. 57, no. 11, 11 September 1964. 35mm transparency. Collection Museum of New Zealand Te Papa Tongarewa. Gift of Wai-man Lau, 2010.

Plate 47
Ancient and Modern
Page 082

02 I *Woman tending bobbins in a synthetic-fiber factory, Beijing, China,* 1957. *Brian Brake: China, the 1950s.* Wellington: Museum of New Zealand Te Papa Tongarewa, 1995. 35mm transparency. Collection Museum of New Zealand Te Papa Tongarewa. Gift of Wai-man Lau, 2001.

Plate 23
Making Reputations
Page 55

STEVE MCCURRY BIOGRAPHY AND PLATES IN ALPHABETICAL ORDER

Steve McCurry has been one of the most iconic figures in contemporary photography for more than thirty years. Born in Philadelphia, Pennsylvania, in 1950, McCurry studied cinematography at Pennsylvania State University, before going on to work as a photographer for a regional newspaper, *Today's Post*, in 1974. In 1978, McCurry made the first of many trips to India. Traveling with little more than a bag of clothes and film, he made his way across the subcontinent, exploring the country with his camera.

In May 1979, he crossed the Pakistan border into rebel-controlled Afghanistan, prior to the Russian invasion in December. His photographs were among the first to document the conflict there. Emerging after months embedded with the Mujahideen guerrilla fighters, McCurry made his way over the Pakistan border with his film sewn into his clothes. An image of Mujahideen observing an enemy convoy was published in the *New York Times* in September 1979. He went on to cover the war for *Time* magazine, and was awarded the Robert Capa Gold Medal for "best published photographic reporting from abroad requiring exceptional courage and enterprise".

In 1984, while on assignment for *National Geographic*, he photographed the young Sharbat Gula, soon recognized internationally as "Afghan Girl". He was awarded the Magazine Photographer of the Year from the National Press Photographers' Association. Many more awards followed, including four first prizes in the World Press Photographers' competition.

His many book publications include *The Imperial Way* (1985), *Monsoon* (1988), *Portraits* (1999), *South Southeast* (2000), *Sanctuary: The Temples of Angkor* (2002), *The Path to Buddha: A Tibetan Pilgrimage* (2003), *Steve McCurry* (2005), *Looking East* (2006), *In the Shadow of Mountains* (2007), *The Unguarded Moment* (2009), *The Iconic Photographs* (2011), and *Steve McCurry: India* (2015).

McCurry has worked for many of the leading international magazines and journals, including *National Geographic*, *New York Times Magazine*, and *Life*. His work has been exhibited widely, in most of the major cities in the world, and most recently at La Venaria Reale north of Turin in Italy.

He travels constantly, from a base at Steve McCurry Studios in Long Island City, NY, where his staff maintain a website (www.stevemccurry.com), a Facebook page (www.facebook.com/stevemccurrystudios/), a blog (https://stevemccurry.wordpress.com) and an extensive Instagram account (www.instagram.com/stevemccurryofficial/?hl=en).

01

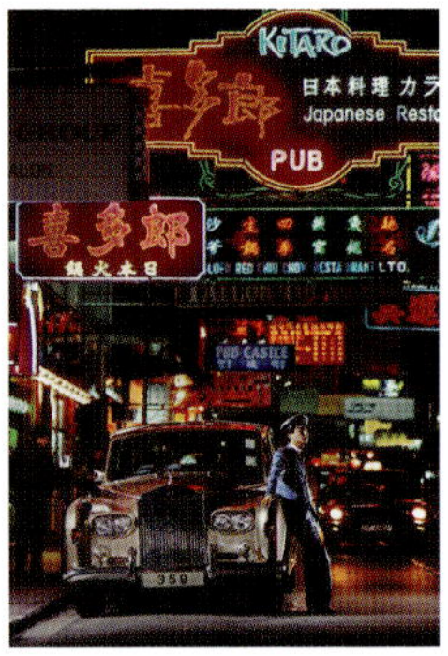

02

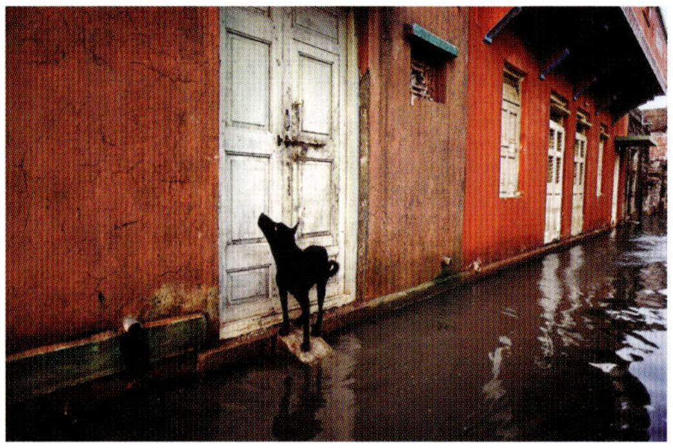

03

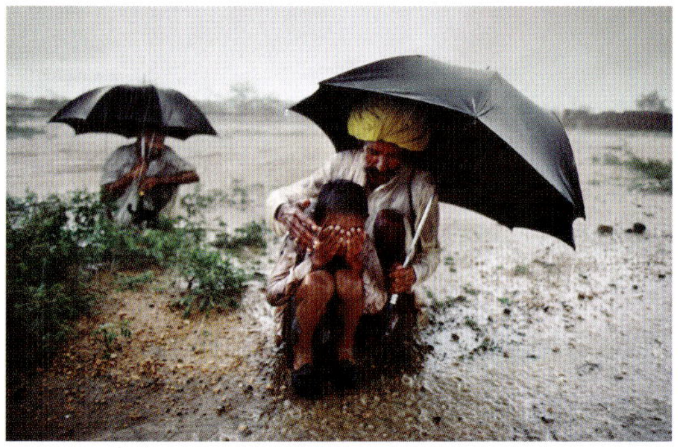

04

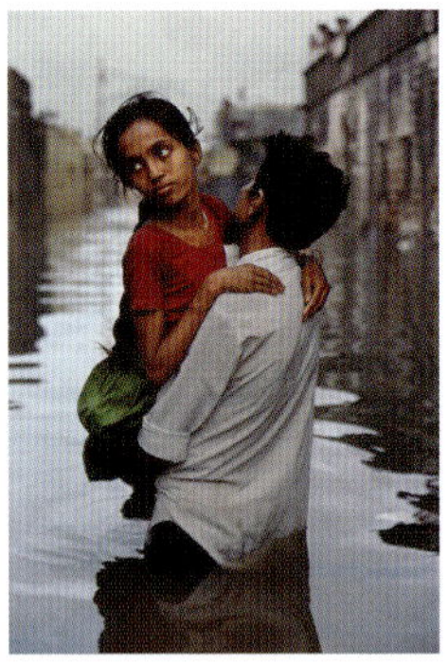

05

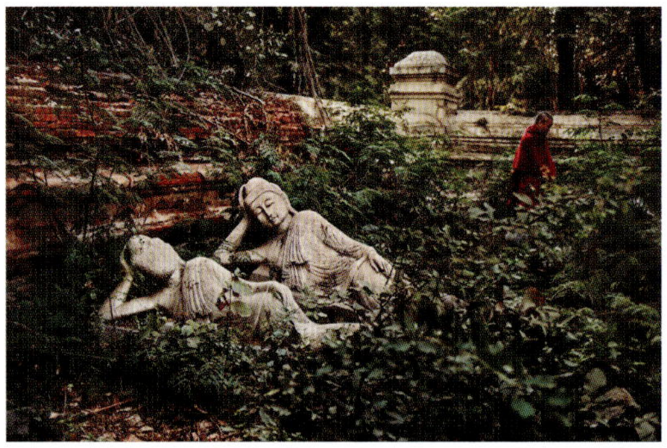

06

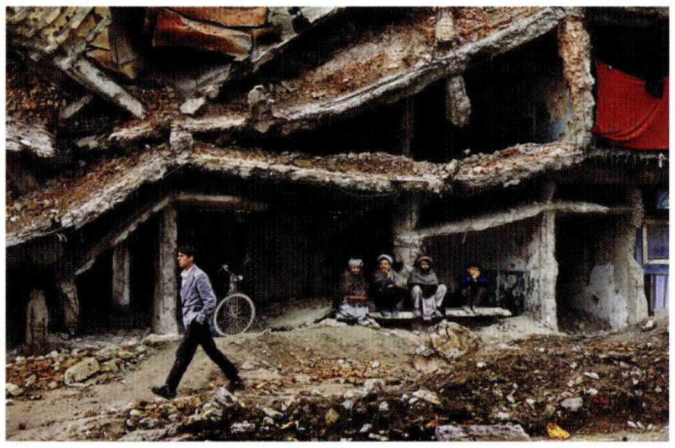

01 I *A chauffeur leans against his car, Hong Kong, China,* 1985. "Exotic, Enticing Hong Kong". *National Geographic Traveler,* vol. III, no. 4, Winter 1986/87. © Steve McCurry.

Plate 89
"Exotic, Enticing Hong Kong"
Page 127

02 I *A dog caught in a monsoon, Porbandar, India,* 1983. *Monsoon.* New York: Thames & Hudson Ltd., 1988. © Steve McCurry.

Plate 19
Monsoon Meeting
Page 050

03 I *A father and son, Rajasthan, India,* 1984. *Monsoon.* New York: Thames & Hudson Ltd., 1988. © Steve McCurry.

Plate 15
Monsoon Meeting
Page 046

04 I *A flooded street, Porbandar, India,* 1983. *Monsoon.* New York: Thames & Hudson Ltd., 1988. © Steve McCurry.

Plate 17
Monsoon Meeting
Page 048

05 I *A monk walks past reclining Buddha statues, Schwedagon Pagoda, Rangoon, Burma/Myanmar,* 2010. Unpublished. © Steve McCurry.

Plate 62
Ancient and Modern
Page 098

06 I *A ruined building, Kabul, Afghanistan,* 2002. "Afghanistan Between War and Peace". *National Geographic,* vol. 204, no. 5, November 2003. © Steve McCurry.

Plate 41
Making Reputations
Page 077

07

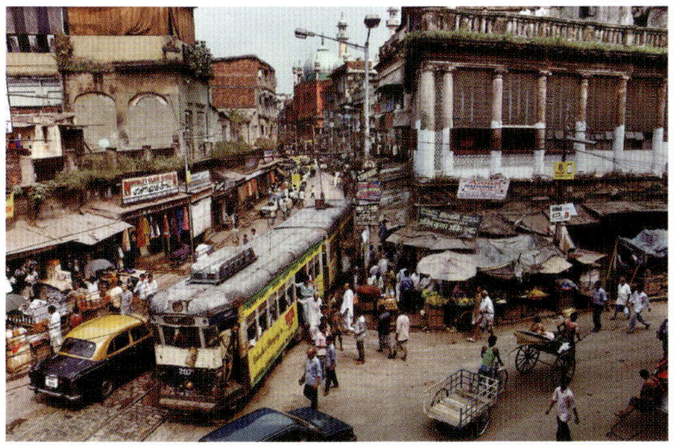

08

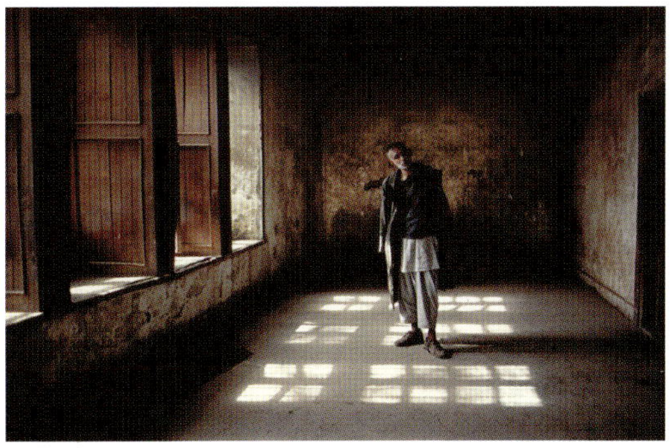

09

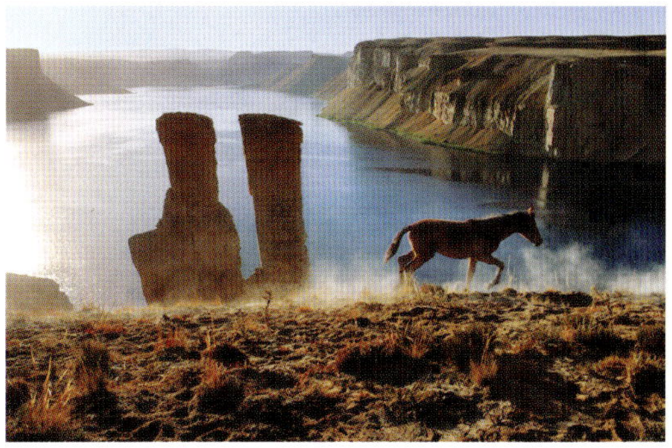

10

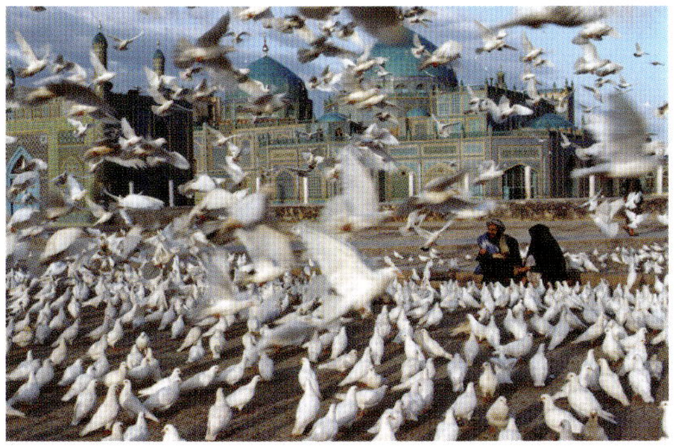

11

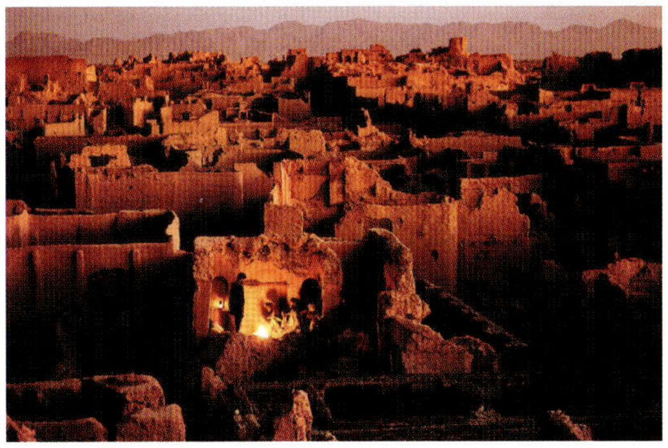

12

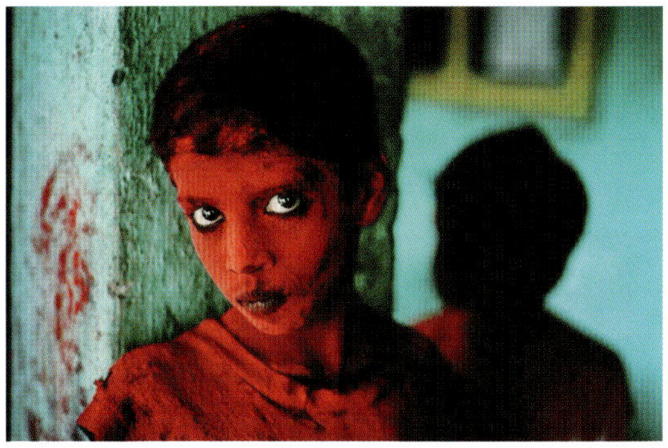

07 | *A tram, Calcutta, India,* 1996. “India: Fifty Years of Independence”. *National Geographic,* vol. 191, no. 5, May 1997. © Steve McCurry.

Plate 79
Signature Styles
Page 115

08 | *Asylum, Kabul, Afghanistan,* 1992. “Afghanistan’s Uneasy Peace”. *National Geographic,* vol. 184, no. 4, October 1993. © Steve McCurry.

Plate 40
Making Reputations
Page 076

09 | *Band-i-Amir, Bamyan, Afghanistan,* 2002. “Afghanistan Between War and Peace”. *National Geographic,* vol. 204, no. 5, November 2003. © Steve McCurry.

Plate 36
Making Reputations
Page 072

10 | *Blue Mosque, Mazar-i-Sharif, Afghanistan,* 1991. South Southeast. London & New York: Phaidon Press, 2000. © Steve McCurry.

Plate 33
Making Reputations
Page 068

11 | *Bombed townscape, Herat, Afghanistan,* 1992. “Afghanistan’s Uneasy Peace”. *National Geographic,* vol. 184, no. 4, October 1993. © Steve McCurry.

Plate 38
Making Reputations
Page 074

12 | *Boy at Ganesh Chaturthi festival, Mumbai, India,* 1996. “India: Fifty Years of Independence”. *National Geographic,* vol.191, no. 5, May 1997. © Steve McCurry.

Plate 84
Signature Styles
Page 120

01

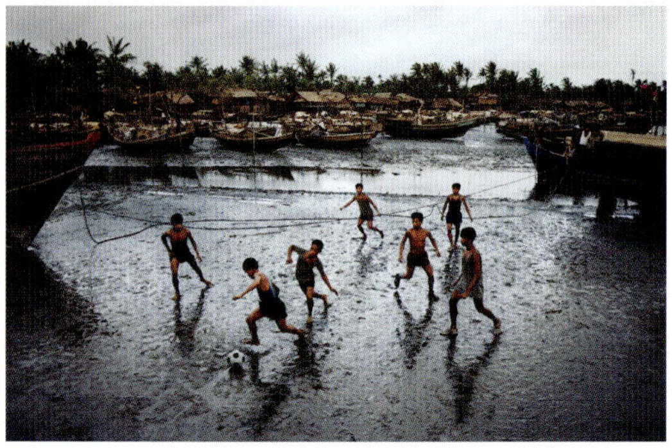

02

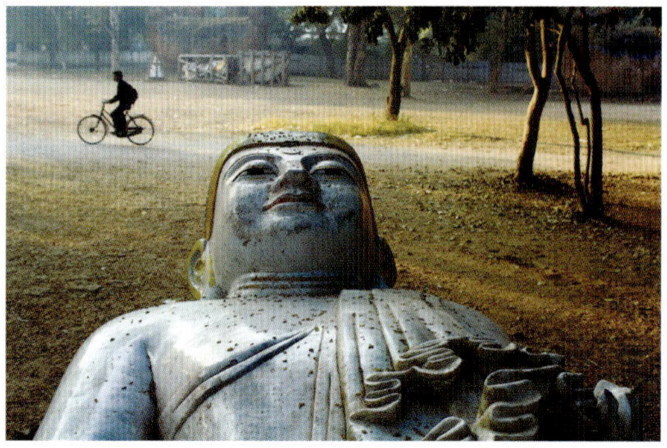

03

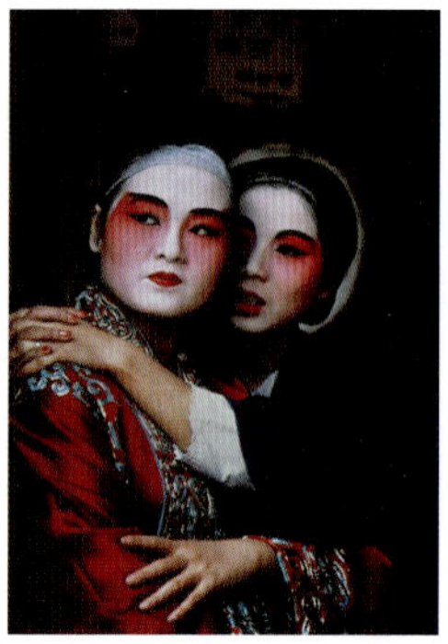

04

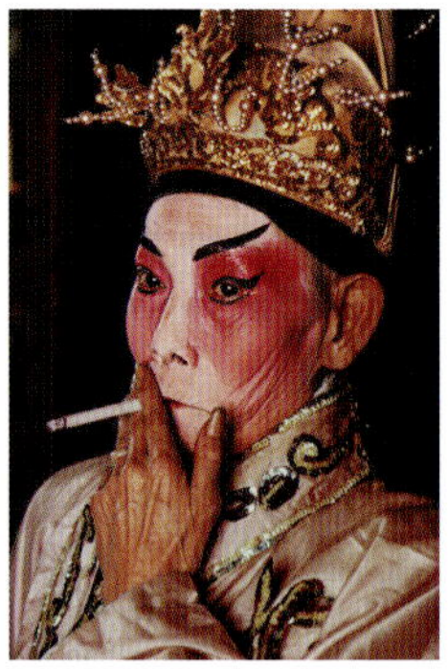

05

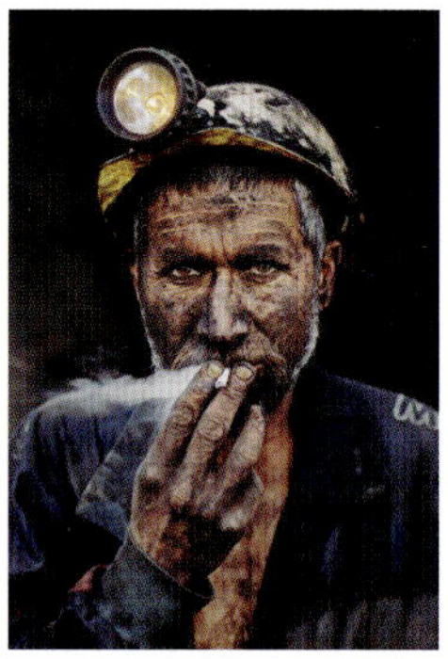

06

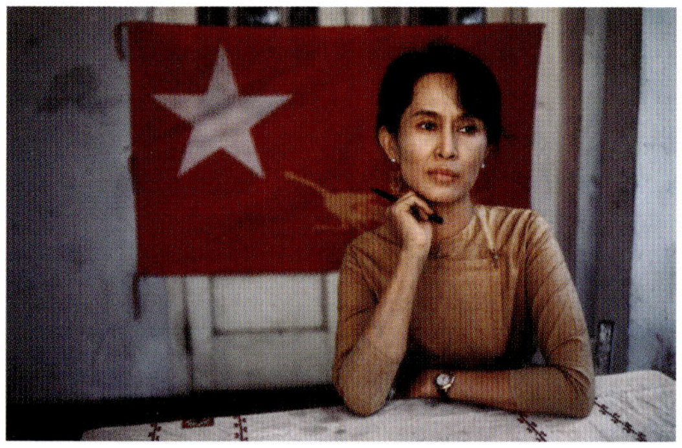

01 I *Boys playing football, Sittwe, Burma/ Myanmar,* 1994. *The Iconic Photographs.* London & New York: Phaidon Press, 2010. © Steve McCurry.

Plate 59
Ancient and Modern
Page 094

02 I *Buddha statue in Mandalay, Burma/ Myanmar,* 2008. *The Unguarded Moment.* London & New York: Phaidon Press, 2009. © Steve McCurry.

Plate 61
Ancient and Modern
Page 097

03 I *Chinese opera performers backstage, Hong Kong, China,* 1984. *Portraits.* London & New York: Phaidon Press, 1999. © Steve McCurry.

Plate 93
"Exotic, Enticing Hong Kong"
Page 132

04 I *Chinese opera star at the Ming Dynasty Theatre, Hong Kong, China,* 1998. *Portraits.* London & New York: Phaidon Press, 1999. © Steve McCurry.

Plate 94
"Exotic, Enticing Hong Kong"
Page 133

05 I *Coal miner, Pol-e Khomri, Afghanistan,* 2002. Bannon, Anthony. *Steve McCurry.* London & New York: Phaidon Press, 2005. © Steve McCurry.

Plate 83
Signature Styles
Page 119

06 I *Daw Aung San Suu Kyi, Rangoon, Burma/Myanmar,* 1995. *The Unguarded Moment.* London & New York: Phaidon Press, 2009. © Steve McCurry.

Plate 58
Ancient and Modern
Page 093

07

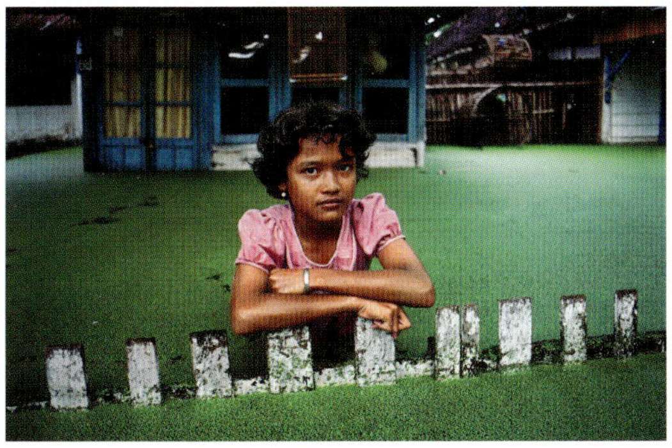

08

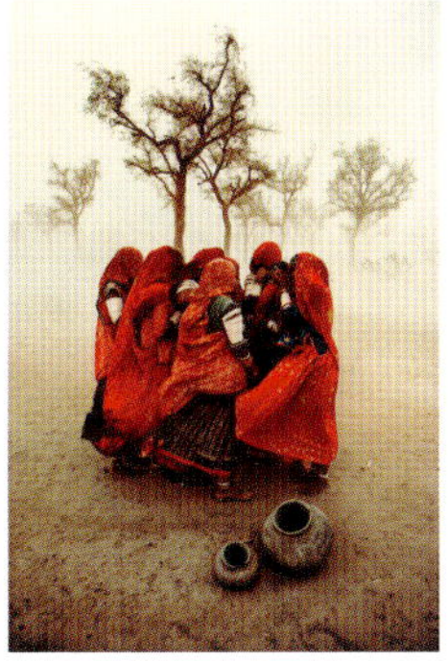

09

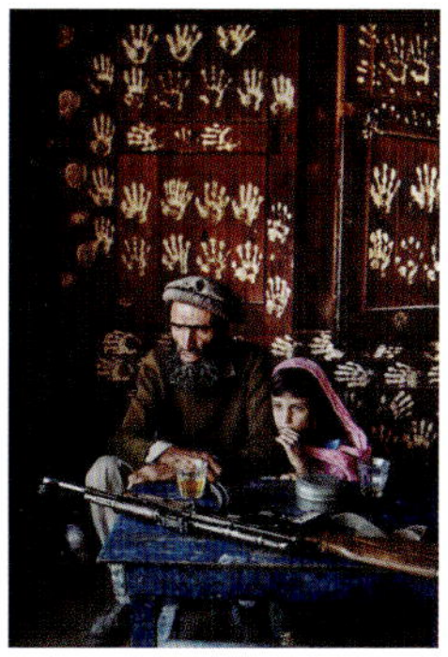

10

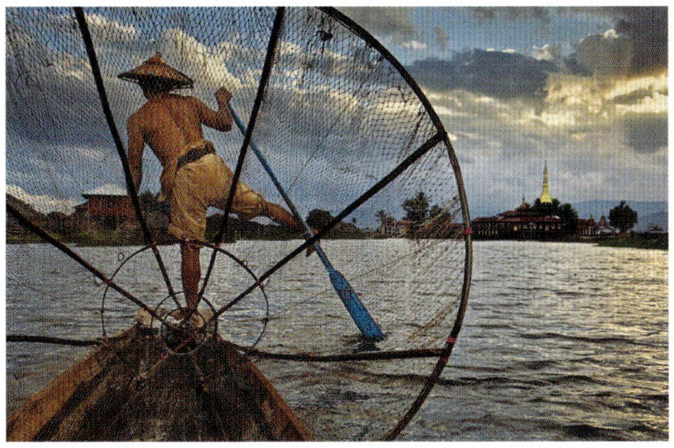

11

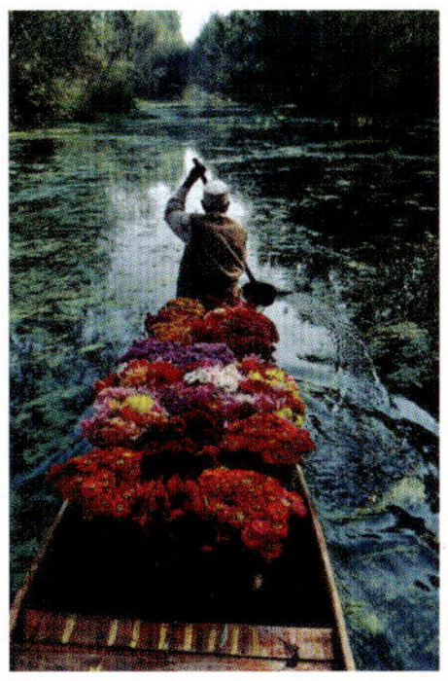

12

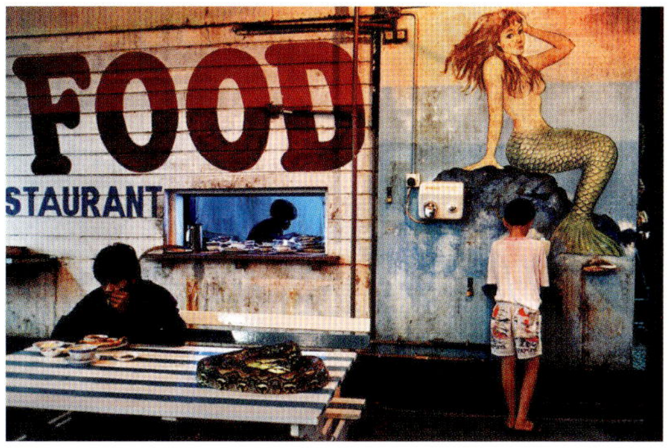

07 | *Duckweed carpets the water in a girl's front yard at Bojonegoro, Java, Indonesia,* 1983. *Monsoon.* New York: Thames & Hudson Ltd, 1995. © Steve McCurry.

Plate 18
Monsoon Meeting
Page 049

08 | *Dust storm, Rajasthan, India,* 1983. *Monsoon.* New York: Thames & Hudson Ltd., 1988. © Steve McCurry.

Plate 12
Monsoon Meeting
Page 044

09 | *Father and daughter at home, Kamdesh, Afghanistan,* 1992. *In the Shadow of Mountains.* London & New York: Phaidon Press, 2007. © Steve McCurry

Plate 34
Making Reputations
Page 070

10 | *Fisherman on Inle Lake, Burma/ Myanmar,* 2008. *The Iconic Photographs.* London & New York: Phaidon Press, 2010. © Steve McCurry.

Plate 60
Ancient and Modern
Page 096

11 | *Flower Seller at Dal Lake, Srinagar, Kashmir,* 1996. "Kashmir: Trapped in Conflict". *National Geographic*, vol. 196, no. 3, September 1999. © Steve McCurry.

Plate 77
Signature Styles
Page 112

12 | *"Food", Rangoon, Burma/Myanmar,* 1994. *South Southeast.* London & New York: Phaidon Press, 2000. © Steve McCurry.

Plate 42
Ancient and Modern
Page 078

01

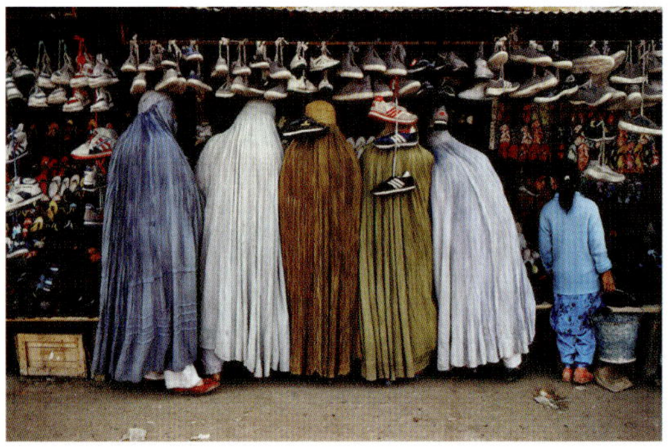

02

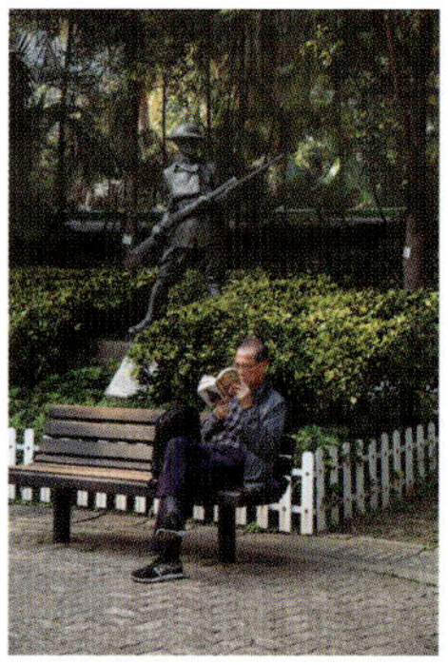

03

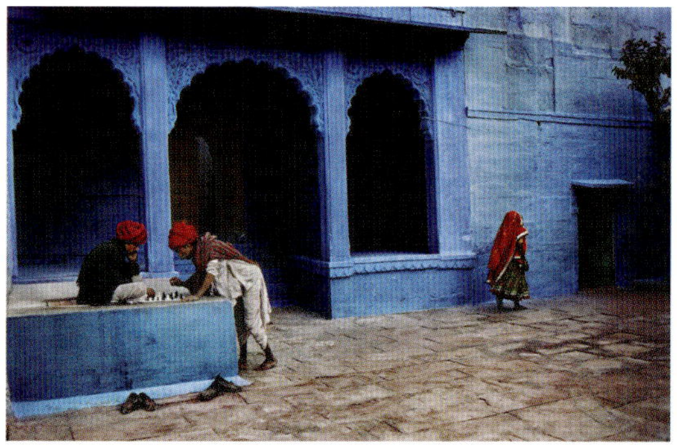

04

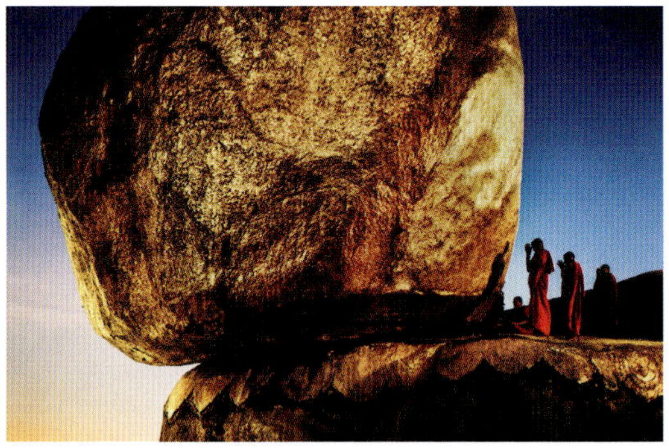

05

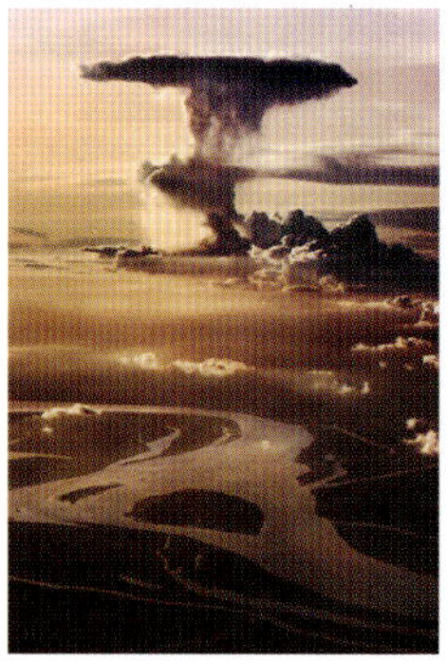

06

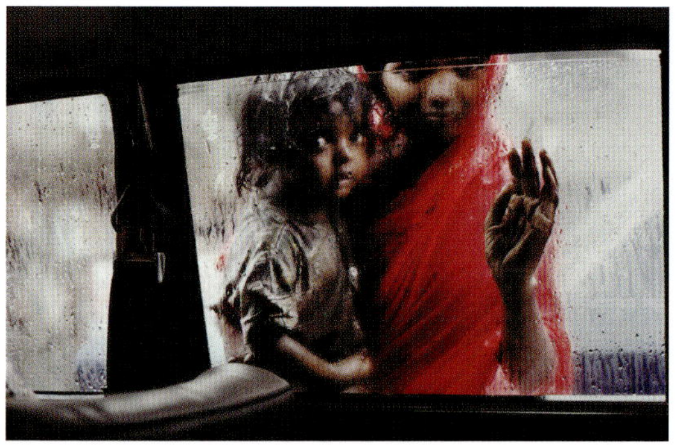

01 I *Kabul, Afghanistan,* 1992. “Afghanistan’s Uneasy Peace”. *National* Geographic, vol. 184, no. 4, October 1993. © Steve McCurry.

Plate 37
Making Reputations
Page 073

02 I *Man reading on a bench in Hong Kong, China,* 2014. Unpublished. © Steve McCurry.

Plate 95
“Exotic, Enticing Hong Kong”
Page 134

03 I *Men playing chess, Jodhpur, Rajasthan, India,* 1996. *South Southeast.* London & New York: Phaidon Press, 2000. © Steve McCurry.

Plate 78
Signature Styles
Page 113

04 I *Monks praying at Golden Rock, Kyaiktiyo, Burma/Myanmar,* 1994. “Burma: The Richest of Poor Countries”. *National Geographic,* vol. 188, no. 1, July 1995. © Steve McCurry.

Plate 54
Ancient and Modern
Page 088

05 I *Monsoon skies over Bihar, Northeast India,* 1983. *Monsoon.* New York: Thames & Hudson Ltd., 1988. © Steve McCurry.

Plate 86
Signature Styles
Page 123

06 I *Mother and child at car window, Mumbai, India,* 1993. “Bombay: India’s Capital of Hope”. *National Geographic,* vol. 188, no. 3, March 1995. © Steve McCurry

Plate 13
Monsoon Meeting
Page 045

07

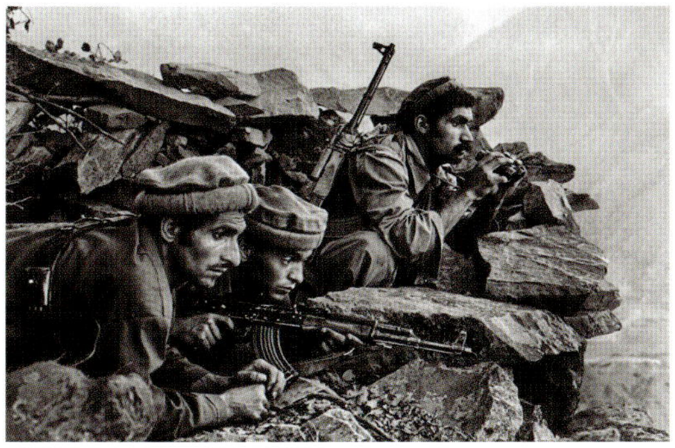

08

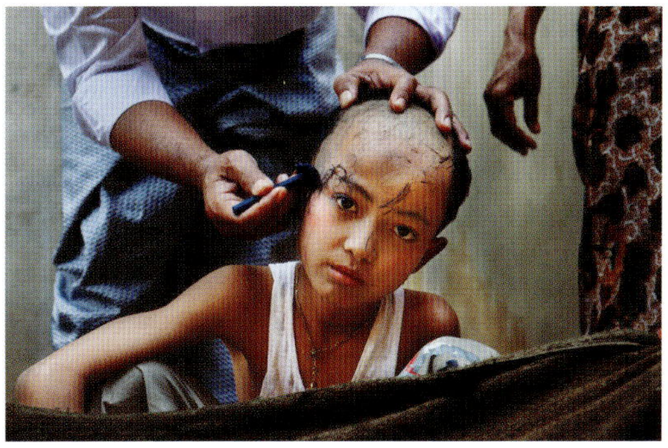

09

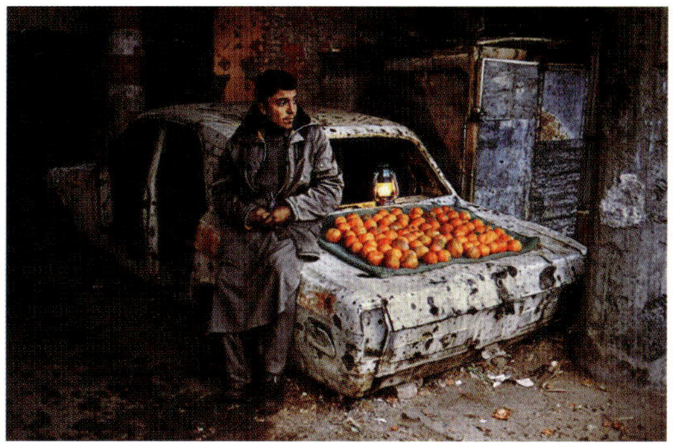

10

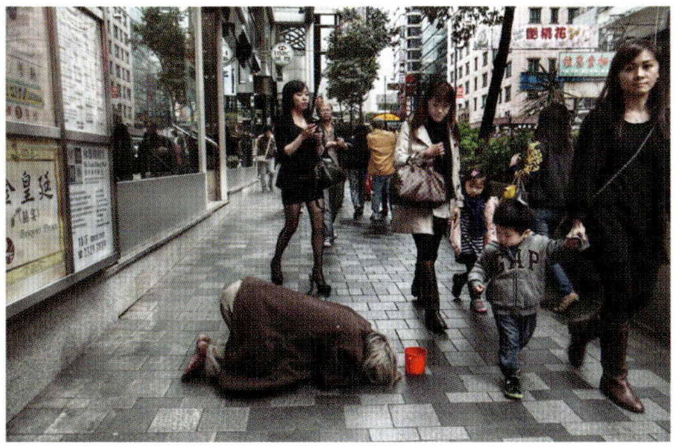

11

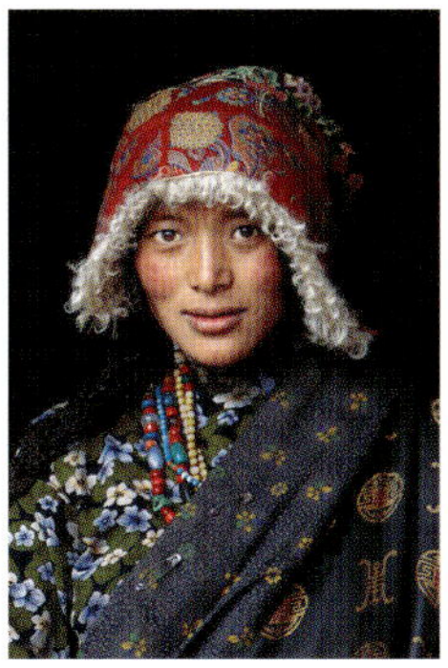

12

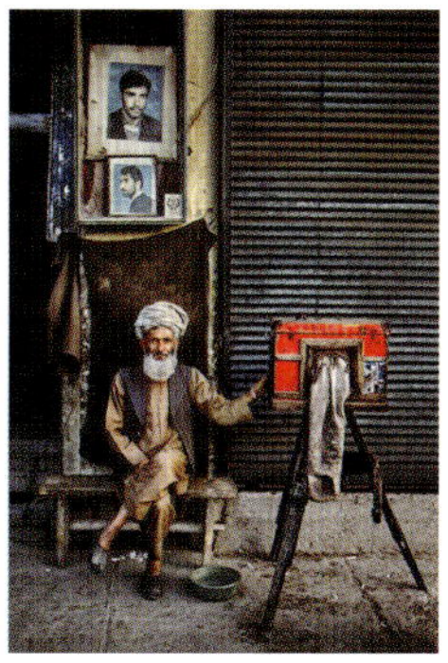

07 | *Mujahideen fighters watch convoy, Nuristan, Afghanistan,* 1979. Bannon, Anthony. *Steve McCurry.* London & New York: Phaidon Press, 2005. © Steve McCurry.

Plate 39
Making Reputations
Page 075

08 | *Novice getting his head shaved, Burma/Myanmar,* 2011. Unpublished. © Steve McCurry.

Plate 57
Ancient and Modern
Page 092

09 | *Orange seller, Kabul, Afghanistan,* 2003. *In the Shadow of Mountains.* London & New York: Phaidon Press, 2007. © Steve McCurry.

Plate 35
Making Reputations
Page 071

10 | *People walk past a beggar on the sidewalk, Hong Kong, China,* 2014. Unpublished. © Steve McCurry.

Plate 96
"Exotic, Enticing Hong Kong"
Page 135

11 | *Pilgrim at a stupa, Amdo, Tibet,* 2001. *The Path to Buddha.* London & New York: Phaidon Press, 2003. © Steve McCurry

Plate 82
Signature Styles
Page 119

12 | *Portrait photographer, Kabul, Afghanistan,* 1992. *In the Shadow of Mountains.* London & New York: Phaidon Press, 2007. © Steve McCurry.

Plate 63
Signature Styles
Page 100

01

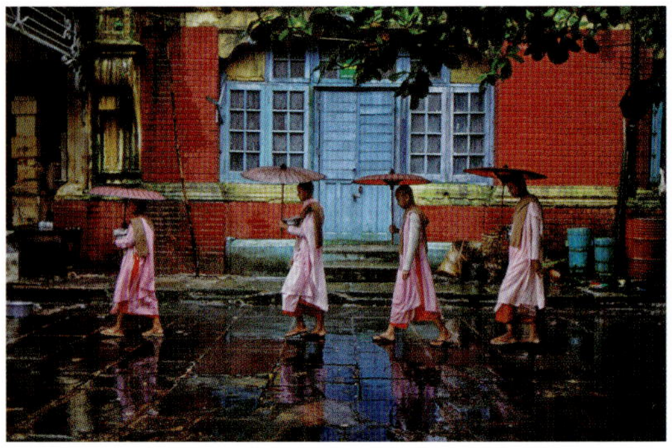

02

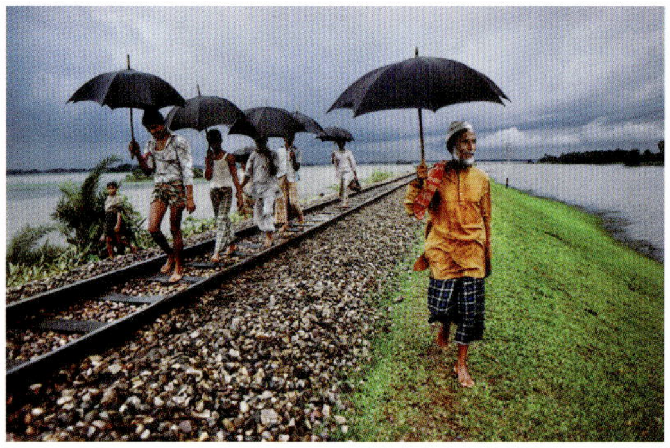

03

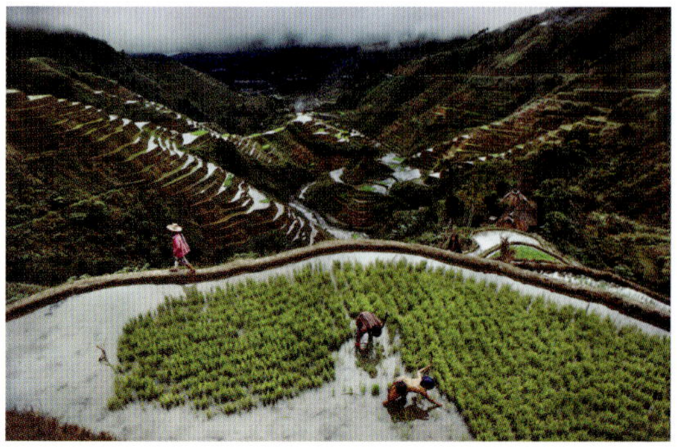

04

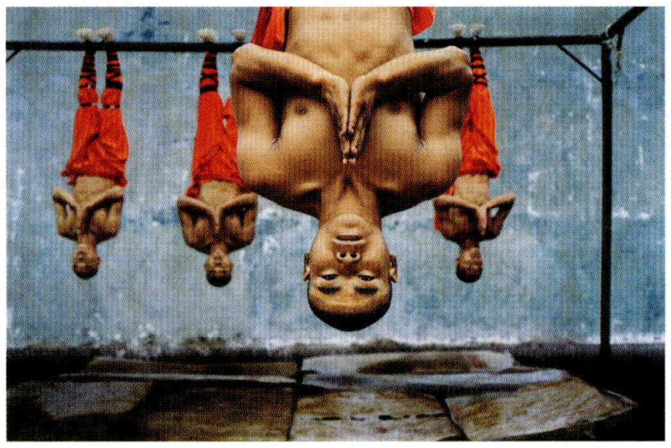

05

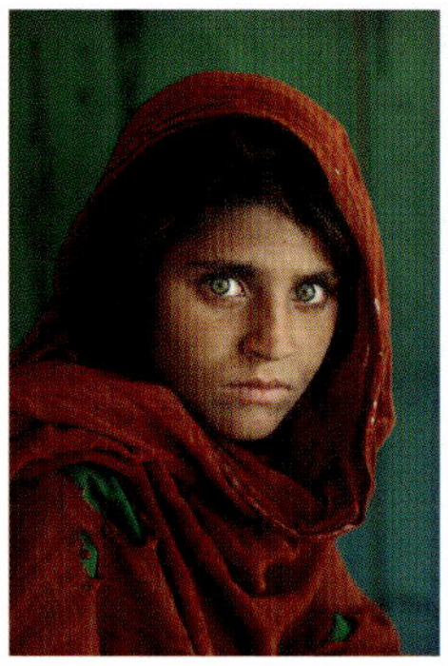

06

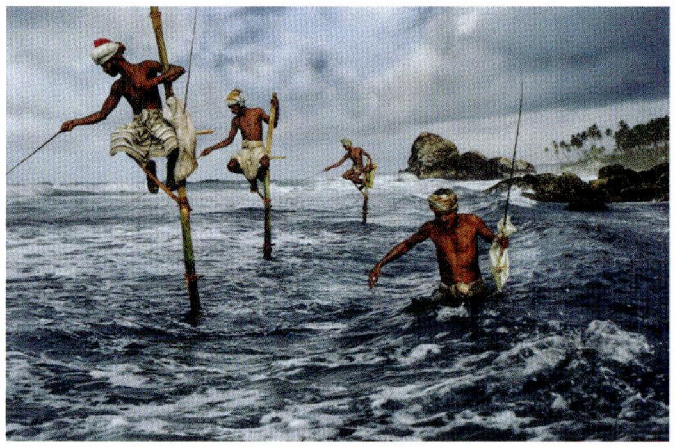

01 | *Procession of nuns, Rangoon, Burma/ Myanmar,* 1994. "Buddha Rising: Out of the Monastery, Into the Living Room". *National Geographic*, vol. 208, no. 6, December 2005. © Steve McCurry.

Plate 56
Ancient and Modern
Page 091

02 | *Railway track, Bangladesh,* 1983. McCurry, Steve and Paul Theroux. "The Imperial Way: By Rail Across the Indian Subcontinent". *National Geographic,* vol. 165, no. 6, June 1984. © Steve McCurry.

Plate 14
Monsoon Meeting
Page 045

03 | *Rice paddy fields, Banaue, Philippines,* 1985. "The Philippines: A Time of Hope and Danger". *National Geographic*, vol. 170, no. 1, July 1986. © Steve McCurry.

Plate 16
Monsoon Meeting
Page 047

04 | *Shaolin monks training, Zhengzhou, China,* 2004. The Iconic Photographs. London & New York: Phaidon Press, 2010. © Steve McCurry.

Plate 81
Signature Styles
Page 118

05 | *Sharbat Gula, "Afghan Girl", at Nasir Bagh refugee camp near Peshawar, Pakistan,* 1984. "Along Afghanistan's War-torn Frontier". *National Geographic,* vol. 167, no. 6, June 1985. © Steve McCurry.

Plate 20
Making Reputations
Page 052

06 | *Stilt Fishermen, Weligama, Sri Lanka,* 1995. "Sri Lanka: A Continuing Ethnic War Tarnishes the Pearl of the Indian Ocean". *National Geographic,* vol. 191, no. 1, January 1997. © Steve McCurry.

Plate 80
Signature Styles
Page 116

07

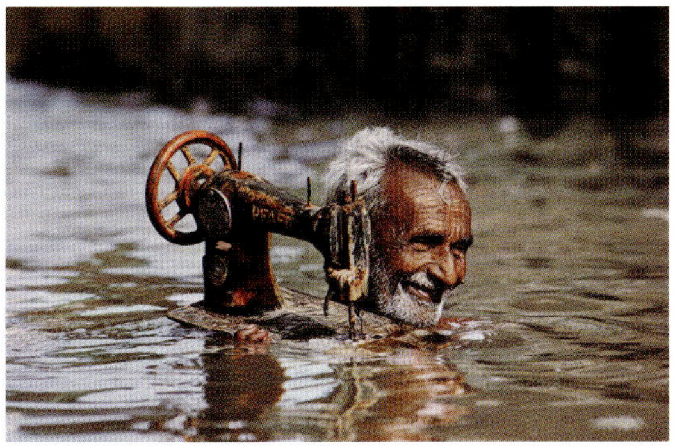

08

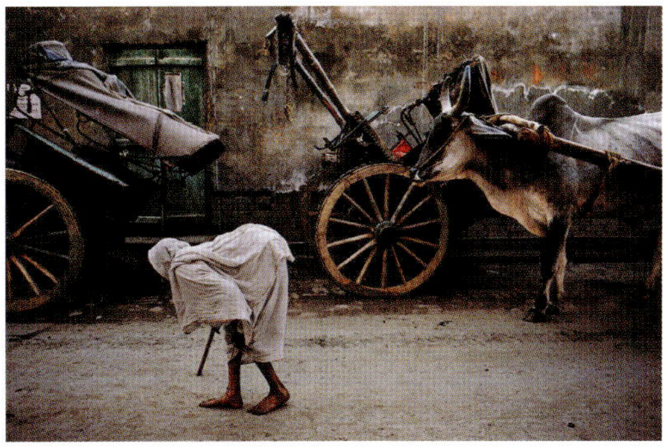

09

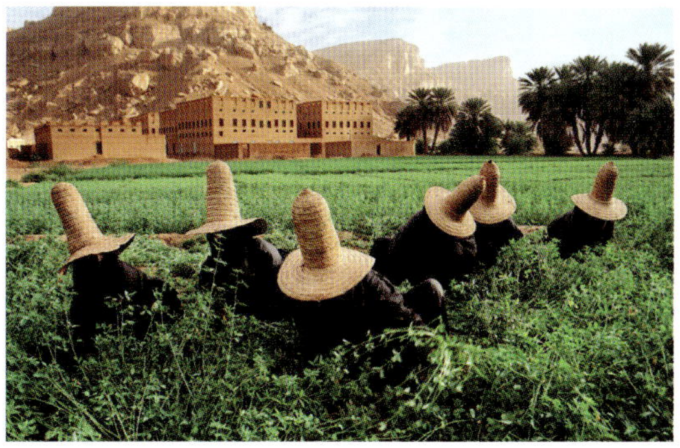

10

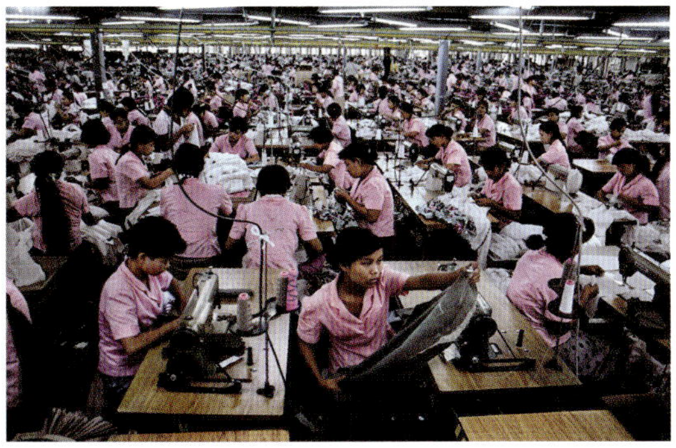

07 I *Tailor in monsoon, Porbandar, India,* 1983. "Monsoons: Life Breath of Half the World". *National Geographic,* vol. 166, no. 6, December 1984. © Steve McCurry

Plate 02
Monsoon Meeting
Page 033

08 I *Widow returning from her ashram, Vrindavan, Uttar Pradesh, India,* 1995. *South Southeast.* London & New York: Phaidon Press, 2000. © Steve McCurry.

Plate 85
Signature Styles
Page 122

09 I *Women gather clover, Shibam, Wadi Hadhramaut, Yemen,* 1999. "Yemen United". *National Geographic,* vol. 197, no. 4, April 2000. © Steve McCurry.

Plate 87
Signature Styles
Page 125

10 I *Women in a garment factory, Rangoon, Burma/Myanmar,* 1994. *The Iconic Photographs.* London & New York: Phaidon Press, 2010. © Steve McCurry.

Plate 55
Ancient and Modern
Page 090